ACCOUNTING
IRREGULARITIES
AND
FINANCIAL
FRAUD

ACCOUNTING IRREGULARITIES AND FINANCIAL FRAUD

A Corporate Governance Guide

Edited by

MICHAEL R. YOUNG

 Harcourt
Professional Publishing

SAN DIEGO   NEW YORK   CHICAGO   LONDON

The publisher has not sought nor obtained approval of this publication from any other organization, profit or nonprofit, and is solely responsible for its contents.

Printed in the United States of America

ISBN: 0-15-606998-9

00   01   02   03   MG   4   3   2   1

CONTRIBUTORS

Jack H. Nusbaum, Chairman
Willkie Farr & Gallagher

Stephen Greiner, Litigation Partner
Willkie Farr & Gallagher

Joseph T. Baio, Litigation Partner
Willkie Farr & Gallagher

Benito Romano, Litigation Partner
Willkie Farr & Gallagher

John Oller, Litigation Partner
Willkie Farr & Gallagher

Harvey R. Kelly, Partner
PricewaterhouseCoopers LLP

Ty R. Sagalow, Chief Underwriting Officer
*National Union Fire Insurance Company
of Pittsburgh, Pa. (AIG)*

CONTENTS

Foreword ix

Preface xi

Acknowledgments xii

About the Authors xiii

About the Computer Disc xvii

Detailed Table of Contents xix

Chapter 1: The Origin of Financial Fraud 1

Chapter 2: So Who Gets the Blame? 21

Chapter 3: The Immediate Aftermath 41

Chapter 4: Getting New Audited Financial Statements 55

Chapter 5: Digging Out the Fraud: The Lawyers 73

Chapter 6: Digging Out the Fraud:
            The Forensic Accountants 89

Chapter 7: Class Action Lawsuits 111

Chapter 8: Dealing with the D&O Insurer 133

Chapter 9: Dealing with the Regulators 157

Chapter 10: Criminal Investigations 179

Chapter 11: What's an Audit Committee to Do? 211

Chapter 12: Accounting Irregularities and
            the Future of Financial Reporting 255

Appendix A: New Rules of the Securities and Exchange
             Commission Regarding Audit Committee
             Disclosure 270

Appendix B: New Rules of the New York Stock Exchange
             Regarding Corporate Governance and
             Audit Committees 296

Appendix C: New Rules of the National Association of
              Securities Dealers Regarding Corporate
              Governance and Audit Committees 308

Appendix D: SEC Staff Accounting Bulletin No. 99—
              Materiality 320

Appendix E: SEC Staff Accounting Bulletin No. 100—
              Restructuring and Impairment Charges 331

Appendix F: SEC Staff Accounting Bulletin No. 101—
              Revenue Recognition in Financial Statements 348

Using the CD-ROM 367

CD-ROM Contents 371

Index 379

by Mario M. Cuomo

The unprecedented era of spectacular growth over the last decade has unleashed cascading new wealth in the financial industry and created a new American world of glorious possibilities and challenges. One of the challenges is the disconcerting outbreak of "accounting irregularities," a nice euphemism for what amounts to the deliberate manipulation of bookkeeping to disguise regrettable realities with desirable illusions. In my old neighborhood that was usually called "fraud."

In the pages that follow, you will learn about the corporate environment that causes it, how it spreads, the kind of crises it can create for the company, and the best ways to deal with them. Experts will offer advice on the conduct of the initial investigation and the first meeting of the board of directors. They will give insights dealing with insurance, indemnity, and the possibility of class action lawsuits, and demonstrate how to restore corporate and individual credibility after the event.

There are also helpful ideas about how to strengthen the company against a recurrence of lapses in judgments and ethics. To do that we have to understand the dynamics and temptations that help spawn the manipulations: the corporate pressure that can push honest people into doing dishonest things, how an executive can be trapped by what seems an easy escape from the embarrassment of disillusioned earnings expectations. Business people with firsthand experience show how, in the process, the executive overlooks the possible cost in dollars and reputation and marketability, not just to the offending company and all those implicated by the company, but even to honest competitors in the rest of the industry whose reputations suffer by association.

All of that is described, clearly and vividly, from the cumulative experience of knowledgeable professionals, making this volume the first authentic "how to" book on dealing with accounting irregularities.

It can also prompt some badly needed reflection on the larger economic and fiscal context in which we find ourselves.

A lot has happened to economics and business in the last 30 years. So much so that a new language is being developed to describe our changing world. Words like "transparency" are suddenly and obviously recurrent in the pages of financial journals, on paper and on the computer screen. Thirty years ago the word "transparency" was used only infrequently and almost never by economists. Today that word means that if you want help from the IMF or the World Bank, or if you want credibility in your fiscal practice here at home, your books and accounting records ought to be clean, honest, and comprehensible.

Most dictionaries still don't list that particular meaning. But it is found in almost every speech by former Treasury Secretary Robert Rubin and current Chairman of the Federal Reserve Board Alan Greenspan.

And only a few years ahead of "transparency," the words "interconnectedness" and "interdependence" resurfaced. Wendell Willkie, who ran against FDR in 1941, had used those words over a half a century ago in his book *One World*, while predicting the inevitable emergence of another new word, "globalization." Four decades later, Mikhail Gorbachev and Vaclav Havel resuscitated Willkie's words and now they regularly appear when the point is being made that the financial world and the rest of the planet are intensifying dealings with one another all over the globe. Horizons have broadened, borders have become infinitely elastic. Mergers and mega-mergers, joint ventures and affiliations, stretching the reach of companies across seas and over continents, have created tremendous new opportunities and fearsome new competition at the same time.

The message in this book is that, in this world of exciting new options and intense new competition, financial regularity and transparency will be a *sine qua non* to success. Only the enterprise that can be believed and depended upon will survive. Our hope is that the contributions we offer will make that case clearly enough that, before much longer, this kind of fraud will become so rare we won't need clumsy euphemisms like "accounting irregularities" at all.

It only takes a phone call. One moment you're a titan of corporate management. You are, among other things, an outside director of a company that has, yet again, reported stellar results. The stock price is up. Senior management is happy with their well-deserved bonuses. And you're basking in the glow of a favorable article that has just appeared in *Business Week*.

Then, with a single phone call, everything changes. You're told that accounting irregularities have surfaced at the company. Inexplicably, the CFO has confessed. An emergency board of directors meeting is being called for the next day. There will be one item on the agenda: How to deal with a crisis.

Increasingly, boards of directors, audit committee members, and senior executives are finding themselves in precisely this situation. For virtually all of them, it will be the first time that they will go through it. For that matter, it will probably be the first time for their outside law firm, the certified public accountants who serve as their outside auditors, and almost everybody else involved. Some will choose the proper course of action almost as a matter of instinct. But, experience teaches, many will not.

This book is intended to provide a step-by-step guide to the crises enveloping a company in the wake of fraudulent financial reporting—and how to prevent it from happening in the first place. It is directed to almost everybody involved: outside directors, audit committee members, senior executives, CFOs, CPAs, in-house lawyers, and outside law firms. Experience teaches that, where fraudulent financial reporting surfaces, the root causes and effects are almost always the same. Also the same are the strategies for dealing with them.

Michael R. Young

ACKNOWLEDGMENTS

The authors would like to thank the following for their invaluable contributions to this book:

Laila Abou-Rahme, Willkie Farr & Gallagher

William T. Allen, Independence Standards Board

Joseph G. Davis, Willkie Farr & Gallagher

Paul A. Ferrillo, American International Group, Inc.

Alan S. Fox, PricewaterhouseCoopers LLP

Paul V. Gerlach, Securities and Exchange Commission

Vinita M. Juneja, National Economic Research Associates, Inc.

Alison M. Lehr, Willkie Farr & Gallagher

Michael G. Marks, Willkie Farr & Gallagher

D. Edward Martin, Richard A. Eisner & Company, LLP

Scott S. Rose, Willkie Farr & Gallagher

Diane M. Tokarz, Willkie Farr & Gallagher

Lynn E. Turner, Securities and Exchange Commission

William U. Westerfield, Price Waterhouse LLP (retired)

John O. Whitney, Columbia University Graduate School of Business

ABOUT THE AUTHORS

Editor

Michael R. Young is a litigation partner of Willkie Farr & Gallagher specializing in securities and financial reporting. For more than a decade, Mr. Young has served as a counsel to the American Institute of Certified Public Accountants, and he has accordingly assisted in such matters as the formulation of the federal securities tort reform legislation of the mid-1990s, the drafting of generally accepted auditing standards, the enactment of the Uniform Accountancy Act, and the submission to the United States Supreme Court and Courts of Appeal of *amicus curiae* briefs on matters of importance to financial reporting. Mr. Young also actively investigates and defends companies, officers and directors, accounting firms, and others in matters involving financial reporting and liability, and he has been involved in some of the most significant accounting irregularities matters of the past twenty years. He is a member of the American Bar Association's Committee on Law and Accounting and writes and lectures frequently on financial reporting and liability issues.

Foreword

Mario M. Cuomo, before he entered public service, had been a law clerk to the Honorable Adrian P. Burke of the New York State Court of Appeals, an Adjunct Professor of Law, and a practicing attorney who had appeared in every level of the New York State courts and before the Supreme Court of the United States. As Secretary of State and then Governor of New York for 12 years, he took a leading role in the enhancement of the laws of public disclosure and integrity in public reporting. As Secretary of State, Mr. Cuomo helped write the first public disclosure laws in New York State and drafted the first reform of New York's lobbying laws in over 70 years. As Governor, he proposed and signed the first ethics law for public officials; the law requiring the application of generally accepted accounting principles to the state budget; and the first state statute requiring regular and independent audits of all executive agencies, including the Comptroller's Office, the State Inspector General's Office, and his own Office of the Governor. As a partner of Willkie Farr & Gallagher, Mr. Cuomo has played an active role in advising public companies, boards of directors, and audit committees on issues of corporate governance and financial reporting, and he has engaged in a broader practice specializing in national and international corporate law. Mr. Cuomo is the author or editor of more than a half-dozen books, including *The Blue Spruce, Reason to Believe, The New York Idea: An Experiment in Democracy, More Than Words, Lincoln on Democracy, Diaries of Mario Cuomo,* and *Forest Hills Diary.*

Contributing Authors

Jack H. Nusbaum is Chairman of Willkie Farr & Gallagher and leads the firm's Mergers and Acquisitions Practice Group. Mr. Nusbaum also actively advises public companies, senior executives, and professionals in matters relating to financial reporting and accounting irregularities, and he headed the team responsible for the 1998 Report to the Audit Committee of the Board of Directors of Cendant Corporation. Mr. Nusbaum is also a director of a number of publicly held corporations, including W.R. Berkley Corporation; Pioneer Companies, Inc.; Prime Hospitality Corp.; Neuberger Berman, LLC; Strategic Distribution, Inc.; and The Topps Company, Inc. He also serves on the board of directors of Hirschl & Adler Galleries, Inc. Mr. Nusbaum is a trustee of The Robert Steel Foundation, Prep for Prep, and The Joseph Collins Foundation.

Stephen Greiner is a litigation partner of Willkie Farr & Gallagher specializing in securities litigation. Throughout his career, he has represented officers and directors, financial services organizations, accounting firms, and other businesses in a broad variety of securities matters, including litigation and investigations initiated by the Securities and Exchange Commission and other regulatory agencies. He has also specialized in conducting internal investigations, including matters involving accounting irregularities and other financial reporting issues.

Joseph T. Baio is a litigation partner of Willkie Farr & Gallagher and a member of the firm's Executive Committee. Although his practice is not limited to any area, he regularly represents individuals and companies involved in litigations arising out of large commercial or securities transactions. He has defended companies and corporate officers in connection with Securities and Exchange Commission, Department of Justice, and FBI investigations and in proceedings before the New York Stock Exchange and the National Association of Securities Dealers. Mr. Baio is a frequent lecturer on business law at the Columbia University School of Business and is a regular speaker for the Directors' Network, an organization that instructs members of boards of directors about their responsibilities and potential liabilities under state and federal law.

Benito Romano has been a litigation partner of Willkie Farr & Gallagher and head of its white collar crime practice group since November 1989. Mr. Romano has represented numerous companies and individuals in criminal investigations involving allegations of financial fraud, fraud against the government, and regulatory offenses. Before his return to private practice, Mr. Romano served as United States Attorney for the Southern District of New York. Before assuming the position of United States Attorney, Mr. Romano served in a variety of supervisory and executive positions in that office, including Chief Appellate Attorney for the Criminal Division, Executive Assistant United States Attorney and Chief of the Public Corruption Unit, and Associate United States Attorney.

John Oller is a litigation partner of Willkie Farr & Gallagher. Since joining the firm in 1982, Mr. Oller has specialized in complex commercial litigation with particular emphases on federal securities litigation and internal and independent corporate investigations. He was a principal author of the 1998 Cendant Report, based on the internal investigation of Cendant Corporation on behalf of its audit committee, which the *New York Times* called a definitive case study in the area of accounting irregularities and fraud.

Harvey R. Kelly is a certified public accountant and a partner in the Financial Advisory Services practice of PricewaterhouseCoopers LLP. Mr. Kelly specializes in forensic accounting investigations and litigation consulting and has conducted forensic investigations into alleged accounting errors and irregularities on behalf of companies, directors, creditors, and shareholders. Mr. Kelly has also been called upon to provide litigation consulting services and expert witness testimony in related securities litigation and regulatory investigation proceedings and has served as a court-appointed examiner charged with investigating fraud allegations. He is an experienced financial statement auditor and has audited the financial statements of public and private companies in a wide range of industries. Mr. Kelly is a frequent lecturer on the topics of forensic accounting investigations and securities litigation.

Ty R. Sagalow is senior vice-president, chief underwriting officer, and chief legal officer for the National Union Fire Insurance Company of Pittsburgh, Pa., a member company of American International Group, Inc., and has authored most of National Union's insurance policies since 1987. Mr. Sagalow is on the faculty of the National Association of Corporate Directors and has spoken before numerous legal and insurance forums throughout the nation on issues affecting directors' and officers' (D&O) liability and corporate governance, including Stanford University's *Director's College*, Watson Wyatt's *D&O Symposium*, and the American and New York Bar Associations. Mr. Sagalow has also written a number of articles on director and officer liability which have appeared in such publications as *Bank Director* and *Director's Monthly*. He was both guest editor and a contributing author for the *Special Issue on D&O Liability, Indemnification and Insurance* appearing in *Director's Monthly*. Most recently, he co-authored the chapter "Directors and Officers Insurance" appearing in *Directors & Officers Liability: Indemnification and Insurance*. Mr. Sagalow is vice chairman of the American Bar Association's standing committee on Directors, Officers and Professional Liability for the Tort & Insurance Professional Liability section.

ABOUT THE COMPUTER DISC

System Requirements

- IBM PC or compatible computer with CD-ROM drive
- Microsoft® Word 6.0 for Windows™, WordPerfect® 7.0 for Windows™, or compatible word processor
- Version 4 or above of either Netscape® Navigator or Microsoft® Internet Explorer™
- 3 MB available on hard drive

The CD-ROM provided with *Accounting Irregularities and Financial Fraud* contains electronic versions of the latest SEC initiatives against earnings management; Staff Accounting Bulletins 99, 100, and 101; the new rules of the NYSE and the NASD regarding corporate governance and audit committees; and a variety of primary source material. See pp 367–378 for information about using the CD-ROM and for a listing of its contents.

Subject to the conditions in the license agreement and the limited warranty, which is displayed onscreen when the disc is installed and which is reproduced at the end of the book, you may duplicate the files on this disc, modify them as necessary, and create your own customized versions. Installing the disc contents and/or using the disc in any way indicates that you accept the terms of the license agreement.

The data disc is intended for use with your word processing software. There are versions of each document in Microsoft® Word 6.0 and WordPerfect® 7.0, both for Windows™. If you do not own either of these programs, your word processing package may be able to convert the documents into a usable format. Check your owner's manual for information on the conversion of documents.

DETAILED TABLE OF CONTENTS

Chapter 1: The Origin of Financial Fraud 1

Let's Step Back 2

What Is an *Accounting Irregularity*? 3

So How Do Accounting Irregularities Come About? 6

Isolating the Elements 11

The Danger of "Managed Earnings" 13

The Audit Committee, the Internal Audit Department, and the
    Outside Auditor 15

The Fraud Surfaces 19

A Crisis for the Board 19

Chapter 2: So Who Gets the Blame? 21

Blaming the Outside Auditor 21

The Treadway Commission 23

Consequences of the Treadway Commission Report 26

Further Developments 28

So Who Gets the Blame? 30

The Levitt Initiatives 34

Chapter 3: The Immediate Aftermath 41

The Preliminary Investigation 41

The Initial Board Meeting 42

Insurance Issues 48

Action Plan 49

The Initial Press Release 49

Other Issues 50

Chapter 4: Getting New Audited Financial Statements.......... **55**

Initial Involvement of the Outside Auditor 56

Effect on Previously Issued Audit Reports 56

The Element of Mistrust 58

Benefits of Continuing the Audit Relationship 59

The Independent Forensic Accounting Team............................... 61

Responsibility for Restated Financial Statements 62

Restatement Requirements 63

The Audit Process.. 66

Representations to the Auditor 69

Effect of Lawsuits on Auditor Independence 70

The Bottom Line.. 72

Chapter 5: Digging Out the Fraud: The Lawyers **73**

Purposes of the Investigation.. 73

Who Conducts the Investigation? 75

Time Frame of the Investigation 76

Tasks to Perform.. 77

Lack of Subpoena Power and the Interview Process.................... 79

Unresolved Questions.. 82

The Report 83

Can the Report Remain Privileged? 85

Is the Investigators' Work Product Privileged?............................ 86

**Chapter 6: Digging Out the Fraud: The Forensic
  Accountants** **89**

What Is a Forensic Accountant? 89

Why Hire a Forensic Accountant?... 89

The Difference between a Forensic Investigation and an Audit ... 94

Immediate Objectives 96

Framing the Issues 98

Conducting the Investigation 104

Interacting with the Lawyers and the Attorney-Client Privilege . 105

Coordination with the Outside Auditor 106

Knowing When to Stop 108

Chapter 7: Class Action Lawsuits 111

What Is a Class Action? 111

The Commencement of Class Action Litigation 112

The Likely Defendants 113

Sorting Out Parties and Counsel.. 115

The Consolidated Complaint 116

Liability Implications of the Initial Press Release 119

The Motion to Dismiss 121

The Prospects of an Early Settlement 122

The Process of Discovery 123

Dynamics Favoring Settlement 127

Securities Law Damages 129

Ultimately a Settlement 130

Chapter 8: Dealing with the D&O Insurer 133

The Structure of a Typical Policy 134

Analysis of a D&O Policy 135

The D&O Policy and Accounting Irregularities 148

So How Does All This End Up?... 154

The Best Approach 155

Chapter 9: Dealing with the Regulators **157**

The SEC: The Power to Investigate, Correct, and Punish 157

Dealing with Self-Regulatory Organizations 169

Chapter 10: Criminal Investigations **179**

The Initial Grand Jury Phase 182

The Testimonial Grand Jury Phase... 191

Corporate Criminal Liability for Employee Actions 198

Plea Discussions and Sentencing Considerations........................ 202

Other Responsibilities of Counsel for a Target Company 207

Parallel Proceedings 209

Chapter 11: What's an Audit Committe to Do? **211**

Financial Reporting and the Audit Committee 212

An Approach to Audit Committee Oversight............................... 214

A Properly Configured Audit Committee 218

The Biggest Challenge: Information 230

Getting Information from Senior Management 231

Getting Information from the Outside Auditor............................. 232

Getting Information from Internal Audit...................................... 246

Making the Tools Work.. 248

**Chapter 12: Accounting Irregularities and the Future of
Financial Reporting** **255**

A Real-Time World 256

A 1930s Financial Reporting System 257

So Enter the Analysts 258

A Consequence Is Accounting Irregularities............................... 259

Other Capital Market Inefficiencies 261

There's Another Way 264

Appendix A: New Rules of the Securities and Exchange
Commission Regarding Audit Committee
Disclosure 270

Appendix B: New Rules of the New York Stock Exchange
Regarding Corporate Governance and
Audit Committees 296

Appendix C: New Rules of the National Association of
Securities Dealers Regarding Corporate
Governance and Audit Committees 308

Appendix D: SEC Staff Accounting Bulletin No. 99—
Materiality 320

Appendix E: SEC Staff Accounting Bulletin No. 100—
Restructuring and Impairment Charges 331

Appendix F: SEC Staff Accounting Bulletin No. 101—
Revenue Recognition in Financial Statements 348

ACCOUNTING IRREGULARITIES AND FINANCIAL FRAUD

CHAPTER 1

THE ORIGIN OF FINANCIAL FRAUD

Michael R. Young

On top of everything else, today's senior executive, outside director, and (in particular) audit committee member now face a growing problem that seems to have appeared in the financial headlines almost overnight. It is the problem of so-called accounting irregularities. That is to say, it is the problem of deliberately misreported financial results.

The accounting irregularities to attract the most public attention, of course, were those that surfaced at Cendant Corporation in April 1998, where the announcement of misstated financial results at Cendant's newly acquired CUC International unit led to a $14 billion loss in market capital in just a few hours. But Cendant is far from alone. Highly publicized financial misreporting problems have also surfaced at McKesson, Livent, Mercury Finance, Donnkenny, Rite Aid, Boston Scientific, Informix, Sunbeam, Micro Warehouse, Northstar Health Services, Paracelsus Healthcare, Penguin, Photran, Sensormatic, Thor Industries, BT Office Products, Guildford Mills, Bankers Trust, and Physician Computer Network. And that's just to name a few.

Evidence of an increase in accounting irregularities is more than anecdotal. A series of surveys conducted by PricewaterhouseCoopers shows that claims based on alleged accounting irregularities have increased from 25% of securities claims in 1997 to 49% just two years later. A similar study concluded that between 1992 and 1998, the number of securities lawsuits based on the need to restate audited financial statements increased by 750%. A separate survey of chief financial officers, conducted on a strictly anonymous basis, found that fully two-thirds had recently been subjected to pressure within their companies to misrepresent financial results. According to the survey, 55% had successfully resisted. At the same time, 12% had not.

The Securities and Exchange Commission (SEC) is understandably up in arms. At a seminal speech at New York University on September 28, 1998, SEC Chairman Arthur Levitt threw down the gauntlet to the financial community and announced a series of initiatives to combat accounting fraud. These included heightened SEC scrutiny of certain types of reporting practices, the formation of a Blue Ribbon Committee to study the effectiveness of corporate audit committees, and an effort to reexamine the outside audit function. In the ten months following that September 28 speech, the topic of accounting irregularities was the subject of no fewer than 21 speeches by the SEC's Chairman, the Chief Accountant, the Director of Enforcement, or others within either the Office of the Chief Accountant or the Division of Enforcement.

Under prodding from the SEC, others within the financial community are taking action. The New York Stock Exchange (NYSE) and the National Association of Securities Dealers (NASD), based on the recommendations of their newly formed Blue Ribbon Committee on Improving the Effectiveness of Corporate Audit Committees, have adopted a new set of rules to combat financial fraud. The Committee of Sponsoring Organizations of the Treadway Commission (COSO) has published the results of an extensive study on the underlying causes of fraudulent financial reporting. The Public Oversight Board—a collection of elder statesmen charged with oversight of the audit profession—has launched a new initiative to scrutinize the audit function. And the Financial Accounting Standards Board (FASB) is subjecting technical pronouncements to new scrutiny. Even entirely private groups, such as sponsors of seminars, law firms, and bar associations, have convened conferences and programs to explore why a wholesale breakdown in financial reporting systems seems to be taking place.

Let's Step Back

At one point, someone is bound to ask the following questions: Are we witnessing a collapse of honesty and morality in financial America? Have we finally reached the point in the evolution of business practice where dishonesty has become the norm rather than the exception? If we have not reached that point, how do we explain a statistic that tells us that two-thirds of corporate America is putting pressure on its accounting departments to commit fraud?

These questions can be answered. But first we need to step back and take an objective look at what is really going on.

To begin, there is little question that reported instances of accounting irregularities are on the rise. The evidence is anecdotal, statistical, and convincing. More and more companies are experiencing some level of financial misreporting, and the evidence suggests that the misreporting is not always innocent.

But that does not mean that corporate America is slipping into an abyss of dissembling and dishonesty. On the contrary, ample evidence exists that the individual integrity of those running public companies today has never been at a higher level. Never before have we seen such attentiveness to the welfare of employees and their families, the effect of corporate activity on the environment, or the need for a corporation to act, in the words of one recent book (*Corporate Compliance*, Murphy and Wallace, Practising Law Institute, 1996), like "a good corporation citizen." Those who would argue that corporate managers behave less responsibly and with a greater level of dishonesty than their predecessors have a tough argument to make.

So how can these seemingly inconsistent trends be reconciled? How do we reconcile an increase in financial misreporting with increasing executive interest in proper corporate behavior? The answer lies in an understanding of the root causes of financial misreporting. In particular, it lies in the recognition that financial misreporting—even deliberate financial misreporting—does not, at root, start with dishonesty. Rather, financial misreporting stems from a certain type of corporate environment. Where that kind of environment exists, accounting irregularities can develop and grow undetected at companies whose senior executives are ostensibly of unimpeachable integrity.

What Is an *Accounting Irregularity*?

Before we go further in dissecting the origin of financial fraud, we need to establish some basics. In particular, we need to make sure we have a common vocabulary as to exactly what financial writers mean when they refer to an *accounting irregularity*.

The term has its origin in the obscure (and, ironically, now superseded) authoritative literature of the accounting profession. (See Exhibits 1–1 and 1–2.) Perhaps out of a belief that the word *fraud* was too rude for its au-

---

Exhibit 1–1. A Word about Nomenclature

The now ubiquitous term *accounting irregularities* comes from one of the standards explicating generally accepted auditing standards—Statement on Auditing Standards (SAS) No. 53 (The Auditor's Responsibility to Detect and Report Errors and Irregularities). SAS-53 defines *irregularities* as "*intentional* misstatements or omissions of amounts or disclosures in financial statements."

Ironically, just as the term *irregularities* has come into vogue, SAS-53 has been superseded by a new standard on the same subject—SAS-82 (Consideration of Fraud in a Financial Statement Audit). Although SAS-82 does not seek to alter the auditor's responsibility for detecting fraud, it does serve to heighten auditor awareness of that responsibility and, in the process, completely drops the reference to irregularities and adopts the term *fraud.*

Technically, a distinction can be drawn between an irregularity and fraud insofar as an irregularity consists of an intentional misstatement in financial statements, whereas an irregularity evolves into fraud only when those financial statements are shown to another who then justifiably relies on them to his or her detriment. In common parlance, though, the terms are being used interchangeably and they will largely be used interchangeably in this book.

---

thoritative literature, accountants have historically avoided the term *fraud* altogether and, instead, divided financial statement misstatements into two categories: errors and irregularities.

The difference between the two has nothing to do with the accuracy of the reported numbers—one or the other may apply even where numbers are equally wrong. The difference has to do with the intent of the individual by whom the incorrect numbers have been provided. *Errors* are defined to be accidental inaccuracies. *Irregularities* are defined to be inaccuracies that are deliberate.

Why does the literature distinguish between the two? Because the distinction between an accounting *error* and an accounting *irregularity* is comparable (to paraphrase one American jurist) to the difference between a dog

---

Exhibit 1–2. Statement on Auditing Standards No. 53's Definition of *Errors and Irregularities*

The term *errors* refers to unintentional misstatements or omissions of amounts or disclosures in financial statements. Errors may involve:

- Mistakes in gathering or processing accounting data from which financial statements are prepared

- Incorrect accounting estimates arising from oversight or misinterpretation of facts

- Mistakes in the application of accounting principles relating to amount, classification, manner of presentation, or disclosure

The term *irregularities* refers to intentional misstatements or omissions of amounts or disclosures in financial statements. Irregularities may include fraudulent financial reporting undertaken to render financial statements misleading and misappropriation of assets. Irregularities may involve:

- Manipulation, falsification, or alteration of accounting records or supporting documents from which financial statements are prepared

- Misrepresentation or intentional omission of events, transactions, or other significant information

- Intentional misapplication of accounting principles relating to amounts, classification, manner of presentation, or disclosure

---

that has been stumbled over and a dog that has been kicked. Where a company finds an accounting error, it does its best to fix it and move on. If the accounting misstatement has truly been accidental, in many cases the federal securities laws will not even allow shareholders to sue.

Where the misstatement is an irregularity, the situation is completely different. When financial statements are misstated because of an irregularity, someone has not made an innocent mistake. Someone has deliberately lied. And the resulting concern is that somebody (best scenario) or a group of people (worst scenario) is dishonest and is lying to everyone about financial performance. So the company is not in a position in which it can just fix the numbers and move on. Some level of corporate housecleaning is going to be involved.

None of this means that an irregularity implies that everyone in an organization was in on the fraud or even that executives were in on the fraud. Unfortunately, an irregularity can be brought about by just one bad apple. But, when we see the label "accounting irregularity," we know that someone within the organization has deliberately misstated some aspect of financial performance, and that misstatement has seeped its way into the company's publicly reported results.

So How Do Accounting Irregularities Come About?

Accounting irregularities start and grow within a certain type of corporate environment. The key to understanding this kind of financial fraud—and the key to its prevention—is to understand that environment and the way it influences individual conduct.

Example

To illustrate, let's consider a situation that many will recognize as all too familiar. Hypothesize a manufacturing company that went public not too long ago at a time when the market was hitting new highs and an economic expansion was surpassing all records. Accordingly, management has been able to announce a series of record-breaking quarters. In the meantime, management has struggled to attract the attention of Wall Street analysts whose attention is, management believes, necessary if the company's laudable earnings history is to be fairly reflected in the stock price. Several analysts are following the company's stock and, in fact, among the company's stockholders are momentum investors who are investing based on an anticipation of a continuing upward trajectory to ever-increasing heights.

There is, though, a problem. The company's industry—which, quarter after quarter, had enabled continued expansion and double-digit earnings growth—is starting to slow down. Management perceives this slowdown in growth, moreover, before its potential effects are fully appreciated by the investment community. In particular, the slowdown largely seems to escape the notice of the Wall Street analysts following the stock.

Therefore a mismatch exists. Wall Street is expecting a new record quarter (and the analysts have got it nailed down to the exact penny). But management sees that a new record quarter is not likely to happen. For the first time, the company is facing the specter of a failure to attain analyst expectations.

The more seasoned members of the business community might recognize that it's time for the company to take its lumps and move on. But this company is somewhat lacking in seasoned managers—it's only been public for a few years. For management, the thought of missing analyst expectations—and the specter of momentum investors fleeing the stock—is more terrifying than it can endure. So what happens? Executives' feet are to be held to the fire. The word goes out to all division heads: Pull out the stops. Specific earnings targets are distributed to various divisions. Along with the targets comes an admonition: There is to be no slippage. A failure to attain the target will be viewed as unforgivable.

So now key elements of a certain kind of corporate environment are in place. There is pressure. There is an aggressive earnings target. And there is a vivid recognition that, one way or another, that earnings target must be attained.

Let's now shift our attention to someone who's on the receiving end of all this—a division president, a graduate of the finest schools, and an individual whose personal integrity has heretofore been unchallenged. He is now facing the most difficult crisis of his career.

For it is plain to our division president that, excruciating pressure or no, he cannot meet his earnings target. The business simply isn't there. He has already cut expenses to the bone. He has already admonished his sales force to make every effort. But, as he comes to the end of the quarter, he's just not going to make it.

Our division president has one of two choices. One, of course, is that he can report up the chain-of-command that he has failed. Admitting failure, though, is never an attractive option, especially in an environment in which failure is viewed as unforgivable. Our division president, though, sees another alternative. He can take a hard look at his numbers and see if there's enough flexibility in his division's financial reporting system to find a way to come up with the specified earnings.

What can he do? Because the president works for a manufacturing company, he sees a simple solution. He realizes that during the last few days of the quarter he can bring in overtime help and accelerate shipments. He does the math and sees that shipment acceleration would give him a couple of extra pennies in earnings. By the way, he doesn't think he's planning to do anything wrong. His understanding is that, under generally accepted accounting principles (GAAP), if you ship the goods, you are actually entitled to recognize the revenue. (He views it as sort of a hazy area of financial reporting.) And he figures that this is only going to be a one-quarter thing. He's confident that next quarter he'll have enough business to more than make up for what he is borrowing for this quarter.

So that's what he chooses to do. As the quarter comes to a close, he brings in overtime help. He accelerates shipments. He generates a couple of extra pennies in earnings. He meets his earnings target. And in the company he's a big hero.

But—now he's got a new quarter. And with the new quarter comes a new earnings target. And he finds that the business has not bounced back the way he hoped it would. Now the president has twice the problem. First, he's got to meet his earnings target for this new quarter. Second, he has to make up for what he borrowed out of the new quarter for the previous quarter.

So what's he do? Again, he decides to accelerate shipments. This time, though, he sees that shipment acceleration by itself won't be enough. So he thinks this might be a good time to take a look at some of his reserves. His gut tells him that his reserve, say, for returns is too big, and if he can reduce his reserve for returns, that can translate into a couple of extra pennies in earnings.

So that's what he does. In addition to again accelerating shipments, he reduces his reserve for returns. And, again, he meets his earnings target.

But—now he's got a new quarter. Now the problem is three times as bad. He's got a new earnings target, plus he's got to make up for what he's borrowed out of this quarter for the previous two quarters. And what makes it a little worse is that this happens to be the fourth quarter. For soon the auditors of the financial statements are going to show up.

Still, the division president isn't overly concerned. First of all, it's far from clear to him that he's done anything wrong. He figures you're allowed to second-guess reserves. He figures you're allowed to ship early. Besides, at this point everything is so small, and the real issue isn't asset values as much as quarterly timing, so there is very little likelihood that the outside auditors are going to pick it up. He's pretty confident of that, by the way, because he used to be a manager at the Big Five accounting firm that audits his company's financial statements. He basically knows how the firm goes about its audit. More than that, audit fees have been under some pressure lately, and there is no reason to think that this year the auditors will undertake more than their standard audit steps.

So he makes it through the audit without a problem. And, in fact, reported earnings for the year are terrific. Stock analyst expectations have been met. The stock price is up. He gets a nice bonus. And a complimentary article appears in *Business Week*.

But—now he's got a new quarter. Now he's got a bunch of quarters from the previous year to make up for, and it's becoming increasingly clear that the business is not going to bounce back. Now little beads of sweat appear. Soon he is creating charts with earnings on one side and Wall Street expectations on the other. For the president, the preoccupation of financial reporting is no longer accurately reflecting the operations of the business. It has become: How are we going to meet this quarter's street expectations?

So he goes through the year. As the quarters proceed, he finds himself keeping bad accounts receivables, delaying the recognition of expenses, altering inventory levels. At one point, dispensing with all formality, he finds himself directing his accounting staff to cross out real numbers and insert false ones. More and more he feels like he's on a treadmill on which he has to run faster and faster just to stay in place. (See Exhibit 1–3.)

Now it's audit season again. Now there's reason to be a little nervous. The word goes out to others within the division who have to deal with the auditors: Extra caution is to be used in providing the auditors with certain kinds of information. Supporting documentation for questionable entries comes to be manufactured by people within the accounting department to try to respond to questions that the auditors will inevitably raise. Members of the accounting department convene meetings for the sole purpose of talking about how to survive the audit.

Now a fair question would be: What's the president's exit strategy? The answer is: He hasn't got one. He didn't intend for this to happen. This was supposed to be a little glitch in the numbers that came and went away in a single quarter. But somehow it got away from him. And now, quarter to quarter, the president is basically scrambling for his life.

And let's pause to look at what's happened. At this point, the physical implementation of what's going on, and in particular the need to deal with the outside auditors, has broadened participation beyond one or two people. By the time a fraud surfaces, it's not unusual to have a large percentage of the entire accounting department involved. It's not that these people are fun-

---

Exhibit 1–3. The Treadmill Effect

- Shipments accelerated
- Quarters kept open
- Reserves reduced
- Revenue recognized on anticipated orders
- Consignment sales improperly recognized
- Bill-and-hold sales improperly recognized
- Accounts receivable manipulated
- Expense recognition delayed
- Intercompany credits used
- Acquisition reserves adjusted
- False inventory "in transit" recorded
- Phantom inventory created
- Phony shipments recorded
- Unsupportable general ledger revisions made
- Unsupportable top-side adjustments made

---

damentally dishonest or evil. In fact, typically, very few people actually see the whole picture.

But as the quarters proceed, ostensibly innocent people within the accounting department know that they've been asked to make entries without understanding why. They know they've watched numbers on their computer screens change for reasons they don't completely understand. They know they've been asked to second-guess reserves without understanding the underlying reason. They don't know that they are now participants in a fraud. But they suspect it. And it begins to eat at them. And it eats at their conscience. And they worry.

And at one point, they see it. They see that they are up to their eyeballs in a massive financial fraud. The problem is that, by the time that light bulb has gone on, it's too late. They are participants.

Isolating the Elements

Even though the example is hypothetical, those knowledgeable of fraudulent financial reporting will recognize a pattern. Let's break out the key elements and focus on each one.

1. *It doesn't start with dishonesty.* The starting point is the recognition that fraudulent financial reporting ordinarily does not start with dishonesty. It does not start because the CEO is dishonest. It does not start because the CFO is dishonest. It does not start because the company has had the misfortune of hiring a group of dishonest people in its accounting department. In fact, the level of honesty of the individual participants has very little to do with it.

2. *It starts with pressure.* Rather than starting with dishonesty, fraudulent financial reporting starts with a certain kind of environment. In particular, it starts with an environment in which two things are present. The first is an aggressive target of financial performance. The second is a vivid realization that a failure to attain that target will be viewed as unforgivable. In other words, fraudulent financial reporting starts with pressure.

   Now the example described above assumes—as is very much the case in today's volatile stock market—pressure created by the market expectations created by Wall Street analysts. But that's not the only potential source of pressure. The pressure can come from almost anywhere. It may come from a hard-driving CEO who wants to make a name for himself by attaining a certain return on equity. The pressure may come from the need to satisfy the performance demands of one or more large shareholders. For a bank, the pressure may come from an unwillingness to report increased loan loss reserves to the FDIC. For some, the pressure may come from a senior executive who simply is not a very good manager.

   But whatever the source, deliberate financial misreporting starts with pressure. It starts with pressure to attain an aggressive performance target and with a vivid realization that a failure to attain that target will be viewed as unforgivable.

3. *It starts out small.* Massive financial fraud does not start with a grand plan or conspiracy. It does not start with a group of executives in a conference room in which someone volunteers, "Let's perpetrate

a massive fraud." In fact, its origin typically is precisely the opposite. It starts out very small—so small that the one or two participants don't even appreciate that they are stepping over the line. Then, as the need to disguise past performance inadequacies is compounded by the need to make up for new ones, the problem starts to grow.

4. *It starts with hazy areas of financial reporting.* Rarely does even a lone participant in a large-scale financial fraud start with a deliberate decision to do something dishonest. Now it is true, of course, that some people are dishonest and that they make deliberate decisions to lie, cheat, and steal. But rarely do those kinds of individuals survive long in a company, and they almost never make their way up the ranks to the senior levels.

So when we're talking about massive financial fraud, we're talking about a fraud that is being perpetrated by people who are not by nature or training the type to step over the line. What do they do? They exploit what they perceive to be ambiguities in the rules. They exploit ambiguities with regard to revenue recognition. They exploit the need to exercise judgment in the establishment and adjustment of reserves. They exploit areas where the dictates of GAAP do not lead inexorably to any particular number. Then, as the fraud grows deeper, they end up taking positions that should have objectively been viewed as <u>indefensible</u>.

5. *The fraud grows over time.* If the financial misreporting came and went away in a single quarter, that would be the end of it, and no one would be the wiser. That wouldn't make it right, but it wouldn't make it a massive financial fraud.

The problem is that the nature of financial misreporting makes it difficult to create and correct the misreporting in one quarter. By its nature, financial misreporting typically starts out in the form of borrowing from future quarters. Whether it be through changes in revenue recognition practices, the adjustment of reserves, the delay of expenses, or whatever, the nature of the fraud at its origin is such that the participants are almost always borrowing from Peter to pay Paul.

As the quarters progress, therefore, the problem is mathematically incapable of staying the same. Insofar as the perpetrator is always borrowing from future quarters to meet the present one, the fraud mathematically has got to get worse—in the absence of a dramatic business upturn. The fraud grows, moreover, not only in terms of its numerical significance, but also in terms of the number of people needed to perpetrate it. As the fraud numerically grows larger, the efforts of increasing numbers of individuals are needed simply to keep up with its implementation. Thus, the fraud grows beyond the original one or two perpetrators and, by the time it surfaces, may have, in one way or another, involved close to everyone in the accounting department.

6. *There's no way out.* In a sense, getting caught up in accounting irregularities is a one-way street. It's easy to start down the road, but it's almost impossible to turn back.

That's not to say that the participants will not be looking for a way out. As fear turns to desperation, those involved may dream of some kind of extraordinary event—a massive restructuring, a corporate acquisition, a divestiture—that will create enough smoke around the company's accounting that the improper entries may be removed from the books.

Indeed, it may be that the dream of such an extraordinary event—combined with the lack of any other alternative—is what keeps the fraud going. All the while, though, it keeps getting larger and larger, and the hoped-for event remains like a mirage on the horizon.

The Danger of "Managed Earnings"

Such an understanding of the origin and growth of fraudulent financial reporting points to the underlying weakness in the argument of those who would seek to defend the practice of what has become known as *managed earnings*. Now in talking about managed earnings, one has got to be careful. There are two types of managed earnings. One type is simply conducting the business of the enterprise in order to attain controlled, disciplined growth. The other type involves deliberate manipulation of the accounting in order to create the *appearance* of controlled, disciplined growth—when, in fact, all that is happening is that accounting entries are being manipulated.

The topic at hand, of course, is the latter—the manipulation of accounting entries in order to create the appearance of controlled, disciplined growth.

Still, the practice of even this kind of managed earnings has its defenders. The argument goes like this. In today's volatile stock market, precise reporting of the sharp edges of business upticks and downturns can turn a stock price into a roller coaster. That kind of volatility serves no one. It is far better, therefore, for management to use its judgment in the application of GAAP to take a longer-term view and smooth out earnings as they are reported. Such smoothing can be attained, for example, by putting away extra reserves (i.e., overestimating expenses and establishing concurrent liabilities) when times are good and tapping into them during temporary business downturns by acknowledging previous periods' expense overstatements and reversing them in the current period. According to one publication, some financial officers of public companies "see it as their duty to take the rough edges off operating results." The *Wall Street Journal*, in a much-discussed editorial in February 1998, came close to accepting just this kind of approach.

Certainly some can argue that aspects of the objectives of this kind of managed earnings are to an extent laudable. A long-term approach is obviously better than an approach that is limited only to the present quarter. And the volatility in many companies' stock prices has genuinely reached the point where it can seem almost unbearable.

A major fallacy in the argument for managed earnings, however, lies in its implicit premise that the practice can be neatly packaged and controlled. The problem is that it cannot be. True, establishing cookie-jar reserves in good times is easy enough and, in a different era, might have even been defended as good, conservative financial reporting. However, when downturns arrive it can be more difficult for management to make the decision that investors should be permitted to see the truth. Nor can a normal manager be expected accurately to forecast which downturns are only the result of the normal ebb and flow of the business, and therefore theoretically appropriate for use of the cookie-jar reserves, and which signify a more serious reversal in the company's prospects. More than that, once any cookie-jar reserves were exhausted, the temptation to exploit other reserves—ones that had been *appropriately* estimated—would have to be almost irresistible. It is easy to see how even such well-meaning management would find itself on a treadmill.

That is not to ignore other problems with the defense of accounting adjustments to smooth out earnings. Probably a more obvious one is its advocacy of distortion of a company's true operations in order to accommodate the investment expectations of financial analysts and the public. The fulfillment of expectations can be rewarding, but when it is achieved through distortion, it rarely works out in the long run.

Still another problem with a managed-earnings approach to financial reporting is the effect it can have on a company's financial reporting culture. Managerial acceptance of managed earnings, and in particular the use of such cookie-jar reserves, can send an extraordinarily dangerous message to the troops: "Where it is for the good of the corporate enterprise, it is all right to camouflage the truth." Once that genie is out of the bottle, it will never go back. Managers at all levels will perceive themselves as having license, if not encouragement, to do what they have internally tried to resist all along—camouflage their own dismal inadequacies by subtle rearrangement of the numbers. Where that should happen, investors, creditors, and suppliers will never be in a position to trust the numbers again. Not even management itself will be certain it is getting the truth. Under such a circumstance, lack of rigor in financial reporting can be expected to infect every fiber of the enterprise and become part of the corporate culture. If a company should get to that point, probably the best move is to sell the stock short. It is only a matter of time.

The Audit Committee, the Internal Audit Department, and the Outside Auditor

Any public company, of course, is supposed to have in place systems of corporate governance and internal control that keep any of this from happening. In particular, modern scholars of corporate governance would point to a triumvirate of internal control elements whose principal objectives would include the prevention of financial fraud: the audit committee, the internal audit department, and the outside auditor. To understand the origin of accounting irregularities, therefore, we have to consider how accounting irregularities are able to get by each of them.

The Audit Committee

Let's start with the audit committee. Under modern systems of internal control and corporate governance, it is the audit committee that is to be at the vanguard in the prevention and detection of financial fraud. What kinds of failures do we typically see at the audit committee level when financial fraud is given an opportunity to develop and grow undetected?

There is no single answer, but several audit committee inadequacies are candidates. One inadequacy potentially stems from the fact that the members of the audit committee are not always genuinely independent. A typical audit committee will have three members, and it may be that those members in substance, if not in form, had ties to the CEO or others that made any meaningful degree of independence awkward if not impossible.

Another inadequacy is that audit committee members are not always terribly sophisticated. Frequently, companies that are most susceptible to the demands of analyst earnings expectations are new, entrepreneurial companies that have recently gone public and that have engaged in a heroic struggle to get outside analysts to notice them in the first place. Such a newly hatched public company is unlikely to have exceedingly sophisticated or experienced financial management, let alone the luxury of sophisticated and mature outside directors on its audit committee. Rather, the audit committee members may have been added to the board in the first place because of industry expertise, because they were friends or even relatives of management, or simply because they were available.

A third inadequacy is that audit committee members are not always clear on exactly what they're supposed to do. Historically, the rules of the NYSE, as well as the NASD, in this regard have been somewhat vague. Even the new rules, while providing some detail as to the proper configuration of audit committees, decline to explicate all the specifics of audit committee activity, and instead implicitly assume that the audit committee will correctly exercise some level of oversight of the financial reporting function. For many audit committee members, however, that "oversight" will translate into listening to the outside auditor once a year. The concept of active oversight of the financial reporting process and establishing broad objectives for the outside auditor would strike many audit committee members as completely backward.

Some or all of the above audit committee inadequacies may be found in companies that have experienced accounting irregularities. Almost always there will be an additional one. That is that the audit committee—no matter how independent, sophisticated, or active—will have functioned largely in ignorance. It will not have had a clue as to what was happening within the organization. The reason is that a typical audit committee (and the problem here is much broader than newly public startups) will get most of its information from management and from the outside auditor. Rarely is management going to reveal financial manipulations. And, for reasons explained later, reliance on the outside auditor for the discovery of the accounting irregularities is hazardous at best. Even the most sophisticated and attentive of audit committee members have had the misfortune of accounting irregularities that have unexpectedly surfaced on their watch.

The unfortunate lack of access to candid information on the part of the audit committee directs attention to the second in the triumvirate of fraud preventers: the internal audit department.

Internal Audit

It may be that the internal audit department is one of the least understood, and most ineffectively used, of all vehicles to combat financial fraud. Theoretically, internal audit is perfectly positioned to nip in the bud an accounting irregularity problem. The internal auditors are theoretically trained in financial reporting and accounting. The internal auditors theoretically have a vivid understanding as to how financial fraud begins and grows. Unlike the outside auditor, internal auditors do not merely appear once a year: they work at the company full time. And, theoretically, the internal auditors should be able to plug themselves into the financial reporting environment and report directly to the audit committee what they have seen and heard.

The reason all of these theoretical vehicles for the detection and prevention of financial fraud have not been effective is that, where massive fraud has surfaced, the internal audit department has been somewhere between nonfunctional and nonexistent. In part, this may be the result of an unfortunate cultural tradition in which, as one business leader has put it, internal auditors are viewed as the Rodney Dangerfields of corporate governance—they get no respect. Whatever the explanation, where massive financial fraud has surfaced, a viable internal audit function is typically nowhere to be found.

The Outside Auditor

That, of course, leaves the outside auditor which, for most public companies, means some of the largest accounting firms in the world. Indeed, it is frequently the inclination of those learning of an accounting irregularity problem to point to a failure by the outside auditor as the principal explanation. Recent criticisms made against the accounting profession have included compromised independence, a transformation in the audit function away from data assurance, the use of immature and inexperienced audit staff for important audit functions, and the perceived use by the large accounting firms of audit as a loss leader rather than a viable professional engagement in its own right.

Each of these is certainly worthy of consideration and inquiry, but the fundamental explanation for the failure of the outside audit to detect financial fraud lies in the way that fraudulent financial reporting typically begins and grows. Most important is the fact that, as discussed earlier, the fraud almost inevitably starts out very small—well beneath the radar screen of the materiality thresholds of a normal audit pursuant to generally accepted auditing standards (GAAS)—and almost inevitably begins with issues of quarterly timing. Quarterly timing is not normally a subject of intense audit scrutiny; the auditor, rather, is concerned with financial performance for the entire year. The combined effect of the small size of an accounting irregularity at its origin and the fact that it begins with an allocation of financial results over quarters almost guarantees that, at least at the outset, the fraud will escape outside auditor detection.

These two attributes of financial fraud at the outset are compounded by another problem that enables it to escape auditor detection. That problem is that, at root, massive financial fraud stems from a certain type of corporate environment. Of those involved, perhaps no one is worse positioned to detect that type of environment than the outside accountants conducting the annual audit. The typical audit may involve fieldwork at the company once a year. That once-a-year period may only last for eight or 12 weeks. During the fieldwork, the individual accountants are typically secreted by themselves in a conference room. In dealing with these accountants, moreover, employees are frequently on their guard. There exists, accordingly, little opportunity for the outside accountants to get plugged into the all-important corporate environment and culture, which is where financial fraud has its origins.

As the fraud inevitably grows, of course, its materiality increases as does the number of individuals involved. Correspondingly, also increasing is the susceptibility of the fraud to outside auditor detection. However, at the point where the fraud approaches the thresholds at which outside auditor detection becomes a realistic possibility, deception of the auditor becomes one of the preoccupations of the perpetrators. False schedules, forged documents, manipulated accounting entries, fabrications and lies at all levels—each of these becomes a vehicle for perpetrating the fraud during the annual inter-lude of audit testing. Ultimately, the fraud almost inevitably becomes too large to continue to escape discovery, and auditor detection at some point is by no means unusual. The problem is that, by the time the fraud is suffi-ciently large, it has probably gone on for years.

That is not to exonerate the audit profession, and certainly profession-wide improvements should be considered. These might include greater in-volvement of the outside auditor in quarterly data, the reduction of materi-ality thresholds, and a greater effort on the part of the profession to assess the corporate culture and environment. Nonetheless, compared to, say, the potential for early fraud detection possessed by the internal audit depart-ment, the once-a-year outside auditor is at a noticeable disadvantage.

The Fraud Surfaces

So, having been missed for so long by so many, how does the fraud typi-cally surface? One of several ways. Sometimes there's a change in person-nel, either from a corporate acquisition or a change in management, and the new hires stumble onto the problems. Sometimes the fraud—which quarter to quarter is mathematically incapable of staying the same—grows to the point where it can no longer be hidden from the outside auditor. Sometimes detection results when the conscience of one of the accounting department people gets the better of him. All along he wanted to tell somebody. And it gets to the point where he can't stand it anymore and he does. Then you have a whistle-blower.

Now there are exceptions to all of this. But in almost any big accounting irregularity problem, one will almost inevitably see some or all of these ele-ments. We need just change the names of the companies and the people and the industry.

A Crisis for the Board

So that's the origin of an accounting irregularity. And when it surfaces, prob-lems will come out of the woodwork like nothing the board of directors has ever seen. Those problems will involve crises of corporate governance; of disclosure; and with creditors, employees, insurers, and shareholders. And that's just in the first two hours.

Before we get to this myriad of corporate problems, though, it is worth pausing to take stock of the plight of an unfortunate outside director who suddenly learns of an accounting irregularities problem on an otherwise uneventful afternoon. He didn't have a clue of any financial misreporting. He knew nothing of undue pressure for financial performance or that the company was not doing as well as it said. Now he's being told of massive financial fraud and asked to report for an emergency board meeting the next morning. The urgency of the request makes clear to him that he had better put aside everything else and oblige.

Such a director could hardly be blamed, however, if he momentarily turned away from critical issues of corporate operations and financial reporting to consider just briefly his own vulnerability: Will he get sued? Did he do everything he was supposed to? Is responsibility for this problem in part his? Or will the blame go entirely to the outside auditor and to the director of internal audit? (Actually, our director is not even sure who the director of internal audit is.)

All of the director's questions are valid. So before turning to the immediate crises engulfing a corporation in the wake of a massive financial fraud, let's take on some of this director's questions. When accounting irregularities surface, who is going to get the blame?

CHAPTER 2

SO WHO GETS THE BLAME?

Michael R. Young

Pausing to think about who will get the blame is not a frivolous exercise by any means. Once an irregularity has been exposed, class action litigation is only days away. That litigation is sure to include as defendants almost anyone within the vicinity of the accounting irregularity or the company's financial reporting function. Beyond that, investigations by the Securities and Exchange Commission (SEC) and the National Association of Securities Dealers (NASD) (or, for larger companies, the New York Stock Exchange [NYSE]) will quickly follow. The targets of investigation and inquiry will quickly fall into three categories. One is those who will be viewed as guilty. The second is those who will be viewed as not guilty. The third is those who could go either way.

Focusing on the allocation of responsibility for the financial misstatements, therefore, is a natural first step. However, determining that allocation is not easy. At bottom, it requires an understanding of an evolution of responsibility for financial reporting that has taken place over roughly the last 15 years (Exhibit 2–1). Spurred in part by privately commissioned groups, the SEC, and the accounting profession, the principal theme of the evolution has been a shift in responsibility for financial reporting. In particular, the prevalent theme has been a shift in responsibility for financial reporting to those within the reporting entity itself. That is not to suggest the evolution is complete. With the advent of an entire set of new initiatives and rules by the SEC, the evolution continues to this day.

Blaming the Outside Auditor

To begin, let's go back about 20 years—to the early part of the 1980s. Back then, things were not quite so complex and the target of blame for financial

---

Exhibit 2–1. The Evolution of Financial Reporting

- Treadway Commission Report (1987)
- Expectation Gap revision of Statements on Auditing Standards (1989)
- Private Securities Litigation Reform Act (1995)
- Independence Standards Board (1997)
- Levitt Speech at New York University (1998)
- Securities Litigation Uniform Standards Act (1998)
- Report of Blue Ribbon Committee on Improving the Effectiveness of Corporate Audit Committees (1999)
- New rules of the SEC, NYSE, NASD, and American Stock Exchange (1999)

---

misreporting was fairly straightforward. It would be blamed on the outside auditor. There were several reasons, but most of them revolved around the fact that the auditor had money. In the inevitable litigation, a typical outside director, or for that matter senior executive, might simply testify, "I was relying on the outside auditor," to the general satisfaction of all.

All, that is, except the auditor. For its part, the auditor quickly came to realize that it was in a no-win position. Given the way that financial fraud develops, by the time an accounting irregularity had surfaced the auditor would typically be in the unenviable position of having missed it for years. Subsequent scrutiny of the auditor's workpapers would by definition show that, sure enough, had the auditor undertaken this or that additional task, the fraud would have been exposed.

Once the auditor actually entered the courtroom, the situation only became more difficult. There, the contention of fraud detection as an auditor's responsibility fed into a jury's normal inclination to view the auditor as providing a "guarantee" of accuracy or "a clean bill of health," which was accompanied by only a hazy understanding of what generally accepted auditing standards (GAAS) actually required the auditor to do. The common courtroom scenario would involve the auditor getting blamed from all sides. The auditor's defensive-sounding response that it should be viewed as a fellow victim of the fraud, rather than a participant, could be a tough sell.

In this context, the law was no help at all. To the contrary, courts came to view the accounting profession almost as a vehicle for risk diversification. Thus, one state supreme court justified an expansion of audit liability through an observation that "independent auditors have apparently been able to obtain liability insurance . . . to satisfy their financial obligations." Other courts similarly expanded the categories of plaintiffs who, when accounting problems surfaced, were entitled to sue. Federal courts, interpreting the federal securities laws, came to the conclusion that investors could be found to have relied upon audit reports they had never even seen.

Within the accounting firms during the first half of the 1980s, therefore, two things grew. One was their in-house legal departments. The other was their exposure to liability. Data collected by the then Big Six firms showed that those firms by themselves would ultimately end up facing legal liability of around $30 billion—roughly $3.8 million per partner.

It was thus somewhat understandable that, by the mid-1980s, the accounting profession had come to view the liability landscape with a blend of frustration and terror. On the one hand, its exposure to liability seemed to be increasing almost exponentially as financial community frustration intensified over the profession's seemingly inexplicable inability to detect fraudulent financial reporting before it got out of hand. On the other hand, the ability of a typical outside auditor to discover fraud at the outset was limited. Key members of the financial community came to the fairly vivid realization that it was time to rethink, and to rationalize, the allocation of responsibility for fraudulent financial reporting between the outside auditor and others. The question was how to do it.

The Treadway Commission

The stage was thus set for what would prove to be a watershed in the evolution of financial reporting and corporate governance: The formation of the National Commission on Fraudulent Financial Reporting, which later came to be known as the Treadway Commission after its chairman, former SEC Commissioner James Treadway. The task to be undertaken by the Treadway Commission went to the crux of the matter. The Commission's task was to investigate the underlying causes of fraudulent financial reporting, to examine the role of the outside auditor in the detection of fraud, and to analyze the extent to which corporate structure may allow fraudulent financial reporting to take place.

The Treadway Commission began its study in 1985 and over a two-year period undertook an exhaustive investigation of the root causes of financial fraud. Subjects of investigation and analysis included internal control systems, internal auditing, the significance of intra-corporate pressures for performance, management failures, and inadequacies of the accounting profession. Ultimately, the Commission undertook more than 20 separate research projects and briefing papers. In addition, the Commission investigated the views and perceptions of key financial regulatory agencies and groups, including the SEC, the FDIC, the Comptroller of the Currency, the American Institute of Certified Public Accountants (AICPA), the Auditing Standards Board, the Financial Executives Institute, and the Institute of Internal Auditors. Twice the Commission appeared before the House Committee on Energy and Commerce's Subcommittee on Oversight and Investigations as part of that subcommittee's inquiry into the adequacy of auditing, accounting, and financial reporting practices. Prior to its publication, 40,000 copies of an exposure draft of the Commission's report were publicly distributed for comment.

The resulting Report of the National Commission on Fraudulent Financial Reporting was published in October 1987. Among other things, it concluded the following: Foremost, "fraudulent financial reporting usually does not begin with an overt intentional act to distort the financial statements." Rather, the Treadway Commission found that fraudulent financial reporting frequently came about as "the culmination of a series of acts designed to respond to operational difficulties." What tended to happen, the Commission concluded, was that initially "the activities may not be fraudulent, but in time they become increasingly questionable" until, finally, someone steps over the line.

The Treadway Commission also found that, behind the individuals stepping over the line into financial fraud, was almost always undue pressure. It might be "unrealistic pressures, particularly for short-term results" or "financial pressure resulting from bonus plans that depend on short-term economic performance" or pressure from "the desire to obtain a higher price for a stock or debt offering or to meet the expectation of investors." At the core of fraudulent financial reporting, though, the Commission almost inevitably found pressure. The Commission stated:

The Commission's studies revealed that fraudulent financial reporting usually occurs as the result of certain environmental, institutional, or individual forces and opportunities. These forces and opportunities add pressures and incentives that encourage individuals and companies to engage in fraudulent financial reporting and are present to some degree in all companies. If the right, combustible mixture of forces and opportunities is present, fraudulent financial reporting may occur.

Any effort to combat fraud, therefore, had to start at the top. In particular, responsibility for reliable financial reporting had to reside "first and foremost at the corporate level." Thus, top management had to establish the proper "tone at the top"—an attitude that demanded truth and candor in financial reporting and that, just as important, saw to it that pressures for financial performance did not get out of hand. Such a tone at the top then had to penetrate every fiber of the enterprise so that it became part of the corporate culture. The Commission summarized: "The tone set by top management—the corporate environment or culture within which financial reporting occurs—is the most important factor contributing to the integrity of the financial reporting process."

The problem with the Treadway Commission's determination to place foremost responsibility for financial reporting on the tone set by top management was that, of all groups within an enterprise, it was probably top management that was most vulnerable to pressures from outside forces. Those forces might include investors, financial analysts, bankers, owners, or others—some of whom may not be expected to appreciate fully the importance of the tone at the top and who may rather maintain a greater interest in the bottom line. For top management, establishing the right amount of pressure to achieve results, while at the same time ensuring that at no level of the enterprise did the pressure get out of hand, would pose a formidable challenge.

It is for this reason that the Treadway Commission posited a key role in financial reporting beyond that of senior management. That key role was to be filled by the board of directors and, in particular, by its audit committee. Through "establishment of an informed, vigilant and effective audit committee to oversee the company's financial reporting process," a board of directors could thereby act as a backstop for senior management and undertake to ensure that a proper tone at the top and financial reporting system remained in place. The centrality of the audit committee's function to financial reporting was emphasized by the Commission's formulation of eight separate recommendations regarding audit committees that were directed to public companies:

- The board of directors of all public companies should be required by SEC rule to establish audit committees composed solely of independent directors.

- Audit committees should be informed, vigilant, and effective overseers of the financial reporting process and the company's internal controls.

- All public companies should develop a written charter setting forth the duties and responsibilities of the audit committee. The board of directors should approve the charter, review it periodically, and modify it as necessary.

- Audit committees should have adequate resources and authority to discharge their responsibilities.

- The audit committee should review management's evaluation of factors related to the independence of the company's public accountant. Both the audit committee and management should assist the public accountant in preserving his independence.

- Before the beginning of each year, the audit committee should review management's plans for engaging the company's independent public accountant to perform management advisory services during the coming year, considering both the types of services that may be rendered and the projected fees.

- Management should advise the audit committee when it seeks a second opinion on a significant accounting issue.

- Audit committees should oversee the quarterly reporting process.

To complement the efforts of the audit committee, the Treadway Commission also recommended an effective internal audit function that would report directly to the audit committee and thereby be positioned to act as the audit committee's eyes and ears. (See Exhibit 2–2.)

Consequences of the Treadway Commission Report

The reason the Treadway Commission report is central to any modern day assessment of those who stand to be blamed for financial misreporting is

Exhibit 2–2. Key Recommendations of the Treadway Commission for Public Companies

Recommendation 1:   Top management must identify, understand, and assess the factors that may cause the company's financial statements to be fraudulently misstated.

Recommendation 2:   Public companies should maintain internal controls that provide reasonable assurance that fraudulent financial reporting will be prevented or subject to early detection.

Recommendation 5:   Public companies should maintain an effective internal audit function staffed with an adequate number of qualified personnel that is appropriate to the size and the nature of the company.

Recommendation 9:   The board of directors of all public companies should be required by SEC rule to establish audit committees composed solely of independent directors.

Recommendation 10:   Audit committees should be informed, vigilant, and effective overseers of the financial reporting process and the company's internal controls.

Recommendation 13:   Both the audit committee and management should assist the public accountant in preserving his independence.

Recommendation 17:   Management should advise the audit committee when it seeks a second opinion on a significant accounting issue.

Recommendation 19:   Audit committees should oversee the quarterly reporting process.

that the report's publication basically marked a sea of change in the allocation of financial reporting responsibility. Implicit in the report's findings and recommendations was the notion that reliance for the prevention of fraud on mechanisms outside the corporate structure—and, in particular, on the annual audit function—was not enough. Indeed, the Treadway Commission explicitly relegated the outside auditor to "a crucial, but secondary role" and cautioned that outside auditors could not be viewed as "guarantors of the accuracy or the reliability of financial statements." Rather, the genesis of financial fraud took place as a consequence of pressures and a tone within the company and, if financial fraud was to be prevented and detected at the outset, the mechanisms to do so must exist within the corporation itself. An effect of the Treadway Commission's findings and recommendations, therefore, was to shift responsibility for accurate financial reporting onto the shoulders of senior management, outside directors, internal audit, and—most important—audit committees.

Upon the report's publication in October 1987, the findings and recommendations of the Treadway Commission garnered almost extraordinary attention and support. Members of Congress instantaneously came to view its recommendations as authoritative. Legal writers discussed at length the Treadway report and advocated a level of diligence consistent with its recommendations. The national accounting firms separately took steps to apprise the directors and officers of their client companies as to precisely what was now expected of them according to the report's recommendations. Thus, the accounting firms published their own monographs, duly distributed to corporate officials, that highlighted the recommendations of the Treadway Commission and outlined their views as to what corporate officials, and audit committees in particular, should be doing. Management letters, typically issued at the conclusion of an audit engagement, explicitly or implicitly began to assume Treadway Commission recommendations as important criteria against which the corporate-governance aspects of internal control systems were to be measured. The Treadway Commission's recommendations in effect became the touchstone for the evaluation of financial reporting systems.

Further Developments

The effect of the Treadway Commission's report did not, moreover, stop with the Commission's findings and recommendations themselves. The

Commission also affected a series of subsequent financial reporting initiatives and developments. Even beyond the four corners of the report, therefore, Commission findings and recommendations influenced the evolution of financial reporting. Among the effects was a further shift of responsibility for financial reporting to those within the reporting entity.

One of these further developments was a concerted effort by members of the accounting profession to make clear to the public that it was performing—in the words of the Treadway Commission—only a "secondary" role. Within the profession, this became colloquially known as the effort to close the expectation gap—the gap perceived to exist between what juries in accountant malpractice litigation seemed to assume to be the auditor's role and the auditor's role in fact. The impetus behind this initiative was a concern, rooted in the experience of individual CPA firms in audit malpractice litigation, that the public assumed a much greater level of responsibility on the part of the outside auditor than the outside auditor under professional standards was prepared to fulfill. That responsibility, the accounting profession sought to demonstrate, really belonged to management.

Here, too, one of the more significant results was a clearer allocation of responsibility for financial reporting between corporate officials and the outside auditor. One visible consequence was a revision of the standard form of auditor's report, which now stated explicitly on the face of the report what had earlier been buried in the underlying literature articulating GAAS: that the "financial statements are the responsibility of the Company's management," whereas the auditor's responsibility is only to "express an opinion on these financial statements based on our audit." Although the expectation-gap initiative also involved some assumption by the auditor of increased responsibilities for the detection of fraud, it highlighted the primary responsibility as that of corporate management.

Still another development operated to affect the allocation of responsibility for financial reporting between corporate officials and auditors. That is the much-touted "litigation crisis" and the very real concern that, if the accounting profession remained at the forefront of liability for fraudulent financial reporting, every national accounting firm was going to be driven out of business. Headlines advertised not only extraordinary jury verdicts but extraordinary settlements as well. Ernst & Young's $400 million settlement with the federal government appeared in giant headlines on the front page of the *New York Times*.

The resulting appearance of professional vulnerability was furthered by business decisions made by the individual CPA firms: They started firing their clients. Accordingly, the financial press began to report impediments to expanding enterprise owing simply to the unavailability of financial statement audits. A March 1, 1993 article in *Business Week* is typical. In an article titled "Big Six Firms Are Firing Clients," *Business Week* reported:

> With growing regularity, major public accounting firms are turning their backs on many smaller banks, thrifts, and fledgling companies. Deloitte & Touche, for one, declined to audit about 60 companies trying to go public last year, more than half the 103 initial public offerings they actually evaluated.

Business Week described the reason as "no mystery." It was because "[i]n recent years, accounting firms have been forced to fork over hundreds of millions of dollars to settle lawsuits."

The prospect of accounting firms going out of business or firing clients turned the conventional wisdom—underlying the allocation of responsibility between management and the outside auditor—on its head. The conventional wisdom, typified by a 1983 decision by the New Jersey Supreme Court, had been that the placement of broad responsibility for financial reporting upon the outside auditor would operate, among other things, as a mechanism to enhance financial reporting and, at the same time, to diversify risk. The analysis was proved incorrect. The system was in trouble.

All of this culminated in broader scrutiny as to responsibility for financial reporting and a broader assessment of the extent to which corporate officials, rather than outside professionals, should be at the forefront of those held accountable for financial fraud. Courts began to take notice. In the thick of this reawakening emerged decisions such as the California Supreme Court's opinion in *Bily v. Arthur Young & Co.*, which scrutinized the role of an outside auditor and precisely what level of responsibility an auditor of financial statements was assuming (See Exhibit 2–3). Decisions placing broad responsibilities on auditors such as that in New Jersey came to be undermined or, in the case of the New Jersey decision itself, reversed by the legislature.

So Who Gets the Blame?

The principal consequence of all this is the resulting focus on those within the corporate entity as the principal safeguard against fraudulent financial

Exhibit 2–3. Evolving Perceptions of Auditor Responsibility

"By certifying the public records that collectively depict a corporation's financial status, the independent auditor assumes a public responsibility transcending any employment relationship with the client. The independent public accountant performing this special function owes ultimate allegiance to the corporation's creditors and stockholders, as well as to the investing public. This 'public watchdog' function demands that the accountant maintain total independence from the client at all times and requires complete fidelity to the public trust."

United States v. Arthur Young & Co., 465 U.S. 805, 817–18 (1984).

"An auditor is a watchdog, not a bloodhound.... As a matter of commercial reality, audits are performed in a client-controlled environment. The client typically prepares its own financial statements; it has direct control over and assumes primary responsibility for their contents.... The client engages the auditor, pays for the audit, and communicates with audit personnel throughout the engagement. Because the auditor cannot in the time available become an expert in the client's business and record-keeping systems, the client necessarily furnishes the information base for the audit. Thus, regardless of the efforts of the auditor, the client retains effective primary control of the financial reporting process."

Bily v. Arthur Young & Co., 3 Cal. 4th 370, 399–400 (1992).

reporting. This is not to say that management and boards of directors may no longer rely upon outside professionals for assistance. Nor is it to suggest that it will be incumbent upon executives and directors to aggressively second-guess the judgment of professionals or that outside professionals—be they auditors, lawyers, underwriters, or others—are to be exonerated from any responsibility for a failure of financial reporting systems. The point, rather, is that responsibility for financial reporting has evolved in such a way that ultimate responsibility for the integrity of the financial reporting system will be placed on those within the reporting entity. In other words, where fraudulent financial reporting should surface, among the candidates to share in the blame will be executives and directors themselves.

What will they get blamed for? The answer depends on the particular circumstances at issue, but it is not difficult to pinpoint the fundamental aspects of a financial reporting system that investigators may conclude had broken down.

1. *Too much pressure.*   Foremost, if the integrity of the financial reporting system has been compromised as a result of excessive pressure for performance, blame may find its way to those senior executives by whom that pressure was placed. True, investigators will hopefully understand that all executives place upon operating personnel some level of pressure for performance and that, in the absence of some degree of pressure, optimal performance may not be attained. Nonetheless, senior executives may be criticized where the pressure reaches a level that compromises the truthfulness of the company's financial disclosures.

2. *An inadequately configured audit committee.*   Where fraudulent financial reporting surfaces, both senior executives and outside directors may find themselves sharing in the blame in the absence of an adequately configured audit committee staffed with sufficiently independent, sophisticated, and diligent members. Particularly as a result of new independence and financial sophistication requirements by the NYSE and NASD (see Chapter 11), an audit committee whose membership consists, for example, of family members, professionals charging large fees to the enterprise, or individuals with little expertise in matters of financial reporting may be found not to measure up.

3. *An insufficiently diligent audit committee.*   If an appropriately configured audit committee is in place, it may nonetheless find itself subject to criticism to the extent it has failed to deploy its talents by actively overseeing the company's system of financial reporting. This is not to suggest that an outside director, upon becoming a member of an audit committee, must immediately resign his day job and become a micro-manager, directing his energies to the inspection of general ledgers for suspicious-looking transactions. The audit com-

mittee members will be expected to remain at an oversight level. At the same time, though, the audit committee may be called upon to look into whether the basics of a sound financial reporting system are in place and, in particular, to seek the installation of mechanisms whereby the audit committee is provided with regular and reliable information as to just what is happening within the enterprise. Among other things, for example, the audit committee will want to inquire as to whether the financial reporting function is adequately supervised by a sufficiently sophisticated chief financial officer and whether the accounting department is adequately staffed and logistically capable of producing reliable reports.

4. *Lack of internal audit.* As financial reporting further evolves, executives and directors at larger companies may begin to suffer criticism in the absence of a viable internal audit function. An important function of internal audit would be to obtain direct information as to what is happening within the company and, in particular, the effect that the tone at the top or the environment is having on accuracy in financial reporting. At the moment, the role of internal audit in public companies has probably not developed to the point where the absence of a viable internal audit capability would subject audit committee members or outside directors to a substantial risk of criticism. On the other hand, things could be heading in that direction.

5. *Insufficient demands for information from the outside auditor.* Beyond effective use of internal audit, the audit committee may increasingly be faulted if it has failed to exploit fully the information available from the outside auditor. Audit committees are increasingly being encouraged to engage in an open and frank dialogue with the auditor while, at the same time, the accounting profession is encouraging auditors to respond in kind. Executives and directors may find themselves criticized where they do not seek to take advantage of the enhanced opportunity for information.

How serious is the exposure where there is a failure to install these basics? At the moment, financial reporting responsibilities are in a state of flux, owing to the uncertainty introduced into the established standard of care by the accelerating pace of change. Indeed, to put all this in context, today any number of well-meaning executives and directors, acting entirely in good faith, could probably be found to have in place financial reporting systems which, measured against the above criteria, are less than optimal. It goes without saying, moreover, that a failure of financial reporting systems by itself does not come anywhere close to demonstrating executive or director complicity in a fraud. Still, where the basics of a viable financial reporting system have not been established, senior executives, outside directors, and audit committee members may find themselves getting blamed from all sides. Increasingly, for example, even diligent audit committee members are being targeted as defendants in class action litigation and, at the same time, class action law firms are focusing on failures of internal control systems as an underlying predicate for securities claims. Regulators are looking askance at boards of directors and audit committees that fail to seek the installation of viable financial reporting systems. Corporate executives and directors may even find themselves liable to their outside auditor, which, under recent legal developments, may itself be entitled to sue corporate officials for fraud and negligence where the auditor has been deceived as to the existence of accounting irregularities in a company's underlying books and records.

The manner in which corporate officials' financial reporting responsibilities have expanded over the last 15 years, moreover, contributes to the existence of a lengthy paper trail pointing to corporate officials' financial reporting and corporate governance responsibilities. Recall, for example, the accounting firm monographs and newsletters mentioned earlier that assumed Treadway-style financial reporting systems as a basis for recommendations on internal control system improvements. Such information, calculated to increase awareness, may place a corporate executive, director, or audit committee member on the defensive to the extent that he has failed to act upon them. Consider as well the plethora of internal memoranda, correspondence, board packages, or even press reports on issues of potential inadequacies in, or improvements to, financial reporting systems. The net effect of such information is that, throughout corporate America, the bar is being raised. Those who fail to act in response may potentially find themselves defending their inactivity should fraudulent financial reporting surface on their watch.

The Levitt Initiatives

The most recent chapter in this saga took place at New York University on September 28, 1998, when SEC chairman Arthur Levitt announced a new set of initiatives in response to the SEC's perception that accounting irregularities are on the rise (Exhibit 2–4). These Levitt initiatives spanned a wide range of subjects and included regulatory and private-sector proposals to address a variety of potential accounting abuses.

The most notable aspect of the Levitt initiatives, however, was their fundamental reliance on the Treadway Commission's financial reporting concepts for their predicate. Accordingly, at the core of the Levitt initiatives was the concept of "qualified, committed, independent and tough-minded audit committees":

> And, finally, qualified, committed, independent and tough-minded audit committees represent the most reliable guardians of the public interest. Sadly, stories abound of audit committees whose members lack expertise in the basic principles of financial reporting as well as the mandate to ask probing questions. In fact, I've heard of one audit committee that convenes only twice a year before the regular board meeting for 15 minutes and whose duties are limited to a perfunctory presentation.
>
> Compare that situation with the audit committee which meets 12 times a year before each board meeting; where every member has a financial background; where there are no personal ties to the chairman or the company; where they have their own advisers; where they ask tough questions of management and outside auditors; and where, ultimately, the investor interest is being served.

Exhibit 2–4. Arthur Levitt's September 28, 1998, Speech

Plans to improve the reliability and transparency of financial statements:

- Technical rule changes by regulators to improve the accounting framework

- Improved outside auditing in the financial reporting process

- A strengthened audit committee process

- Cultural changes on the part of corporate management and the financial community

---

> The SEC stands ready to take appropriate action if that interest is not protected. But, a private sector response that empowers audit committees and obviates the need for public sector dictates seems the wisest choice. I am pleased to announce that the financial community has agreed to accept this challenge.

The consequences of the Levitt initiatives are still unfolding, but an important one was the formation of the Blue Ribbon Committee on Improving the Effectiveness of Corporate Audit Committees. After hearings on the effectiveness of financial reporting systems and, in particular, corporate audit committees, the Blue Ribbon Committee in February 1999 issued a series of recommendations for new rules by the NASD, the NYSE, the American Stock Exchange, the SEC, and the AICPA, which, to a large extent, either duplicated or carried further the recommendations made by the Treadway Commission 13 years before. Again, we see an emphasis on the centrality of audit committees in the prevention of fraudulent financial reporting, accompanied by renewed emphasis on the role of internal audit.

In substance, the committee's recommendations, some of which were directed only to companies with a market capitalization of $200 million or more, were these:

- Audit committees should be comprised solely of independent directors.

- Members of an audit committee shall be considered independent only if they have no relationship to the corporation that may interfere with the exercise of their independence from management and the corporation.

- A non-independent director may be appointed to an audit committee only if the board, under exceptional and limited circumstances, determines that membership on the committee by the individual is required by the best interests of the corporation and its shareholders and the board discloses, in the next annual proxy statement subsequent to such determination, the nature of the relationship and the reasons for that determination.

- Audit committees should be comprised of a minimum of three directors, each of whom is financially literate (as described in a section of the report titled "Financial Literacy") or becomes financially literate within a reasonable period of time after his or her appointment to the audit committee. At least one member of the audit committee should have accounting or related financial management expertise.

- Audit committees should (i) adopt a formal written charter that is approved by the full board of directors and that specifies the scope of the committee's responsibilities and how it carries out those responsibilities, including structure, processes, and membership requirements, and (ii) review and reassess the adequacy of the audit committee charter on an annual basis.

- The SEC should promulgate rules that require audit committees to disclose in the company's annual proxy statement whether the audit committee has adopted a formal written charter and, if so, whether the audit committee satisfied its responsibilities during the prior year in compliance with its charter, which shall be disclosed at least triennially in the annual report to shareholders or proxy statement.

- The audit committee charter for every listed company should specify that the outside auditor is ultimately accountable to the board of directors and the audit committee, as representatives of shareholders, and that these shareholder representatives have the ultimate authority and responsibility to select, evaluate, and, where appropriate, replace the outside auditor (or to nominate the outside auditor to be proposed for shareholder approval in any proxy statement).

- The audit committee charter for every listed company should specify that the audit committee is responsible for ensuring its receipt from the outside auditor of a formal written statement delineating all relationships between the auditor and the company, consistent with Independence Standards Board Standard 1, and that the audit committee is also responsible for actively engaging in a dialogue with the auditor with respect to any disclosed relationships or services that may affect the objectivity and independence of the auditor and for taking, or recommending that the full board take, appropriate action to ensure the independence of the outside auditor.

- GAAS should require that a company's outside auditor discuss with the audit committee the auditor's judgments about the quality, not just the acceptability, of the company's accounting principles as applied in its financial reporting; the discussion should include such issues as the clarity of the company's financial disclosures and degree of aggressiveness or conservatism of the company's accounting principles and underlying estimates and other significant decisions made by management in preparing the financial disclosure and reviewed by the outside auditors. This requirement should be written in a way to encourage open, frank discussion and to avoid boilerplate.

- The SEC should require all reporting companies to include a letter from the audit committee in the company's annual report to shareholders and Form 10-K Annual Report disclosing whether or not, with respect to the prior fiscal year, (i) management has reviewed the audited financial statements with the audit committee, including a discussion of the quality of the accounting principles as applied and significant judgments affecting the company's financial statements; (ii) the outside auditors have discussed with the audit committee the outside auditor's judgments of the quality of those principles as applied and judgments referenced in item (i) under the circumstances; (iii) the members of the audit committee have discussed among themselves, without management or the outside auditors present, the information disclosed to the audit committee described in items (i) and (ii); and (iv) the audit committee, in reliance on the review and discussions conducted with management and the outside auditors pursuant to items (i) and (ii), believes that the company's financial statements are fairly presented in conformity with GAAP in all material respects. The SEC should adopt a "safe harbor" applicable to any such disclosure.

- The SEC should require that a reporting company's outside auditor conduct a SAS-71 (Interim Financial Review) review before the company files its Form 10-Q.

- SAS-71 should be amended to require that a reporting company's outside auditor discuss with the audit committee, or at least its chairman, and a representative of financial management, in person, or by telephone conference call, the matters described in AU Section 380 (Communications With the Audit Committee) before filing Form 10-Q (and preferably before any public announcement of financial results), including significant adjustments, management judgments and accounting estimates, significant new accounting policies, and disagreements with management.

In the months following their publication, these Blue Ribbon Committee recommendations were the subject of vigorous debate. On the one hand, advocates of improved corporate governance maintained that the adoption of these recommendations was critical to improved financial reporting systems. Indeed, a report by the Committee of Sponsoring Organizations of the Treadway Commission caused some to suggest that, insofar as the report found that accounting irregularities tended to strike with frequency at smaller companies, the recommendations of the committee should be made applicable to companies with even less than the $200 million market capitalization proposed by the committee in certain instances as a cutoff. On the other hand, corporate defense lawyers understandably raised concerns about the corresponding increase in legal liability to boards of directors and, in particular, audit committees.

On December 15, 1999, the SEC approved a series of new rules as a consequence of the Blue Ribbon Committee recommendations. In substance, virtually all of the Blue Ribbon Committee's recommendations were adopted. Thus, the new rules:

- Required audit committees to include at least three members and generally be comprised solely of "independent" directors who are financially literate

- Defined *independence* more rigorously for audit committee members

- Required companies to adopt written charters for their audit committees

- Gave the audit committee the right to hire and terminate the auditor

- Required at least one member of the audit committee to have accounting or financial management expertise

- Required companies' interim financial statements to be reviewed by independent auditors before filing

- Required companies to provide in their proxy statements a report from the audit committee that discloses whether the audit committee reviewed and discussed certain matters with management and the auditors and whether the audit committee recommended to the board that the audited financial statements be included in the Form 10-K

- Required companies to disclose in their proxy statements whether the audit committee has a written charter and to file a copy of the charter every three years, and

- Required companies whose securities are listed on the NYSE or AMEX or are quoted on Nasdaq to disclose certain information about any audit committee member who is not "independent."

The liability concerns raised by opponents of the new rules were legitimate ones, but to some extent they were being raised too late. The horse was already out of the barn. Even before publication of the Blue Ribbon Committee recommendations, plaintiffs' lawyers were vividly aware of the increased expectations being placed upon audit committees and, as a matter of course, were naming audit committee members as defendants in class action litigation where accounting irregularities had surfaced. Adoption of the Blue Ribbon Committee recommendations, therefore, is likely to have a limited effect on the extent to which audit committee members will get sued. If audit committee members want to avoid becoming defendants, the best way is to prevent accounting irregularities from happening in the first place.

CHAPTER 3

THE IMMEDIATE AFTERMATH

Jack H. Nusbaum and John Oller

Once a potential accounting irregularity has been uncovered, the board of directors must immediately begin the process of investigating the matter and dealing with the crisis atmosphere that is likely to pervade the company in the immediate aftermath of the discovery. Indeed, crisis management is a phrase that aptly describes what happens in the first few days following the uncovering of a financial fraud. Although there is no standard time frame for when the aftermath begins once an accounting irregularity is discovered—it may be a day, a week, or three weeks after the discovery—there are typical events and issues that the company will need to consider in those first few days.

Chapter 3 addresses the period from the time a potential fraud is uncovered to the time the company concludes that the problem is real and sufficiently serious that it needs to be publicly disclosed and made the subject of an independent, full-scale investigation.

The Preliminary Investigation

An important factor to keep in mind at the outset is that the company does not want to jump to conclusions. After all, it has imperfect information at this early stage. Hypothesize, for example, that a whistleblower has come forward in the manner described in Chapter 1. It may be that this individual misunderstood the facts, or lacks first-hand knowledge, or is withholding information. The whistleblower also may have overstated the problem or understated it. Perhaps he is holding a grudge. The whistleblower may be wrong, and the company may be dealing with accidental accounting errors rather than irregularities or fraud.

In any event, the company will need to conduct a preliminary investigation to verify the problem and to determine how substantial it is. The preliminary investigation could be conducted by any number of people. Financial management could conduct it, unless the company believes financial management was involved in a fraud. Other options include the company's regular outside auditor, internal auditors, general counsel, or outside counsel. Or the preliminary investigation could be carried out by a combination of these people.

Early on in the preliminary investigation, the investigators will have to ask the company's chief financial officer and high ranking accounting and financial personnel what they know about the whistleblower's allegations. Perhaps after talking to these more senior financial personnel the investigators will conclude that a problem does not exist and it was a simple misunderstanding. Chances are, however, that it will not be as simple as that.

It is possible that some of the key financial people will confess when they are confronted with the preliminary facts. They may even go so far as to provide the investigators with a secret schedule that explains what happened. Even if their confessions are not so complete, they may acknowledge that they cut some corners, or bent some accounting rules, but still deny they did anything wrong. In either event, the company has now confirmed that there's at least substance, if not total truth, to the whistleblower's assertions and the problem is not going to go away.

The Initial Board Meeting

Let us now assume that the company reaches the point in its preliminary investigation where it has what it considers to be solid information that there's a serious potential or even likelihood that accounting irregularities occurred. That means that purchasers and sellers of the company's securities are likely to be trading on the basis of materially misleading financial statements. At this point, the company is going to want and need to disclose something as soon as feasible, if only to stop the daily increase in liability arising from each new trade based on false information in the market.

The next point in our aftermath timeline is the initial board of directors meeting, which needs to be convened very quickly—immediately, really—after the preliminary investigation has verified the existence of potential irregularities. The last thing the company's management wants is to have the board read about serious problems with the company for the first time in the newspaper.

Only someone who has been through a number of these initial board meetings can fully appreciate what it is like to be there, the types of problems the board typically faces, and the issues that typically arise. The following is intended to capture some of the flavor and substance of what typically transpires in these meetings.

Again, the environment in which the board finds itself can best be described as a crisis. People are basically in shock. The company has probably never faced anything like this before, and this is probably the first time any of the board members have gone through an exigency of this sort. In short, there is a lack of precedent to guide the board.

Not only do the board members have to go through an exercise they have no experience for, they also must do it with little information to guide them. Although the preliminary investigation may have clarified some things, there will be many more questions than answers at this point. The questions that will naturally occur include the following:

- How bad is the fraud?
- How far back does it go?
- Who did it? Who knew about it?
- Who should have known about it (even if they didn't know)?
- Which employees can the company keep?
- Who, if anyone, should the company fire?
- Who should the company hire to do a more thorough investigation?
- How does the company maintain operations?
- How long will the investigation take?

And finally, of considerable personal interest to the individual board members:

- Is there director and officer (D&O) insurance to cover the board against liability and legal fees?

The board needs to act quickly in getting answers to most of these questions for many reasons, including perhaps the most pressing: every minute that goes by until the company makes a public disclosure about the irregularities, the company's shares are being traded on the basis of faulty financial statements.

And yet it is difficult for the board to get answers and make decisions, because the board is dealing with a situation where information is imperfect, suspicions are running high, people are nervous, and the entire environment is less conducive to the kind of open communication that's usually necessary for effective problem-solving. Indeed, the people with the real information may be actively trying to conceal it because they need to protect themselves.

Following are some likely answers to some of the above questions:

1. *How bad is the fraud?*   The company can't know for sure, but it is probably worse than anyone thinks. That is, the company probably has a greater number of problematic transactions that affect more areas of the company (e.g., units, divisions, and subsidiaries) than first apparent. Unless the company is lucky enough to catch the fraud in the first stages, the fraud usually is not discovered until it has spread well beyond the area that the whistleblower described.

2. *How far back does it go?*   The fraud probably goes back further than anyone thinks, again because fraud is usually detected after it has been occurring for a while. The nature of financial fraud is that it typically starts small. The perpetrator only wants to manipulate a single quarter's numbers in order to make that quarter's financial targets. However, it usually continues until more and more people are required to implement the fraud and more elaborate measures are required. Soon the fraud becomes so great that it can no longer be hidden.

3. *Who did it? Who knew about it?*   The CFO and other senior accounting personnel will be suspects in many cases. The great and often unanswered question is whether the CEO (or other senior non-financial personnel) knew about or condoned the fraudulent conduct, or at least should have known. These questions are difficult to answer because there won't always be a clear paper trail leading directly to the senior-most people.

   So while the board is in its initial meeting trying to resolve some problems, some board members may be wondering whether some of the people in the room are knowing participants in the fraud. The board may ultimately find that the chairman or CEO, the very person running the board meeting, is a participant.

4. *Who does the company keep/fire?* In some cases there may be a temptation to want to terminate everyone who is suspected of having had anything to do with the fraud. The problem is that at this preliminary stage, before a full investigation has been completed, no one knows who was involved or the degree of their involvement. Some of the involved employees may have employment contracts, which may require some fairly stringent standard of cause in order to fire them or to terminate lucrative benefits to which they would otherwise be entitled. Following is a sample clause:

> Cause shall mean (i) conviction of any crime constituting a felony or involving moral turpitude, dishonesty, or theft; (ii) gross neglect or misconduct in the performance of employee's duties hereunder; (iii) willful failure or refusal to perform such duties; (iv) engaging in any conduct that is materially injurious to the company or the reputation of the company.

While engaging in financial fraud may well constitute cause as set forth in the sample clause, proving that an officer or employee actually is guilty of such behavior is not always easy, especially where the individual strenuously denies any allegation of wrongdoing.

On the other hand, the company may want to retain the employees who confessed (particularly lower-level employees or a whistleblower) to help the company conduct the investigation and assist in preparing restated financial statements.

5. *How long will the investigation take?* Everyone will want the investigation done yesterday—and for good reasons. But there will be a tension between this time pressure and the need to conduct a thorough investigation. Realistically, these investigations must be done and can be done in a manner of a few months, although for small, more contained problems it may be possible to shorten that time frame.

6. *How does the company maintain operations?* In order to keep the company functioning, the company needs quickly to reestablish credibility with a variety of different constituencies (Exhibit 3–1). These include lenders, suppliers, customers, regulators, and financial markets.

   - **Lenders**—Fraud might put the company in violation of debt covenants, or in jeopardy of not being able to renew credit lines. The following is a typical debt covenant that could be implicated by financial fraud:

     12.   REPRESENTATIONS AND WARRANTIES

     * * *

     12.4 *Financial Statements and Projection.* (a) The Borrower has delivered to the Bank the audited balance sheet and related statements of income and cash flow for the Borrower and its consolidated Subsidiaries as of December 31, 1998, for the Fiscal Year then ended . . . . All such financial statements have been prepared in accordance with GAAP and present accurately and fairly the financial position of the Borrower and its consolidated Subsidiaries as of the dates

---

Exhibit 3–1. Restoring Credibility

The company's board of directors will need to restore credibility with the following:

- The SEC
- Securities exchanges
- Auditors
- Lenders
- Suppliers
- Customers
- Shareholders
- Financial markets

---

thereof and their results of operations for the periods then ended.

13.   EVENTS OF DEFAULT

13.1. *Events of Default.* It shall constitute an event of default if any one or more of the following events occurs for any reason whatsoever:

* * *

(c)   Any representation or warranty made by the Borrower in this Agreement, any Financial Statement, or any certificate furnished by the Borrower or any Subsidiary at any time to the Bank shall prove to be untrue in any material respect as of the date on which made.

Based on such provisions, the bank now has the power basically to call in the loan. If it wants to be, the bank is in the driver's seat and will have be dealt with.

- **Suppliers and customers**—They need to believe in the financial solvency of the company and the integrity of the people they're doing business with so that they continue to ship merchandise, give credit, and in the case of customers, keep buying the company's product.

- **Regulators**—It will frequently be important to show the SEC, and perhaps other regulatory agencies, that the investigation is being handled properly and that the company is acting responsibly. The company may even want to consider contacting the regulators rather than awaiting regulatory inquiry.

- **Financial markets**—The company must restore credibility with shareholders and the market if it is to maintain the ability to raise capital, attract institutional investors, and retain the confidence and interest of Wall Street analysts.

For all of the above constituencies, the company will need to put out corrected numbers and audited financial statements quickly so that people can have confidence in the company. If the company is a public one, it essentially cannot function without audited financial statements. That is ultimately the only way the company can restore credibility and keep itself operational.

Insurance Issues

It is important to know that, for a variety of reasons, D&O insurance policies typically decline to provide coverage for deliberate fraud. Consider the following fairly standard clause:

> EXCLUSIONS
>
> The Insurer shall not be liable to make any payment for Loss in connection with a Claim made against an insured:
>
> (a) arising out of, based upon, or attributable to the gaining in fact of any profit or advantage to which an insured was not legally entitled;
>
> * * *
>
> (c) arising out of, based upon, or attributable to the committing in fact of any criminal or deliberate fraudulent act.

However, not all directors and officers named as defendants in the inevitable litigations will necessarily be knowing participants, and the fraud of wrongdoing directors and officers is not usually imputed to innocent directors and officers under the policy. But there is one exception: D&O policies sometimes provide that if the insurance application was signed by one of the perpetrators of the fraud, that person's knowledge can be imputed to other insured persons and to the company so that coverage can be denied completely on the basis of a material misrepresentation in the application.

So one thing that needs to be checked immediately is who signed the insurance application. And the board should be made aware of the insurance company's potential right to rescind the policy, and thereby deny any coverage, if the application was signed by one of the guilty parties.

Usually, the affected parties attempt to resolve insurance issues through negotiation rather than litigation, though exceptions do exist. It is not, however, uncommon for these issues to take a long time, sometimes years, to resolve. Will an insurance company deny coverage entirely if a perpetrator signed the application? Experience suggests that they rarely will, though they may have the right to do so. But it is a negotiating tool in their hands and a mortification for directors and officers.

Action Plan

One thing that must come out of the first board meeting is a clear action plan with the right persons designated to implement it. (See Exhibit 3–2.) If the right people are not selected, then the action plan will simply consist of a lot of people milling around and nothing will get done. The board needs to find people to do the following tasks: look at insurance questions and make sure the proper notices are sent to the carriers, address the issue of potential communication with the SEC and other regulatory agencies, coordinate the process of interviewing and hiring the professionals to do the investigation, and think about publicity and getting out a press release.

The Initial Press Release

That brings us to the initial press release. This communication is the one that tells the world the bad news that the company has uncovered a problem and that the financial statements can no longer be relied on.

The tension the company always faces in the initial press release is to balance the need for early disclosure against the desire for accuracy. The issue, put simply, is whether to put out a revised number or not. That is, should the company seek to estimate the amount by which it will need to restate earnings and for what years?

Exhibit 3–2. Implementation Checklist

The company's board of directors will need to make sure the following items are completed to ensure a thorough investigation and to alleviate damages from the fraud:

- Prepare initial press release
- Form a special committee to investigate the fraud
- Retain forensic accountants
- Retain outside counsel
- Make personnel decisions
- Notify insurance carriers

The reality is that the company desperately wants to put out a number (or at least a range); otherwise, the market may assume the worst. The countervailing concern is that whatever number the company puts out may turn out to be wrong: The fraud may be bigger or it may go back further. The problem is that a company almost never gets pleasant surprises once it discovers fraud.

Thus, the well-intentioned press release may end up being a disclosure document on which a brand new class of plaintiffs will seek to sue.

The following is a hypothetical press release that might be issued during the immediate aftermath of discovery of a potential accounting fraud:

> New York, NY, March 15, 1999—ABC Corporation (Nasdaq: ABC) has reached a preliminary determination as to the need to restate earlier reported financial results. A preliminary investigation has indicated that revenues were incorrectly recognized during the second and third quarters of 1998 and that earnings for each of those quarters will need to be restated. The preliminary investigation suggests that earnings may be restated from $.32 to $.25 per share for the second quarter and from $.41 to $.19 per share for the third quarter. The company has not yet determined whether it will need to restate any results for fiscal years 1997 or 1996. At the present time, all such previously reported financial results should not be relied on.
>
> Yesterday evening the independent directors of the board of directors terminated the employment of Chief Financial Officer John L. Jones. At the request of the board of directors, Chief Executive Officer Alan S. Smith has voluntarily taken a temporary paid leave of absence from the company.
>
> The audit committee of the board of directors has hired Monroe, Tyler & Van Buren as special legal counsel to conduct an independent investigation of the matter and to explore the possibility of litigation against culpable parties. The law firm has hired the accounting firm of Pabst and Pabst LLP to conduct an independent investigation.
>
> ABC Corporation is a leading manufacturer of ladies dresses and sportswear. With wholesale delivery capability to 124 nations, it provides a full line of ladies wear for the office, home, and social gatherings. It has twice won the coveted Stellar Award for women's fashions.

Other Issues

Once the initial press release is issued, the board of directors must then turn to myriad additional issues. These include the following:

1. *Form a special committee.*   The board will likely want to appoint a special committee to investigate the fraud. The special committee serves a variety of purposes, all related to getting to the core of the problem quickly and reestablishing credibility promptly by assuring all constituencies that an independent group untainted by the scandal is looking into the matter.

    There are a number of candidates for a seat on the special committee. The existing members of the audit committee are logical candidates. Or some other group such as all outside directors might make sense. The guiding principle here is to be satisfied that the committee is independent and can objectively oversee the investigation.

    The concept of independence need not mean that committee members cannot have any ties whatsoever to management; very few board members, after all, are completely without any such ties. Nor is an audit committee member who held his or her position at the time of the fraud necessarily disqualified from overseeing the investigation. In fact, that person may bring valuable experience and insight to the process. But these are issues for the full board to consider when it is trying in those first few days to put together a special committee to supervise the independent investigation.

2. *Retain forensic accountants.*   The company will potentially need to hire an independent accounting firm—one with experience providing financial-investigative or "forensic" services—to find the correct numbers. That is, the forensic accountants will have to uncover and piece together all the irregularities to facilitate the restatement of financial results.

    The forensic specialists, however, will not necessarily be the ones to audit and render an opinion on the restated financial statements. Companies often hire their regular outside auditors to issue the actual audit opinion. In fact, one of the most important decisions the company will need to make early on is whether to retain its regular outside auditor to opine on the restated financial statements, or whether to bring in a new firm for this task. On the one hand, the incumbent auditor may be in the best position to complete the audit most quickly, which gets the company to its goal of restated financial statements most rapidly. In some cases, however, there may be a concern about the incumbent auditing firm's independence stemming from the possible allegation down the road that it should have uncovered the problem itself. These competing concerns must be balanced on a case-by-case basis.

3. *Retain outside counsel.*   Next, the special committee (or audit committee) will need to select an independent outside counsel (i.e., not the company's regular outside counsel) to do the following:

- Conduct and advise at the meetings

- Direct the investigation

- Conduct the interviews of company personnel and others who can shed light on the problem

- Write an investigative report, assuming there is to be a written report

- Deal with other counsel (for the company, for employees, for the SEC, for other regulatory agencies, etc.)

4. *Install new management.*   The company may need to hire new management (if old management has been suspended or fired), and it may have difficulty retaining valuable old management, because they may be demoralized and looking to leave a troubled situation. It is normal for the company's stock price to drop substantially following the initial press release, so any stock options management holds, which provide much of its compensation, may now be much less valuable or even worthless. At some point the company may want to consider appropriate incentives to induce critical personnel to stay with the company.

5. *Securities delisting.*   For companies whose shares are quoted on Nasdaq, revelation of accounting irregularities also raises the specter of Nasdaq delisting. Nasdaq has fairly stringent listing requirements, including that the company stay current in filing audited financial statements with the SEC. In the event the company's outside auditor were to withdraw its previous audit opinions, or withdraw from its current engagement, causing a delay in the filing of audited financials, Nasdaq could elect to delist the company's securities, thereby relegating them to the old pink sheets. Nasdaq may also delist in the extreme circumstance where the company's stock drops

below a specified level in trading value. Of course, the company may apply for reinstatement if and when it resumes compliance with the Nasdaq requirements, but in the meantime it will have had its credibility and reputation in the marketplace badly damaged. A company whose shares are traded on the New York Stock Exchange may face analogous problems with that exchange.

6. *Secure documents.* The board should promptly try to secure company documents and computer records from the perpetrators to keep them from being destroyed. In this increasingly technological age, it may not be enough just to lock suspected perpetrators out of their offices. The company may also have to retrieve the laptops the perpetrators carry home with them every night.

7. *Handle class-action lawsuits.* Class action lawsuits are certain to roll in within a day or two after the initial press release. Although many corporate executives may have come to think of securities class actions as meritless annoyances, the types of class actions the company faces in the wake of an accounting irregularity disclosure may not fall into this category. Keep in mind that the company's initial press release in all likelihood will have admitted at least one important element of a securities law claim.

8. *Indemnification.* The company's by-laws and charter need to be checked to see whether the company has an obligation to indemnify and provide defense costs, including for those who are suspected wrongdoers. Most bylaws these days generally provide for indemnification of the company's officers and directors to the maximum extent permitted by the corporation law of the company's state of incorporation.

   A typical state corporate law (Delaware, for example) provides that a corporation may indemnify:

> . . . any persons, including directors and officers, who are, or are threatened to be made, parties to any threatened, pending or completed legal action, whether civil, criminal, administrative or investigative . . . by reason of the fact that such person is or was a director, officer, employee or agent of such corporation, or is or was serving at the request of such corporation as a director, officer, employee or agent of another corporation or enterprise [such as a corporate subsidiary]. The

> indemnity may include expenses (including attorneys' fees), judgments, fines and amounts paid in settlement . . . provided such director, officer, employee or agent acted in good faith and in a manner he reasonably believed to be in the corporation's best interests. . . .

Even if the company believes a particular officer or director did not act in good faith or in the best interests of the company, it is difficult to resist advancing defense costs to such person in the absence of an actual adjudication of wrongdoing. At least this is true where the by-laws provide that indemnification "shall" (rather than "may") be provided to the fullest extent permitted under state law, which is usually the case. Thus, the company may find itself in the rather unpalatable position of having to pay the legal fees of separate counsel for persons whom the company believes were responsible for the fraud. Even though the company can (and often must) require an undertaking from the directors and officers to repay defense costs if they are ultimately found to have acted dishonestly or for improper personal gain, this will be small solace since, by the time the company is ready to collect, the line of creditors will be long, and assets to pay creditors probably long gone.

CHAPTER 4

GETTING NEW AUDITED FINANCIAL STATEMENTS

Harvey R. Kelly

What do the real numbers look like? What is the true financial condition of the company? How far back do the accounting problems go?

The instant potential accounting irregularities come to light, a company is sure to have to answer these and similar, endless questions. The questions emerge from everywhere. As the company's owners, its shareholders demand reliable financial information. Lenders, concerned about the company's financial stability and compliance with loan covenants, may threaten to cut off credit lines and demand loan repayments. Customers or vendors may seek to delay, renegotiate, or even cancel purchases or sales. Major transactions, such as mergers or pending financing transactions, may hang in the balance. And, of course, the Securities and Exchange Commission (SEC), stock exchanges, and other regulatory bodies will have a keen interest in exactly what has gone wrong. Frequently, regulators will halt trading in a company's stock pending receipt of adequate additional financial information.

Amidst all this uncertainty, one point becomes clear: the marketplace will demand to see corrected financial statements. Realizing the need for corrected or "re-audited" financial statements is the easy part—getting there is often more of a challenge. Chapter 4 explores issues that companies often confront in their attempts to get new audited financial statements right after the discovery of accounting irregularities.

Initial Involvement of the Outside Auditor

When potential accounting irregularities initially surface, the first task for the board of directors is to get the facts. However, the need to understand what has happened creates a very real dilemma for the board: Who is familiar enough with the company's accounting systems to quickly size up the problem, but at the same time is entirely free of suspicion? Directors rarely know enough facts in the early stages to allay fears that the CEO, the CFO, the controller, or other senior members of financial management may be directly involved. Indeed, experience shows that the very executives on whom the board typically relies for financial information often turn out to be somehow implicated in the fraud.

Unless such concerns are quickly demonstrated to be groundless, the immediate involvement of the outside auditor is therefore likely. The outside auditor has the expertise, experience, knowledge of generally accepted accounting principles (GAAP), and history with the company that make it the logical first choice to help the board of directors assess the situation. In fact, calling potential accounting irregularities to the immediate attention of the outside auditor typically has several important advantages to the company, such as:

- Making available the necessary expertise and resources to quickly determine whether accounting irregularities exist
- Limiting reliance on company personnel to evaluate the potential irregularities at a time when the identity of the perpetrator(s) may be unknown
- Enabling the auditor to fulfill its professional responsibility to evaluate the effect of suspected irregularities on previously issued audit reports

Consequently, one of the first things a board of directors typically does when faced with accounting irregularities is to bring in the incumbent outside auditor.

Effect on Previously Issued Audit Reports

Once called to the scene, the auditor may take as little as a few days to substantiate that the company does indeed have an accounting irregularity problem. When that fact has been determined, the auditor is immediately confronted with a serious issue: the possibility, if not likelihood, that the fraud goes back to the most recently filed Form 10-K, which includes not only the company's annual financial statements but the auditor's report on them. Thus, the discovery of irregularities may force the auditor to act to prevent further reliance on the previously issued audit reports, as required by American Institute of Certified Public Accountants (AICPA) professional standards when an auditor becomes aware of new information that relates to previously audited financial statements.

In situations involving material accounting irregularities that affect prior-years' financial statements, an auditor will almost inevitably conclude that reliance on previous audit reports must be discontinued. Under such circumstances, the auditor will advise the company to make appropriate disclosure to those who the company knows to be relying on, or who are likely to rely on, the financial statements and audit report.

One way the company can make that disclosure, if the effect of the accounting irregularity on the financial statements can be promptly determined, is to issue revised audited financial statements. However, the effect on the financial statements often cannot be determined without a prolonged investigation; thus, the prompt issuance of revised financial statements is frequently not an option. In such a circumstance, the auditor will ordinarily suggest that the company notify those who use the statements that the financial statements and accompanying audit report should no longer be relied upon. The auditor will also likely advise that the company tell the statement users that restated financial statements will be issued once the company completes an investigation. The auditor may also insist that the company notify the SEC, stock exchanges, and other appropriate regulatory agencies.

The board of directors must take the auditor's recommendation for such notification seriously. If the board fails to act on the auditor's suggestion, the auditor could notify:

- Regulatory agencies that the audit report should no longer be relied on
- Each person known to be relying on the financial statements that the audit report should no longer be relied on. (In the case of public companies, this can be accomplished by the auditor requesting that the SEC, the stock exchange, or other regulatory agency take whatever steps are deemed necessary to accomplish the required disclosure.)

The board might be tempted to avoid these disclosure obligations by excluding the auditor from the process; however, such an approach is ill-advised. Exclusion of the auditor may expose the company to even greater litigation and regulatory risk and almost certainly would destroy any working relationship between the auditor and the board. In any event, once accounting irregularities have surfaced, the involvement of the auditor is inevitable.

The Element of Mistrust

Unfortunately, the very mention of an accounting irregularity often leads to premature accusations and mistrust. Company executives, directors, and others almost without fail begin to accuse the auditor and ask questions such as:

- Where was the auditor?
- How could the auditor have missed this?
- Is it possible that the auditor was in on the fraud?
- Should we fire the auditor for not doing its job thoroughly?

At the same time, the auditor inevitably must face the following questions:

- Who at the company knew about the accounting problems?
- Which company personnel lied to us during the audit?
- Were documents deliberately withheld from us?
- Did the company forge documents?
- Who at the company can we trust?
- What other problems are out there?

Such accusations at the outset are understandable but counterproductive. They create a certain level of tension, which, if allowed to fester, can be disastrous. Such an environment may cause the auditor to terminate the relationship and withdraw all previously issued audit reports, effectively leaving the company without audited financial statements. The company would then have to disclose publicly the auditor's resignation in SEC filings, which could elevate the concerns of regulators and shareholders. At a time when interested parties are already nervous about the company's financial condition, the abrupt departure of the company's auditor can be operationally unfortunate as well as a public relations disaster. Moreover, as described later, changing auditors will almost certainly delay the procurement of revised audited financial statements, which, the board of directors will quickly come to realize, is one of the most important tasks that it faces.

Usually, a more constructive approach for both the auditor and the company is to reserve judgment until the facts are known. Because the procurement of revised, credible financial statements is of paramount importance, the energies of management and the auditor should generally be placed on working with, not blaming, each other.

Benefits of Continuing the Audit Relationship

Once the auditor has reported back to the board of directors that corrected financial statements are necessary, the board then must decide who should assist in correcting them. In particular, the board must decide whether to stay with its incumbent auditor or to bring in a new auditor. (See Exhibit 4–1.)

The answer is not always obvious. Among the arguments for a new auditor will be the notion that "a new broom sweeps clean" and that the incumbent auditor may be a co-defendant in class action litigation. At the same time, the element of mistrust in the auditor-client relationship will be obvious to everyone, and some will inevitably view the retention of a new auditor as an opportunity to eliminate the resulting stress.

All of those views may be sound; however, they are largely trumped by one that is more important: Once an accounting irregularity has surfaced, of utmost concern to the board of directors will be the procurement of restated financial statements accompanied by a reliable audit report. As the days and weeks progress, the board will find that it is difficult for a public company to function without audited financial statements. The company's banking relationships will founder. Its lines of credit will dry up. The company will face significant inquiry from the SEC. It will be threatened with delisting by its stock exchange. Suppliers will begin having second thoughts and may demand cash on delivery. Customers will become skeptical as to the company's reliability. And, as time progresses, the doubts will only increase.

The biggest issue in the audit relationship, therefore, is not the level of comfort with the incumbent auditor or whether a new broom will sweep clean. The biggest issue is getting re-audited financial statements as fast as humanly possible. In balancing the benefits and costs of continued use of

---

Exhibit 4–1. Selecting an Auditor

- Benefits of a new auditor
  - — Fresh look
  - — Clean break from the past
  - — Less tension in auditor relationship
- Benefits of continuing with the incumbent auditor
  - — Ability to audit restatements faster
  - — Access to information gathered in past audits
  - — Buy-in of past auditor to restatement requirements
  - — Ability to reaffirm opinions on unaffected years
  - — Avoids challenges of finding new auditor in a fraud environment
  - — Less burden on company personnel

---

the incumbent auditor, the following considerations will favor the incumbent auditor's continued retention:

1. *Speed.* The incumbent auditor can do it faster. In the absence of evidence to the contrary, the incumbent auditor will generally be able to rely on audit work it has already performed. Conversely, in order to be able to render an opinion on the financial statements as a whole, any new auditor would need to perform extensive audit procedures beyond areas affected by the accounting irregularities. Such additional efforts can be particularly time-consuming where the irregularities have affected multiple years.

2. *Information.* Often, the auditor's working papers will contain documents that shed light on the origin and parties responsible for the irregularities. For example, an auditor may have copies of altered documents (although such alterations may not have been previously apparent to the auditor) or evidence of misrepresentations made to the auditor by company personnel. Termination of the auditor may hinder the investigation by delaying or even precluding audit workpaper access.

3. *Concurrence.* If a company opts to engage a different auditor, it increases the risk that the former auditor will later publicly contest the restatement. Such disputes can cast further doubt on the integrity of the company's financial statements at a time when the company can ill-afford such uncertainty.

4. *Prior-year audit reports.* When accounting irregularities are determined not to extend back to multiple years, a company may wish to continue to rely on prior-years' audit reports. For example, applicable rules and regulations generally require a company to keep on record a total of three successive years of audited financial statements. If the company terminates its incumbent auditor or otherwise isolates the auditor from the investigation findings, the auditor may withhold its consent to incorporate its audit reports from prior years. Conversely, an auditor that is sufficiently familiar with the investigation findings should be in a position to reaffirm previously rendered audit reports on years unaffected by the irregularities.

5. *New auditor reluctance.* At this particular moment in its corporate history, the company is not exactly a dream audit client. At least some members of management have probably committed fraud. Among the victims of the fraud is the incumbent auditor. It is not necessarily the case, therefore, that termination of the incumbent auditor will be followed by an onslaught of other auditors fighting to pick up the engagement. Depending on the circumstances, each of the other Big Five accounting firms (if your incumbent auditor is a Big Five firm, already you're down to four) may decide it is better to let this one pass. The enthusiasm of the other national or regional firms may not be any greater. Termination of the existing auditor— at least until another firm is lined up—can therefore leave the company in the completely untenable position of having no auditor at all. Again, a public company basically cannot function for very long without audited financial statements.

The Independent Forensic Accounting Team

All of these considerations do not mean that a company must rely exclusively on its incumbent auditor to conduct an investigation. After all, many will (fairly or unfairly) point to the fact that the incumbent auditor did miss the fraud once. Moreover, the "audit sampling" and "professional skepticism" approaches of a normal audit pursuant to generally accepted auditing standards (GAAS) are not necessarily optimal where deliberate misrepresentations have surfaced. Therefore, it frequently makes sense to bring in a separate accounting firm with special expertise in digging out fraud to complement the incumbent auditor's efforts. Thus will be introduced to the process the "forensic" accounting team.

The engagement of forensic accountants usually is controlled by a special committee of the board of directors charged with the responsibility of conducting the investigation. Although the scope of the forensic accountants' responsibilities can differ from investigation to investigation, their role normally will include the investigation of data that will assist the auditor in issuing a new audit report. Among other contributions, the forensic accountants are frequently called upon to facilitate the financial statement restatement by:

- Serving as technical accounting advisors to the board of directors and its lawyers
- Identifying and compiling documentary support that will be needed by both the company and its auditors to determine the proper financial statement presentation
- Acting as intermediaries between the company's management and auditor with respect to specified accounting issues
- Providing the company's auditor comfort that a credible, independent investigation into the irregularities is being performed
- Communicating relevant investigation findings to the auditor

The role of the forensic accounting team and its interaction with the outside auditor are discussed in greater detail in Chapter 6.

Responsibility for Restated Financial Statements

Notwithstanding the involvement of a battery of auditors and forensic accountants, the ultimate responsibility for preparing restated financial statements remains with company management. Management, with the assistance of its newly formed army of accounting investigators, must make its own determination as to whether accounting irregularities have occurred. If management concludes that irregularities resulted in financial statements that violated GAAP, the company must process accounting adjustments and issue revised financial statements that comply. Before the auditor issues an audit report on the restated financial statements, it will require appropriate members of the company's management to provide written representations that the financial statements are management's responsibility and have been fairly presented in accordance with GAAP. Management must, therefore, fully understand and document the corrections.

Although it may seem obvious that management should be knowledgeable about its own financial statements, the time-sensitive, pressure-filled environment of an investigation into accounting irregularities usually is unfamiliar territory to management personnel. In some cases, high-level financial managers, new to their positions as a consequence of personnel changes after irregularities have surfaced, may be dedicating most of their time to other newly obtained responsibilities. Often, irregularities are identified and quantified initially by the forensic accountants or an auditor rather than company personnel, who may find themselves largely or entirely left out of the picture. However, even in instances in which well-respected auditors and forensic accountants have identified, quantified, and documented restatement adjustments, management must ensure that the company maintains appropriate documentation of the nature and composition of such adjustments and takes responsibility for concluding that such adjustments are appropriate.

Restatement Requirements

A re-audit of previously issued financial statements can potentially uncover all kinds of issues—if only because time has passed since the original audit and things inevitably have not turned out exactly as previously estimated. Not every issue that surfaces, however, will require restatement of the financial statements. (See Exhibit 4–2.) Indeed, restatement to accommodate certain kinds of issues is forbidden by GAAP. Thus, one task facing management and its auditor will be to determine which issues require restatement and which do not.

As a general matter, the issues uncovered during a re-audit will fall into one of the following five categories:

1. *Errors.* Errors are unintentional misstatements or omissions of amounts or disclosures in financial statements. Errors may involve the following:

Exhibit 4–2. Restatement Guidance

Accounting issues that require restatement:

- Misstatements arising out of errors
- Misstatements arising out of irregularities
- Misstatements arising out of illegal acts
- Misstatements arising out of bad faith estimates

Accounting issues that do not require restatement:

- Misstatements arising out of a revision of earlier good faith estimates
- Misstatements arising out of a change in accounting principle

---

- Mistakes in gathering or processing data from which financial statements are prepared
- Unreasonable accounting estimates arising from oversight or misinterpretation of the facts
- Mistakes in applying accounting principles relating to the amount, classification, manner of presentation, or disclosure in the financial statements

2. *Irregularities.* Irregularities (under the revised audit standards they are now called *fraud*) are intentional misstatements arising from fraudulent financial reporting practices, such as:

- Manipulation, fabrication, or alteration of accounting records or supporting documents from which financial statements are prepared
- Misrepresentation in, or intentional omission from, the financial statements of events, transactions, or other significant information
- Intentional misapplication of accounting principles relating to the amounts, classification, manner of presentation, or disclosure in the financial statements

3. *Illegal acts.* Illegal acts involve violations of laws or governmental regulations.

4. *Inaccurate estimates.* Subsequent events may demonstrate that accounting estimates used in preparing the financial statements later proved to be inaccurate. Examples of accounting estimates that can be called into question include inventory valuation reserves, bad debt reserves, loss contract reserves, percentage-of-completion revenue recognition estimates, sales returns and allowance reserves, and warranty reserves.

5. *Changes in accounting policies.* Accounting policies represent the methods adopted by a company to account for transactions in accordance with GAAP. Sometimes two or more acceptable methods of accounting exist for certain types of transactions (the use of FIFO or LIFO to account for inventory being a good example).

The nature of the accounting issues determines whether previously issued financial statements require restatement. Misstatements arising out of newly discovered errors, irregularities, or illegal acts will require a restatement unless the amounts are not material or, in some instances, the financial statements are outdated.

On the other hand, the identification of inaccurate estimates underlying the financial statements does not necessarily call for restatement of prior-year financials. Virtually every company that prepares financial statements later discovers that its accounting estimates differed from how things actually turned out. For example, an entity's actual receivable write-off experience may be worse than a reserve for bad debts previously accrued due to unforeseen customer financial difficulties. Under GAAP, changes in estimates generally should not be accounted for by restating amounts reported in prior periods. Instead, the effects of changes in accounting estimates should be accounted for in the period the company changes its estimate and, in certain circumstances, in future periods.

The distinctions between these different types of accounting issues can be blurry. Distinguishing between an incorrect estimate that is the result of an error (which requires a restatement) and an incorrect estimate that is the result of reasonably unforeseen subsequent events (which does not) can be exceedingly subtle. The context in which the distinctions must be made, moreover, virtually guarantees that all such determinations will be heavily second-guessed. Thus, the restatement process frequently involves much discussion and debate among management, the auditor, and the lawyers.

Further complicating the process may be a natural desire on the part of management to seize the opportunity to change preexisting accounting policies even though those preexisting accounting policies already complied with GAAP. For example, to increase its credibility with the financial community, management may decide to adopt new accounting policies that, while still complying with GAAP, are more conservative than those previously used.

If a company elects to change from one proper accounting policy to another, the nature and justification for the change and its effect on income are to be disclosed in the financial statements in the period in which the company makes the change. Although GAAP provides for certain exceptions, companies generally are to report most changes in accounting principles by recognizing the cumulative effect on net income of the period of the change rather than as a restatement of prior-period results.

The Audit Process

Once the re-audit has commenced, management is often taken aback by the auditor's adoption of new procedures in conducting the actual audit testing (Exhibit 4–3). The audit process, never a complete pleasure even under the best of circumstances, can become more exasperating once the auditor has been told that it was earlier the victim of lies. The auditor must then be more thorough and cautious during the re-audit, to the point where genuinely innocent employees may get frustrated as their integrity seems to be repeatedly called into question.

That frustration may be increased insofar as company personnel fail to appreciate exactly what the auditor is trying to accomplish during a re-audit. Common misconceptions among company personnel about the re-audit include:

- The auditor will confine itself to revisiting only those prior-year issues that the company has called to its attention
- The auditor can fully rely on work done and conclusions reached by the independent forensic accountants, so the auditor will not have to perform much additional work

---

Exhibit 4–3. What to Expect from Auditors Auditing Fraud-Related Restatements

- New and expanded test procedures

- Increased demand for third-party corroboration

- Voluminous document requests

- More visible involvement of senior personnel and national office technical experts

---

- The auditor will only require the company to provide the same level of documentation as customarily requested in prior audits

- The company will only be dealing with the same personnel from the auditing firm that performed past audits of the company

In general, company employees should expect audits of restated financial statements, particularly those resulting from prior fraudulent financial reporting, to involve heightened auditor skepticism, more extensive evidence gathering, and expanded audit teams. All in all, it will generally be an entirely unpleasant experience for company personnel.

Evidence of a new approach in the audit, moreover, will be everywhere. The auditor might seek additional documentary evidence from outside the company. For example, if the fraud involved improper revenue recognition, the auditor may request expanded confirmations from the company's customers on issues such as contract terms, the existence of side letters, acceptance criteria, delivery and payment terms and timing, the extent of any continuing company obligations, and cancellation or return provisions.

Such an additional level of audit scrutiny can be burdensome and frustrating. The auditor may request documents that are voluminous, that have been sent to off-site storage, or, even worse, that cannot be found. The auditor may demand to see original documents when previously it accepted photocopies. The company may be asked to prevail upon its customers to research and confirm (or perhaps re-confirm) details about the customers' business with the company dating back several years. Management may believe it has provided the auditor sufficient explanation or documentation, yet the auditor will seek still more. Even innocent senior executives may get the feeling that its overzealous auditor no longer trusts anything anybody says.

Such a characterization usually is something of an exaggeration, but it does highlight an important dynamic that occurs in instances of financial fraud. Auditors, always obligated to conduct independent audits with an attitude of professional skepticism, must consider how the fraud previously escaped detection both by the company's internal control system and by the auditor. Once the auditor concludes that one or more members of management consciously committed fraud, the auditor may question the reliability of every representation or piece of evidence received from those individuals. The auditor may also question the reliability of every representation or piece of evidence prepared by subordinates of those determined to have perpetrated the fraud.

All of this is made more difficult for company personnel by the auditor's likely introduction of new audit team personnel to supplement (or replace) the previous engagement team, with which the company personnel may have been comfortable. The auditor may involve personnel not previously involved in the company's audit to ensure that the audit team possesses the knowledge, skill, ability, and experience commensurate with the risk. The addition of new accountants to the audit team, moreover, will not only take place among those individuals at the company's offices during the duration of the auditor's fieldwork: Beyond those in the field, the audit team will probably now include significant participation by the most senior technical representatives of the accounting firm's national office. In all likelihood, company personnel will notice constrained flexibility and discretion in those areas that require some level of judgment. Correspondingly, the process of decision making may be slowed. To some extent, company personnel may get the impression that the CPAs in the field are very much under the thumb of those at the auditing firm's national headquarters. In many instances, that impression will be correct.

The auditor's task can be further confounded by management confusion over how its incumbent auditor and its newly retained forensic accountants are supposed to interact. Thus, executives and employees sometimes mistakenly assume that the investigation performed by the forensic accountants from a different accounting firm will obviate the need for the auditor to perform much testing. After all, cannot the auditor accept the findings of these other professionals and still render an unqualified opinion? The answer is no. GAAS requires an auditor on its own to obtain sufficient competent evidential matter to afford a reasonable basis to express an opinion on the financial statements.

Representations to the Auditor

One issue that rarely creates a problem in a normal GAAS audit, but which can pose quite a significant problem after accounting irregularities have been discovered, is the auditor's need to obtain management representations.

The auditor's procurement of management representations is mandated by GAAS. Before the audit report is issued, the auditor is to obtain a representation letter setting forth, among other things, the representations of responsible executives that the financial statements are set forth in accordance with GAAP and that all pertinent information has been provided to the auditor. That representation letter is to be signed by executives whose knowledge of the financial reporting system is such that an adequate basis for the representations exist. Beyond the formal representations of the representation letter, any number of executives and accounting personnel will make separate representations during the course of the audit that sometimes will be noted by the auditor in its workpapers.

What can be routine in a normal audit, however, can become more of a problem once fraud has been discovered. Suddenly the normal procurement of management representations can be difficult, or even potentially impossible, insofar as executives from whom the representations would normally be obtained—such as senior financial executives or the CEO—may have been terminated or, even if not terminated, may no longer be viewed as completely reliable. In instances in which key management personnel have been terminated, moreover, the company may have filled newly vacated positions with individuals not previously associated with the organization.

New members of management may add credibility to the company, but they can also pose a challenge to the audit process. The auditor will demand from management written representations covering all previous years upon which the auditor must express an opinion. Executives new to the company may resist taking responsibility for the propriety of financial reports about which they, in truth, know little. Under GAAS, management's unwillingness to furnish written representations constitutes a limitation on the scope of the audit sufficient to preclude an unqualified opinion. It is also enough to cause the auditor to disclaim an opinion or to withdraw from the engagement.

Needless to say, an auditor disclaimer or resignation is the last thing management wants. Neither is likely to restore the confidence of shareholders, creditors, regulators, or others. The need for management representations can therefore delay the release of audited financial statements if not dealt with early in the audit process. At the outset, company management and its auditor should do their best to achieve a clear understanding of the personnel from whom the auditor will require written representations and exactly what those representations will consist of. Of course, even the best of planning in this area may be ruined if the investigation finds fault with individuals from whom the auditor planned to obtain representations.

Effect of Lawsuits on Auditor Independence

Amid all the uncertainty of the re-audit and investigative process, one matter is a virtual certainty—lawsuits will be filed. One question that often arises involves the effect of such lawsuits on the auditor's ability to continue in its capacity as the company's auditor.

Public accountants are governed by a code of professional ethics that requires them to be "independent" of the companies whose financial statements they audit. Beyond that, for an auditor to be able to render an informed, objective opinion on financial statements, the relationship between the auditor and the company being audited must be characterized by complete candor and full disclosure. There must also be an absence of bias on the part of the auditor so that the auditor can properly exercise professional judgment on the financial reporting decisions made by management.

Litigation concerning the propriety of a company's previous financial statements and the accompanying audit report can potentially interfere with the auditor's independence. For one thing, litigation that names both the company and the auditor as co-defendants can potentially turn the auditor and management into adversaries—and thereby chill the complete candor that, under GAAS, must characterize the audit relationship. Often, both the company and the auditor will come to the strategic recognition that lashing out against each other in litigation is foolish and counterproductive. Still, the potential for compromised independence poses a risk to issuance of a new audit report.

Whether independence is in fact deemed to be compromised involves a complex area of GAAS that is to be governed by the particular circumstances at issue. As a general rule, the following matters are considered to impair the auditor's independence and therefore would result in the auditor's resignation:

- The commencement of litigation by present company management against the auditor alleging deficiencies in audit work on the company's financial statements
- Under certain circumstances, the threat of litigation by present management of the company against the auditor alleging audit deficiencies if the auditor deems the filing of such a claim to be probable
- The commencement of litigation by the auditor against present management alleging management fraud or deceit

Conversely, litigation by shareholders or other third parties against the company and/or its auditor alleging violations of the securities laws or similar issues normally does *not*, in and of itself, necessarily affect the auditor's independence. Therefore, such lawsuits do not automatically result in the company's need to find a new auditor. Even such third-party litigation, however, can lead to an impairment of auditor independence under certain circumstances. Independence may be compromised if, for example, the company files a cross-claim against the auditor alleging that the auditor is responsible for financial statement deficiencies. A cross-claim filed by the auditor alleging fraud by present company management may also impair the auditor's independence.

On the other hand, the existence of cross-claims filed by the company, its management, or any of its directors merely to protect the right to legal redress in the event of a future adverse decision in the primary litigation (or, in lieu of cross-claims, agreements to extend the statutes of limitations) would not normally impair the auditor's independence, unless there was thereby created a significant risk that the cross-claim would result in a settlement or judgment in an amount material to the accounting firm or the company.

The issues are obviously complicated, and the complexities of the litigation environment preclude the formulation of hard-and-fast rules governing auditor independence in all actual, threatened, or possible circumstances. Accordingly, the best approach is probably to raise the issue of independence at the outset of the re-audit so that both the auditor and company management are completely familiar with the risks and can develop a common understanding of how those risks will be addressed.

The Bottom Line

The bottom line is that a public company that has experienced accounting irregularities needs to get restated financial statements fast. To be sure, the company and its employees start out behind the eight ball—the auditor, having already been the victim of a fraud once, will not want it to happen again. Therefore, management must convince the auditor that it has management's full support; that management has every interest in digging out all of the fraud; and that management will be completely candid and forthcoming in complying with all of the auditor's requests for data, information, and corroboration. These tasks will not be pleasant or easy, but for a public company, audited financial statements are a prerequisite for continued existence.

CHAPTER 5

DIGGING OUT THE FRAUD: THE LAWYERS

Stephen Greiner and John Oller

The auditors are only the first of a long list of constituents who may want to know what happened. Others include the Securities and Exchange Commission (SEC), the National Association of Securities Dealers (NASD), the New York Stock Exchange (NYSE), the company's creditors, its insurance company, and (though the incentives are a little different) shareholders and their class action lawyers. All of this means that the board of directors has to conduct a thorough investigation.

Purposes of the Investigation

In this chapter we discuss the investigative process. Generally, this refers to an in-depth investigation conducted by lawyers and forensic accountants retained by the company's audit committee, its outside directors, or some other independent committee of the board of directors. Chapter 5 focuses on the investigative process from the lawyers' standpoint. Chapter 6 will focus on the role of the forensic accountants.

The principal purpose of the accounting irregularities investigation is to answer two fundamental questions: What happened? and Who did it?

The first question involves the determination and quantification of the irregularities affecting the company's publicly filed financial statements. The investigation needs to identify, substantiate, and quantify all of the various irregularities (and distinguish them from any additional errors not involving fraud) before the company can achieve its primary goal of issuing restated audited financials.

This is not an easy task, for it will frequently be the case that what the company initially believed to be a relatively isolated, confined problem will turn out to be much more widespread, not only in terms of the number and seriousness of irregularities, but also in terms of the areas or business units affected, the time periods implicated, and the people involved. Thus, questions such as the need to investigate one area or another where no evidence of wrongdoing has yet surfaced or to question financial and accounting personnel at various subsidiaries or divisions that seem not to be involved will take on real importance.

This is especially true if a pattern of fraud emerges—if the same people seem to be involved in or directing the irregularities, or the same accounts tend to be affected. In such instances, it may become necessary to probe into those areas that fit the pattern even in the absence of any specific indication of wrongdoing. For example, if the company's controller is found to have engaged in fraud at corporate headquarters regarding the parent company's financials and that person has had regular dealings with assistant controllers at the company's various subsidiaries, it is reasonable to question whether any subsidiary's books might likewise have been tainted by irregularities.

In most cases, the fraud will prove to be more widespread, more complex, will involve more people, and will implicate more fiscal periods than initially thought. This means that the investigation is likely to expand accordingly and will require more time, effort, and expense than initially hoped. As such, the investigative team must be prepared to go wherever the evidence leads it.

There are no guidelines that the investigators can use to determine when they should feel comfortable that all irregularities have been found; they will need to be alert to any red flags or patterns that suggest a need for further inquiry. Yet experience suggests that there is a high likelihood that the objective of answering "What happened?" will be achieved and that the investigation will allow the company to issue accurate restated financials. This is generally true even if the fraud is widespread and complex.

The second question—"Who did it?"—is really several questions: Who directed, who participated in, and who had knowledge of the accounting irregularities? The investigation may also seek to answer the more difficult question of who should have been aware of the accounting irregularities or perhaps some variant of that question.

These questions about culpability and responsibility will be of intense interest, as well they should be. They are really the questions on everyone's mind. And they will be questions that are the subject of intense speculation within and outside the company. The SEC, as well as other regulators, will be interested in questions of culpability and responsibility from an enforcement standpoint. The financial press will be writing and speculating about who knew what and when, and employees within the company—many of whom will be working side by side—will be wondering the same thing about their colleagues.

In the end, many of the principal architects and participants will almost certainly be identified. Perhaps all will be. But there may be some persons about whom suspicions run high whose involvement cannot be definitively determined, for reasons discussed below.

Who Conducts the Investigation?

In a typical case, and almost always in more complex investigations, outside counsel will be retained by the company (or more likely, by the audit committee or other special committee commissioned to oversee the internal investigation). The selection of outside counsel will often be made by or with substantial input from the company's general counsel and/or the chairperson of the audit or special committee.

Outside counsel should be *independent* in the sense that it has no significant ties to the members of company management who conceivably may have been involved in the fraud. This will generally mean that a law firm other than the company's regular outside counsel will be hired to conduct the investigation. Outside counsel will also perform a number of noninvestigatory tasks, such as advising the audit or special committee at meetings; advising on press releases concerning the status of the investigation and other matters; and dealing with counsel for other constituencies, such as the company, individual employees, and the SEC.

Outside counsel, in turn, will generally retain what are known as *forensic accountants* to assist in the investigation. Forensic accountants are specially trained in ferreting out financial fraud from a complex set of accounting and financial records and their focus is more on the who, what, when, and how of what happened, rather than on auditing a set of financial statements. Forensic accountants tend to be more skilled in interviewing techniques, are more cognizant of issues such as attorney-client privilege and other issues that may become relevant later in litigation, and are more experienced in retrieving data from computer systems than are regular auditors. In general, forensic accountants from a firm other than the company's regular auditors will participate in the independent investigation. (The respective roles of the forensic accountants and the company's regular outside auditors, along with related issues, are discussed in greater detail in Chapter 6.)

One reason the forensic accountants are generally retained by the law firm (rather than directly by the company or special committee) is that this can enhance the argument that the work product of the accountants is privileged and can be kept confidential. Generally, the work product of attorneys, and agents working for attorneys, is entitled to be kept confidential, at least until it is voluntarily disclosed to others.

Both the lawyers and the forensic accountants conducting the investigation will need to work closely with people inside the company to gather the necessary facts and data. Indeed, from the outset of the investigation, swarms of lawyers and accountants may virtually take up residence at the company for weeks on end, securing various company and individual employee files and requiring assistance from clerical personnel such as secretaries and file clerks. Inevitably, this will cause some disruption to the company's day-to-day operations, which will require sensitivity on the part of the investigative team in going about its business.

Time Frame of the Investigation

The board of directors will frequently want to know, as early as possible, how long the investigation will take. In many instances, it will want the investigation done yesterday. As a result, there is an inevitable tension between the desire to resolve the matter quickly and the need to get it right the first time. One restatement is unpleasant enough. A second is not something that the company will want to experience.

For smaller, more confined problems that stay that way, it is quite possible to complete a detailed investigation in a matter of a few weeks or less. On the other hand, large, complex frauds may take several months to investigate fully. It would be highly unusual, however, for even the most complex investigation to drag on interminably, as the imperatives of the marketplace and the demands of the company generally will not allow for it. It is hard to overemphasize the pressure to complete the investigation as soon as humanly possible.

The government's investigation of the matter is quite another thing. Often, the government's investigations and inquiries will take years, so individuals who are potentially implicated in the fraud will not know where they stand until long after the internal investigation has been completed. In addition, private lawsuits by civil parties, such as shareholders, may take several years to be resolved. That means, again, that even after the internal investigation has been completed, the company will continue to be required to provide documents and files, and individual officers and employees (including former employees) may be required to provide testimony about their activities during the period in question. In many ways, the internal investigation is merely the beginning, rather than the end, of the process.

Tasks to Perform

Whatever the time frame involved, a great deal of work must be performed during the internal investigation (see Exhibit 5–1):

1. *Procure documents.* Foremost, relevant documents must be identified, secured, reviewed, and understood. Depending on the circumstances, such documents may include:

    - Individual correspondence files

    - Company central files

    - Accounting records (e.g., general ledgers, journal entries, balance sheets, trial balances, memoranda, and other documents supplied to outside auditors)

    - Budgets and projections (both company-wide and by division, subsidiary, or operating unit)

    - Operating reports (e.g., monthly sales and revenue reports, expense reports, and profit and loss reports, again on a company-wide and unit basis)

Figure 5–1. Investigative Tasks

- Gather documents

- Retrieve e-mails and other computer data

- Interview witnesses

- Prepare a report

- Personnel records (which may contain sensitive and confidential personal information)
- Telephone records
- Vendor files, including contracts and invoices
- Expense account forms and receipts
- Personal calendars, diaries, appointment books, and telephone messages
- Minutes of meetings of the board of directors and its committees, as well as agendas and presentation books
- Notes and memoranda from meetings and other interoffice memoranda
- Research analysts' reports

The task of obtaining such documents may entail preventing those who are suspected of being involved in the fraud from having access to their offices and may require removal of their files into secure locations.

2. *Retrieve database information.* Databases must be accessed and efforts made to retrieve information that has been deleted. As illustrated by the recent Microsoft antitrust trial, e-mails are a potentially rich source of evidence in any case. E-mail communications tend to be more casual than formal interoffice memoranda and therefore either more or less reliable indicators of the truth, depending on one's point of view. Many corporate executives may not even realize that, depending on the company's software system, the e-mails, computer files, and other documents they thought had been deleted might actually be retrievable.

3. *Understand the accounting system.* A thorough understanding of the accounting systems and the functions of various accounting and financial personnel must be developed.

4. *Interview witnesses.* Witnesses must be interviewed—frequently more than once. The list of people to be interviewed would normally include at least the following:

- Financial and accounting personnel at corporate headquarters and any relevant operating units
- Senior level executives in management

- The company's outside auditors
- Internal auditors
- Members of the board of directors and relevant committees (such as the audit committee during the relevant time period)
- The company's legal counsel and compliance officers
- Public relations or other personnel who communicated with the public and research analysts on financial matters

5. *Prepare a report.*   Finally, a report generally must be prepared.

To accomplish the above tasks, a large team will be needed—probably larger than one might guess. To give some indication, as many as thirty or more forensic accountants and seven or eight lawyers may be needed in a large and complex investigation. The expense can be enormous.

Lack of Subpoena Power and the Interview Process

Unlike government investigators, or private litigants in a civil lawsuit, the investigating team does not have subpoena power. The reason is that the internal investigation is essentially a private matter conducted voluntarily by the company and not as part of a lawsuit or regulatory action where the law provides for subpoenas.

The absence of subpoena power is significant and will shape the outcome of the investigation in many ways. It means, first, that the ability to interview witnesses is dependent on their voluntary cooperation, including their willingness to appear and to speak fully. It is particularly important to have the cooperation of at least some of the perpetrators, because these people can best point the investigators in the right direction so that they can ask the right questions and obtain the key documents.

Unfortunately, the atmosphere that will likely exist as the interviewing process begins could hardly be less conducive to obtaining cooperation. By this time:

- Employees will be largely aware of the problem
- Outside accountants and lawyers may have taken up residence at corporate headquarters and taken control of various files
- Rumors will be rampant

- Personnel in the accounting and financial areas will wonder whether they are suspected
- They will also wonder whether they did something wrong that they do not know about

Putting employees at ease in this setting and coaxing them to tell what they know are challenges. Nonetheless, experience suggests that most people will cooperate. Current officers and employees may be required to appear for interviews, because refusal may constitute grounds for termination. Many others will agree to be interviewed because they do not want to appear uncooperative or because they feel (rightly or wrongly) that they have done nothing wrong and have nothing to hide.

Still others may suspect (or even acknowledge) that they or their co-employees might have done something improper and they will want to appear to put their best spin on their own behavior (perhaps by explaining that they did not understand the complete picture or were directed by their superiors to engage in the acts in question).

Other people, however, may conclude that it is not in their best interest to appear unless they get advance briefings on the questioning and evidence or an opportunity to review documents before the interview. For example, they may ask for a specification of the allegations (if any) against them by other employees, a list of questions (or at least subject matters) that they will be asked, copies of any documents that will be shown to them at the interview, and copies of any significant documents on which their name appears (either as author, recipient, or cc). In other words, they or their lawyer will want to know what the investigators know before they decide whether to tell what they know. Although providing such information in advance may seem to facilitate and streamline the interview process (by ensuring that the witness is better prepared), it also has the potential to impair the kind of spontaneity that is conducive to learning the whole truth.

Some witnesses will ask to have their own counsel present during their interviews. The company may in fact be paying for such counsel where its by-laws require it, thereby creating a significant additional expense for the company.

The company generally has no legal obligation to honor an employee's request to have counsel present for the interview, and there is no particular reason for the company to encourage employees to retain counsel during the investigative stage. As a practical matter, though, witnesses will usually be permitted to have their lawyer present if they wish, even if no formal charges have been made against the employee. The presence of such counsel may actually facilitate the fact-finding process, although, again, there may be some tradeoff in terms of the witness's level of spontaneity.

It normally should be made clear to the person being interviewed that the attorneys conducting the interview do not represent him or her personally and, instead, that the attorneys represent the special committee or other independent body. As a result, witnesses generally should be advised that their discussions and statements during the interview may not remain subject to an attorney-client privilege and that their statements may later be communicated to the company or outside parties such as the SEC. Even if a privilege applies, the company could elect to waive the privilege later and voluntarily provide to third parties the employee's interview statements. In some states, the lawyers conducting employee interviews may be ethically bound to advise the employee of these considerations, at least where it appears that the company's interests are adverse to the employee's.

In any investigation there may be some persons who see no reason to help and will decline to be interviewed altogether. Individuals such as former employees, including those discharged after the preliminary investigation and those who resign in the course of the investigation, may conclude that the risks of giving a statement for the record at an early stage are too great in light of the potential civil litigation, regulatory, and criminal problems that they may face. For example, employees may be sued as part of a shareholder class action; the SEC could bring an enforcement action against them (the result of which could be a civil fine or other penalty); and, most daunting of all, the U.S. attorney's office or other prosecutorial body could bring a criminal indictment. Thus, the familiar observation that "anything you say can and will be used against you" is one that employees will be advised to take into consideration in deciding whether to be interviewed.

Questioning at the interviews will generally be done by the lawyers or accountants or both. On occasion, a member of the independent committee may ask to be present, and such a request may be honored because the committee is the client of the lawyers conducting the investigation.

Another important consequence of the lack of subpoena power is that witnesses cannot be questioned under oath and therefore the laws against perjury do not apply. The interview setting will be less formal than in a courtroom or even in a pre-trial deposition. Generally, a court reporter or a stenographer will not be present to take down, verbatim, what the witness says.

Most investigators will elect not to tape record the interview for fear of intimidating the witness and chilling candor. Rather, the lawyers will typically make handwritten notes of the interview (which will later be typed), and it is always possible that a witness may subsequently deny having said at the interview what the notes record (although such outright denials are rare). As a result, some witnesses may perceive that they will not suffer the same adverse consequences from not telling the truth as they might from testifying falsely under oath. Or they may be less than completely forthcoming in their answers.

All of this may mean that the evidentiary record may not be as complete as one would like. But that does not mean that the fact-finding process under discussion is not extremely effective. In fact, it is. The documentary information will provide much of what is needed, and many witnesses with relevant information will be willing to be interviewed and to tell what they know. Indeed, for some the discomfort of having had information about the fraud bottled up for months or years may lead to almost extraordinary candor. The informal setting of the investigative interview and the fact that information is not being taken under oath and transcribed will operate to encourage witnesses to talk freely.

Unresolved Questions

It should not be surprising, though, that there may be certain persons whose knowledge and participation cannot be definitively determined. They may have been implicated in some way by persons who have been interviewed. Or their positions may have been such as to make it seem probable that they must have been involved. But they themselves may have appeared for interviews and denied any wrongdoing. And there may be no documents that clearly demonstrate their participation or knowledge.

What then? Are the investigators and the special committee free to draw conclusions about such individuals from whatever available information exists? Should determinations be made as to issues of credibility based upon the known facts or even upon demeanor at their interviews? Can the investigators and special committee act, in effect, as jurors and, if so, what standard of proof do they use? Should the investigators in these circumstances simply report the disputed facts, leaving to others with subpoena power (e.g., regulators, prosecutors, private litigants) the task of further inquiry and leaving to any ultimate fact-finders (e.g., the court, the jury) the determinations of guilt, innocence, or liability?

These are among the interesting and difficult questions that are likely to be faced as the conclusions of the investigation are formulated. Each investigative team and each special committee will have to decide under the particular circumstances just how far they wish to go in drawing inferences or conclusions from the available information.

Even in the absence of clear proof of knowledge of accounting irregularities, the evidence will often be sufficient to allow the board of directors to determine whether various personnel should be terminated, even though it may leave issues of employment and severance benefits and the like to be sorted out later in negotiation or litigation. That is because the investigation is very likely to provide information about whether there was a tone of some kind within the organization—in effect, an acceptance or encouragement of what occurred. And this type of information may well be the basis on which the board decides that changes must be made. In fact, there may be instances where, even if it cannot be definitively determined who knew what, the company will feel compelled to clean house simply because the fraud is found to be so egregious and widespread. Care must be taken, however, not to publicly malign individuals whose culpability is not clear; otherwise, the company may face the prospect of suits for defamation. Under some states' laws, moreover, employees who can prove they were unjustly terminated, i.e., without cause, may be able to successfully sue for damages (although probably not for reinstatement).

In the end, the company can reasonably expect that the investigation will accomplish most of what it set out to accomplish: It will identify the accounting irregularities and many of the individuals involved and will allow directors to make appropriate judgments as to which officers and employees should be terminated.

The Report

Reports in accounting irregularities investigations run the gamut from oral presentations to lengthy written documents that review the evidence in great detail. The nature, length, and level of detail of the report will depend on the complexity of the case, the number of individuals interviewed, the time pressure to complete the report, and strategic considerations.

A number of factors should be considered in deciding whether to prepare a written report (see Exhibit 5–2). The company may want a written report to document the results of the investigation and to exonerate the innocent and identify the guilty. A written report may also help restore the company's credibility by demonstrating, quite tangibly, the efforts and lengths to which the company has gone to investigate wrongdoing and take corrective action. A written report that explains to the world what happened and who was involved in a clear and comprehensive manner may put to bed many rumors and prior speculation. Recent reports in these cases have been widely disseminated to the public, including on the Internet.

A written report also avoids the need for repeated oral presentations and the ambiguities and lack of precision inherent in that process. Without a written report, it is possible that the lawyers who conducted the investigation will have to make multiple oral presentations of their findings to various groups (e.g., management, the board, the special committee, insurers, outside auditors, regulators, the courts). The recipients of these oral presentations will undoubtedly recall the presentations somewhat differently and they may take notes which, if later scrutinized, could on their face seem inconsistent and be taken out of context. A single written report can largely avoid such problems.

Figure 5–2. Pros and Cons of a Written Report

Advantages of a written report:

- Assists in exoneration of the innocent
- Avoids lack of precision in oral presentations
- Avoids need for multiple oral presentations
- Regulators expect written report
- Thorough report enhances company's credibility

Disadvantages:

- Provides roadmap for plaintiffs
- Conclusions may be binding on the company and others

Regulators, such as the SEC, may expect to receive a written report at the conclusion of the investigation. In those situations where the company may be seeking to convince the regulators not to take any further action (for example, because the investigation has concluded that no wrongdoing occurred), a written report may be a virtual necessity.

Regulators cannot require that a written report be prepared, but they will generally view a well-written, thorough report as a positive in the company's favor and a valuable tool in conducting whatever further investigation they make themselves. A comprehensive report will also provide a good road map to the regulators as to what areas are of importance, who the key players are and what they have said, and what documents are most critical (generally, the report will include an appendix or separate volume of relevant documents, including many or most of the documents referred to in the text of the report).

It is true that a written report will provide a clear trail for subsequent litigants, whether they be investors suing the company, officers or directors defending against such suits (or against suits by the company itself), or auditors involved in litigation. The conclusions in the report will generally not be binding in subsequent litigation on most of the individuals mentioned, but may very well include admissions that may be binding on the company. The report or its conclusions might also be binding on certain individuals, such as audit committee members or directors who endorse and act upon the report's conclusions.

To the extent the company views creation of a litigation road map to be undesirable, it will need to balance that concern against the considerations identified earlier that largely favor a written report. Another factor to bear in mind is that, even if the report is not written, subsequent litigants may be able to discover the essence of the report's findings and conclusions through other means (such as obtaining the investigative team's interview notes, memoranda or other work product, or the notes taken by recipients of oral presentations). That leads to the next topic, concerning the applicability of various privileges to the report and underlying work product.

Can the Report Remain Privileged?

Generally, if a written report is prepared by the investigative team and given to the special committee that oversaw the investigation, that report will constitute an attorney-client communication. If the report receives no wider distribution it can effectively be kept confidential, if that is the committee's (and company's) desire.

However, for the reasons discussed earlier, the company may wish to distribute the report to the regulators, who undoubtedly will request a copy. If the company voluntarily provides the report to the government, the company may be deemed to have waived the attorney-client privilege. If the privilege is waived, then other outside parties (besides the selected recipients) will be able to obtain the report in the course of any subsequent litigation by serving a subpoena for its production.

The company might be able to secure an agreement by the government to keep the report confidential. Such an agreement may offer some protection against waiver of the privilege, but it is no guarantee.

Apart from the regulators, the company may wish to give the report to various other outside parties, such as its lenders, its D&O insurer, or the company's outside auditors (all of whom will be anxious to obtain a copy). Again, if the company elects to provide the report to any such parties, it may be deemed to have waived any privilege that otherwise might apply. To the extent the report is used for operational decision making or to determine those to be discharged or retained, that may also impede the applicability of the privilege.

As a result, it is prudent for the company and the investigative team to assume, from the outset, that the privilege may end up being waived and that the report will eventually become public.

Is the Investigators' Work Product Privileged?

Apart from the actual report, the company may desire to keep the interview notes, memoranda, and other work product of investigative counsel and the forensic accountants confidential. Such work product would likely be protected against disclosure by virtue of one or more legal privileges, but, again, there is a possibility that the privilege could be waived. For example, if the company provides the actual report to regulators or other parties, this could be deemed a waiver as to any documents (such as interview memoranda and notes) that constitute the backup for the report.

The government will often request the company to turn over not just the report but also the interview memoranda and other underlying documents themselves. If the company elects to do so, this could also constitute a waiver of any privilege as to those backup materials. Again, prudence dictates that, due to the uncertainty and the possibility of waiver, the company and investigative counsel should proceed from the outset on the assumption that all work product relating to the report and investigation will eventually become public.

CHAPTER 6

DIGGING OUT THE FRAUD: THE FORENSIC ACCOUNTANTS

Harvey R. Kelly

Although highly skilled, lawyers experienced in digging out the truth behind fraudulent financial reporting typically cannot do it alone. They need the technical expertise, the skills, and the familiarity with the intricacies of generally accepted accounting principles (GAAP) that public accounting firms possess. Frequently, however, not just any accountant will do. It is often of great advantage to retain those accounting professionals experienced in special investigations and, in particular, rooting out fraud. Such specialists are informally known as *forensic accountants*.

What Is a Forensic Accountant?

The term *forensic accountant* does not represent an officially recognized professional designation, such as certified public accountant (CPA), and *forensic accountant*, accordingly, can mean different things to different people. As a general matter, though, the term connotes a specialized type of financial professional whose expertise and experience is targeted to the excavation of the underlying facts in connection with financial misreporting. Where accounting irregularities have been detected, forensic accountants are frequently retained by the special committee to assist the special committee's law firm in digging out the fraud.

Why Hire a Forensic Accountant?

A special committee investigation into accounting irregularities will not get too far, if it gets started at all, without the recognition that the special committee's outside law firm will need the technical assistance of experienced accountants. Certainly, the special committee lawyers can do much of the investigatory work—interviewing witnesses, reviewing business files, interacting with the special committee and others involved. However, typically the investigation quickly plunges into depths of analysis beyond the ken of the average attorney not schooled or deeply experienced in accounting and financial reporting. In particular, areas of the investigation requiring the expertise of specialized accounting professionals include the following:

- **Generally accepted accounting principles.** Most obvious, an investigation into accounting irregularities requires extensive knowledge and experience in working with GAAP. The ultimate question, of course, is whether the financial statements conformed to GAAP as represented in the company's financial statements and Securities and Exchange Commission (SEC) filings. Insofar as those manipulating the books will have frequently undertaken to misreport results by exploiting potential ambiguities in GAAP, hazy areas of financial reporting, and highly technical rules of accounting, intimate and extensive familiarity with those rules is critical.

- **Accounting conventions.** Beyond intimate familiarity with the technical rules, an accounting irregularity investigation requires knowledge of the conventions of accounting practice in the particular industry at issue or, more broadly, in the context of financial reporting overall. Frequently, the accounting irregularities will surface in areas in which GAAP do not necessarily provide crystal clear answers and the propriety of the accounting will turn on what is generally accepted. Therefore, the lawyers will need the help of those who have not only mastered the black-and-white pronouncements that constitute GAAP but also the conventions as to how they are applied.

- **Bookkeeping and accounting systems.** In addition to expertise in GAAP and the conventions of financial reporting, the investigators will also need the availability of expertise in bookkeeping and accounting systems. The most important and revealing evidence is often tucked away in obscure and hard-to-find general ledger entries, records of reserves, sales cut-off documents, bills of lading, account reconciliations, and other components of the company's bookkeeping process. Expertise in accounting systems allows the investigators to go right to the potential trouble spots.

- **Manpower.** Uncovering accounting irregularities can literally be like looking for a needle in a haystack. The perpetrators will have deliberately selected the most hard-to-find places in which to bury obscure and hard-to-detect entries. Without their cooperation (and with the specter of prison hanging over their heads, they frequently will not cooperate), uncovering the fraud can involve untold man-hours of combing books and records. Although law firms specializing in the area frequently have teams of attorneys ready to start working, it is not unusual for a massive financial-fraud investigation to require more manpower than a law firm has readily available. For example, one recent large accounting-irregularity problem involved the full-time efforts of approximately 80 professionals—a number that, by itself, is greater than the size of many law firms. For the national accounting firms, with their thousands of partners and tens of thousands of employees, literally no investigation is too big—even if they have to fly in CPAs from surrounding cities in order to staff the investigation.

- **Lower billing rates.** If a special committee is still in doubt about retention of a team of forensic accountants, the next issue usually wins it over: billing rates. Although the top rates of the most senior public accountants can easily match or exceed those of senior partners in law firms, the billing rates of those at the most junior levels will frequently be lower for accountants than for lawyers. Not all aspects of the investigation are rocket science and for much of the investigation (e.g., checking the dates through years' worth of bills of lading), a junior-grade professional will be more than adequate. Though cost is not usually the foremost concern in fraud investigations, to the extent it can be considered, cost also militates in favor of the substantial involvement of forensic accountants to supplement the lawyers.

So far, all of the factors listed support the involvement of accountants to assist the lawyers. None of them, though, suggests the need for a forensic accountant rather than, say, use of the investigatory capabilities of the company's incumbent auditor. CPAs from the incumbent audit firm meet most of the requirements: they are familiar with GAAP, understand the conventions of financial reporting, understand the company's bookkeeping and accounting systems (probably better initially than would a newly introduced forensic team), can presumably make available the necessary manpower, and have billing rates that are competitive with the other firms. Why not, therefore, use the incumbent auditor not only to obtain new audited financial statements (see Chapter 4), but to dig out the fraud as well?

In truth, the answer is not always obvious. Sometimes, it may make sense to use the incumbent auditor to assist in the investigation, and special committee investigations have been conducted with complete success on that basis. On the other hand, additional factors frequently support the need for a specialized forensic team from a different firm (Exhibit 6–1). Among those factors are the following:

- **Awareness of the gravity of the situation.** Though it may seem strange, sometimes the discovery of accounting irregularities is sufficiently outside the experience of normal financial statement auditors that the CPAs on the incumbent engagement team may not immediately appreciate the seriousness of the situation. They may not, therefore, react with a dramatic and intense response. In one instance, for example, an audit engagement team partner responded to the potential discovery of accounting irregularities by asking if the matter could wait several weeks to be addressed—apparently failing to appreciate that, all the while, investors would be trading on potentially fraudulent information.

  Forensic accountants, in contrast, have been through the drill before. Because of their experience with accounting irregularities, they fully understand that, in all likelihood, the survival of the corporation is hanging in the balance. Frequently, they will be prepared to begin working within hours of having been retained, with a full army of experienced professionals who know precisely where to go and what to do during the critical first 72 hours. They will understand what they have to do and will act accordingly.

- **Objectivity.** It is entirely possible that the incumbent auditor will be able to field an investigative team every bit as energetic as another

---

Exhibit 6–1. Key Benefits of Using Outside Forensic Accountants

Forensic accountants:

- Add objectivity and credibility
- Provide the investigation team with accounting expertise
- Supply much needed manpower in a time of crisis
- Enhance effectiveness and efficiency by adding individuals experienced in rooting out fraud

---

firm's forensic accountants. Even where that is the case, though, an additional factor, depending on the particular circumstances, may militate in favor of the retention of new forensic accountants from another firm: objectivity.

Of course, CPAs are trained in objectivity and independence, and many excellent professionals will be able to rise above more parochial concerns to investigate with zeal, tenacity, and earnestness every path and trail—no matter to whom they may lead. In some cases, the special committee may be convinced that its incumbent auditor can field a group of forensic accountants that will be completely objective.

Complete objectivity is one thing. The *appearance* of objectivity is another. Even under circumstances where the outside auditor is capable of being fully objective, some special committees may nonetheless determine that the appearance of objectivity favors the retention of a new forensic accountant.

To whom will that appearance of objectivity be important? Pretty much anybody whose responsibilities include oversight of, or interaction with, the company, and who, therefore, has an interest in its credibility and integrity. Those who may be interested in an objective investigation include the Securities and Exchange Commission (SEC); the New York Stock Exchange (NYSE); and the company's banks, suppliers, customers, venture capitalists, large investors, and shareholders. When accounting irregularities first surface, all of these parties will ask themselves whether the company can be expected to do the right thing. Retention of an outside forensic accountant with unquestioned objectivity may be a necessary step in satisfying everyone.

• **Experience with forensic investigations.** A final factor favoring the retention of forensic accountants is their experience in dealing with financial fraud. In truth, a normal outside auditor does not have to wrestle with fraud very often. It is not unusual for a CPA in an audit department to go through the entirety of his career without ever once having accounting irregularities surface on his watch.

This lack of experience with fraud investigations can cause delays because, unlike those experienced in such investigations, the inexperienced accountant does not know that the fraud tends to take place in the same areas over and over again. Those experienced in the ways of forensic investigations can immediately zero in on the likely areas and quickly target questionable transactions and entries. An experienced forensic accountant will have been through it all before. When time is of the essence, such experience helps.

The Difference between a Forensic Investigation and an Audit

Implicit in the discussion so far is the notion that a forensic investigation, of the sort to be undertaken by the special committee where accounting irregularities have surfaced, is somehow different than a normal generally accepted auditing standards (GAAS) audit. To those not steeped in the ways of the accounting profession, such a disparity may seem something of an anomaly. It is conventional wisdom that normal outside auditors have some responsibility for the detection of fraud. Can the fulfillment of that responsibility in a normal year-end audit pursuant to GAAS and the investigation of fraud pursuant to a forensic engagement be all that different?

The answer is yes. In essence, an audit pursuant to GAAS and a forensic investigation into fraud fulfill their objectives in two completely different ways. Although the goal of each is correctly stated financial statements, the avenues to those goals are noticeably different.

The main difference between a conventional audit and a forensic investigation involves the principal assumption that constitutes the engagement's predicate. In a normal GAAS audit, the predicate is that, absent evidence to the contrary, everyone is generally trying to tell the truth. That is not to say that an auditor is entitled to accept everything at face value. That is certainly not the case. However, a normal auditor under GAAS—again, absent evidence to the contrary—is entitled in the first instance to believe that documents have not been forged, that books and records have not been deliberately manipulated, and that management's representations to the auditor are true. Although the auditor does not assume the unquestioned honesty of management, neither does the auditor assume management to be dishonest. The technical term describing this predicate is *professional skepticism*. At its core, professional skepticism requires the auditor to be something of a skeptic but not to assume the falsity of everything everybody says.

That is not to say that the auditor consistently assumes that no fraud has taken place—though years ago testing for fraud was not even required. Today, the auditor is called upon by GAAS to make an informed and reasoned judgment about the risk of fraud and, in light of that judgment, to design audit tests that provide the auditor reasonable assurance that any such fraud would be detected in the audit if it were material to the company's financial statements. Even here, though, the predicate is not that the company is infected with defrauders.

In a forensic investigation, that predicate changes to the complete opposite. Once it has been established that the bookkeeping has been infected by defrauders, the issue for the forensic accountant is: How deep and widespread does it go?

Therefore, everyone is a suspect. Each member of the board of directors, each senior executive, those in middle-level management, right down to the truck driver transporting potentially fictitious goods—all must initially be subject to the forensic accountant's withering probe. True, most will not stay suspects for long. But at the outset, the forensic accountant takes nothing for granted.

As a practical matter, this means that all suspicious areas—and even those areas that are only potentially suspicious—will be investigated. Whereas, in the absence of evidence to the contrary, the outside auditor would ordinarily assume the genuineness of documents, forensic accountants exhaustively search for evidence that either validates key documents or establishes their falsity. Similarly, forensic accountants must be extraordinarily suspicious of the veracity and completeness of the statements of company personnel made during the investigation. Such statements may be unduly influenced by self-serving motives. For those within the company, credibility is something that now must be earned.

The principal features that distinguish a forensic investigation from a normal GAAS audit are these:

- **Purpose.** The principal purpose of a forensic investigation is to dig out the fraud. It is, in other words, to find out the who, what, when, where, and how of what happened. The purpose is not simply to audit the financial statements through sampling techniques, as is the case in a normal GAAS audit.

- **Documentary evidence.** A forensic investigation into accounting fraud will almost inevitably uncover forged documents. Thus, forensic accountants view all documents with what might politely be referred to as a "heightened degree of skepticism." Documents falling into suspect areas must be corroborated, supported, and verified. The documentation behind questionable transactions must be inspected, inquired into, and inspected again.

- **Other evidence gathering.** Forensic accountants employ additional evidence-gathering techniques beyond those used in an audit. Extensive interviews of company employees and third parties, often in the presence of lawyers, are typical. Searches of company computer files (including those thought to have been deleted by employees) are sought to provide further clues to the truth. Reviews of employee desk files are not uncommon.

- **Scope and materiality.** Forensic accountants typically are asked to investigate irregularities without regard to their materiality to the financial statements taken as a whole. Thus, small transactions, unlikely to be examined in a normal GAAS audit, may be scrutinized with care. On the other hand, a forensic investigation may leave entirely untouched areas that would be subject to significant testing in a normal GAAS audit. The level of scrutiny by a forensic accountant turns largely on the susceptibility of a particular area to manipulation and fraud.

- **Urgency.** Investigations into potential accounting irregularities almost always involve extreme urgency. As a result, the number of forensic accountants and other investigators that descends upon a company can easily exceed the size of the company's entire accounting department. Even if they are not bountiful in number, the investigation team will submit substantial information requests and expect to receive responses quickly. The forensic investigators, in other words, will operate on the assumption that expedited completion of the investigation is of paramount concern for everyone involved. On the other hand, a normal GAAS audit has to take place in a way that does not unduly interfere with the company's ongoing operations.

Immediate Objectives

If the special committee decides to retain a team of forensic accountants, some of the newly hired accountants will often begin working within hours of being engaged (see Exhibit 6–2). The first objective will be to learn everything possible about the fraud based on available sources. Who, what, when, where, how—all of these will be the subject of immediate questioning by the forensic accountants, even while the complete forensic team is in the process of being assembled. The forensic accountants, of course, will be under no delusions. It is almost inevitable that, whatever information they obtain at the outset, the fraud will turn out to be deeper and more widespread than initially described. Still, the accountants have to start somewhere, and the available pool of information is obviously the right place.

Part of the initial inquiry into the fraud will involve examining the telltale documents that have surfaced to date. Frequently, the initial detection of accounting irregularities will be accompanied by suspicious documents,

---

Exhibit 6–2. Typical Approach of Forensic Accountants

- Focus on the who, what, when, where, and how of what happened
- Consider all suspects
- Be on the alert for forged documents
- Conduct extensive searches of company documents and computer files for evidence of fraud
- Formally and informally interview key company employees

---

such as forged bills of lading, mysterious schedules of reserves, or, possibly, memoranda providing a window into the fraud. Members of the forensic team will be dispatched to explore clues that the initial set of documents will, in all likelihood, present.

All the while, the forensic accountants will be gaining an understanding of the business. Metaphorically speaking, the forensic accountants' role requires that they plunge into the deep end without more than a quick understanding of a company's operations, accounting system, or perhaps even the complete nature of its business. Thus, initial inquiry into the specific areas of fraud will be accompanied by an assessment of broader aspects of the business—who runs it, what it does, how it is set up.

With some level of initial orientation complete, an immediate objective becomes assisting the lawyers in the preservation of evidence from the likely malefactors. Today, with core financial records almost entirely computerized and frequently accessible from home, this can be more difficult than one would think. If it has not been done already, the supervisor of management information systems will be requested to preserve all computerized information and to shut down access by those who are suspected of participation in the fraud. To preclude physical destruction of paper, locks on doors may be changed and security personnel instructed to physically impede the reentry of suspected participants. In one instance of accounting irregularities, the local police force was summoned to physically stand guard at company headquarters with a directive to bar any attempted access by the newly discharged CEO and CFO.

Needless to say, all of this can be extraordinarily disruptive to the company's normal operations—many of which, in all likelihood, will suddenly grind to a halt. An additional objective of the forensic accountants, therefore, will be to determine those aspects of the accounting system and the documentary evidence that require isolation and to free up operating personnel to get back to work in those areas that are theoretically unaffected. Even if it completely uncovers the fraud, a forensic investigation is not a success story if it destroys the company in the process.

Framing the Issues

With the completion of an initial orientation and preservation of key evidence, it is time for the forensic accountants and the lawyers to sit down together and determine the issues to be explored. By this point, both the forensic accountants and the lawyers will have a fair handle on the principal areas of fraud and a sense as to what additional areas may be involved. Based on that knowledge, they will together agree upon a strategy for turning over every stone so that the totality of the deceptions may be uncovered and corrective statements made.

To the uninitiated, this may seem somewhere between a daunting task and an impossible one. A normal public company keeps thousands or millions of documents. Do the team members assume every one is false? If not, how do they distinguish between those that need to be checked and those that do not? And what about employees, officers, and directors? Is everyone from the chairman of the board down to the messengers in the mailroom to be the subject of interviews?

Obviously, no investigation could proceed in such a way. Still, one financial restatement is horrific; a second is unacceptable. The extent of the fraud, therefore, is no excuse for lack of thoroughness in uncovering the deceptions wherever they may be. Framing the issues, therefore, largely entails important judgments as to those areas to be explored.

It is at this point that the experience of the forensic accountant again proves its worth. Experience will have shown that financial fraud tends to involve the same areas over and over again. Therefore, each new investigation does not necessarily involve completely starting from scratch. Given an initial orientation into the nature of the fraud, experienced forensic accountants will start out with a pretty good idea of where to look.

And where is that? In essence, it is in those areas of the company's financial statements that involve flexibility or the use of judgment in the application of GAAP. These are the areas where fraud typically begins largely because the corresponding lack of clarity and black-and-white rules render the fraud (at least at its origin) difficult to detect. As the fraud proceeds, the need for more extreme manipulations causes it to branch out into other areas. Even then, though, areas involving judgment and lack of clarity are preferred by the perpetrators.

Thus, one typically does *not* find fraud in areas where the rules are clear and the account balances objectively verifiable. An example is cash. When it comes to cash, the rules under GAAP are straightforward and the balances are easy to check—they can simply be confirmed with the bank. Similarly, physical assets, such as plant, property, and equipment, are not exactly easy to manipulate. It would be difficult to explain, for example, the reason that the recorded value of a company warehouse suddenly tripled when, under GAAP, the proper value to be set forth is the warehouse's depreciated cost.

Still, that leaves plenty of areas of the company's financial reporting that are susceptible to manipulation (see Exhibit 6–3). Some of the more common areas are discussed below.

Revenue Recognition

These days, revenue recognition is one of the first places to look. There are two reasons. First, today financial misreporting seems to be driven by the need to meet analyst quarterly expectations, which itself leads to the recognition of revenue as a prime candidate for manipulation. Second, management often resorts to creative sales techniques involving complex revenue recognition rules as a way to come up with at least a few extra pennies of earnings. One study of alleged accounting irregularity cases found that, over a two-year period, issues involving revenue recognition were implicated 40% of the time.

What are the devices by which revenue recognition may be manipulated? The most obvious is the one discussed hypothetically in Chapter 1: accelerating shipments. Frequently, financial fraud starts with shipment acceleration, which, as the treadmill effect goes into full gear, evolves into keeping the quarter open for a day or two and then longer and thereafter recognizing revenue on post-quarter orders or, after that, orders that have not been received at all. The evolution of the fraud, accordingly, tends to follow a natu-

---

Exhibit 6–3. Common Accounting Fraud Areas

Revenue recognition
- Premature recognition of sales
- Phantom sales
- Improperly valued transactions

Reserves
- Bad-faith estimates
- One-time charges

Inventory
- Overvaluation
- Nonexistent inventory

Expenses
- Delayed expense recognition
- Improper capitalization of expenses

Other
- Related party transactions
- Acquisition accounting

---

ral progression. It starts out in an ostensibly innocuous way and evolves into a manipulation of records that is blatantly indefensible.

Quarter-end shipment manipulations, though, are only one of the more obvious ways that revenue recognition is susceptible to fraud. Another frequent area involves *bill-and-hold transactions*—transactions in which revenue can be recognized even though the product has not been shipped. Revenue recognition on bill-and-hold transactions involves compliance with a laundry list of criteria. Where accounting irregularities have surfaced, it is not unusual to find revenue recognized even when the specific criteria have not been met.

Similarly, consignment sales have historically been fertile ground for fraud. A consignment sale, of course, involves the placement of a product in another location, such as a retailer, with an obligation to take back the product in the event it is not sold. Whereas GAAP delays the recognition of revenue until the product is sold by the consignee, manipulators of financial records have on occasion seized upon shipping documents as a basis to recognize revenue before the actual sale has taken place.

Special discounting constitutes still another area where manipulations historically have been found. Special discounting frequently comes about based on a need for a spike in revenue as quarter-end is rapidly approaching. In order to obtain the necessary orders, the sales force may be instructed to offer special terms that then are not candidly reported to the company's accounting department. The result is a recognition of revenue, part of which (if, for example, the special terms involve a discount in price) or all of which (if, for example, the terms involve a particular right to return) should not have been taken into account.

Another area in which fraud is frequently found involves so-called barter transactions, that is, transactions in which the medium of exchange is not cash but a product or service of theoretically equivalent value. Barter transactions can be notoriously difficult to value insofar as their economic effect must be translated into cash when, in fact, no cash has changed hands. The resulting ambiguity is rife with opportunity for exploitation.

Reserves

Beyond revenue recognition, another area with the potential for manipulation involves the use of reserves. Although the term *reserves* is used broadly, in this instance we are talking about pools based on an estimate that either reduces the value of an asset (e.g., an allowance or reserve for bad debts) or establishes a liability for costs expected to be incurred in the future (e.g., damages relating to a lawsuit).

The reason reserves may be candidates for manipulation is straightforward. Reserves by their nature almost always involve some element of prediction. The precise number, therefore, can never be known. Under GAAP, the appropriate reserve level is determined according to the best estimate of management based upon its reasoned and informed judgment.

With regard to some reserves, the opportunities for manipulation are fairly constrained. If, for example, a company has consistently experienced a 90% collection rate on its receivables over the last 20 years, it is hard to argue that suddenly the reserve should be reduced from 10% to 2% absent any demonstrable changes in circumstances that would dramatically improve collections. Frequently, though, the appropriate reserve is not clear. That is particularly the case in new or evolving industries where the track record of performance is either nonexistent or short.

In recent years, reserves in the form of restructuring charges taken at the time of a merger or corporate reorganization have become a controversial topic (and a particular hot-button with the SEC). Restructuring charges are supposed to cover one-time costs, such as the costs of consolidating two companies, relocating or eliminating redundant operations, or paying severance to terminated employees. The charge is generally recorded and labeled as a special or unusual charge in the company's financial statements.

The danger inherent in such reserves arises from the potential desire by management to overstate the restructuring charge (i.e., create an excess reserve) so that the excess can be used to bolster income in future periods. Many believe that Wall Street analysts tend to ignore or discount the effect of restructuring charges as one-time or extraordinary, so the company's managers may reason that they are better off taking a hit to income up front and later reversing the excess reserve into income (thereby improving profits).

Inventory

For those defrauders interested in tradition, inventory manipulation is the vehicle of choice. One of the most famous frauds of the century— McKesson-Robbins during the 1930s—involved inventory fraud. It was specifically because of the inventory fraud at McKesson-Robbins that GAAS were rewritten to require auditor observation of a client's inventories and inventory-measurement processes.

Today, inventory remains rich with opportunity for cooking the books. One reason is the need to record inventory at the lower of cost or market. Although cost is objectively verifiable, market value may not be as readily demonstrable. GAAP necessitate judgments as to the point at which recorded inventory levels should be reduced or, perhaps, written off completely.

Another problem with inventory involves the clumsiness inherent in physical inspection and verification. Although GAAS generally require an auditor to undertake some level of physical observation of inventory, even here the auditor relies on techniques of statistical sampling and random tests. In the event of fraud, such tasks are never foolproof. Fraud perpetrators have been known to go to such extremes as filling boxes with bricks, sealing the boxes, and labelling and counting the boxes as though they contained valuable inventory. Other methods used to circumvent the physical inspection and verification process include manipulating inventory counts at locations not visited by the auditor and falsifying records regarding inventory reported to be in transit at the time the auditor visited the site.

Expenses

Although manipulation of expenses is not a vehicle of first choice, a defrauder may turn to it to help cover his tracks. The manipulation of expenses is more difficult than, say, the manipulation of reserves, because expense amounts are normally objectively verifiable and, under GAAP, there is little room for discretion. Nonetheless, expense recognition can be delayed, thereby artificially enhancing the calculation of profitability.

One aspect of the recording of expenses, moreover, is more susceptible to fraud than the others. That involves the distinction between expenditures that are to be expensed and expenditures that are to be capitalized. Insofar as the distinction under GAAP can involve judgments regarding the nature of the cost and/or its future benefit to the organization, the opportunity for manipulation is enhanced.

Each of these areas will be a potential candidate for investigation as the lawyers and forensic accountants determine their approach to the special committee investigation. As to each area where inquiry is warranted, the discussion will involve the location of relevant documents, those in a position to participate in the fraud, and the possible extent of misreported amounts.

At no point, though, will either the lawyers or the forensic accountants allow themselves to be deluded into thinking that this initial framing of issues will be the last one that takes place. Rather, each will fully appreciate the extent to which fraud tends to start out small in one area and then, as it grows, spread into other areas. Insofar as minor account manipulations are harder to detect than large ones, in the early stages the fraud will likely have resulted in modest manipulation to multiple accounts. Only when the opportunity for modest revision in many accounts has been exhausted will the perpetrators allow the fraud to grow to noticeable levels in any particular one of them.

Any initial framing of the issues, therefore, is going to be temporary. The parameters of the investigation will always be changing as the weeks and months proceed.

Conducting the Investigation

Once the issues have been framed, the investigative team sets forth on its quest to find the truth. Ultimately, many avenues will be explored. At this stage, though, the quest begins with a fundamental undertaking: to develop a detailed understanding of the company's accounting system, with particular focus on the computerized general ledger.

Today, virtually all public companies maintain a computerized general ledger system. This general ledger represents the primary accounting tool of the company. Each and every transaction is recorded on the ledger. Each entry into the general ledger will include background information that, for the experienced forensic accountant, is abundant with potential clues.

Among the wealth of information potentially stored in the company's general ledger, for example, may be the following:

- The journal entries that the company recorded to implement the fraud
- The dates upon which the company recorded fraudulent transactions
- The sources for the amounts recorded (e.g., an automated sub-accounting system, such as purchasing or treasury, versus a manually prepared journal entry)
- The company employee responsible for entering the journal entries into the accounting system
- Any adjusting journal entries that may have been recorded

The general ledger journal entries, therefore, give an investigator a key starting place into the who, what, when, where, and how of the manipulated entries. Dates, amounts, key-punching employees, and related data may immediately become available. That is not to suggest that the general ledger will provide all of the answers. But it is an excellent place to start.

Examination of other aspects of the general ledger system—and the company's accounting system as a whole—will yield other clues. For example, inspection of quarter-end or year-end journal entries may reveal patterns of reserve manipulation, revenue enhancement, or other peculiar activity taking place as each financial reporting period draws to its close. Unusual manual entries—potentially the result of senior executive directives—may surface. Anything that appears out of the ordinary, in the context of the normal flow of the company's operations, may be a candidate for investigation.

The investigation obviously does not stop with clues gleaned from the general ledger or other aspects of the accounting system. Much more is involved. For example, frequently, a useful step is to assess the extent to which a company has accounted for certain transactions in accordance with their underlying terms. Thus, the forensic accountants will often scrutinize the terms of contracts and other documents underlying important or suspicious transactions. Such scrutiny may include a search for undisclosed terms, such as those that may be included in side letters or pursuant to oral agreements. The forensic team may coax information from knowledgeable company personnel outside the accounting function, such as those in sales, about the possible existence of special terms or other considerations not reported to the accounting department. It is not unusual for the forensic accountants to contact those outside the company to corroborate important records as they become available.

Although the avenues of investigation may be somewhat straightforward at the outset, before long they will look like a road map of Paris. Inevitably, therefore, no matter how well-framed the issues at the outset, the investigation will largely depend upon the experience and gut instincts of the forensic investigative team. Although manipulative patterns are almost certain to exist, inevitable as well are unique tricks and manipulations owing to the creativity of the perpetrators and their particular needs of the moment. In the end, the adequacy of the investigation will come down to the zeal, tenacity, and ingenuity of the forensic team.

Interacting with the Lawyers and the Attorney-Client Privilege

As the investigation progresses, one mechanical issue involves the division of labor between the lawyers and the forensic accountants. What is to be done by whom? Related to that is the extent to which attorneys must participate in every discussion in order to maximize applicability of the attorney-client privilege.

As to the division of labor between lawyers and forensic accountants, there are no clear rules of delineation and the best approach depends upon the particular circumstances at issue. Important interviews of senior financial executives may be conducted jointly—with both a lawyer and an accountant in attendance. At the other end of the spectrum, interviews of lower-level accounting department personnel may involve only the accountants. Interviews of others may involve only the lawyers.

One aspect of the interview process that will become apparent fairly quickly is the practical impossibility of lawyer participation in every interview—at least in an investigation of any meaningful scope. Many or most interviews conducted by the forensic accountants will not be structured in any formal sense; rather, they will take place in momentary intervals throughout the day as documents surface, need to be explained, and then lead to new documents and explanations in turn. Concerns regarding efficiency, staffing, cost, and simply the availability of manpower will largely preclude the possibility of attorney participation in all such conversations. One thing the lawyers will need to check, therefore, will be the extent to which conversations between the forensic accountants and company personnel will be privileged even absent the involvement of a lawyer. If the company's lawyer has directed it, as the lawyer's client, to communicate with an accountant engaged by the lawyer, who is then to interpret the accounting aspects so that the lawyer may give better legal advice, then communications by the client reasonably related to that purpose ought to be privileged. The forensic accountants will typically inquire as to the structure of the investigation in order to maximize the applicability of the privilege.

One characteristic that both the attorneys and the forensic accountants will need to have in common is a capacity to put people at ease and to solicit candid information—a task that is particularly difficult in the context of an investigation into fraud. In all likelihood, certain employees will have already been discharged. Company operations will be in something of a state of turmoil. Entirely new faces will be combing through filing cabinets, asking difficult questions, setting up ad hoc offices in every inch of available space. And employees will be keenly sensitive to the fact that preservation of their employment may depend on the substantive answers given in interviews.

Soliciting information under such circumstances is difficult at best. The forensic accountants, like the lawyers involved, therefore will need to possess the interpersonal skills and diplomacy that cultivate an atmosphere in which employees are willing to talk.

Coordination with the Outside Auditor

Coordination with the lawyers spearheading the investigation, though, may turn out to be easy compared to the challenge of coordination with another group of professionals investigating the fraud at the same time. That group of professionals is the engagement team of the company's incumbent outside auditor.

The problem is this: The company needs its incumbent auditor. As discussed in Chapter 4, the company needs audited financial statements fast, and the quickest route to the procurement of audited financial statements is a re-audit by the incumbent auditor. Already having been lied to once, the incumbent auditor will not be in a particularly good mood. At best, the relationship between the company and its auditor will be strained.

Add to this already-strained relationship another accounting firm whose mission it is to second-guess, among other things, the reasons the fraud took place and was not discovered. One of the last things the incumbent auditor wants to hear is that now a new accounting firm (by the way, a competitor) will be combing through the books and records and finding out just who missed what. The forensic accountants undertaking that investigation, moreover, will probably have a fairly good sense of GAAS and will be almost unable to avoid second-guessing the diligence with which they were applied.

A natural consequence would be for the incumbent auditor and the forensic accountant simply to avoid each other. That, though, is a luxury that neither can afford. Ironically, each needs the other. The forensic accountant needs the incumbent auditor because the incumbent auditor has possession of knowledge and workpapers that can get the forensic investigation off to a more rapid start. Information about period-end adjusting journal entries, conversations with management regarding suspicious transactions, even important aspects of the audit chronology—all of these will be just sitting in the incumbent auditor's workpapers waiting for the forensic accountant's review.

But the need for information is not simply a one-way street. The incumbent auditor also needs information from the forensic accountant. In particular, as extra protection regarding the integrity of its re-audit, the incumbent auditor needs to know the results of the forensic accountant's investigation. Was the CEO in on the fraud? The CFO? Which individuals within the accounting department were involved in the fraud? These are all key questions that, to the extent not determined during the audit, will need to be answered before the auditor is prepared to issue a new audit report. For the incumbent auditor, simply turning away from the forensic accountant and offering no cooperation is not a realistic option.

An uneasy truce will therefore be established: The incumbent auditor will normally allow the forensic accountant access to its workpapers to assist in the speed and efficiency of the forensic investigation, and the special committee will agree that formulation of a conclusion as to the adequacy of the incumbent auditor's work is not a purpose of the special committee investigation. That is not to say that no aspect of the investigation will turn up evidence that might ultimately be used against the auditor. The mere fact that the auditor did not catch the fraud probably makes the discovery of some such evidence inevitable. But the special committee will agree that, with regard to the incumbent auditor, it will not try to make things worse than they already are.

As the forensic investigation and the re-audit of the financial statements simultaneously draw to their conclusions, one issue that can be potentially troublesome is the manner in which the special committee's conclusions are to be presented for outside auditor consideration. For understandable reasons, the auditor may prefer to receive a written report outlining the scope of the investigation, the details of the fraud, those found to have been participants, and the quantification of numerical consequences. The company, however, for equally understandable reasons involving the class actions, may not want such a written report to be drafted. If such a report is drafted, moreover, the company may not want to provide the report to its outside auditor, which could then potentially compromise applicability of the attorney-client privilege.

No written rules determine the manner in which the results of any investigation are to be transmitted to the outside auditor or, for that matter, that the results should be transmitted at all. The mechanism by which information is to be transmitted, therefore, depends upon the particular needs of the company and the auditor under the unique circumstances at issue.

Knowing When to Stop

With incomplete witness interviews, lost or destroyed records, and seemingly endless accounting records and transactions, how do the forensic accountants know when to end the investigation?

No fraud investigation concludes with absolute assurance that all irregularities have been identified or all wrongdoers caught. Nonetheless, the investigation should be sufficient to assist the directors and company management in forming their determination as to:

1. Whether previously issued financial statements require restatement
2. Which company personnel bear responsibility for the irregularities
3. What steps can be taken to minimize the risk that accounting irregularities will recur in the future

There will be no guarantee that every improper transaction has been completely uncovered. On the other hand, there *should* be a strong level of conviction that the investigation has been as thorough and complete as the circumstances will permit.

CHAPTER 7

CLASS ACTION LAWSUITS

Michael R. Young

After the first several weeks of an accounting irregularity crisis, it may be that the board of directors will have occasion to be almost amazed at the speed and efficiency with which it has addressed many aspects of the problem. If all has been properly handled, the board will have undertaken an investigation, alerted the public through a press release, terminated the employment of those whose complicity was clear, and handled innumerable problems involving creditors, employees, suppliers, and others. Looking back, individual board members may be genuinely astonished at the alacrity with which difficult issues have been handled.

There is at least one aspect of the problem, however, where speed and efficiency of resolution most notably will not be the case. That is the aspect dealing with the inevitable class action litigations. For the board, the litigation will likely proceed with exasperating inefficiency, delay, and expense. It is to this process of dealing with class action lawsuits that we now turn.

What Is a Class Action?

Broadly stated, a *class action* is a type of lawsuit in which a single representative individual is permitted to sue on behalf of an entire group of similarly situated individuals known as a *class*. In the wake of an accounting irregularity, a class action theoretically comes about when an aggrieved shareholder contacts a lawyer and explains that he has been harmed. The law then generally permits that single shareholder to sue on behalf of all similar shareholders.

Although the conceptual justification for class action litigation begins with the predicate of an aggrieved shareholder reaching out to a lawyer to seek redress, the reality is somewhat different. Shareholder class action litigation tends to be prosecuted by just a small number of highly specialized law firms and, over the years, these firms have developed practices and relationships that enable them to take the lead in commencing shareholder litigation almost on their own. A practical consequence is that, within 24 hours after issuance of a press release revealing the occurrence of accounting irregularities, the class action lawyers will normally have their lawsuits already prepared.

The Commencement of Class Action Litigation

The catalyst for commencement of the litigation will be the initial press release (see Exhibit 7–1), which will tell the class action lawyers pretty much everything they feel they need to know to prepare their first complaint. Among other things, the lawyers will glean from the press release that accounting irregularities have surfaced, that earlier Securities and Exchange Commission (SEC) filings are false, which line items on the financial statements are affected, and the board of directors' preliminary information as to how far back the accounting irregularities go. With that information in hand, the class action lawyers will quickly extract from their word processor an earlier complaint filed in a similar case and quickly insert the specifics regarding the particular company at hand. In their haste to be the first to file a

---

Exhibit 7–1. Typical Stages of a Securities Class Action

- Initial press release
- Series of complaints
- Consolidated complaint
- Motion to dismiss
- Document productions
- Depositions
- Settlement (if necessary)
- Trial (almost never)

---

lawsuit, the process of revision is not always completely thorough. In one famous instance, class action lawyers described Philip Morris as being part of the toy industry.

From the perspective of the board of directors, the consequence will be that, within a day or two after the issuance of the company's initial press release, the directors will begin receiving a number of seemingly duplicative lawsuits in which the only significant difference seems to be the name of the representative shareholder seeking to represent the interests of the class. In truth, a shareholder gains no meaningful strategic advantage over the defendants in rushing to be named the class representative. In the end, only one class of similarly situated shareholders will be certified and only one complaint ordinarily will survive. Rather than trying to get a strategic advantage over the defendants, the interest of a plaintiff in rushing to be named the class representative is to get an advantage over the other plaintiff shareholders—or, more precisely, their lawyers. For a class action plaintiff's lawyer, having one's client named the class representative opens the door to the lion's share of the legal fees.

The Likely Defendants

Although the class action complaints may not be precisely identical, in all likelihood they will focus upon the same general group of individuals and companies as defendants. The candidates of those likely to be named in the class action complaints are as follows:

- **The company.** The corporate entity will almost inevitably be named a defendant. Also named may be a parent company or holding company. The plaintiffs will argue that the corporate entity or entities are responsible for the wrongdoing of their individual officers and directors.

- **Any officers who have resigned, been terminated, or placed on leave.** It may be that the initial press release will have identified particular officers who have resigned, been terminated by the board, or placed on paid or unpaid leave. The plaintiffs' lawyers will infer from any such corporate action the officers' complicity in wrongdoing. Such officers, therefore, will almost inevitably be named as defendants in the complaint.

- **The CEO and the CFO.** Prime candidates to be included as defendants in the class action lawsuits include the chief executive officer and the chief financial officer. The plaintiffs will infer from their positions some level of complicity. To the extent that they have signed what have now turned out to be incorrect SEC filings, such as a Form 10-K or Forms 10-Q, the likelihood of them being named as defendants increases.

- **Particular officers.** Beyond the CEO and CFO, other officers may be named as defendants depending upon the nature of the fraud (as described in the press release) and a particular officer's proximity to it. For example, if the fraud involved improper revenue recognition on consignment sales, the plaintiffs may seek to include as a defendant the officer or officers with responsibility in that area. Similarly, if the fraud involved improprieties at some remote location, those responsible for operations or the financial reporting function of that location may be named.

- **Members of the audit committee.** Increasingly, class action complaints are including as defendants members of the audit committee. The reason apparently stems from the trends discussed in Chapter 2, whereby responsibility for the prevention and early detection of fraudulent financial reporting has shifted to those within the corporate enterprise and, in particular, the individual audit committee members. From the existence and growth of undetected accounting irregularities, the class action plaintiffs will infer that the audit committee has not done its job.

- **Outside directors.** At the moment, the extent to which outside directors tend to be included as defendants in class action complaints is in a state of flux. Historically, all outside directors would be named as defendants almost as a matter of course. Congress's passage of federal securities law tort reform in the mid-1990s, however, operates as an important impediment to the inclusion of the entire board—at least in the absence of evidence suggesting an individual director's knowledge or complicity. Some plaintiffs' law firms still seek to bring in the entire board as defendants. Others, however, do not.

- **Underwriters.** An emerging trend in class action litigation is the inclusion as defendants of underwriters where the company has had occasion to publicly issue stock within the last three years. For the corporate issuer, this is particularly unfortunate insofar as typical under-writing documents will provide for corporate indemnification of the underwriter in the absence of the underwriter's own wrongdoing. The desirability from the plaintiffs' perspective of inclusion of the under-writer is not entirely clear, though it may result from a hope that, in-demnification or not, the mere inclusion of the underwriter as a de-fendant will act as an incentive for the underwriter to pay some amount in settlement to get out.

- **Selling shareholders.** An issuance of public stock within the prior three years may also open the door to the inclusion as defendants of any shareholders who participated as sellers in the offering. Plaintiffs may seek to show their complicity in the accounting irregularities based upon inferences drawn from their natural desire to see the stock price sustained or increased during the period prior to their sale.

- **The outside auditor.** Several years ago, inclusion of the outside audi-tor in an accounting irregularities case occurred almost without excep-tion. Today, the inclusion of the outside auditor as a defendant—at least in the first complaint—has become something of a rarity. As with the inclusion of outside directors, the reason stems primarily from the federal securities law tort reform legislation in the mid-1990s, which erected barriers to naming the outside auditor, at least without particu-larized facts showing auditor complicity. It would not be unusual, therefore, for the initial wave of class action complaints to completely omit the auditor from among the numerous defendants.

  However, that is not to say that the auditor will be left out forever. An important preoccupation of the plaintiffs will inevitably be assem-bling detailed evidence sufficient to make claims against the auditor stick. At that point, the auditor will in all likelihood join the ranks of defendants in the case.

Sorting Out Parties and Counsel

Although the intensity of the initial barrage of lawsuits may create an ap-pearance that the class action litigation will proceed with ferocity, that ap-pearance will quickly change as the case gets bogged down almost from the outset. There will ordinarily be several reasons but foremost will be the need for the plaintiffs and their law firms to sort themselves out. Typically, any number of plaintiffs and law firms will have filed complaints but theoretically only one plaintiff under the law is to become the lead plaintiff and only one law firm is to become lead counsel. The filing of class action complaints, therefore, will be followed by a series of discussions and negotiations among various plaintiffs' law firms as to which will emerge as the leader of the others. Given the potential fees at stake for the plaintiffs' law firm, this is arguably one of the two most important negotiations that will take place.

For the defendants, the resulting hiatus will provide a welcome respite. The main reason stems from the fact that the initial class action complaints will arrive within days of the initial press release, a time during which the defendants will already be preoccupied with operational and financial crises and emergencies that seemingly must be handled on a daily basis. More than that, the defendants will have some sorting out to do among themselves. Among other things, they will want to sort out their own representation.

A complicating factor in arranging for the defendants' representation will be that, unfortunately, not every defendant will have precisely the same interests as every other. At one extreme, for example, will be those defendants by whom the accounting irregularities were perpetrated. At the other extreme will be those defendants who are falsely accused and who, in truth, are entirely blameless. Those two groups—and others that fall somewhere in the middle—may not share precisely the same interests on every issue that will arise in the case. Accordingly, the need for different lawyers to represent different groups of defendants will soon become apparent. At the same time, any outside professionals who have been named as defendants will in all likelihood seek their own representation.

The initial weeks of class action litigation, therefore, will be largely occupied with the plaintiffs, the defendants, and their new lawyers trying to sort themselves out.

The Consolidated Complaint

At one point, both sides will have successfully coordinated among themselves to the point where they are ready for the battle to begin, and it will be incumbent upon the plaintiffs to fire the first salvo. The projectile will be in the form of a *consolidated complaint*—that is, a single complaint that consolidates all of the material allegations, legal claims, and parties of the others. In essence, the consolidated complaint will reflect a distillation of the information and charges hastily thrown together into the earlier separate complaints. In drafting the consolidated complaint, the plaintiffs may decide to add claims, delete claims, add defendants, delete defendants, expand the time frame at issue, shorten the time frame at issue, or otherwise adjust the contours of the plaintiffs' contentions. Although the particulars of any consolidated complaint will depend upon the circumstances at issue, certain claims will be included almost inevitably. They are the following:

- **Section 10(b).** The one claim that is sure to be a fixture of any accounting irregularities lawsuit is a claim pursuant to a provision of the Securities Exchange Act of 1934, known as Section 10(b), and a corresponding SEC rule, known as Rule 10b-5. Directed against fraud in the secondary market of publicly traded securities, Section 10(b) makes it unlawful for any person directly or indirectly "to use or employ, in connection with the purchase or sale of any security," any "manipulative or deceptive device or contrivance" in violation of SEC regulations. In substance, Section 10(b) makes it unlawful to say anything of consequence that is false or misleading in connection with the purchase or sale of a security. Among the data subject to the prohibitions of Section 10(b) are significant inaccuracies in a company's financial statements that are filed as part of its Form 10-K or Form 10-Q.

  Although Section 10(b) is broad in its scope, a critical prerequisite of a claim limits its applicability. Section 10(b) imposes liability only upon those who acted with *scienter*—that is, with "intent to deceive, manipulate, or defraud." In other words, Section 10(b) does not impose liability on those who accidentally make false or misleading statements, even where the person who made the statements was negligent.

  Exactly what is needed to plead and prove "intent to deceive, manipulate, or defraud" is an issue that plaintiffs' and defendants' lawyers have been arguing about for more than 20 years—ever since the United States Supreme Court declined to reach the issue in the famous footnote 12 of its 1976 decision in *Ernst & Ernst v. Hochfelder*. The key point is that Section 10(b) does not impose liability for mere accidents or negligence.

- **Section 20.** A claim pursuant to Section 20 is frequently a companion to a claim pursuant to Section 10(b). Section 20, also a provision of the Securities Exchange Act of 1934, operates to impose liability on those who control another person who makes a significant false or misleading statement in SEC filings "unless the controlling person acted in good faith and did not directly or indirectly induce the act or acts constituting the violation or cause of action." Thus, for example, a consolidated complaint might allege that a large shareholder of a company at which accounting irregularities were discovered should be equally liable with the company. An inside director or high-ranking officer may also be alleged to control the corporation. The actual facts and circumstances that constitute control under Section 20 are frequently an issue of significant dispute.

- **Section 12(a)(2).** Unlike Sections 10(b) and 20 of the 1934 Act, Section 12(a)(2) of the Securities Act of 1933 (often still referred to as "Section 12(2)" based on the original statutory provision) does not apply to false or misleading statements in connection with secondary market purchases or sales of securities. The role of Section 12(2), rather, is much more limited: It applies only to false or misleading statements that are made in a prospectus, which has been interpreted to mean that only shareholders who bought in a public offering may sue under this statute. Although Section 12(2)'s scope is more limited, proving a violation of Section 12(2) is easier for a plaintiff than proving a violation of Section 10(b), because a Section 12(2) claim does not require proof that the false statement was deliberate. Under Section 12(2), therefore, when the statutory elements are met, even a person who accidentally says something that is false can be held liable.

  Courts have held that in the typical firm-commitment underwriting of a public offering (where the shares are sold by the company to the underwriter and then to the public), only the underwriter (and others who directly solicited the plaintiff's purchase) can be liable under Section 12(2). Defendants can avoid liability, however, by showing that they conducted a reasonable "due diligence" investigation of the information in the prospectus.

- **Section 11.** In some respects, Section 11 of the Securities Act of 1933 (applicable to registration statements) is the most draconian of them all. It potentially imposes liability on every person who signs a company's false or misleading registration statement, every person who is a director of such a company, every accountant who prepared or issued a report on a part of the registration statement, and every underwriter of the security at issue. In substance, Section 11 operates to make each of these potentially liable where the registration statement contains false or misleading information, although everyone except the company has a defense to the extent they conducted a reasonable investigation and had "reasonable ground to believe" that the registration statement was true, which they have the burden of proving. (The law also recognizes that it is easier for non-experts to justify the reasonableness of their beliefs as to those parts of the registration statement prepared by an expert, such as an auditor of the financial statements.) Under Section 11, the company can be held liable whether it had reasonable ground to believe in the truthfulness of the statements or not.

- **Section 15.** Analogous to Section 20, Section 15 of the 1933 Act operates to impose liability on "every person who . . . controls any person liable under Section 11, or 12."

While each of these provisions is relegated to a particular context of the securities markets, their collective thrust is the same: It is unlawful to make significant false or misleading statements. Where a significantly false and misleading statement has been made, liability may potentially be imposed upon the company; those who control the company; and the company's officers, directors, underwriters, and accountants.

Liability Implications of the Initial Press Release

These provisions obviously pose a particular problem where a company has issued a press release announcing the discovery of accounting irregularities. The press release by itself could operate to establish some of the key elements of a securities law claim against the company and individuals directly associated with it, the most notable of which being the fact that a significant false statement has occurred. One reaction to the company's press release would be that, once it is issued, there would seem to be very little left to argue about.

In fact, however, the imposition of liability under the securities laws, even after issuance of a press release conceding that accounting irregularities have taken place, can give rise to exceedingly vigorous litigation. There are several reasons, including the fact (as discussed more fully below) that the amount of damages allegedly suffered by the plaintiffs' class will be hotly disputed. Another reason that litigation may be intense, even after a company's "confession" of false financial statements, involves the fact that the various individual defendants directly associated with the company, in all likelihood, will fall into one of the three categories outlined in Chapter 1. One category is those who will be perceived as plainly guilty. A second category is those who, when the facts become available, will be perceived as plainly innocent. The third category is those who could go either way.

Some of the most significant battles in the class litigation will revolve around those who should fall into the third category. The reason is that often this third category is where the money is. As to those individuals in the first category—those who are plainly guilty—they frequently will not have personal assets worth pursuing. Nor will they typically be eligible for coverage under the company's director and officer (D&O) insurance policy, insofar as D&O policies generally exclude coverage for deliberate acts of fraud. For the plaintiffs, therefore, those individuals who are plainly guilty will ordinarily be of little financial interest.

Of even less interest will normally be those falling into the second category—those who are plainly not guilty. Though the legal system may be somewhat inefficient, it nonetheless ultimately serves to impede the prosecution of claims against those who did nothing wrong. For this reason, this category of defendants, too, will be of little financial interest to the plaintiffs.

That naturally leaves the third category—those individuals who may or may not bear some blame. True, their financial assets may be no more substantial than the plainly guilty. However, the D&O insurance policy will treat them somewhat differently. The absence of unequivocal evidence establishing their guilt at the outset will in all likelihood cause the D&O insurer to begin financing their defense. At the same time, the D&O insurer's mindset will shift to acceptance of the proposition that these individuals are not deliberate defrauders but, instead, those who are at worst guilty of reckless fraud—something for which the D&O insurer will pay. The battle over the liability of those falling within this third category of defendants, therefore, is in substance a battle over the proceeds of the D&O policy. Depending upon the amount of the policy, that battle can become quite intense.

Of those directly associated with the company, that leaves one defendant: the company itself. A key to assessing the company's vulnerability will obviously involve those facts to which the company has already admitted in its initial press release. As mentioned earlier, almost inevitably the company will have admitted a misstatement of fact insofar as it is precisely such a misstatement that has triggered the need for a press release in the first place. Moreover, to the extent the company has announced the discovery of accounting irregularities, it will have revealed that at least someone within the corporate enterprise has misstated financial results deliberately.

It does not necessarily follow, however, that the company will be the principal target of the class action plaintiffs. Keep in mind that many of the class action plaintiffs will still be shareholders and, to the extent that they use the judicial system to extract a cash payment from the company, they are in a sense simply taking money from one pocket and placing it in another— through a judicial vehicle involving enormous transaction costs, insofar as a significant percentage of each dollar thereby extracted goes to the class action lawyers. On the other hand, to the extent that the class includes those who are no longer shareholders, their reluctance to seek a cash payment from the company will be significantly less pronounced. Another complicating factor, moreover, results from the fact that, where accounting irregularities have surfaced, the company's cash position may be somewhat tenuous. As discussed in Chapter 3, for example, the company may be in violation of debt covenants. To the extent that cash is not available, the interest of the class action plaintiffs in the company as a defendant correspondingly decreases.

In any event, with the consolidated complaint having been prepared and filed, the ball, so to speak, is now in the defendants' court. It is incumbent upon the defendants to respond. The preferred vehicle is through a *motion to dismiss*.

The Motion to Dismiss

A motion to dismiss is a document filed with the court and served on the plaintiffs' lawyers that assumes as its predicate (as it must) that the allegations of the consolidated complaint are true. Nonetheless (the motion goes on to contend), the plaintiffs may not prevail because the law provides no remedy based on the pleaded and assumed facts. Thus (the motion will conclude), the lawsuit should be judicially terminated without further ado.

The precise defenses to be raised in such a motion depend upon the unique facts and circumstances of any particular case. Almost inevitably, though, one defense in particular will be included in such a motion. Where Section 10(b) claims have been alleged—as they almost always will have been—the defendants will call into question whether, as to each separate defendant, the consolidated complaint has adequately alleged a sufficient awareness of the facts to render that particular defendant culpable. In the technical jargon of the procedural rules, the defense will be presented that the consolidated complaint does not adequately allege scienter.

The need to adequately allege scienter stems from the fundamental principle that Section 10(b) imposes liability only upon those possessed of an "intent to deceive, manipulate, or defraud." Federal procedural requirements—designed with the goal of protecting innocent citizens from baseless allegations—require a plaintiff seeking to allege a Section 10(b) claim to set forth with specificity the precise circumstances making clear that such an "intent to deceive, manipulate, or defraud" did in fact exist. Thus, the complaint must allege, for example, participation in a conspiratorial meeting, receipt of a telltale memorandum, or other circumstances laying a factual predicate for the allegation that an "intent to deceive, manipulate, or defraud" was possessed by each defendant.

Whether a consolidated complaint does, or does not, adequately plead scienter is something that, in a typical accounting irregularities case, plaintiff and defense lawyers may end up arguing about for months. Among the issues of contention will be such things as the legal requirements of a satisfactory complaint (the courts disagree with each other), the types of factual allegations that will satisfy those legal requirements (as a practical matter, the court has a great deal of discretion), and the extent to which a plaintiff failing to include adequate allegations should be given the opportunity to amend its consolidated complaint in order to make another try. By the time the adequacy of the complaint's allegations is ultimately resolved, more than a year may have gone by.

This passage of time, though, is not necessarily to the disadvantage of the defendants. The reason is that, under the tort reform legislation of the mid-1990s, during the pendency of the motion to dismiss, the plaintiffs' pretrial investigation (formally known as *discovery*) may not proceed. The filing of a motion to dismiss, therefore, largely puts the class action litigation on hold and gives the defendant officers and directors time to deal with other pressing business problems.

The Prospects of an Early Settlement

Throughout the initial stages of the litigation, one thought that will never be far from either the plaintiffs' or the defendants' minds is the possibility of an early resolution of the case through a negotiated settlement. Logically, an early resolution would seem to make eminent sense. If a material accounting irregularity has surfaced, then both sides should theoretically recognize the strong likelihood that a number of shareholders have been harmed. The principal remaining obstacle would seem to be the calculation of resulting damages under the law and the negotiation of an appropriate settlement amount. Neither would seem like an insurmountable obstacle.

Moreover, strategic considerations would seem to heavily favor an early negotiated resolution. For the plaintiffs, an early settlement can maximize recovery by tapping into the reservoir of D&O insurance when it is at its fullest point (i.e., before it is depleted by the expenditure of defense costs) and, for that matter, can result in a recovery for shareholders before the incurrence of substantial legal fees. For the defendants, an early settlement brings a prompt end to the unpleasantness and helps individuals of questionable complicity keep their reputations intact. A particular advantage of an early settlement for the company stems from the removal of the horrific distraction of time-consuming litigation at a time when the company has more important operational and financial issues on which to focus.

Nonetheless, although some preliminary discussions of settlement may take place, an early resolution of the litigation is by no means assured and, in fact, is relatively rare. The normal reasons are not particularly profound. Usually the plaintiffs want more money than the defendants (or, more precisely, the defendants' insurance companies) are willing to pay. That is not to say that early settlements never happen, but they are the exception rather than the rule.

The Process of Discovery

In the absence of a settlement, the court will be given the time it needs to resolve the motion to dismiss. Although, with resolution of the motion, some or even most defendants may find themselves dismissed from the case, it is entirely possible that some defendants will remain. For those remaining defendants, the next step is to begin the pretrial investigation known as *discovery*.

The process of discovery has two main components. One is that the parties will request each other's documents as well as the documents of nonparticipants in the litigation who may have interesting information. The other component involves taking sworn testimony through depositions. Discovery involves other investigative techniques as well, such as written questions known as *interrogatories*, but the production of documents and the taking of depositions are the two main vehicles for gathering information.

Unfortunately for the defendants, in a class action, discovery tends to be entirely a one-way street. That is to say, it is almost entirely a process in which the plaintiffs investigate the defendants. The reason is straightforward: The plaintiff shareholders rarely have much information of importance to the case. One securities defense lawyer has analogized the role of a defendant in a class action to that of a punching bag. You take punch after punch but get to give very little in return.

The Production of Documents

The first step to the discovery process will be a *document request*. This consists of a list of documents to be made available to the plaintiffs. The list will normally seek documents such as board packages, board minutes, internal financial reports (e.g., snapshot reports, flash reports), monthly financial statements, and less generalized documents pertinent to the particular irregularities at issue. Under the rules, the defendants get 30 days to respond, though this is almost always extended to add at least another month.

It is usually during the process of collecting documents that the defendants are given the first opportunity to experience remorse that the case did not settle during the pendency of the motion to dismiss. The reason is that something unfortunate almost always turns up. This is not to fault the diligence of the directors at the time of the operative events. It is merely a consequence of the fact that, with the benefit of hindsight, seemingly wholesome financial reports or operating documents may contain clues that arguably should have put directors on notice that something was afoot.

What's an example? Assume a board of directors has spent the past year reviewing monthly and quarterly financial statements at a time when, unbeknownst to the board, the company was improperly seeking to accelerate revenues at quarter-end by prematurely shipping merchandise to customers who did not want it. As time passed, things looked fine to the board of directors and, in fact, the board was pleased to see earnings maintain a fairly steady pace of disciplined growth. With the accounting irregularities having been exposed, however, the seemingly innocuous financial statements now suggest a different story. A comparison of monthly revenues reveals that, for the first month of each quarter, revenues were almost non-existent; in the second month, revenues started to trend upward; and, in the third month, they accelerated dramatically. Absent some peculiarity in the buying practices of customers, careful scrutiny of the revenue pattern at the time might have given rise to questions as to the reason for the pattern.

Still, such documents must be turned over to the plaintiffs who will then scrutinize them for exactly this kind of information. That is not to suggest that the defendants' lawyers will turn over all requested documents without a fuss. Compliance with some requests for documents may be so burdensome, disruptive, or seemingly redundant that the defendants will formally refuse, thereby giving rise to another dispute to be resolved by the court. The process of requesting, producing, and arguing about documents may be expected to take another few months.

The plaintiffs' request for one document in particular may be expected to give rise to especially vigorous litigation. That is the plaintiffs' attempt to procure the investigative report of the special committee or audit committee (which was discussed in Chapters 4 and 5) if a written report has been prepared. For the plaintiffs, procurement of the report would be invaluable. Insofar as it reflected candid interviews conducted by the committee's own counsel, it would provide to the plaintiffs' lawyers the best information to date as to exactly what happened, how it happened, which financial statement items were influenced, the reasons behind the accounting irregularities, and the varying degrees of guilt of each of the potential participants. Extraction of such information through the discovery process—in which witnesses will inevitably be more guarded and less candid—could literally take years. In the committee report, the information may be neatly packaged and available for the price of a photocopy.

Resolution of the plaintiffs' ability to get such a report will, in all likelihood, ultimately involve the court. The extent to which the plaintiffs should be entitled to such a report has been the subject of extensive judicial rulings and a plethora of published decisions. Alas, the decisions give support both to plaintiffs who would seek production of the report and defendants who would oppose it. Resolution of this issue, too, can be expected to take months.

Addition of the Outside Auditor

It is typically during the document-production phase of discovery that efforts will begin in earnest to add as a defendant the outside auditor. The principal reason will be that the auditor is no doubt heavily insured and therefore provides an exceedingly deep pocket from which to fund a substantial verdict. Moreover, if the accounting irregularities have gone on for more than one year, as they almost inevitably will have, the auditor would have issued an audit report that, insofar as it offered assurance as to the financial statements' conformity to generally accepted accounting principles (GAAP), was incorrect. As the plaintiffs delve into the defendants' documents, therefore, a key objective will be uncovering telltale memoranda, financial reports, or other documents implicating the auditor in the accounting irregularities.

For the company, the prospect of inclusion of its outside auditor as a defendant in the case presents dilemmas that are both significant and strategically difficult to sort out. At best, the company's reactions will be mixed. On one level, the addition of a deep pocket to the group of defendants may be perceived to offer the prospect of a reduction in the damages that will be sought from the original members of the defendant group. To that extent, addition of the auditor as a defendant would seem to work to the company's advantage. Countervailing business considerations, though, may strongly militate in the other direction for reasons discussed in Chapter 4. Keep in mind that, while the litigation is proceeding, one of the company's most important goals will be to procure restated audited financial statements, and the most efficient way to get restated audited financial statements is to stick with the existing auditor. If the auditor is named a defendant, for reasons discussed above, that potentially jeopardizes the auditor's independence. Therefore, the addition of the auditor as a defendant carries with it the risk of enormous business problems.

As one examines the issue more deeply, moreover, the strategic complications only get worse. Inevitably, some of the more removed outside directors will feel betrayed by the auditor insofar as the auditor failed to expose the fraud. For them, the thought of claims against the auditor might seem to make sense. Those closer to the center of wrongdoing, in contrast, may have a sense that, in truth, it was the company and its personnel who actively conspired to defraud the auditor. If anyone has a claim against anyone else, they might surmise, it is the auditor who has a claim against them. On close inspection, even the benefit of an additional "deep pocket" as defendant may not operate to the company's advantage. Recent statistical evidence suggests that where the auditor is included as a defendant, the portion of the overall now-increased settlement amount paid by the company increases significantly.

Mercifully, whether the auditor ultimately gets named as a defendant or not is not a decision the defendants will get to make. It will be up to the plaintiffs and, after that, to the judge on the auditor's inevitable motion to dismiss. If the auditor is to remain a defendant in the case, experience teaches that the minimization of hostilities among defendants will, in all likelihood, work to all of the defendants' advantage as the litigation proceeds.

The Taking of Depositions

As the process of document discovery draws close to its conclusion, the parties will turn to the second phase of the pretrial discovery process: the taking of depositions.

Any number of senior executives or outside directors have been through the process of a pretrial deposition. Basically, it is the process by which one sits in a conference room while the plaintiffs' lawyer asks questions and a court reporter transcribes both the questions and the witness's answers. Throughout the deposition, lawyers will interpose objections to particular questions being asked. One recent development is to videotape the entire process.

The deposition process usually offers a second opportunity for the defendants to regret that the case has not settled, insofar as the process itself frequently brings to the surface information that, in hindsight, might have indicated to innocent executives or outside directors the possibility of financial reporting improprieties. More than that, the process itself is fraught with peril stemming from the fact that potentially incriminating documents from previous years can be extracted from the files and the witness quizzed about their content as if he or she saw them only yesterday. The opportunities for failed recollection, inadvertently inconsistent testimony, or simply honest mistakes exist at every turn. Although corporate defendants will normally be exceedingly well prepared for the process, the process by its nature inherently presents substantial risk.

Dynamics Favoring Settlement

As the case proceeds further through discovery, for everyone the prospects of a negotiated resolution will begin to look more attractive. "Everyone," by the way, may include not only the defendants and their insurance companies but also, in all likelihood, both the defendants' lawyers (whose legal experience may stop short of actually having to appear in front of a jury) and the lawyers for the plaintiffs (who at trial would actually be at risk of losing the contingency fee they at this point view as their birthright). As the case proceeds, therefore, the dynamics between the opposing parties will gradually shift in the direction of a pretrial resolution.

The biggest catalyst for a pretrial resolution, though, may not come from the lawyers for the plaintiffs or the defendants but from the trial judge itself. Generally speaking, a normal federal trial judge will view a multi-month jury trial about GAAP as about as much fun as a root canal. More than that, such a trial would upset the court's calendar, distract the judge from other urgent judicial business, and overwhelm the judge's staff with paperwork. The judge will view a failure of the case to settle as something akin to a personal failure.

At a propitious moment in the discovery process, therefore, the judge will likely convene what is known as a *settlement conference*. The ostensible purpose of the conference will be for the judge to use his authority to try to move the parties to a mutually acceptable damage amount. Attending the settlement conference will be attorneys for the plaintiffs, attorneys for the defendants, attorneys for the insurance carriers, and representatives of the clients with settlement authority themselves. In fact, only one group will not be in attendance: the actual plaintiff-shareholders. They are left out of the process completely.

The settlement conference itself proceeds in a fairly predictable way. Once the assembled attorneys and clients have settled down (they will frequently fill almost to capacity the judge's courtroom), the judge will normally begin by asking to speak privately with the plaintiffs' lawyers. In that meeting, he will dutifully listen to the plaintiffs' carefully rehearsed presentation, write down their damages estimate, and then tell them what a terrible case they have. Next, the judge will ask to speak privately with the defendants' lawyers. He will then listen to *their* carefully rehearsed presentation, write down *their* damages estimate, and then tell them what a terrible case *they* have. He will then reconvene a meeting of everyone in his courtroom and announce that the prospects of settlement are dim because the parties appear to be very far apart.

Indeed, they will be. Before the settlement conference, each side will have hired a *damages expert*, essentially an economist schooled in calculating damages to be as high (for the plaintiffs) or as low (for the defendants) as the confines of the numerical evidence will allow. At this stage in the litigation, it is not unheard of for the estimates of the plaintiffs' expert and the defendants' expert to be literally hundreds of millions of dollars apart. At an initial settlement conference, therefore, there will typically exist a wide chasm between the plaintiffs and the defendants to be closed.

Securities Law Damages

The underlying explanation for the disparity in damage estimates lies in the fact that the estimation of damages for securities law violations—and, for this purpose, we will discuss principally Section 10(b)—is not entirely a precise exercise in mathematics. Under the securities laws, the amount of damages is measured by the difference between the price a shareholder paid and what the price *would* have been if the truth had been known at the time of purchase. The first of the two numbers—what the shareholder actually paid—is easy. It is the second of the two—what the price would have been had the truth been known—that opens the door to advocacy.

Estimating damages thus becomes largely an exercise in speculation aided by all of the stock valuation methods and tools of the most sophisticated teams of economists that money can buy. Topics for debate include the extent to which the stock price was influenced by market factors (rather than fraud), the performance of the industry, the performance of comparable companies, and the non-fraud performance of the stock itself.

For a single share of stock purchased on a single day, this would be complicated enough. In a typical accounting irregularities case, at issue normally will be millions of shares of stock purchased and sold over a period of years at wildly different prices through industry ups and downs. Trading patterns among plaintiff shareholders, moreover, will have varied dramatically. Included as part of the class of shareholders may be momentum investors (who arguably pay little or no attention to value), day-traders (who may have traded hundreds of times a day), mutual funds (whose trading patterns would have varied depending upon their stated objectives and goals), and institutional investors (who may not have traded at all). Throw into the mix warrants, options, and short-sellers, and there is much to argue about.

Everyone has complete confidence, of course, that a jury would easily figure it out. For the judge, he is looking forward to his next slip-and-fall case.

Ultimately a Settlement

For all of these reasons, no matter how determined the parties, it is an unusual class action that settles in the first settlement conference. In fact, the judge may have to convene several more spanning a period of several months. Slowly, however, and with painstaking deliberateness, the parties will start to move toward each other. Recalcitrant directors will be prevailed upon to show flexibility. Participating deep pockets (i.e., the accounting firm, underwriters, investment banks) will think hard about the toll the inevitable bad press is taking on their reputations. The plaintiffs' lawyers will increasingly focus on the potential loss of their contingency fee. Thus, the numbers of each will start to move toward each other.

So at some point the parties will probably come to an agreement. A form of settlement agreement will be extracted from one of the law firms' computers (probably in a form that these very lawyers have used many times before), marked up to reflect the precise terms of the resolution, and signed. The most difficult part will be over.

Successful execution of a settlement agreement, though, will not completely end the matter because, to this point, one group will have remained completely unaccounted for. That group is the plaintiff-shareholders themselves. The normal process of resolution will leave them out completely and, although the law presumes their interests have been protected by their counsel, the danger always exists that their lawyers' concern with the anticipated contingency fee may appear to cloud their judgment as to what's best for the shareholders themselves. The law thus imposes an additional procedural device to protect the shareholders. That device is the requirement of court approval, after notice to the shareholders, of any settlement terms.

The next step once the settlement agreement has been signed, therefore, is to give notice to all shareholders so that each can individually decide whether to participate in the settlement or not. Among other things, the names and addresses of the class member plaintiffs need to be ascertained, the class notice must be sent to each, a hearing on the settlement terms must be held, class members will be called upon to submit proofs of claim setting forth the particulars of their stock purchases and sales, and these proofs of claim must then be scrutinized to isolate those for which a recovery is genuinely warranted.

This process, too, can add several months. Once the settlement terms have been agreed upon, though, these procedural requirements are left largely to the plaintiffs' attorneys and their retained administrators to work out. For the defendants, it will be time for them to lick their wounds and vow never to let it happen again.

DEALING WITH THE D&O INSURER

Ty R. Sagalow and Michael R. Young

The commencement of class action litigation will bring to the fore a document whose principal function to that point will have been to sit quietly in a filing cabinet. That document is the director and officer (D&O) insurance policy. Among other things, the defendant officers and directors, and perhaps the company itself, will seek to call upon the D&O policy to pay lawyers, to finance damages experts and, they hope, to finance all or a portion of any settlement. When an accounting irregularity first surfaces, the newly named defendants will no doubt be comforted by their understanding that D&O insurance generally provides coverage for conventional securities class actions and that, assuming compliance with the notice provisions and other prerequisites of the policy, reputable D&O carriers are fairly straightforward in abiding by the policy requirements.

Unfortunately, a situation involving accounting irregularities does not necessarily give rise to a conventional securities class action of the sort that D&O policies are specifically designed to address. The reason is that, in a conventional class action, the defendants will normally have available the defense that they told, or at least tried to tell, the truth. In an accounting irregularities class action, in contrast, that defense largely will not be available. At least one person within the organization, and frequently more than one, will have deliberately lied. The company, moreover, will have already admitted that it got the numbers wrong.

In a situation where accounting irregularities have surfaced, therefore, the insurance posture changes somewhat. And the defendant officers, directors, and company will likely find themselves facing, among other things, a policy exclusion that explicitly disclaims coverage for deliberate fraud. When accounting irregularities have surfaced, accordingly, officers, directors, and the company itself soon find themselves encountering significant issues as to coverage under the policy.

Chapter 8 explores D&O insurance issues. First, it provides an overview of the typical D&O policy and focuses on important policy provisions relevant to securities class action litigation. Then it zeroes in on those provisions that can be troublesome where accounting irregularities have surfaced.

The Structure of a Typical Policy

The typical D&O policy is an elaborate system of parts, each with a separate function. At root, the traditional policy is typically built around two central promises that reflect the dual purposes of this type of insurance. In older policy forms, the separate promises were treated as separate policies. Most modern policies, however, treat the two promises as two insuring clauses in one policy form. One promise, typically called Coverage A or the *individual side* coverage, promises to pay or reimburse officers and directors for losses they have suffered as a result of wrongful acts for which they are not indemnified by the company. The second promise, frequently called Coverage B or *company reimbursement* coverage, promises to reimburse the corporation for amounts that it has had to pay as indemnification of officers and directors for losses they have suffered as a result of wrongful acts within the meaning of the policy. Today, many policies also contain a third promise, entity coverage, that provides direct coverage for certain claims against the corporation itself.

The front page of a typical D&O policy is a *declarations page*, which functions as something of a specification sheet for the policy. The declarations usually state the following:

- **The policy period.** Since the mid-1980s, the policy term has most often been a year, but beginning in 1996, two- or three-year terms became increasingly available.

- **The name of the parent or named corporation.** The typical policy will cover the directors and officers of the named corporation and its subsidiaries, as defined.

- **The limit of liability of the insurer.** That is, the maximum combined amount that the insurer is liable to pay with respect to all claims, in the aggregate, made during the policy period or any extended reported period.

- **The retention or deductible amounts.** The amounts by which the company and the individual insured are agreeing to self-insure each of their losses.

- **Coinsurance.** The amounts, expressed as a percentage, of every loss by which the company and the individual insured are agreeing to self-insure.

- **The premium and any surcharges or installment terms.** This is simply the price of the insurance.

For purposes of analysis, it may be helpful to think of the body of the policy as consisting of several principal parts, regardless of whether the policy writer presents them separately in the text. The insuring clauses, as discussed above, form the initial principal part of the policy. These are the promises that form the heart of the bargain between the insureds and the carrier. The second part is the defining terms, which must be carefully reviewed, as they materially affect the extent of coverage offered by the policy. The third part is an exclusion section, which describes broadly those areas of liability that are not covered under the policy. The next part sets forth general terms and conditions of the policy, which establish important procedures, presumptions, and conditions to coverage, including provisions relating to notice of claims to the insurer, the insured's and insurer's rights with respect to the defense of a claim and subrogation of losses, circumstances in which the policy may be canceled, the right of the insured to elect an extended reporting period or discovery period, and, sometimes, an agreed mechanism for alternative dispute resolution. A particularly important provision in this part of the policy is one that describes the circumstances in which the insurer will advance costs to the insured. The final part is the endorsements—a series of side agreements between the insureds and the carrier reflecting points of negotiation and adjustments to the premium. This customized section of the policy has enormous practical impact, as it can either diminish or enhance the value of the policy to the company and the insured officials.

Analysis of a D&O Policy

Because of the complexity of the policies and the huge effect the exceptions and conditions imposed in them have on coverage, the best way to understand D&O insurance may be to go through the policy as would an insurer when faced with a claim.

Three preliminary tests must be satisfied before a claim can be considered for coverage under the policy:

1. A *claim* must have been made against the insureds during the policy period.

2. The claim must be for a *wrongful act* committed by the insureds.

3. The insureds must have experienced a *loss*.

These tests arise, logically enough, under the policy's *insuring clause*. If these preliminary tests are satisfied, then a review of the policy's exclusions and other conditions must be made in order to make a final determination of coverage. (See Exhibit 8–1.) All of these are examined in the following section.

A Claim Must Have Been Made During the Policy Period

D&O policies, like professional malpractice and other similar liability policies, are *claims-made* policies. That is, they provide coverage only for *claims* that have been made first against an insured during the policy period.

Some policy holders may confuse the claim on which a claims-made policy is predicated with the claim that must be made by an insured when it gives the insurer notice of an insured loss. The claim referred to in the term

---

Exhibit 8–1. D&O Insurance Issues

- Existence of a *claim* made during the policy period
- The claim must be against an *insured*
- The claim must be for a *wrongful act*
- The insured must have incurred a *loss*
- The claim must not be *excluded*
- The insurer must be timely notified

---

claims-made does not refer to the notice by the insured to the insurer, but to a demand by a third party against the insured seeking to hold the insured responsible for the consequences of some alleged wrongful act.

The first inquiry, therefore, focuses on what constitutes a claim. Surprisingly, in the past it was not uncommon for a D&O insurance policy not to contain a definition for claim. In the absence of a defining term in the contract, as the years progressed the meaning of claim became subject to conflicting judicial interpretations. Because of the potential ambiguity and expense associated with judicial interpretations of undefined terms, policy holders increasingly grew to demand that important terms be defined. Accordingly, almost all modern D&O policies contain a definition of the term claim.

Under some policies, especially those written years ago for higher-risk coverage, the term claim is fairly restrictive. Given prior judicial determinations, a basic definition of claim for most risks would generally contain four types of coverage:

- Civil proceedings, such as lawsuits
- Criminal proceedings (post-indictment)
- Administrative proceedings (post notice of charges)
- Monetary or nonmonetary damages or relief for all of the above

A typical definition of *claim* that fulfills all these requirements would be the following:

1. A written demand for monetary or nonmonetary relief, or
2. A civil, criminal, or administrative proceeding for monetary or non-monetary relief that is commenced by:
   a. service of a complaint or similar pleading, or
   b. return of an indictment (in the case of a criminal proceeding), or
   c. receipt or filing of a notice of charges.

Recently, the definition of claim has been the beneficiary of several additional, and significant, enhancements. These enhancements were brought on by civil, criminal, administrative, or regulatory investigations, and by grand jury proceedings. D&O policies are claims-made policies and cover only claims that are first made during the policy period.

Closely related to the claims-made concept is the establishment of a retroactive date. A *retroactive date* or *prior acts date* is a starting point for coverage under the policy—the first date in which covered wrongful acts may occur. For both the insureds and the insurer, the placement of the retroactive date can be of great significance to the amount of risk covered under the policy. For example, a retroactive date that is concurrent with the inception date of the D&O policy would limit coverage severely. In such a case, both the wrongful acts as well as the claim arising out of those wrongful acts would have to occur during the policy period in order for a claim to be covered. This concept is so central to many D&O policies that some policies actually have a reference to the retroactive date in the insuring clauses. On the other hand, sometimes policies can be negotiated with no retroactive date. In such instances, wrongful acts occurring at any time in the past or during the policy period would be covered.

The Claim Must Be Made Against an Insured

The definition of *insured* plays an important role in a coverage determination. Until recently, the term *insured* usually meant those directors and officers whose acts were protected. However, recent policies have greatly expanded the definition to include the company for certain designated claims, in particular securities claims. Modern D&O policies, therefore, will include as insureds officers, directors, and the company itself.

As a general matter, the term *director* describes those individuals who are elected by the shareholders of the corporation. Similarly, the term *officer* describes corporate officers appointed by the board of directors.

In the past, directors and officers had to be listed individually to be insured, and persons who thereafter became directors and officers during the policy period had to be submitted to the insurance company for approval. However, today almost all policies provide blanket coverage for all directors and officers and automatically include all directors and officers elected or appointed after the inception date.

But it should not ever be assumed that individuals hired by management and given generic titles, such as vice president, are automatically covered. Most insurers have the ability to add by endorsement divisional officers or other types of managers or supervisors as insureds to the policy upon request of the parent corporation. In addition, policies may contain endorsements automatically adding all employees as insureds in the cases of employment practices coverage or securities claims coverage. However, the terms of the policy should be checked to verify any information or assumptions.

The Claim Must Be for a Wrongful Act

Assuming that one has a *claim* against an *insured* made during the policy period, the next question is whether the claim alleges a *wrongful act*. The definition of wrongful act will vary somewhat from policy to policy. A typical definition would read as follows:

> Wrongful Act means any breach of duty, neglect, error, misstatement, misleading statement, omission or act by the directors and officers of the company in their respective capacities as such, or any matter claimed against them solely by reason of their status as directors and officers of the company.

Definitions of wrongful act generally require, as a predicate for coverage, that the directors or officers be acting in "their respective capacities as such." A number of issues arise out of this *capacity requirement*. The most common example of a claim that could run afoul of this requirement is a claim made against a director or officer because of his service at the request of the insured corporation on the board of another corporation that is not a subsidiary. Although the director in question might view his service on the other corporation's board as a mere extension of his capacity as a director or officer of the insured corporation, no insurer is likely to agree with him. Claims arising out of such outside directorships are normally excluded from the policy unless such coverage is specifically provided. This restriction in coverage may take the form of an *outside directorship exclusion* or may be inferred from or made explicit in the definition of wrongful act. However, outside directorship coverage is commonly available by endorsement.

An interesting question arises with respect to the capacity requirement when the director or officer is also rendering professional services to the corporation. Carriers take markedly different views as to whether, for example, an officer-attorney rendering legal services to the corporation was acting in a covered capacity if he is sued as a result of those professional services. Other allegations that may fall outside the insured capacity are those that involve conduct by directors and officers that concern acts that are self-interested, such as ventures involving corporate officials but not corporations, or other acts that are not within directors' and officers' official sphere of responsibility. The position of virtually every insurer will be that at least some, and possibly all, such acts would not be covered by the policy even if such coverage were not already barred by public policy or standard policy exclusions, which they generally are. Outside directors who provide legal, consulting, or other services to the corporation not directly related to their service as directors also may find that those activities are not covered.

The Insured Must Have Incurred a Loss

D&O policies require that, in order to qualify for coverage, the insured must have incurred a loss. A *loss* with respect to an individual insured is generally defined as any amount for which the insured is legally liable and that arises out of a claim made against him for wrongful acts. With respect to the corporate reimbursement side of the policy, a loss may encompass any amount for which the corporation indemnifies its directors and officers for covered wrongful acts by such directors and officers. Further, in the event that the policy provides entity coverage, the corporation may also recover for losses it incurs arising out of securities claims made against the corporation itself.

A typical definition of *loss* includes all "damages, judgments, settlements and defense costs" incurred in the defense and investigation of a claim. Losses covered by the policy thus do not include losses incurred by the corporation unless entity coverage is bargained for separately.

It almost goes without saying that the directors or officers must have suffered real legal liability for there to be a loss under the policy terms. In the past, some defendants have attempted to settle a claim without the consent of the insurer, with the proviso that the plaintiff could not look to them for payment, but must proceed directly against the D&O insurance policy. Carriers have resisted such attempts to create what they perceive to be an inchoate or artificial loss and courts have upheld the insurers' position.

It is usual for a D&O policy's definition of loss to be limited by specific exceptions. One illustrative exception, mentioned earlier, prevents payments made pursuant to settlements without legal recourse to the insured. Other typical exceptions include punitive and exemplary damages, fines and penalties, taxes, and "matters uninsurable under the law pursuant to which the policy is construed." The historic logic behind these limitations is that fines, penalties, and punitive damages are really designed to be punishment to wrongdoers, not compensation to wronged plaintiffs, and they are, or should be, uninsurable as a matter of public policy.

Another issue affecting the scope of covered losses is the treatment of interrelated or causally connected wrongful acts. D&O policies typically provide that all claims arising out of *interrelated wrongful acts* are deemed to arise out of the first such claim. Arguably, this provision has benefits for both the insurer and the insured. For the insurer, it ensures that all risks associated with claims arising out of the same or related wrongful acts will be captured within one policy period and thus will be subject to one liability limit. The danger to the insurer of omitting such a requirement is that insurers that fail to include such language may be found liable under separate policy limits for multiple related claims filed over a several-year period. On the other hand, such a provision may also contain benefits for the insured. First, it may permit the insured to move coverage to another carrier, reserving the argument that any future claims arising out of the interrelated wrongful acts of a previously submitted claim will be covered by the former policy. In addition, most policy forms also indicate that all claims that are interrelated for the purpose of imposing a single limit also obtain the benefit of applying a single retention.

The Claim Must Not Be Excluded

If a *claim* occurs during the policy period against an *insured* and alleges a *wrongful act* creating a *loss* for the insured or for the corporate policy holder that indemnifies him, the next avenue of inquiry is whether the claim has been excluded either by the *exclusion section* of the policy or by the *endorsement section*.

In a typical D&O policy, exclusions generally fall under three categories. They are those relating to:

- Specific conduct of an insured
- Coverage provided under other policies
- Issues of public policy or areas of difficult exposure

Most exclusions are found in the basic policy form, but many are often added by endorsement. There are also various fairly standard exclusions that (for historical reasons) are always added by endorsement. Because exclusions block coverage under the policy, it is the insurer that bears the burden, in the event of any coverage dispute, of demonstrating that the exclusion applies and that the language of the exclusion is clearly stated. Typical exclusions are as follows:

Conduct Exclusions

Conduct exclusions preclude coverage of acts that the carriers deem to be uninsurable or inappropriate for coverage. Typical conduct exclusions concern claims based on:

- Illegal remuneration
- Short-swing profits
- Criminal or deliberately fraudulent acts, or the gaining of any personal profit or advantage to which the insured is not legally entitled

As discussed in detail later, the third of these exclusions—for criminal or deliberately fraudulent acts—can play an important role in determining D&O coverage where accounting irregularities have surfaced. For the moment, the important point is to recognize not only the exclusion but the fact that a policy may provide that the exclusion is triggered not merely by allegations, but by a final adjudication or other finding of fact. The reason is that virtually all class action complaints allege deliberate fraudulent acts. If the exclusion were triggered by a mere allegation, the exclusion would swallow the policy.

Exclusions Due to Other Policies

A number of exclusions in the D&O policy are meant to protect the policy from being used to cover claims that are, or should be, covered under another type of policy. Such exclusions include:

- Claims to which an earlier D&O policy was applicable
- Claims arising out of litigation pending as of or completed before the continuity date (the *pending and prior litigation exclusion*)
- Claims based on wrongful acts of a director or officer of a subsidiary corporation occurring either before it became a subsidiary or after it was spun off

- Claims based on or attributable to any failure or omission to effect or maintain insurance
- Claims that are insured against by any other policy or policies, except presumably for D&O policies written specifically to provide excess coverage in addition to the coverage provided by the primary policy

Although these exclusions are rather straightforward in intent, there are nevertheless issues of interpretation of which a corporation should be wary. For example, exclusions preceded by the word *for* are typically interpreted narrowly to exclude only those items specifically stated. For the insureds, such a narrowing of the exclusions is a benefit. In contrast, older policy forms may begin with broader introductory phrases, such as "based upon, arising out of, or attributable to," which is catch-all introductory language that broadens the scope of the exclusions.

One exclusion that is subject to significantly varying interpretations is the seemingly innocent exclusion for *pending and prior litigation.* In its most acceptable form, the exclusion precludes coverage for "claims arising from any pending or prior litigation as of the continuity date, as well as all future claims or litigation based upon the pending or prior litigation or derived from the same or essentially the same facts that gave rise to the pending or prior litigation." Other broader, and therefore less preferable, versions of the exclusion might also exclude any "demand, suit or other proceeding . . . decree or judgment entered against any" director, officer, or the insured corporation.

The Insured v. Insured Exclusion

The purpose of the *insured v. insured exclusion*, now standard in almost all D&O policies, is easy to understand. The underwriting philosophy behind a D&O policy is to provide coverage for claims brought by third parties against an insured corporation's management. There are two reasons classically given for the insured v. insured exclusion. First, providing coverage for a claim brought by an insured against another insured, or brought by the company against an insured, would support potentially collusive arrangements between insiders. Second, even in the absence of collusion, the insured v. insured exclusion is needed to prevent coverage for boardroom infighting.

Although the reasons for the exclusion are understandable, some of the original phraseology used in older policies was overly broad and gave rise to considerable confusion. For example, an early broad form of this insured v. insured exclusion read as follows:

> The Insurer shall not be liable to make any payment for Loss in connection with any claim or claims made against the Insureds . . . which are brought by, or on behalf of, any other Insureds including but not limited to shareholders' derivative suits and/or representative class action suits, brought by one or more past, present or future Directors and/or Officers including their estates, beneficiaries, heirs, legal representatives, assigns and/or the Company against one or more past, present or future Directors or Officers.

Because the broad language of such early forms of exclusion might be deemed to exclude even judgments paid in shareholder derivative actions (coverage of which is one of the principal advantages of insurance over indemnification), policies subsequently came to be modified to clarify the exclusion. Newer forms of the exclusion create significant exceptions for shareholder claims that can be shown not to have been made in collusion with an insured or the company and for wrongful discharge complaints against management by former officers. For example, a modern insured v. insured exclusion might read:

> The Insurer shall not be liable to make any payment for Loss in connection with any claim or claims made against the Directors or Officers . . . which are brought by any Insured or the Company; or which are brought by any security holder of the Company, whether directly or derivatively, unless such claim(s) is instigated and continued totally independent of, and totally without the solicitation of, or assistance of, or active participation of, or intervention of, any Insured or the Company; provided, however, this exclusion shall not apply to wrongful termination of employment claims brought by a former employee other than a former employee who is or was a Director of the Company.

This form of the exclusion is intended to screen out the possibility of suits by the company, or by individuals acting as proxies for the board or the company, while at the same time permitting most non-collusive shareholder class or derivative actions to be covered.

Endorsements

Most of the exclusions listed above are so generally applied that they have
become part of the preprinted policy form. Sometimes, however, exclusions
that are more fitted to the particular circumstances and risks of an individual
company are added by endorsement. *Endorsements*, unlike exclusions, may
be either restrictive or expansive, and thus may best be viewed as the result
of bargaining and customization of the basic policy form.

A sample of some of the restrictive endorsements that might be found in
a typical policy include:

- Deletions from coverage of specific directors or officers against whom
  actions or investigations or known claims are pending when the policy
  is written

- *Reorganization of business* exclusions, which provide for termination
  of coverage in the event of a takeover or insolvency

Endorsements, of course, are also frequently used to expand coverage
under the policy. Examples of such expansive endorsements include those:

- Amending the term *insured* to include divisional officers, employees,
  or other non-officers

- Expanding the definition of the insured company to include founda-
  tions, trusts, partnerships, or other noncorporate affiliates

- Obligating the insurer to advance defense costs, if such advancement
  is not already provided in the boilerplate of the policy

- Expanding or clarifying the worldwide applicability of the policy

- Providing multi-year discovery or run-off periods or making the policy
  applicable to a particular acquisition that the company is contemplat-
  ing

- That are state amendatory endorsements required by state law, which
  typically expand coverage by providing longer advance notification of
  cancellation, the ability to elect discovery periods, and sometimes
  other benefits to policy holders mandated by state law

The Insurer Must Be Timely Notified

Assuming that a *claim* has been made against an *insured* during the policy period alleging a *wrongful act* creating a *loss* and that the claim is not excluded by any of the *exclusions*, the policy will require that the claim be submitted on a timely basis to the insurer. As mentioned earlier, the D&O policy is a *claims-made* contract. A necessary part of the claims-made concept is that both the insured and the insurer know with reasonable certainty at the time the policy is created or renewed whether coverage under the expiring policy has been triggered by a claim. Notification requirements are taken extremely seriously in the claims-made context, and the failure to give timely notice may jeopardize coverage. D&O policies usually require that insureds notify the insurer "as soon as practicable" of any claims made against them during the policy period (or discovery period, if elected). Higher-quality policies might add a small window after the end of the policy to facilitate the submission of claims made against the insured late in the policy period. A typical provision of that type might read as follows:

> The Company or the Insureds shall, as a condition precedent to the obligations of the Insurer under this policy, give written notice to the Insurer of a Claim made against an Insured as soon as practicable and either:
>
> (1) any time during the Policy Period or during the Discovery Period (if applicable); or
>
> (2) within 30 days after the end of the Policy Period or the Discovery Period (if applicable), as long as such Claim(s) is reported no later than 30 days after the date such Claim was first made against an Insured.

Some more restrictive policies may require notice to be given within a certain period—such as 30 days—after the claim is first made.

In addition to the notice-of-claim provisions, most D&O policies also permit insureds to notify the insurer of circumstances that may give rise to a claim in the future. If such notice is given before the policy expires, the insurer will treat any subsequent claims arising out of those circumstances as claims first made within the policy period. A typical provision would read like this:

> If during the Policy Period or Extended Reporting Period (if exercised) an Insured becomes aware of any circumstances which could

give rise to a Claim and gives written notice of such circumstance(s) to the Company, then any Claims subsequently arising from such circumstances shall be considered to have been made during the Policy Period or the Extended Reporting Period in which the circumstances were first reported to the Company.

The Insureds shall, as a condition precedent to exercising their rights under this coverage section, give to the Company such information and cooperation as it may reasonably require, including but not limited to a description of the Claim or circumstances, the nature of the alleged Wrongful Act, the nature of the alleged or potential damages, the names of actual or potential claimants, and the manner in which the Insured first became aware of the Claim or circumstances.

The advantage to the insured of submitting such a notice of circumstances is that it preserves the insured's rights under the existing policy. If a claim arises out of such circumstances after the expiration of the policy period, the policy will treat the claim as if it were made during the policy period and therefore covered. Of course, such a claim likely would be excluded from coverage under a subsequent policy due to that subsequent policy's *prior-notice* exclusion. As a practical matter, therefore, giving notice of circumstances is something that should be approached with caution.

The Loss Must Be in Excess of the Retention Amount and Not Within Any Applicable Coinsurance Percentage

Having properly submitted to the insurer a claim which falls within the scope of the insuring clause and which meets the essential definitions of the policy and is not excluded by the exclusion section, the policy holder finally gets to ask the key question: How much of the loss will be paid by the policy?

This avenue of inquiry relates, in major part, to the retention and coinsurance sections of the policy. Typically, the insurer is liable to pay only that loss that is in excess of the applicable retention or deductible amount and, in the event of coinsurance, in excess of the applicable coinsurance percentage. Both retentions and coinsurance percentages are forms of self-insurance; their effect is generally to lower the amount of premium that the insurer otherwise would require, in exchange for some or all of the insureds' assumption of a portion of the risk.

The D&O Policy and Accounting Irregularities

That's basically how a standard D&O policy works. Where accounting irregularities enter the picture, though, particularly difficult issues of interpretation emerge. The reason, as mentioned at the outset, is that a typical D&O policy is primarily intended to address a conventional securities class action—that is, a class action in which the defendant officers, directors, and company do not admit they've deliberately said anything wrong. Where accounting irregularities have surfaced, that is by definition not the case. If the company has issued a press release admitting to irregularities, it has already gone a long way to conceding the existence of fraud. Even absent the admission of irregularities, the mere acknowledgment of need for an earnings restatement concedes that earlier numbers were incorrect.

Where accounting irregularities have surfaced, therefore, a series of difficult issues needs to be faced. These might be divided into the following five categories:

- The *deliberate fraudulent act exclusion*
- *Imputation* from one insured to another
- The need for a *factual adjudication*
- The problem of "loose cannons on the deck"
- The *application process*

The Deliberate Fraudulent Act Exclusion

The starting point in assessing coverage in the wake of accounting irregularities is ordinarily the *deliberate fraudulent act exclusion*. To reiterate briefly, this exclusion typically provides:

> The Insurer shall not be liable to make any payment for Loss in connection with any Claim made against an Insured:
>
> * * *
>
> (c) Arising out of, based upon or attributable to the committing in fact of any criminal or deliberate fraudulent act;....

Interpreted in accordance with its plain meaning (which the insurer will be wont to do), this means that the D&O policy expressly excludes coverage for deliberate fraudulent acts. That is, the policy excludes coverage for claims arising out of fraudulent acts that the perpetrator intentionally undertook. If the exclusion does not contain the restrictive adjective *deliberate* (and many policies do not), the breadth of the exclusion may be even broader, potentially excluding *all* fraudulent acts. The policy will also exclude coverage for criminal acts, which accounting irregularities may very well involve. If the coverage analysis were to end there, it would seem a fairly straightforward proposition that coverage would be denied.

Fortunately for the officers, the directors, and the company, the analysis does not end there—at least if the policy only excludes coverage for deliberate fraudulent acts. The reason stems from the fact that, although some within the organization may have deliberately misstated financial results, it is not necessarily true that everyone named as a defendant will have knowingly participated—or perhaps participated at all. In particular, among those who were not participants in the irregularity, but who still may nonetheless be named as defendants in the class actions, will frequently be additional officers and directors of the company. Will the insurer deny coverage as to them? Here, the policy provisions may suggest a different outcome. Although an enlightened D&O policy excludes coverage for deliberate fraud, it *provides* coverage for fraud that arises out of recklessness.

One interpretation of the policy, therefore, would have the defendants falling into one of two groups. One group would include those who were deliberate participants in the fraud. The other would include those who were not deliberate participants in the fraud and who, at worst, were only reckless. One possible outcome, therefore, is that the insurance carrier will deny coverage to the former but provide it to the latter.

Imputation from One Insured to Another

If only life were that simple. First, it is not always entirely clear who acted with a deliberately fraudulent intent—particularly when one is focusing upon potential participation in the fraud by a corporation. Second, in determining who possessed the requisite intent and who did not, another important provision comes into play. That is a provision providing for *imputation* from one insured to another—be the insured a natural person or an entity.

As a general matter, imputation works like this: If one person knows of the fraud, but another does not, then (in the absence of imputation) the insurance consequences should follow the separate knowledge of each. The innocent defendant gets coverage; the knowing defendant does not. However, this result can be unfair to the insurance company which, after all, has accepted a risk in good faith reliance on an understanding that it was not being misled. The doctrine of imputation, therefore, will in some instances impute the knowledge of a deliberate wrongdoer into the state of mind of another. For example, under many circumstances, a senior executive's knowledge of wrongdoing might be imputed to the company, thereby making the company, as a matter of law, a deliberate wrongdoer as well. Similarly, knowledge of one officer or director may potentially be imputed to another. This approach, while perhaps understandable from the perspective of the insurance carrier, may nonetheless have harsh consequences for those insureds who are truly innocent. The issue thus arises as to the extent of imputation for purpose of determining insurance applicability.

Here, too, different insurance carriers approach the issue differently, but many insurance policies will contain an imputation provision to address precisely this dilemma. For example, on the issue of imputation from an officer or a director to his company, a policy might provide as follows:

> For the purposes of determining the applicability of the foregoing exclusions . . . only facts pertaining to and knowledge possessed by any past, present or future chairman of the board, president, chief executive officer, chief operating officer or chief financial officer of the Company shall be imputed to the Company.

Similarly, on the issue of imputation from one officer or director to another, the policy might read like this:

> The Wrongful Act of any Director or Officer shall not be imputed to any other Director or Officer for the purpose of determining the applicability of the [deliberate fraudulent act exclusion].

Or the policy might contain a provision that reads:

> For the purpose of determining the applicability of [certain] exclusions, the facts pertaining to and the knowledge possessed by any Insured shall not be imputed to any Natural Person Insured ....

On the issue of imputation, the provisions among various insurance carriers are far from standardized. As a general proposition, though, the extent of imputation from one defendant to another will be determined according to the policy's terms. In the absence of an imputation provision (these days a rarity), the extent of imputation from one defendant to another will be determined in accordance with the applicable state law.

The Need for a Factual Determination

The coverage analysis, though, is still not over. Yet another provision now comes into play. It is the provision, found in many policies, that limits an exclusion of coverage based on deliberate fraudulent acts to instances where there has been a *final adjudication* or other finding of fact. A typical provision may, for example, exclude coverage for deliberate fraudulent acts "if a judgment or final adjudication adverse to the Insured(s) or an alternative dispute resolution proceeding establishes that such criminal or deliberate fraudulent act occurred." Or a provision might indicate that the exclusion is premised upon a factual finding. Where such a provision exists, the insurance carrier may not, therefore, simply premise an exclusion of coverage based upon (for example) a press release admitting the existence of accounting irregularities. Rather, the insurance carrier must first obtain a determination to that effect.

The ease or difficulty with which an insurer might obtain such a determination will largely be driven by the facts. Indeed, factual disputes can exist even where the company has conceded that accounting irregularities have taken place. For example, although the company may be more than willing to blame a particular executive as a perpetrator of the fraud, that executive may not be disposed to agree. He may, rather, point the finger at someone else, say it was all an innocent mistake, or deny the existence of irregularities completely. It is not the case, therefore, that a determination of fact will necessarily be swift or that the outcome is sure. Rather, the parties may be in store for years of document productions, depositions, and perhaps even a trial before the underlying facts can be known and determined.

Making the process still more complicated is the fact that precisely what constitutes a final adjudication (on those policies that use that particular phrase) may not itself be entirely clear. The defendants can be expected to argue that the policy thereby requires a judgment in the class action litigation. Such an interpretation can operate to the singular advantage of the defendants insofar as virtually no class action litigation goes through trial to a final judgment. On the other hand, such a position may have the undesirable consequence of motivating the insurer to withhold consent to a settlement based upon an expectation that a finding of fraud at trial would trigger the exclusion. The insurance carrier may also argue that a final adjudication involves any judicial determination of deliberate wrongdoing. Accordingly, the insurance carrier may assert that a judicial declaration in, say, a separate declaratory judgment action brought by the carrier would suffice under the policy. As in most contract disputes, the actual meaning may largely turn on the understanding of the parties at the time the policy was signed. A definitive resolution of such issues may require a separate judicial determination—and therefore still more litigation.

The Problem of "Loose Cannons on the Deck"

Let's take a moment to recap. Accounting irregularities by definition involve deliberate false statements and therefore potentially trigger the deliberate fraudulent act exclusion of a normal D&O policy. Each defendant will fall into one of two categories: those who were knowing participants and those who were not. Due to the rule of imputation, though, the knowledge of those who were knowing participants may be imputed to some or all of those who were not. But first a factual determination is required.

The further one gets into the analysis, therefore, the messier it becomes. Now it will get even worse. Because strategic and practical concerns may cause the insurer to think twice about a denial of coverage even to those individuals as to whom it has a legal right to do so. The explanation lies in what might be referred to as the problem of "loose cannons on the deck."

The problem comes about as follows. At first blush, it might seem to make all the sense in the world for the carrier to deny coverage where it has the legal right. Given the fractured interests of the defendants in typical accounting irregularity litigation, each defendant or similarly situated group of defendants will frequently need their own law firms as well as their own entourage of experts, forensic accountants, and others. All of these can be exceedingly expensive. It would seem entirely logical, therefore, for the insurance carrier to seize upon the policy's exclusions and limit coverage to the full extent possible.

Except for one thing. That is whether it really makes sense for the insurance carrier to limit coverage. The reason it may *not* make sense is that an outright denial of coverage to the deliberate wrongdoers may mean they will lack the financial resources to retain counsel at all. A foreseeable consequence, therefore, may be that the wrongdoers will end up completely unrepresented by counsel in the class actions. That may operate to no one's interest. Certainly it is bad for the deliberate wrongdoers. But more to the point, it can be exceedingly unfortunate for the other defendants—not to mention the carrier insuring them—insofar as those without lawyers may behave like loose cannons on the deck, careening back and forth through the swells and troughs of the litigation and wreaking havoc in the process. It is not without precedent, therefore, for some insurance carriers to recognize the legal right to deny coverage to some, but to go ahead and provide coverage for them nonetheless. The deliberate wrongdoers become the beneficiaries of their own lack of resources and their ability, through the inadequacy of their own representation, to compromise the defense of others.

The Application Process

We're getting to the end, but still not there yet. One final hurdle needs to be overcome. That is the injection of uncertainty into the insurance coverage arising out of representations and information given to the insurance carrier as a result of the insurance application process itself.

Here is the context. As part of the application process, an insurance carrier will normally seek submission of an application form to be accompanied by financial information on the company. The application will seek background information on the company and will normally be signed by a senior executive, such as the CFO. It may include a representation that the individual executing the application, as well as others in the company, are not aware of any circumstances that would give rise to a claim. The financial information sought by the carrier, in turn, will typically include the company's most recent Form 10-K and, perhaps, more recent quarterly information.

The problem is that, where accounting irregularities have surfaced, the information given to the insurance carrier may in fact be false. The insurance application may be false, for example, insofar as it disclaims knowledge by any officer of circumstances that would give rise to a claim. Correspondingly, the financial information may be false insofar as, to the extent the fraud goes back into prior reporting periods (as it probably does), the financial information is infected by—and, for that matter, may be the same as—the false financial information that is giving rise to the class action litigation. Making matters worse, it is possible, if not likely, that among those signing (or deemed to be signing) the insurance application on the part of the company will have been the CFO, who will frequently himself be implicated in the underlying fraud.

On top of all of the other coverage issues, therefore, is heaped the problem that the insurance carrier itself may be a victim of the fraud. To the extent it can prove the misrepresentations were material and that the policy was issued in justifiable reliance upon them, the carrier may potentially have still another basis to deny coverage and, now, to rescind the policy.

That is not to suggest that an attempt to deny coverage or rescind the policy will necessarily follow. Among the issues the carrier would want to consider would be, as mentioned above, materiality and justifiable reliance, and the carrier may have the uphill burden of proving those prerequisites. Here, too, the issue of imputation may arise. If the carrier acts too aggressively, moreover, there is the potential for a fairly severe downside. Beyond the possibility of harm to the insurer's reputation, the newly uninsured officers, directors, and company may themselves commence bad-faith litigation against the carrier premised upon the contention that the denial of coverage was made in bad faith. Historically, in front of a jury, insurance carriers have not always seemed to stand an even chance. On the other hand, neither the insurance industry nor the public welfare will necessarily be well served by a system of insurance that allows defrauders to obtain insurance coverage based on deliberately fraudulent applications.

So issues arising out of the insurance application process create yet another level of problems for the defendant officers, directors, and company. As if they didn't have enough problems already.

So How Does All This End Up?

When all is said and done, how does the coverage issue end up? Unfortunately, there is no easy answer. The answer, rather, turns on the specific terms of the insurance policy and, frequently just as important, the attitude, size, and reputability of the insurance carrier.

At one end of the spectrum, some carriers will recognize the perils of an outright denial of coverage, be openly disdainful of litigation as a mechanism to resolve insurance coverage disputes, and therefore be a willing participant with the class action defendants in an attempt to mutually define the precise contours of the policy. Among the considerations taken into account may be the carrier's own reputation and its desire to be perceived in the market as a supporter, rather than an adversary, of those it has elected to insure. This is particularly so given the likely innocence of many of those officers and directors named as class action defendants. More than that, an experienced and quality carrier will recognize the value of working as a partner to the insureds in devising a litigation strategy that is assisted by its own deep reservoir of experience in analogous situations—experience that the insureds themselves will typically lack.

But not all insurance carriers approach the issue in that way. At the other end of the spectrum, at least one of the smaller carriers has responded to the detection of accounting irregularities with a complete denial of coverage and the commencement of separate litigation by the carrier against the officers, directors, and company. The ostensible purpose of such litigation is a judicial declaration that the carrier may walk away from the policy completely.

For the officers, the directors, and the company, an outright denial of coverage by the insurance carrier can be catastrophic. The reason has little to do with the need to fund a class action settlement, and everything to do with the more immediate problem of up-front cash. Frequently, as the class action litigation proceeds through the early stages, the cash position of the company will be getting more and more dire. In all likelihood, the company will be in default on lending agreements; lenders may be seeking to withdraw from the relationship; and lines of credit may have suddenly dried up. At the same time, the company will likely be undergoing significant drains on its cash resources—stemming from the need to obtain a re-audit of its financial statements, the need to hire a new law firm to commence a special investigation, and particular needs of operations to sustain the enterprise in a time of crisis.

Of the utmost importance to those named as defendants in the class actions, therefore, will be the immediate availability of up-front cash with which to finance their defense. Making the need all the more pronounced will be the reluctance of outside professionals to become involved absent assurance that their fees can be paid. Putting aside the insurance carrier's ultimate position as to coverage, therefore, the critical issue at the outset is the carrier's willingness to begin financing the defense. Absent up-front cash, the defendants may end up tottering on the brink of litigation default.

The Best Approach

All in all, D&O insurance thus becomes another potential headache for the board of directors and senior executives when accounting irregularities have surfaced. The issues can be difficult, the frustrations many, and the availability of coverage—at least during the early stages—not completely certain. Ideally, both the insureds and the insurance carrier will share a common appreciation for the desirability of an agreed-upon approach to the potential coverage issues. A preferred approach, for example, may be one that permits the parties to settle the underlying class action litigation and then, if necessary, resolve any disputes between themselves through some alternative dispute resolution mechanism, such as arbitration. In the future, it may be that sophisticated carriers will find blended-risk solutions to the insurance problem.

The overriding objective on the part of both the insurer and the insureds, though, is the minimization of disputes between themselves. In that way, they may effectively cooperate to obtain an optimum result for the company and the other insureds in the underlying litigation.

CHAPTER 9

DEALING WITH THE REGULATORS

Joseph T. Baio

Just as class action lawsuits are a predictable consequence of the discovery and disclosure of accounting irregularities, so too are the investigations and formal proceedings that are typically brought by the Securities and Exchange Commission (SEC) and the regulatory arms of the stock exchanges. Unlike class action lawsuits, however, these regulatory matters can proceed relatively quickly, and they must be considered and dealt with by the company's management from the outset of the crisis.

The SEC and the stock exchanges enforce a variety of rules designed to protect investors who buy and sell the stock of public companies. A company that has been providing false financial statements to investors inevitably has violated a collection of these rules, and the consequences of those violations can be severe. The SEC has the power to investigate and punish companies and their responsible agents for misleading the public. The stock exchanges can delist the securities of companies that do not adhere to their quantitative and qualitative requirements. In dealing with these potential repercussions, company managers hope to minimize the penalties that the company will suffer for its past sins, to regain credibility in the eyes of the regulators, and to create an environment where the company can successfully move forward. Although all these goals cannot always be met and each crisis will pose its own unique problems, this chapter identifies some techniques for dealing with the regulatory problems that follow the disclosure of accounting irregularities.

The SEC: The Power to Investigate, Correct, and Punish

The SEC, created by an act of Congress in 1934, is the government agency with principal responsibility for the administration and enforcement of the federal securities laws. The SEC is composed of five members who are appointed by the President, with the advice and consent of the Senate, for five-year terms. The SEC directs a number of divisions, each of which has a large staff of lawyers, accountants, engineers, investigators, examiners, and others.

Describing itself as an "independent, non-partisan, quasi-judicial regulatory agency," the SEC is designed to provide some measure of protection for investors by policing securities markets to keep them fair and honest. The SEC does not assess and relay the value or quality of any particular security; actually, it can be a crime to represent that the SEC has done so. Instead, the SEC works to ensure that companies that sell their stock to a large group of investors—these companies are called *issuers*—publicly disclose the information necessary for investors to make informed choices and to help provide honest markets in which those securities are traded. The SEC's regulatory activities therefore fall into two broad categories: corporate disclosure and market fairness. In its role as enforcer of corporate disclosure rules, the SEC works to identify, investigate, and prevent financial fraud and to punish those who engage in it.

Disclosure Requirements

The first piece of legislation that provides an oversight and enforcement mechanism for the federal securities laws was actually passed shortly before the SEC came into being. The Securities Act of 1933 made it illegal (subject to some exceptions) to offer a security for sale to the public unless that security was registered. An issuer registers a security by filing a registration statement with the SEC. The registration statement contains two parts. One part is the prospectus, which must be provided to every purchaser of the security. The second part, which contains additional information and supporting documents, is available to the public but need not be transmitted to every purchaser.

The 1933 Act identifies some of the information to be included in the registration statement, but it also gives the SEC some discretion to add required material and permit certain omissions. The SEC has exercised this authority to develop a number of different forms suitable for different categories of issuers. Generally, an issuer must provide a description of its business and holdings, a description of the security it is offering with an explanation of the relationship between the new offering and pre-existing securities, information about company management, and financial statements certified by independent public accountants. The registration statement must be signed by the issuer's principal officers and at least a majority of the board of directors.

Some months after passing the 1933 Act, Congress passed the Securities Exchange Act of 1934 which, in addition to establishing the SEC, extended corporate disclosure requirements. Unlike the 1933 Act requirements, which are imposed at the time a registration statement is filed, the 1934 Act disclosure obligations are ongoing. As long as securities of a company subject to the 1934 Act are being traded, the company must file annual and other periodic reports to update continuously the information submitted in the original filing. These requirements extend to most issuers with more than 500 shareholders and $1 million in assets, regardless of whether their securities were listed and traded on a national exchange.

Three basic reports are filed with the SEC under Section 13 of the 1934 Act and they are designed to assure that the public gets accurate and timely information about a company. These are (1) Form 10-K, an annual report; (2) Form 10-Q, a quarterly report; and (3) Form 8-K, a report filed whenever certain specified events occur. Both Forms 10-K and 10-Q include a company's financial statements, and the financial statements in Form 10-K must be audited. The Form 10-K must be signed by the issuer, by the company's principal officers, and by a majority of its board of directors. Thus, corporate disclosure under both the 1933 and the 1934 Acts involves representations by many responsible individuals, all of whom are at some risk if the company's financial statements prove to be false.

Additional Provisions

The 1934 Act doesn't just establish disclosure requirements. As amended over the years, it contains a number of different provisions that hold individuals accountable for violations of the disclosure rules. For example, Section 10(b) of the 1934 Act makes it unlawful for any person directly or indirectly "to use or employ, in connection with the purchase or sale of any security, . . . any manipulative or deceptive device or contrivance" in violation of SEC rules and regulations. This statute can serve not only as the basis for a private, class action lawsuit, as discussed in Chapter 7, but also for an action brought directly by the SEC against the company, as well as those who control it, direct it, operate it, underwrite its financings, and keep its accounts. The same applies to the other anti-fraud sections of the 1934 Act discussed in Chapter 7.

The rationale behind these laws is clear. Companies act through human beings. The SEC cannot effectively enforce corporate disclosure requirements if it cannot regulate those people who act on a company's behalf. The SEC's regulatory reach must extend to *all* of the principal actors, so that one group cannot attempt to shelter itself behind another. By linking anti-fraud provisions to disclosure requirements, the 1934 Act puts the SEC in the business of regulating not only the company itself but also its controlling shareholders, directors, officers, underwriters, accountants, and lawyers.

Financial Fraud Investigations

The SEC has express legislative authority to combat accounting irregularities. Recently, it has become clear that the SEC also has the will to attack the problem. In a series of speeches beginning in the fall of 1998, the SEC's Chairman, Arthur Levitt, has challenged the financial community to stop "accounting hocus-pocus." The SEC views transparency and comparability as the "touchstone" to this country's financial reporting system. The SEC believes that accounting tricks place these two principles in serious jeopardy, and it intends to use its powers of persuasion as well as its powers of enforcement to correct that problem.

The SEC has noted that the fast pace of today's technology-driven market and the market's unforgiving attitude toward failed earnings expectations have combined to cause a "gradual, but noticeable erosion in the quality of financial reporting." Outright fraud is not the only problem, according to the SEC. Rather, all too often, corporations and their accountants are exploiting the flexibility of accounting rules to "manage" their earnings and obscure real-life financial volatility in order to satisfy market expectations. Operating in this "gray area between legitimacy and outright fraud," as the SEC's Chairman has remarked, "jeopardizes the public trust" and threatens to undermine the public confidence that gives the country's markets their stability, not to mention their prosperity.

The SEC's Chairman has focused much of his energy on encouraging the private sector to take an active role in revitalizing financial accounting and disclosure practices, but the SEC is not waiting for the problem to correct itself. The SEC's Director of Enforcement has made combating financial fraud the division's "number one priority." He has warned that the more than 800 members of the Enforcement Division—the part of the SEC that has the power to investigate and litigate against possible wrongdoers—have been directed to focus on financial fraud cases. Because this will result in an increase in the number of SEC investigations that involve accounting and financial disclosure practices, it is important to understand how the SEC conducts those investigations and how a company under investigation or in danger of being investigated should react.

Formal Orders of Investigation and Subpoena Powers

Under the guidance of the Director of Enforcement, the Division of Enforcement monitors the activity and disclosures of public companies; fields complaints from whistle-blowers, investors who have been burned, and anonymous sources; and makes recommendations to the SEC Commissioners as to who should be punished and how severely.

At the outset of an inquiry, the staff members of the Division of Enforcement can informally request information from issuers falling under the SEC's jurisdiction. The staff can also ask that the SEC issue what is known as a *Formal Order of Investigation* if the division believes that there may have been violations of the federal securities laws. The process of seeking and securing a Formal Order of Investigation does not involve the issuer or anyone outside the SEC; it is handled exclusively internally at the SEC, and the company has no right to appear during the process to argue that a Formal Order should not be issued.

The Formal Order itself can be obtained from the SEC by the issuer or subpoenaed parties, but it is not terribly overinformative. It generally identifies the issuer involved (e.g., In re Newco Corporation), the office handling the investigation (e.g., Washington, New York), the possible securities law violations at issue, and the staff members who will be working on the investigation. Most importantly, once a Formal Order of Investigation has been issued, the Division of Enforcement has the power to subpoena evidence and witnesses. The subpoenas may be enforced by the federal courts and failure to comply can lead to fines and other punishments.

Fighting SEC subpoenas on the grounds of irrelevance or harassment almost never succeeds. The staff of the Division of Enforcement, however, will narrow the scope of requests if the company's counsel can convince it that the request is too broad and will require a great deal of time and effort that will likely yield little useful information. As a general matter, the staff's willingness to narrow requests and extend due dates varies directly with the company's level of cooperation with the investigators.

Penalties and Sanctions

If, after its investigation, the Division of Enforcement believes that it can make a case against a company or its representatives, the staff can seek authorization from the SEC to begin administrative or judicial proceedings. At this point, the company and its targeted employees can file a *Wells Submission*, in which they can argue that, as a matter of policy, fact, or law, the SEC should not authorize the commencement of any proceeding.

If the staff of the Division of Enforcement gets authority to proceed and settlement talks lead nowhere, a hearing will follow. Administrative proceedings take place before an administrative judge (who also happens to be an SEC employee). Judicial proceedings occur before federal court judges. Although the money penalties that the SEC can impose often are not as high as civil damages (the SEC is limited in non-insider trading cases to $500,000 or the amount of financial gain realized by the offending party), the SEC has other remedies available to it. It can obtain an injunction against future violations, on penalty of contempt of court, against individual wrongdoers. It can also get "equitable" relief, such as forcing a wrongdoer to undo a transaction made possible or profitable by the fraud. It can prohibit a wrongdoer from ever again serving as an officer or director of a registered company. It can censure, suspend, or bar professionals (including lawyers and accountants) from ever again practicing before it. If the SEC determines that the misstatement was intentional, it also can refer the matter to the United States Department of Justice for criminal prosecution, as discussed in Chapter 10.

Regaining Credibility with the SEC: Fight or Acquiesce?

The premise of this book is that a company has uncovered accounting irregularities and must therefore restate its historical financial numbers. That premise dictates a course of action centered on cooperation with the SEC and conciliation. A different set of problems and a different strategy may arise, however, when the SEC is investigating an ambiguous set of facts: where there are errors but possibly no irregularities; where large reported numbers are involved but possibly not material amounts; where aggressive accounting treatment was employed but possibly not improper accounting; or where the problem is potentially serious but narrowly confined. In such situations, there may be no "special committee" investigation, or, if there is one, the company and its lawyers may conclude in the face of ambiguous evidence and a disbelieving array of regulators that there have been no violations of the federal securities laws. Although confession and contrition can be cleansing, sometimes they are inappropriate.

Thus, a company frequently has defenses against charges of securities fraud, and counsel may seek to advance those defenses zealously in any proceeding before the SEC or the courts. In such situations, questions about whether to retain special counsel to do an internal review, to provide a written report to the SEC, to maintain or waive the attorney-client privilege, and to settle or fight become more complicated and more challenging.

On other occasions, an acknowledgment of past sins and contrition are appropriate, and the uncovering of financial fraud and the restatement of a company's historical financial statements usually presents just such an occasion. In its worst light, a company with restated financial statements has told the world that the numbers that it has been putting out for years were false and that some people at the company knew that they were false. The company, under such circumstances, must purge itself of earlier wrongdoing and rebuild trust. We turn to that process now.

Cooperating with the SEC

A company in the throes of an accounting-irregularities crisis wants to minimize the penalties that the SEC will seek to impose against the company and its innocent agents. It is also in the company's best interest for its officers and directors (at least those not implicated in wrongdoing) to have the opportunity to clean up the company on their own, without SEC prodding. An intense investigation by the SEC, filled with detailed document requests and an avalanche of subpoenas calling for testimony, is one of the last things that a company's executives need when trying to reestablish credibility with investors, sources of capital, suppliers, and customers. It's hard enough to rehabilitate and run a company under such circumstances without the distractions and overhang of an active SEC investigation.

What should a company do to achieve a quiet regulatory environment and a favorable settlement with the SEC after admitting to a major accounting problem? To begin, the company must know what the SEC expects from management when an accounting irregularities crisis erupts. Although the SEC has not provided a checklist to public companies, experience tells us that the SEC will consider the following questions in deciding how closely it will investigate a company, and what it will do to the company and its management, after the discovery of accounting fraud:

- Has the company acted promptly and responsibly to correct previously inaccurate disclosures?

- Has the company taken steps to remove (through suspensions or terminations of employment) the individuals who initiated or advanced the accounting irregularities?

- Is the company undertaking a prompt, thorough, and credible review of its financial statements to determine the extent of the problem? Is that review being undertaken by experienced professionals who have the requisite independence from the company?

- Will the company share with the SEC the results of its internal review, even if that review is otherwise "privileged" and outside the subpoena power of the SEC?

- Has the company taken steps to ensure that accounting irregularities will not be a part of its future?

To answer these questions, the SEC will observe and evaluate the company's conduct in the weeks and months following the discovery of the fraud.

Initial Contact with the SEC

When accounting irregularities first surface, the board of directors may wonder whether it should affirmatively contact the SEC before disseminating the first press release. (If the company has uncovered a significant fraud, it can rest assured that the SEC will almost inevitably be calling on the company's officers and lawyers.) A tangible benefit to calling the SEC first is to begin the process of restoring credibility at the earliest possible moment. Of course, the company may not have a good handle on the severity of the problem on "day one," and any call may be premature. In addition, for lesser problems of questionable materiality, a call might not be warranted at all. Where a massive accounting irregularities problem has surfaced, though, a preemptive call will frequently be advisable. The call can be made to a known branch chief in the Division of Enforcement to brief the individual on what is happening at the company just before the issuance of the first press release.

Early Communication with the SEC

Once lines of communication have been opened with the SEC, the principal contact point typically will be one or more staff members in the Division of Enforcement (who no doubt will be identified in the Formal Order of Investigation). The staff members will want to know what the company is doing to quantify and remedy its problems and to whom subpoenas should be sent seeking the production of documents, the identity of witnesses, and the scheduling of testimony.

In pursuit of the twin goals of rebuilding trust and avoiding a full-scale investigation, counsel for the company should assure the staff of the Division of Enforcement that the SEC will get the company's full cooperation. Counsel should assist the staff in locating former employees and arranging for interviews as they are requested. Counsel should also identify the experts that the board of directors has retained to address the accounting problems, the role of the special committee in overseeing the internal investigative process, and the actions it has taken against responsible agents.

The staff will want to know the expected timetable for the completion of the internal review and restatement of past financial statements. As a general matter, and subject to exceptions, the Division of Enforcement will allow a company to conduct its own internal review without immediate SEC intervention if the staff of the Division of Enforcement concludes that the review will be thorough and unbiased, that it will be conducted expeditiously, and that its results will be made available to the staff promptly after the review is complete. The company should address these concerns honestly and identify realistic timetables that will not have to be repeatedly extended.

Responding to SEC Subpoenas and the Representation of Witnesses

Even though the company is undertaking a thorough internal investigation, the SEC may simultaneously subpoena documents and take testimony of a variety of former and current company representatives to determine what went wrong. (The more high-profile the case, the more likely the SEC will proceed on a faster and more active track.) From the company's perspective, the best course is to have one law firm representing as many individuals as possible. A single counsel increases the likelihood of a coordinated response, enables the company to keep track efficiently of what is going on, and minimizes the financial costs of representation. Under such circumstances, the lawyers for the special committee usually do not represent the company or its officers and directors (other than special committee members), but instead focus on conducting and completing the internal review. Company counsel typically represents the company in responding to document subpoenas, as well as the individual employees, officers, and directors who are not implicated in any wrongdoing.

In many situations, it may be impossible or inappropriate for the same company lawyers to represent all who are called by the SEC to testify. As a matter of the rules of ethics—which vary from jurisdiction to jurisdiction—an attorney generally may not jointly represent parties if they are adverse to one another or if they have sufficiently differing interests such that counsel's ability to represent zealously each client would be impaired by a joint representation. Moreover, joint representations are not appropriate when the parties have significantly differing interests, unless each party agrees to the joint representation after full disclosure of the facts. Former employees may not want to be jointly represented by company counsel, even if the company offers to pay for such counsel. (In fact, the company may be required to supply separate counsel under applicable indemnity obligations.)

If multiple counsel are to be involved, it may be advisable for counsel to enter into a *joint defense* or *common interest agreement*, pursuant to which the parties can exchange information and analyses while maintaining an attorney-client privilege, thereby increasing the data available to all.

Turning Over an Investigative Report to the SEC

On more than one occasion, the SEC will likely make clear that the Division of Enforcement will expect to receive from the company a copy of the final investigative report that the special committee's lawyers and accountants prepared for the committee. The Division of Enforcement staff will also expect to receive all interview memoranda, notes, and supporting materials gathered or prepared in connection with the completion of the report. Although a commitment to turn over such material is usually the linchpin in restoring credibility with the SEC, the disclosure of the report is not without a potential cost: The disclosure will give the plaintiffs' lawyers a strong argument that the report and its backup are no longer privileged and are therefore "discoverable" in the class action litigation. In fact, the plaintiffs' lawyers will argue that, if the special committee and the company intended all along to provide the SEC with a copy of the report, then it was never meant to be a confidential communication between a client and a lawyer and therefore was never privileged to begin with.

Although the risk of losing the "privilege" is a real one and that risk may prevent a company from disclosing privileged material to the SEC in many situations, a company that has conceded accounting irregularities and has restated earnings will frequently have less to lose and more to gain by providing the requested materials to the SEC. Often, the materials are produced in such cases.

Counsel, however, can take steps to protect the materials, even though the report is eventually produced to the SEC. Under current law, the report and underlying data *may* continue to be protected after such a disclosure if the SEC agrees to maintain the confidentiality of the produced materials. In the recent past, the SEC has agreed to do so if the company can demonstrate the reliability of work that was done (i.e., no whitewash) and can identify the benefits that the SEC will receive by entering into such an agreement. In support of the request for confidentiality, therefore, company counsel should be prepared to:

- Demonstrate the independence of the special committee members and their professionals, the complete access to information afforded those professionals in their investigation, and the breadth of the subjects under review.

- Advise the SEC that the company will invoke the attorney-client privilege and work product doctrine and decline to produce the report in the absence of a confidentiality agreement. In this way, the SEC will only receive the benefit of the materials if they agree to maintain them in confidence.

- Specify the extent of the effort undertaken in generating the report (e.g., boxes of documents reviewed, number of employees/witnesses interviewed, hours of lawyer and accountant time expended in analyzing materials and preparing report). The SEC will thereby be given to understand that it gets the benefit of all that effort without governmental cost.

Making Peace with the SEC

Ultimately, probably the best the board of directors can hope for is a negotiated resolution with the SEC. The SEC has a powerful arsenal of weaponry at its disposal. Through a negotiated resolution, those involved may potentially avoid some of the more onerous punishments the SEC might otherwise seek to impose.

In all likelihood, such a negotiated resolution will involve different penalties for different people depending upon their status and complicity. Senior executives who were knowingly involved in deliberate wrongdoing can expect severe punishment. Penalties may include insistence by the SEC on removal from the company, a bar against further service as an officer or director of a public company, an injunction against further violations of the securities laws (which would be punishable by a finding of contempt), and a stiff fine. The SEC may also refer the matter to the U.S. Attorney's Office for criminal prosecution.

For those who were not deliberate wrongdoers but merely negligent, the SEC may seek penalties that are less severe. These might include a cease-and-desist order against further violations.

A difficult issue is presented to the SEC by lower-level employees who were pressured into participation by more senior executives. Such individuals obviously are in a sympathetic position insofar as their complicity may, at the outset, have been entirely inadvertent. Even knowing participation may have resulted from the need to hold on to their jobs. Still, recent informal statements by members of the Division of Enforcement suggest that the SEC will not permit lower-level employees to escape remedial mechanisms entirely. To be sure, it is the senior executives who will be made to suffer the most severe consequences. Nonetheless, representatives of the Division of Enforcement have been crystal clear that "there is no such thing as a good soldier." As one Division of Enforcement staff member has put it, wrongdoers will be pursued "up, down, and sideways." Penalties may include fines, injunctions, cease-and-desist orders (for conduct not warranting an injunction), and insistence by the SEC that the employees be removed from the corporate enterprise.

For CPAs involved in accounting irregularities, the SEC has an additional series of punishments owing to its ability to proceed pursuant to a rule known as Rule 102(e). This is the rule by which the SEC brings proceedings against wrongdoing professionals, and the consequences can be serious for the professionals. Among the frequently employed remedies of the SEC is a permanent or temporary ban from public practice before the Commission. For many professionals, such a penalty can effectively end their careers.

As to the company itself, the penalties resulting from a negotiated resolution with the SEC may include many of those mentioned earlier—including an injunction and a fine. Almost inevitably, though, the remedy sought by the SEC will be supplemented by a dramatic corporate-governance component. Among other things, the SEC may insist that the company bring in additional outside directors, reconfigure its audit committee, hire a new CFO, substantially reorganize its internal-control systems, and remove wrongdoers.

As a general matter, the SEC will seek to understand the facts and circumstances of a particular situation and try to use its enforcement mechanisms to fashion a result that creatively fits its perception of the underlying problem. Many of its penalties may seem harsh. Almost always, though, they will be preferable to a prolonged battle with the SEC.

Dealing with Self-Regulatory Organizations

The SEC isn't the only regulator that companies need to worry about after the discovery of accounting irregularities. The stock exchanges and associations on which companies' securities are traded also have the power to investigate and to punish. Companies must be mindful of what these self-regulatory organizations (SRO) can do to, and what they expect from, companies that restate their earnings.

What "SROs" Are and What They Do

SROs are national securities exchanges, securities associations, or clearing agencies that are registered with the SEC. There are eight active securities exchanges that are so registered: the American Stock Exchange (AMEX), the Boston Stock Exchange, the Chicago Board Options Exchange, the Chicago Stock Exchange, the Cincinnati Stock Exchange, the New York Stock Exchange (NYSE), the Philadelphia Stock Exchange, and the Pacific Stock Exchange. The National Association of Securities Dealers, Inc. (NASD) operates the Nasdaq Stock Market, Inc. (Nasdaq), which is the regulatory body responsible for over-the-counter securities.

The stock of most public companies is bought and sold over one or more of these exchanges. It is important for public companies to be listed on an exchange. The exchanges see to it that there is a liquid market for their listed companies' stock, that the execution of trades occurs quickly, and that the process of buying and selling the stock of listed companies is handled fairly, honestly, and efficiently.

By getting listed on an exchange—particularly the NYSE or the Nasdaq—companies add credibility to their stock and generally experience a higher stock price. The price of admission, however, is that companies must meet specific financial and other requirements to get listed and, to stay listed, companies must maintain defined financial levels and demonstrate good corporate governance. These requirements give rise to a potential problem: Companies suffering from accounting irregularities may be unable to meet the criteria for continued listing and may find themselves the subject of delisting proceedings. But before turning to those standards and the process and effect of a delisting hearing, let's review some important background on the national stock exchanges.

SROs and the SEC

SROs were created by the same New Deal securities legislation that gave birth to the SEC. Rather than impose direct federal regulation of securities exchanges and brokers' associations, Congress decided to allow the exchanges to regulate themselves under the SEC's watchful eye.

In order to qualify for registration with the SEC, an exchange must meet certain organizational requirements specified under law. Broadly speaking, an exchange must have the capacity to enforce compliance by its members with applicable law, to manage fairly its membership and collect membership dues, and to provide an effective and adequate disciplinary procedure. The rules of an exchange must be "designed to prevent fraudulent and manipulative acts and practices, to promote just and equitable principles of trade," and to facilitate a free, open, and competitive market.

The SEC's oversight of the rules and operation of an exchange is perpetual. Since 1975, all proposed changes to the rules of an SRO have been subject to approval by the SEC, and the SEC even has the power to impose new or amended rules. Likewise, a company or individual punished by an exchange typically has a right of appeal to the SEC, and then from the SEC to the federal courts.

An important point to remember is that, if the SEC believes that violations of securities laws or exchange rules are occurring, the SEC has the power to conduct its own investigation, even if the exchange is also conducting an investigation at the same time.

In addition, the SEC can investigate the exchanges themselves if the SEC believes the exchanges are not doing a good job of ferreting out and punishing improper conduct. The SEC exercised this power in 1996, for example, when it issued findings strongly criticizing certain Nasdaq trading practices, including anti-competitive pricing. The SEC and the NASD ultimately arrived at a settlement that required the NASD to allocate significant additional resources to enforcement of its rules and to take specific steps to prevent the criticized trading activity, which led to a major restructuring of the NASD.

Listing Requirements

Subject to approval from the SEC, the exchanges have the authority to determine for themselves which securities qualify for listing. When a company applies to have its securities listed on an exchange, it will have to comply with listing requirements for initial entrance. If the company meets those requirements and the exchange agrees to list its securities, the company must sign a *listing agreement* that will obligate the company to comply with continued listing requirements for as long as its securities are listed on that exchange.

Some of the listing requirements are financial—e.g., minimum market value, minimum number of shares and shareholders, minimum revenues. The exchanges typically refer to these standards as *quantitative listing requirements*. These standards vary widely from exchange to exchange, and if a company (particularly a start-up company) finds the requirements too stringent, it may have to apply for listing on a less desirable exchange.

In addition to setting financial standards, most exchanges also impose *qualitative listing requirements*, which include mandatory standards of corporate governance. Corporate governance standards involve critical subjects such as public disclosure of financial and other material information, the independence of directors and auditors, the existence and configuration of audit committees, voting rights, and preemptive rights. For years, these standards were basic and general, but more recently they have become more specific and pointed—with the trend toward tighter corporate governance standards being expected to continue.

Largely through corporate governance standards, the exchanges are playing an active role in the prevention and detection of financial fraud. Perhaps the most basic corporate governance requirement is that a listed company promptly disclose to the public any information that "might reasonably be expected to materially affect the market for its securities." The NYSE in fact advises that this disclosure requirement is "one of the most important and fundamental purposes of the listing agreement." A company that has discovered a serious accounting irregularity must consider whether it has violated this rule, either because the irregularity prevented accurate disclosure of material financial information or because the irregularity itself, once discovered, was not promptly reported to the public.

Enhanced Exchange Requirements

Accounting and auditing standards are being tightened further. As mentioned in Chapter 2, in late 1998 the NYSE and the NASD convened a Blue Ribbon Committee on Improving the Effectiveness of Corporate Audit Committees. The Blue Ribbon Committee recommended that the NYSE and the NASD:

1. Codify a specific definition for "independent" directors.
2. Require all listed companies with a capitalization greater than $200 million to have an audit committee comprised solely of "independent" directors.
3. Require all listed companies with a capitalization greater than $200 million to have a minimum of three "financially literate" (as defined by the Blue Ribbon Committee) directors on every audit committee.
4. Require the audit committees of all listed companies to adopt a formal, written charter for the audit committee and to review that charter on an annual basis.
5. Specify in the charter the accountability of the company's outside auditor to the board and to the audit committee.
6. Specify in the charter that the audit committee must ascertain and evaluate all relationships between the outside auditor and the company to ensure the auditor's independence.

Given the composition of the Blue Ribbon Committee (it included the chairmen of both the NYSE and the NASD), it is not surprising that the NYSE and the NASD have adopted new rules consistent with the Blue Ribbon Committee's recommendations. (See Chapter 11.)

These new requirements are designed to promote transparency and to prevent financial fraud. However, along with other listing requirements (including quantitative requirements), they also can serve as grounds for an SRO to suspend or remove the securities from the list of securities traded on its exchange—known as a *delisting*—if a company violates the requirements. (See Exhibits 9–1 and 9–2 for the delisting procedures of the NYSE and the NASD.) As listing requirements become more specific and numerous, the grounds upon which an SRO can initiate delisting proceedings in the event of an accounting irregularity will likely expand.

Exhibit 9–1. New York Stock Exchange Delisting Procedures

The NYSE would consider delisting a security of a company in the event of:

- A failure to maintain certain quantitative criteria established by the NYSE
- Reduction in operating assets or scope of activities
- Bankruptcy and/or liquidation
- Authoritative advice to the NYSE that the security is without value
- A registration that is no longer effective
- A failure to solicit proxies for all stockholder meetings
- Violation of agreements with the NYSE
- Operations contrary to the public interest
- A failure to maintain an audit committee in conformity with NYSE requirements

If a decision is made to delist a security, written notice shall:

- Set forth the basis for such decision
- Set forth the specific policy or criterion under which such action is to be taken
- Inform the issuer of its right to a hearing

If the issuer does not request a hearing within 20 days after receiving notice, the NYSE staff will submit an application to the SEC to strike the security. If the issuer requests a hearing, the hearing will be held before a committee of the board of directors of the NYSE.

Exhibit 9–2. Nasdaq Delisting Procedures

Delisting is to occur when:

- The company falls below certain quantitative criteria established by the NASD
- The company fails to meet the NASD's corporate governance requirements
- Any event or circumstance "exists or occurs that makes initial or continued inclusion . . . inadvisable or unwarranted, even though the securities meet all enumerated criteria for . . . inclusion in Nasdaq"

If a decision is made to delist a security, notice shall:

- Describe the grounds for the determination
- Identify the quantitative standard or qualitative consideration that the issuer has failed to satisfy
- Inform the issuer of its right to a hearing

If the issuer does not request a hearing within seven days of the determination to delist, the determination will take immediate effect. If the issuer requests a hearing, the hearing will be held before a Listing Qualifications Panel, and delisting will be stayed pending a written determination by the panel.

Preventing and Handling Delisting Proceedings

In considering how to deal effectively with a company's stock exchange, we look back again to the first day of an accounting irregularities crisis. The board of directors is meeting to determine how to respond. Crisis-response assignments are being distributed. One assignment will be to investigate any potential effect that the irregularities might have on the company's ability to continue to trade its securities on the exchange where the company is listed. The goal, of course, is to prevent a delisting. The mission to accomplish that goal is to take every possible step to provide adequate and proper disclosure of the company's financial position, to rectify past violations of the exchange's listing requirements, to prevent future violations as events unfold, and to meet the ongoing financial standards.

Early Dialogue and Suspension of Trading

As soon as practical, the company should open a dialogue with the responsible listing official of its exchange. Ordinarily, this contact should be made as soon as the irregularities have been discovered. If the company does not have a handle on the magnitude of the problem, the first step usually recommended by the exchange and accepted by the company is to suspend trading in the company's stock.

This interim step often makes sense. The company at this point knows of a real problem with its financial statements but doesn't yet know how big the problem is. A suspension of trading prevents investors from buying or selling based on false financial information and eliminates liability to people who otherwise would have bought stock before a major dip in price. Suspension of trading also gives the company time to straighten out its public disclosures in a non-trading environment.

In dealing with the stock exchange, the company must be careful not to make promises it cannot keep or to misstate either the extent of its understanding of the problem or the problem itself. At the same time, the company should act expeditiously. Although exchanges have listing requirements and other standards, they also have a fair amount of discretion as to how their rules are interpreted and enforced. The rules of most exchanges contain a provision to the effect that the exchange is not bound by the specific, enumerated listing criteria and it can assess suitability for continued listing even though a security meets or fails to meet them. The bottom line is that the company should do what it can as soon as it can to persuade the exchange that, despite whatever violations the company may have committed, it is in the best interest of the exchange and the company's public investors to keep its securities listed.

The company must analyze the facts as it understands them in light of its listing agreement and the applicable listing requirements. It should attempt to identify violations that already have occurred and violations that may occur in the coming weeks and months as a result of the company's (and the market's) response to the problem. Examples of violations that already may have occurred include a failure to disclose information that has a material effect on the market (namely, the true financial picture of the company), an improper or insufficient outside audit program, or a significant conflict of interest that caused inadequacies in financial reporting. Violations of listing requirements that may occur after the irregularity has been discovered might include the failure to disclose promptly all material facts related to the irregularity, the failure to correct deficiencies in the company's accounting system that were identified in the process of handling the crisis, and the sustained devaluation of the company's stock to a level that fails to satisfy the exchange's quantitative listing requirements.

Corrective Measures

As the company continues its investigation of the accounting irregularities crisis, it will have identified one or both of two possible categories of listing violations: those that the company can prevent or correct and those that the company cannot prevent or correct. Violations that can be prevented or corrected should be. The other violations should be identified, assessed, and mitigated to the extent possible. If the company identifies a serious violation that it cannot correct, particularly a violation of the exchange's quantitative listing requirements, it should begin to explore the possibility of listing its securities on a different exchange that may have quantitative or other criteria that the company can meet.

A Two-Pronged Approach to Delisting Proceedings

Despite the company's best efforts, the exchange may nonetheless move to delist the company's securities. If that happens, and if the company believes its securities should continue to be actively traded, the company will probably want to explore two alternatives. If it hasn't already, the company may want to look into the possibility of listing its securities on another exchange. If the company can reach an agreement with another exchange, in all likelihood it will be possible to withdraw its securities voluntarily from the old exchange and list them on the new one, although even a voluntary withdrawal from listing may require that the company demonstrate to the exchange and to the SEC that its decision to withdraw will not unduly harm investors.

The company's second alternative is to prepare to defend its right to continue to be listed on the current exchange. All exchanges have codified some form of delisting procedures. Typically, the applicable procedures require the exchange to provide the company with written notice of its intention to delist the security and the grounds upon which it has tentatively made that decision. The company then has the right to request a hearing before an administrative panel established by the exchange as a tribunal for such matters, and often it must exercise that right within a prescribed period. (Some exchanges also provide another level of discretionary review by the exchange's board of directors or governors.)

If there is a case to be made, it is critical that the company be ready to put into evidence all relevant facts and to present its best case to the exchange's hearing panel. The main reason is that the company may never get another chance to present factual evidence for adjudication. The company can appeal the decision of a hearing panel to the SEC, and the SEC rules give the SEC the ability, in its discretion, to conduct a second hearing, but the SEC is not obligated to conduct a second hearing for the company. And, there is no guarantee that the SEC will exercise its available discretion to see that a second hearing is held.

An additional reason to ensure an effective presentation in the hearing before the exchange is that, although the SEC on appeal would normally take an independent look at the factual record created in the initial hearing, it is likely to give significant weight to the exchange's interpretation of its own rules. Although an SEC decision can be appealed to the United States Court of Appeals, that court almost certainly will apply a standard of review that requires deference to the administrative decisions of the exchange and the SEC. In short, the company's best chance to convince a tribunal that the exchange should not delist its securities is usually at the initial administrative hearing, so the company should make the most of that opportunity.

CHAPTER 10

CRIMINAL INVESTIGATIONS

Benito Romano

It is an exceedingly unfortunate consequence of accounting irregularities that the resulting investigative proceedings may not be limited to civil class action litigation (see Chapter 7) or regulatory proceedings (see Chapter 9). Rather, where accounting irregularities have surfaced at a public company, in all likelihood federal criminal laws, as well as state criminal laws, have been broken (see Exhibits 10–1 and 10–2). Where accounting irregularities have surfaced, therefore, it may be that all other aspects of the problem will need to take a back seat to one that becomes paramount: the commencement of a criminal investigation.

In the federal system, the decision to start a criminal investigation is entirely within the discretion of the United States Attorney in each federal district, who may act merely on the basis of an allegation or a suspicion that a federal crime has been committed. As a result, a criminal investigation of accounting irregularities can originate in all sorts of ways. An investigation may be initiated because of an anonymous tip, information supplied by a conscientious or guilt-ridden employee, or facts discovered in the course of a routine audit of the company's financial statements. The company's public disclosure of financial misstatements may itself lead to the commencement of a criminal investigation.

Whatever its origins, responding to a criminal investigation will almost always have to take priority over everything else. The government's powers to investigate are broad, and a prosecutor, informed of a potential massive fraud at a public company, will likely make the investigation a high priority. Indeed, from the prosecutor's perspective, a massive accounting irregularity problem potentially involves just the sort of dishonesty, deception, and concerted activity that fits neatly into already-tested theories of criminal liability. If a prosecutor has been following reports of accounting irregularities in

Exhibit 10–1. Securities Act of 1933

Section 24. Any person who willfully violates any of the provisions of this title, or the rules and regulations promulgated by the Commission under authority thereof, or any person who willfully, in a registration statement filed under this title, makes any untrue statement of a material fact or omits to state any material fact required to be stated therein or necessary to make the statements therein not misleading, shall upon conviction be fined not more than $10,000 or imprisoned not more than five years, or both.

Exhibit 10–2. Securities Exchange Act of 1934

Section 32. (a) Any person who willfully violates any provision of this title (other than Section 30A), or any rule or regulation thereunder the violation of which is made unlawful or the observance of which is required under the terms of this title, or any person who willfully and knowingly makes, or causes to be made, any statement in any application, report, or document required to be filed under this title or any rule or regulation thereunder or any undertaking contained in a registration statement as provided in subsection (d) of Section 15 of this title or by any self-regulatory organization in connection with an application for membership or participation therein or to become associated with a member thereof, which statement was false or misleading with respect to any material fact, shall upon conviction be fined not more than $1,000,000, or imprisoned not more than 10 years, or both, except that when such person is a person other than a natural person, a fine not exceeding $2,500,000 may be imposed; but no person shall be subject to imprisonment under this section for the violation of any rule or regulation if he proves that he had no knowledge of such rule or regulation.

the financial press, he may even have been looking for such a case in order to make a public example out of an improperly acting company.

Still, even where the existence of accounting irregularities has been conceded, it will be far from clear to a prosecutor that a criminal prosecution should be commenced. Rather, the prosecutor will try to resolve a number of issues bearing on the extent to which an indictment of the company or any executive would be justified. Among these issues may be the following:

- The magnitude and nature of the financial misstatements, both in terms of their quantifiable materiality and whether they involved the fabrication or destruction of documents

- Whether any employee was in good faith mistaken about the relevant accounting rules

- Whether any employee had sufficient knowledge of the entirety of the scheme to justify the conclusion that the suspected perpetrator's conduct was willful and he acted with criminal intent

- Whether any employee personally benefited from the misstatements, or acted primarily to benefit the company, or acted to carry out the instructions of a superior

- Whether the company had in place a system to detect and deter the conduct under investigation, and whether the failure of that system was reasonably foreseeable

- Whether the absence of an effective system of internal control was reckless or deliberate

Chapter 10 examines the role of prosecutors in ferreting out financial fraud involving public-company accounting irregularities. First, it describes the several phases of a typical criminal investigation and possible company responses at each phase (Exhibit 10–3). Then it turns to the responsibilities of the company to gather information in order to comply with the demands of the government, to monitor the progress of the investigation and evaluate the company's exposure to criminal prosecution, and, ultimately, to present its best case to avoid indictment. Finally, it addresses briefly the interplay of the criminal investigation and related civil proceedings and the difficulties of responding effectively in such parallel settings.

Exhibit 10–3. Phases of a Criminal Investigation

- Grand jury subpoena
- Initial contacts with prosecutor
- Production of documents
- Grand jury testimony
- Plea negotiations (if necessary)
- Trial (if necessary)

The Initial Grand Jury Phase

Typically, a company first learns that it is involved in a criminal investigation when it receives a grand jury subpoena, in most instances a "subpoena *duces tecum*," compelling the company or its employees to furnish documents to the grand jury. In an investigation of accounting irregularities, such a subpoena for documents may encompass all the files underlying the company's publicly disseminated financial information, including the records underlying the transactions at issue.

For a company and its executives, the need to respond to the subpoena presents both an opportunity and a dilemma. The opportunity stems from the company's ability, in responding to the subpoena, to learn about the investigation—an education process that will be critical to a successful criminal defense. The dilemma stems from the need to assess the extent to which active and complete cooperation should be pledged to the prosecutor at the outset. The formulation of a response to a criminal subpoena, therefore, constitutes a critical point in the investigatory process. And those involved are thereby placed in the position of needing to make important decisions at an early stage that can have lasting and significant effects.

Once an initial review of the subpoena and its underlying substance is complete, one of the first steps in formulating a response is often for company counsel to make a phone call to the prosecutor to make appropriate introductions and, to the extent possible, to seek background information regarding the investigation. In this initial contact, the prosecutor will be understandably guarded. Nonetheless, some useful information will frequently be shared. A general impression may be gained about the scope and focus of the investigation and the timing of additional subpoenas and testimony. Thereafter, it is not unusual for some kind of initial meeting to be arranged to discuss in greater detail the company's response. One benefit of such a meeting is that some level of additional information may be forthcoming.

It is thus that, from the outset, company counsel will be undertaking a process that is vitally important and that will be ongoing throughout the entirety of the criminal proceedings: learning as much as it possibly can about the prosecutor's case. The reason is that, unlike a civil case, in which broad principles of discovery enable the defendants basically to learn the complete details of the adversary's evidence, a criminal investigation is shrouded in a much greater level of secrecy and complete knowledge of the evidence is not usually available pursuant to the procedural rules. Less formal methods of learning the details of the prosecutor's case, therefore, are critical.

In these initial contacts, the establishment of a sound foundation for the company's dealings with the prosecutor is an additional, critically important aspect of the investigation that will also permeate the entirety of the investigative process. To state it simply, those dealings must be premised upon a foundation of absolute candor. Although it may be appropriate at various stages to decline to discuss sensitive matters, whatever counsel elects to address, counsel should avoid making a factual statement on any subject about which it suspects it may be incompletely or inaccurately informed. This admonition applies to subjects such as the existence and location of files, the burden of producing documents, and the availability of witnesses. It also applies to more substantive matters bearing upon guilt or innocence, although such subjects are unlikely to come up except in the context of a presentation late in the investigation or in discussions of the propriety of extending immunity to a particular witness. An important part of a successful criminal defense is the availability of relevant information. To that end, a relationship with the prosecutor based on trust and confidence is key.

The dilemma posed in these initial contacts—involving the issue of cooperation with the prosecutor—is a difficult one and, unfortunately, no single approach can be devised that will fit every investigation. The basic issue is whether the company should adopt a cooperative or an antagonistic stance. Among the disadvantages of cooperation is the fact that, should the company decide to cooperate fully, it may give up opportunities to assert important privileges that it might otherwise raise. Moreover, complete cooperation with the government serves to educate the government about the company's position. For example, if the company has already completed an internal investigation, it may be asked to waive any applicable privileges and to make a resulting report available. Unlike in a civil proceeding, where cooperation with regulatory authorities (such as the SEC) is almost always the preferred approach, the decision to cooperate with the government in a criminal investigation may be much more difficult, insofar as a subsequent effort to oppose the government (should such a change of heart be necessary) would be impeded by the loss of a significant tactical advantage—the loss of surprise. In criminal cases, the government is not afforded the same broad rights of discovery available in civil proceedings. It is entirely possible for a prosecutor to have no significant knowledge of the defense position until after the start of the trial.

On the other hand, the privileges that the company may assert are limited. There is, most importantly, no Fifth Amendment privilege against self-incrimination for companies. Furthermore, almost any kind of evidence, except illegal wiretaps or privileged material, whether admissible in court or not, can be considered by a grand jury. Therefore, the company's ability to oppose a grand jury investigation is to some extent restricted, and the prosecutor may even consider the company's extensive zeal in such opposition to constitute obstruction of justice. Moreover, the prosecutor's ultimate decisions about indictment of the company may be affected by the extent of the company's cooperation. And corporate management may wish to demonstrate cooperation as a matter of policy or public relations.

One issue that will almost inevitably arise, as the company begins to wrestle with the issue of cooperation, is the extent to which it is appropriate for a public company or its executives to offer anything *other* than complete cooperation with the government. Here, it is useful for executives to appreciate the fact that the U.S. system of justice affords those being investigated certain fundamental rights, and it is not unpatriotic to take advantage of them and, accordingly, to offer a defense that is disciplined and vigorous. Among the available rights is the Fifth Amendment privilege against self-incrimination, though this is available only to individuals and not to the company. Insofar as, in fraud cases, guilt can be established through circumstantial evidence, executives frequently need to understand the importance of the Fifth Amendment privilege and the appropriateness of its assertion even in circumstances in which an executive strongly believes he acted in good faith or made a mere error in judgment. Executives will frequently need to understand that it demonstrates no lack of virtue to take full advantage of those constitutional protections designed to protect the innocent from unwarranted prosecution.

Unfortunately, many of these determinations regarding cooperation, at least as a threshold matter, must be made quickly at the outset of an investigation, at a time when the company may have very little information. Most experienced practitioners find the best stance initially to be one of courteous professionalism, in which the adversary role of counsel is recognized throughout, but in which reasonable accommodations can be extended on both sides. The company should avoid an early appearance of active cooperation, which may arouse a reaction of anger if the cooperation later needs to be withdrawn.

Producing Documents to the Prosecutor

At some point the process of assembling documents in response to the subpoena must commence, and it usually begins with the threshold question of how broad the search of the company's files should be. Typically, the subpoena will be so broad as to comprehend all files of the company relevant to the perceived scope of the investigation. Even with a more narrowly drawn subpoena, questions often arise involving whether an attempt should be made to search every file that might, in any way, bear upon the matter. For example, questions may arise as to whether to review files regarding transactions not directly relevant to the scope of the investigation, but related to it because the same executives were involved, or the same transactions or products were involved in different geographical locations. In this respect, the issues that arise out of a criminal subpoena are comparable to those that arise when a civil request for documents has been received. No single answer can be given as to how broad the scope of the search for documents responsive to a criminal subpoena should be. Overall, the operating principle should be one of reasonableness.

One issue that will frequently surface in a criminal investigation, but not in a civil investigation, arises out of individual executives who have their own files that they consider personal and therefore not called for by a subpoena directed to the company. The company must be diligent in locating such files and should recognize early on that there is no such thing as a "personal" file relating to company business. Such files almost invariably are unearthed, and, although the government attorney usually understands that an initial search will not always turn up every piece of paper, the later new documents are uncovered, the more difficult the situation becomes and the more dangerous the documents can be. For the company, the problem can be serious insofar as the company can be held in contempt for failing to produce subpoenaed documents, even if the employee with physical possession has refused to produce them to the grand jury or to the company based upon his personal Fifth Amendment privileges. Documents maintained by the company are not protected by the Fifth Amendment.

Part of the process of assembling and producing documents may involve selection of a custodian to authenticate the records before the grand jury. The custodian of corporate records may be required to testify as to the authenticity of documents produced in response to a subpoena *duces tecum* and that the documents produced are those called for by the subpoena. A custodian of corporate records may not assert the Fifth Amendment privilege on the ground that the act of production of the documents is itself incriminating, so long as the act of production is not used against the custodian in a subsequent criminal prosecution of the custodian.

If the company has a document retention program pursuant to which documents are periodically discarded or destroyed, upon receipt of a subpoena *duces tecum* the program should be stopped immediately so that responsive documents are not thereby lost. It may be possible, depending on how the document retention program is carried out, to discontinue only a portion of the program so that only documents dealing with the areas apparently under investigation (defined prophylactically in the broadest possible terms) are excepted from periodic destruction.

As noted earlier, subpoenas *duces tecum* are usually very broad—broader typically than the government actually needs for its investigation or, for that matter, usually expects to get. Thus, as soon as possible, company counsel will need to contact the government attorney in charge of the investigation to discuss narrowing the scope of the subpoena and to work out a timetable for producing the documents. The best approach in any particular case will be dictated by the circumstances, and it is for this reason that the attorney must be thoroughly familiar with the company's business and the documents, including the types, volume, and location. The government may accept a staggered production of documents in which the government will specify which categories of documents are to be produced first, with the production of other categories being reserved. It will also be necessary to determine whether the government wants the documents produced directly to the grand jury with a witness to provide authentication, or whether it would be satisfied having the documents produced to an agent of the grand jury.

Counsel should try to reach an agreement in writing with the government before documents are produced stating that, when the proceedings are concluded, the documents will be returned and if anyone other than the grand jury requests access, counsel will be informed and given an opportunity to object. The government will usually agree to return documents and give notice of requests by third parties.

Initial Contacts with Counsel for Individual Employees

While documents are being gathered and produced to the grand jury, it usually makes sense to find out who is representing other recipients of subpoenas and contact them. In an investigation of accounting irregularities, there are likely to be any number of lower-level employees with knowledge of the situation, and it would not be surprising for some to receive personal subpoenas. If the company is taking a stance of cooperation, the identity of such witnesses may be volunteered to the prosecutor. Although a judgment must be made in each case, it is often beneficial for company counsel to share and exchange information with counsel for individual employees. A comparison of the subpoenas issued can sometimes provide leads in determining the scope and focus of the investigation. Such a comparison may also provide insight into whether there are targets and non-targets and provide a basis for predicting the government's plan. On the other hand, on occasion, the company may wish to disassociate itself completely from some executives under investigation and, therefore, may not favor a comprehensive joint defense. In these circumstances, the company may conclude that it is more important not to disclose information than to find out what others know.

To the extent a joint defense is appropriate, counsel should discuss the briefing procedures and the procedures for exchange of statements and debriefing memoranda with regard to witnesses who are later to be called to testify before the grand jury. It is generally the rule that information in documents such as debriefing memoranda prepared by attorneys and exchanged pursuant to a joint defense effort, which would otherwise be protected by the attorney-client privilege, retain their privileged character. The exchange of witness interview documents and debriefing memoranda prepared by lawyers does, though, present some risk of disclosure in discovery in a civil case and that risk must be evaluated.

The risk of disclosure in a civil case presents difficult strategic decisions. If the criminal case is more likely than not to go to trial, counsel must interview witnesses and exchange as much information as possible to enable counsel to prepare. If, however, it appears that the criminal case will not go to trial, interviews of witnesses and debriefing memoranda, if undertaken, present a risk of discovery in a civil case that may outweigh the need for the information in the context of the government investigation. If counsel does not know if the criminal case will go to trial, the safest course is probably to prepare the witnesses jointly and exchange information and memoranda. The first battle will be with the government, and the company cannot afford to be unprepared for the fight.

Employee Interviews

As in civil proceedings, the conduct of witness interviews is an important part of the formulation of a defense. In the context of a criminal investigation, though, the timing of such interviews poses a particular challenge in that the interviews usually can be conducted more effectively if documents are first reviewed, but there ordinarily is an urgent need for the results of the interviews before finalizing negotiations with the prosecutor relating to the subpoena *duces tecum* which, in turn, normally precedes a full-scale file search.

Where a criminal investigation has been commenced, therefore, it is frequently advantageous to follow a sequence in which counsel begins with one or two brief exploratory interviews of executives having general responsibility for the areas of the company's business relevant to the investigation. An experienced lawyer in these circumstances will always be skeptical about the information obtained in the early stages because it may later turn out that the information came from a tainted source, but every effort should be made to identify executives whose conduct is not likely to be the focus of the criminal investigation. These interviews can be followed by a highly selective search of files most likely to contain relevant and sensitive documents. This background helps the lawyers to organize the balance of the fact-gathering process in a reasonable way since they will then have obtained a substantially complete list of significant present and former employees and will have begun the process of document examination.

As in civil proceedings, some employees may refuse to participate in an interview. Presumably, any employer may reasonably require an employee to supply information to counsel on a subject within the employee's scope of employment. If the employee refuses, dismissal is the ultimate sanction. Notwithstanding the probable power to compel an interview, though, it is by no means clear that the power should be exercised. An unwilling employee is likely to be an uncooperative interviewee, and a discharged employee might retaliate by approaching the government and ultimately rendering testimony shaded as much as possible against his former employer. In such a circumstance, outright fabrication of adverse testimony has even been known to occur. As an alternative to discharge, the company may want to consider other means of gaining the desired information. Other, more cooperative employees can provide a framework within which relevant conduct can be considered, and the worst can sometimes justifiably be assumed based on an employee's reluctance to speak.

If a reluctant employee has retained counsel, it will frequently be the case that an interview can proceed on the basis of a joint-defense agreement. As noted earlier, such arrangements can be advantageous as a means of evaluating the probable exposure to prosecution and facilitation of a defense. On the other hand, because such joint-defense arrangements require confidentiality, which can be waived only with the consent of all parties involved, the company may find itself not only associating with positions it would never endorse but also possessing information it is not at liberty to disclose, even if it should desire to take a cooperative stance with the government. For such reasons, it may be best for company counsel and the employee to confer informally before proceeding with a joint-defense arrangement.

Once the interview process has commenced, it is particularly important, in light of the criminal investigation under way, that employees understand the importance of accuracy in describing their recollection of events. The term *accuracy* implies not only truthfulness but also a critical care to convey information on the basis of *testimonial quality* knowledge—that is, based on personal observation and recollection, as opposed to speculation and surmise. Although, of course, counsel should not foreclose the opportunity to hear a witness's suspicions and guesses, it is essential that the employee understand the difference and not get into a pattern of loose talk that will serve him ill if he is eventually called into the grand jury room.

Every experienced trial lawyer has encountered the situation in which, by reason of repeated recounting of a given story by a witness, a point is reached at which the witness is no longer able to draw a cognitive distinction between what the witness actually perceived and what has been discussed on prior occasions. There is considerable propensity for that type of confusion to develop in the course of a criminal investigation, particularly where the witness is repeatedly exposed to documents in an effort to refresh his recollection and suggestions as to the explanations for a given document and alternative descriptions of a particular meeting are pressed upon him by counsel. There is an obvious tension between the desire of counsel to learn as much as possible, as soon as possible, and the vital need to avoid confusing a witness by repeated preparatory interview sessions as the information is being developed. The best interviewer of a witness would, of course, be an attorney who knew exactly what had occurred, because that attorney would be best able to probe the accuracy of the witness's recollection when it deviated from the facts the interviewer knew to be true. Although that ideal can never be achieved in a criminal investigation involving complex transactions, experience suggests the importance of care in the interviewing process, so that when the employee is finally being prepared for his grand jury testimony, counsel will be sufficiently well-informed to contribute to a grand jury appearance in which the witness testifies truthfully and accurately and does not incorrectly implicate his employer. Although counsel cannot remake the facts, careful preparation can minimize the danger that a company will be indicted on inaccuracies and speculation that should not have found their way into the record.

Counsel experienced in criminal matters is also painfully aware that full disclosure from the client is not always easy to obtain. Civil case interviewing techniques may have to be modified to elicit information from persons who believe their own conduct to be criminally suspect, particularly where the conduct involved the circumvention of internal controls or departures from well-established business norms.

As with civil proceedings, development of a relationship with a witness that will produce meaningful disclosure is, of course, a matter of personal style on the part of counsel. Despite the urgency created by the criminal investigation, everyone should recognize that the process of obtaining information may take a little time and perhaps a series of conversations. The selection of counsel to conduct the interview is obviously important. Senior executives are unlikely to "confess" to a multi-person interview team that includes youthful-looking associates. Not infrequently, the interview will have to be conducted solely by a senior member of the team, and the best disclosures have sometimes occurred in a completely informal environment.

During the interview itself, the best interviewing attorneys are respectful and explicitly disavow any function as a judge or critic of the executive's conduct. As the interview proceeds, effective counsel is also sensitive to those areas in which the witness appears reluctant or to be holding back. Counsel may also find it unnecessary in a particular case to encourage a complete confession at a preliminary stage. When a senior executive admits to engaging in conduct that suggests complicity in a crime, it will be apparent that a major criminal problem exists, and at the initial stage it may be preferable to refrain from pressing hard for greater detail.

The Testimonial Grand Jury Phase

Once documents have been produced to the government, and the government has had an opportunity to review them, a criminal investigation typically proceeds into a new phase: the government's procurement of testimony. During this phase, government agents or prosecutors will either seek to interview corporate employees and other witnesses or subpoena them to testify before the grand jury. Frequently, law enforcement agents conduct an initial round of interviews, and the witnesses who are to testify before the grand jury are selected based upon those interviews. On the other hand, in some situations no preliminary interviews are conducted and interviews and grand jury testimony are pursued simultaneously, or the grand jury sessions occur before witnesses are interviewed.

Before a witness actually appears before a grand jury, careful preparation is critical. Memorializing the debriefing of witnesses who have just testified is equally important and, with diligence, defense counsel may become as knowledgeable about the government's case as is the prosecutor. Although some prosecutors may try to interfere with the counsel's debriefings, prosecutors have no right to do so. In addition, some prosecutors will seek to impose an order of secrecy upon the grand jury witness. There is no authority for preventing disclosure by the witness to his attorney.

Preparing a witness to testify before the grand jury is a significant undertaking, even if it is only for the production of documents. The witness is utterly alone in a treacherous situation where the witness must accurately answer questions posed inevitably in a leading fashion by a skeptical, and often hostile, prosecutor. The prosecutor seems irritated with certain answers—which he communicates quite effectively—and the grand jurors have blended into the furniture, save for the occasional snicker, which is produced on cue whenever the prosecutor wants to suggest to the witness that his testimony is not credible. Everything the witness says in this environment is under oath and recorded for possible use later. Anxiety is in no short supply.

And there is no quick relief. A grand jury witness does not have the same rights as someone who has been arrested and is being interrogated by the police. There is no right to refuse to speak unless the witness can assert a constitutional or other privilege. A witness has no recognized right to be advised of his Fifth Amendment privilege not to be compelled to be a witness against himself. A witness has no right to be told that he is a potential defendant or target of the grand jury investigation. A witness has no right to have counsel present in the grand jury room, although a witness may leave the grand jury room to consult with counsel. And there is no constitutional right to have counsel appointed at the grand jury stage because no criminal proceeding has yet been initiated nor is it the equivalent of a custodial police interrogation.

To a limited extent, prosecutorial policy may provide a witness with some minimal protections. For example, it has been the policy of the United States Department of Justice to advise witnesses of their Fifth Amendment privilege against self-incrimination. Similarly, it is the policy of the Department of Justice to advise a witness that he is a target, if such is the case. On the whole, though, the process of testifying before a grand jury is fraught with peril. And once the witness has entered the grand jury room, he is almost entirely on his own.

A particular challenge to the grand jury witness is the preservation of applicable privileges against testimony. These are obviously important to the company's and the witness's criminal defense. They are also important to the defense of the parallel civil litigation. Before the grand jury, four privileges in particular come into play: the Fifth Amendment privilege against self-incrimination, the attorney-client privilege, the attorney work-product doctrine, and the joint-defense privilege.

The Fifth Amendment privilege.   The Fifth Amendment privilege against self-incrimination stands out in importance in a criminal investigation. As mentioned at the outset, the privilege itself is *personal*, meaning that it applies only to natural individuals. For documents, it protects only the compelled production of self-incriminating documents that are the personal property of the person claiming the privilege or papers in the person's possession in a purely personal capacity.

A witness may assert the privilege on the basis that the answers may be incriminating under either state or federal law and may also assert the privilege on the basis that the answers may be incriminating under foreign law, although the authority for that is less clear. The privilege must be asserted in response to each individual question; a blanket refusal to answer is not adequate.

The privilege against self-incrimination can be claimed in any proceeding whether it is civil or criminal, administrative or judicial. As shall be considered later, the privilege may also be asserted at a deposition taken in a civil case. The compelled testimony must expose the witness to possible criminal prosecution. A witness may not refuse to answer because it would place him in danger of physical harm, degrade him, or incriminate a third party.

As a matter of practice, grand jury targets can usually avoid the personally unnerving experience of asserting the Fifth Amendment privilege in front of the grand jurors by providing the prosecutor with a letter confirming the witness's intention to assert the privilege. Justice Department policy states that "if a 'target' of the investigation . . . and his/her attorney state in writing and signed by both that the 'target' will refuse to testify on Fifth Amendment grounds, the witness ordinarily should be excused from testifying unless the grand jury and the U.S. Attorney agree to insist on the appearance." The company may be well-advised to utilize this procedure to avoid potential prejudice and embarrassment and to avoid the not uncommon situation in which an executive is provoked into departing from his Fifth Amendment silence and begins answering questions in the grand jury room.

When a grand jury witness, in response to a question, does not assert the privilege but instead gives an answer that may be incriminating, an express waiver will be deemed to have been made. An unintentional waiver can be exceedingly unfortunate because, once a witness voluntarily reveals incriminating facts, he may not thereafter refuse to disclose the details. Once the waiver has occurred, for each subsequent question the appropriate determination is whether a responsive answer would subject the witness to a "real danger of further incrimination."

A witness who has previously discussed facts relevant to a grand jury investigation with an FBI agent, an investigator, or a government attorney may still assert the Fifth Amendment privilege before the grand jury as to testimony concerning those same facts. Likewise, a witness who has testified before the SEC or in a civil deposition may still assert the Fifth Amendment privilege before the grand jury as to the same facts.

The attorney-client privilege. As in civil proceedings, the attorney-client privilege is applicable in proceedings before a grand jury. The privilege excuses a witness from testifying about (a) a communication, (b) made in confidence, (c) to an attorney by a person who is, or is about to become, a client, (d) for the purpose of obtaining legal advice from that attorney. The privilege is available to corporate clients as well as to individuals. It applies to communications from the attorney to the client as well as those from the client to the attorney.

Of particular significance to grand jury testimony is the fact that the attorney-client privilege may be waived where there has been a *voluntary* disclosure of otherwise privileged matter. Disclosure made pursuant to court order is not voluntary. Disclosure made pursuant to grand jury subpoena *duces tecum*, in contrast, *is* voluntary, insofar as the claim of attorney-client privilege can be asserted and maintained by a timely objection to the subpoena. Accordingly, as in response to a civil document request, preservation of the attorney-client privilege before a grand jury requires a thorough review of documents to eliminate privileged materials before supplying them to the grand jury.

The attorney work-product doctrine. The attorney work-product doctrine often operates closely with the attorney-client privilege. The doctrine protects written statements, private memoranda, and personal recollections prepared or formed by the attorney "in the course of preparation for litigation after a claim has arisen." It does not cover work performed for independent reasons that may have some application to a litigation later. The privilege is a *qualified* one, meaning that, upon a showing "of undue hardship" or "substantial need," documents otherwise covered by the doctrine may be ordered produced.

Both the attorney-client privilege and the work-product doctrine are subject to an important limitation. That is the so-called crime fraud exception. Pursuant to that exception, otherwise-privileged communications that further an ongoing or future crime or fraud are not protected as work product or, for that matter, as attorney-client confidences. To the extent that the privilege has been invoked to prevent disclosure of communications with counsel regarding ongoing misreported items in the company's financial statements, the privilege's applicability may be challenged.

The joint-defense privilege. The joint-defense privilege, already mentioned earlier, is applicable when otherwise-privileged information is disclosed to actual or potential co-defendants in the course of a joint defense. The privilege applies, at its broadest, to any exchanges made for the purpose of a common defense. These might include discussions between a potential defendant and counsel for other potential defendants, disclosures to agents retained by counsel for purpose of pursuing a common defense, and possibly even to discussions among potential co-defendants themselves.

For reasons discussed earlier, the joint-defense privilege is particularly important in the context of a criminal investigation arising out of accounting irregularities, given the usefulness of communications among those involved as a means of learning the focus and scope of the investigation. It is therefore of great importance that, in such a criminal investigation of accounting irregularities, a sufficient *community of interest*, at least among some of those involved, will frequently exist so that the joint-defense privilege may be properly invoked. The joint-defense privilege applies even if those sharing the information are not allies in all respects as long as the information disclosed is in furtherance of some common interest. Ordinarily, subjects and targets of a grand jury will have a sufficiently common defense interest so that their disclosures will be covered by the privilege.

The joint-defense privilege cannot be waived by disclosure to third parties without the consent of all parties who share the privilege. Such a disclosure by a member of the defense group would waive the privilege only as it applied to that party. As a practical matter, this may limit the advisability of the company entering into a joint-defense arrangement insofar as nondisclosure might violate otherwise applicable disclosure responsibilities or render any cooperation with the government less valuable.

Two additional points should be made regarding the joint-defense privilege. First, although the privilege applies to communications between various clients and counsel involved in joint-defense efforts, it is in practice inadvisable for executives themselves to attend all joint-defense meetings. Executives attending such meetings may come away with information they did not know before, and such information can influence the executive's memory of events or may convince the executive to make a proffer with the required information. It is possible that a nervous executive will inadvertently disclose joint-defense material during an interview with the government or in grand jury testimony, and such disclosure can waive the privilege as it applies to that executive. The more prudent approach is to limit the group to defense attorneys and for each attorney to relay joint-defense information to the executive when the attorney feels it appropriate.

Second, any joint-defense group member may waive his right to invoke his privilege by compromising the confidentiality of the information shared, even though such a waiver does not waive the privilege for all participants. Because the attorney-client privilege may be waived even through inadvertent disclosure, it is important to keep tight control on the dissemination of the information to ensure that it not reach parties beyond the joint-defense group. A joint-defense agreement that binds the participants to strict confidentiality should be drafted.

Prosecutorial Status and Immunity

The government divides witnesses into three categories: targets, subjects, and witnesses. A *target* is a putative defendant, someone as to whom the government has information that at least currently suggests that this person will likely be indicted. A *subject* is a person about whom the government is not sure. This person could possibly have criminal liability or could be merely a witness. His status could also change during the course of the investigation and frequently does. A person who is a *witness* is one who the government believes has no possible culpability but who is simply asked to give testimony because he or she happens to have some knowledge that would further the investigation. For example, a secretary who might be called to testify that she typed a particular document for her boss would almost certainly be regarded as only a witness. An employee who can supply background information as to the identity of individuals with various responsibilities or the nature of certain corporate procedures would also be a witness.

For those called upon to give testimony to a grand jury, one issue of the utmost importance involves the grant of *immunity*. As a general matter, absent a Fifth Amendment claim of privilege, the duty to give testimony to the grand jury is absolute. However, because it is only from the mouths of those having knowledge of the conduct under investigation that the facts can be ascertained, the government often has no choice but to take evidence from those who would be implicated by what they have to say. Under such circumstances, the government must provide immunity to those whom it compels to testify if such testimony would incriminate the witness. Unless immunity is granted, such testimony will be suppressed along with its fruits if it is compelled over a valid claim of Fifth Amendment privilege.

Two broad categories of formal immunity are recognized: transactional immunity and use immunity. *Transactional immunity* precludes the government from prosecuting a witness for any offense (or *transaction*) related to the witness's compelled testimony. *Use immunity* precludes the government from using directly or indirectly a witness's compelled testimony in a prosecution of that witness. In the federal system, a grand jury witness who is faced with a Fifth Amendment problem may be accorded statutory use immunity in return for testifying. Formal transactional immunity, in contrast, is not available in the federal courts, but can be obtained by an agreement with the prosecutor in the form of a promise not to prosecute. Use immunity is not available to a company because it is contingent upon an assertion of the Fifth Amendment privilege that the company does not have.

Informal immunity, as opposed to the statutory use immunity described above, is sometimes provided by the government. *Informal immunity*, sometimes known as *letter immunity*, is often used to permit an interview of a witness outside the grand jury, frequently as a step in a process resulting in an agreement to cooperate with the investigation. Prosecutors regard the use of informal immunity as a tool to enhance the effectiveness and efficiency of an investigation and curtail the use of grand jury time. Informal immunity is not governed by statute but is essentially a matter of contract. A witness who has been granted such immunity sometimes later enters into a nonprosecution agreement, essentially conferring a form of transactional immunity whereby if the witness fully cooperates and testifies truthfully pursuant to the terms of the agreement, the government promises not to prosecute him for the crimes about which he has testified. This promise is generally binding only in the district in which it is made; unlike formal immunity, it may not apply in other federal districts or in state courts. It is not as safe a guarantee for the witness, not only because it is not binding in other districts, but also because a failure by the witness to abide by the agreement's terms may enable the government to prosecute the witness, using the information the witness has already provided. When formal immunity is granted, the government can never use the testimony against the witness, except as part of a prosecution for perjury.

Informal immunity is almost always conferred by a letter addressed to the witness and signed by the prosecutor or his supervisor. Most typically, the letter will recite that the government agrees to forbear from making direct or indirect use of the witness's statements in any subsequent criminal proceeding involving the witness for violations of specific crimes that are then under investigation arising out of the witness's conduct within a specific geographic area or during a specific period of time. The letter typically will also provide that the statements of the witness in the interview may be used against the witness to impeach the witness's testimony in any subsequent proceeding, including a subsequent prosecution of the witness, and either for impeachment or substantive evidence in any subsequent case against the witness for perjury or making false statements under oath. The informal letter will also make it explicit that no other agreement exists between the witness and the government.

Because obtaining statutory immunity is a somewhat elaborate internal process within the Department of Justice, informal immunity in the form of an agreement not to prosecute is granted much more frequently, particularly when time does not allow for the more elaborate process to be used.

Corporate Criminal Liability for Employee Actions

Employees who seek to advance the interests of a company in ways that are criminal may cause the imposition of vicarious liability on the company. A criminal investigation of a company's accounting irregularities, accordingly, inevitably poses the risk of criminal liability for the company. Indeed, as the investigation proceeds, the company's liability may be so thoroughly established that the company's stance, to the extent it has been adversarial, will shift to one of cooperation and possibly plea discussions.

Theoretically, a corporation's ability to disassociate itself from the criminal acts of its employees should be aided by the principle of *vicarious liability*. Under that principle, corporate liability for employees' criminal acts is limited to those instances in which the criminal acts were undertaken within the scope of an employee's authority. But what falls within the scope of an employee's authority is interpreted broadly, so broadly that even if an employee acts contrary to instruction or policy, the corporate employer may still be liable. Moreover, the law often imposes on an employer the duty to supervise and control the actions of an employee performing almost any job-related activity. Failure to control an employee's conduct can suggest that the employer *adopted and ratified* the conduct. Or an employee's action may be found to be within the scope of his apparent authority.

It is no impediment to vicarious corporate liability that the offense required a culpable mental state, such as intent or knowledge. For corporate liability to be so imposed, however, the wrongdoing employee must have acted with an intent to benefit the company. This intent-to-benefit rule avoids the anomaly of imposing liability on a company that is the victim, rather than the putative beneficiary, of its employee's criminal conduct. Depending on the particular circumstances, the conduct involved in a deliberate misstatement of a company's financial statements, if serious enough to be the subject of a criminal prosecution, may be found to have been undertaken to benefit the company.

Ironically, a company can also be held accountable for a crime when there is no single employee that could be convicted. This is the result of the *collective-knowledge doctrine*, pursuant to which knowledge can be imputed to a company based on the aggregate knowledge of its employees as a group. Therefore, a company may be found to have knowingly engaged in a crime based on evidence that one employee knew the facts relating to one element of the offense and a second or third employee knew facts relating to additional elements.

Corporate Indemnification for Counsel Fees

Every state (including Delaware and New York, home to a large number of public companies) has legislation providing for corporate indemnification of expenses (including legal fees) of directors, officers, and sometimes other corporate personnel in defending legal action brought against them in their official capacities. These statutes vary but, generally, in order to be eligible for indemnification, the executive must have acted in good faith for a purpose he believed to be in the best interest of the company. When there is a criminal proceeding, an executive normally must have had no reasonable cause to believe that his conduct was unlawful. However, indemnification may be appropriate even if the executive is convicted. And in Delaware and New York, as well as some other states, if the executive is successful on the merits, the law requires that he shall be indemnified. Authorization for indemnification is generally made by the board of directors, provided that the directors are not parties; by the board upon the written opinion of independent legal counsel; or by the shareholders. Notice to the shareholders is sometimes required. Frequently, advance payments are authorized, with the proviso that the executive must undertake to reimburse the company if it is ultimately determined that he is not entitled to indemnification.

Where the executive is designated a *target* of the investigation, the company may generally withhold advancements of counsel fees and ultimately have no obligation to pay these expenses. The company may nevertheless choose to advance these expenses on the basis of the presumption of innocence unless and until the executive is indicted or persuasive evidence of guilt is developed. The same considerations arise when the executive is designated a *subject*, although here the company may conclude that it has a greater obligation to pay attorneys' fees. In either case, the company may want to require an undertaking that it will be reimbursed in the event that it turns out that the executive is culpable. As with any undertaking, if enforcement appears likely to be problematic, adequate security can be arranged.

There may be instances in which the prosecutor or an investigator seeks to obtain the cooperation of a corporate executive by encouraging the company to discipline executives who do not cooperate. For example, if an executive indicates that he intends to assert his Fifth Amendment privilege against self-incrimination, the investigator might ask the company to coerce him into testifying. Similarly, for its own policy reasons the company may wish to dissuade an executive from asserting the Fifth Amendment privilege. There are considerable reasons to resist the pressure to do so. To begin with, there may be some danger of liability if the company fires or disciplines an executive for exercising a constitutional right. Second, the imposition of such discipline implicitly reflects a judgment that any executive who refuses to testify is necessarily guilty. It may well be that the executive is being advised by his attorney not to cooperate without immunity, not because the attorney thinks the executive has any liability, but because the attorney is simply being appropriately cautious.

If the government appears to be proceeding on a theory that the company is a target and the executive is also a target or a subject of an investigation because he furthered the company's interest by criminal means, the company will frequently advance payment of the executive's legal expenses. Particularly at the outset of an investigation, when the executive has not even been formally accused, much less convicted of a crime, allegations that he has furthered the company's interest by illegal means indicate that his need for an attorney arises out of his employment by the company. Under these circumstances, the company may justifiably conclude that it is obligated to pay his legal expenses.

Depending on his level of seniority and the extent of ostensible wrong-doing, a company's refusal to pay an employee's legal expenses in these circumstances can have a serious effect on the morale of its workforce and might be viewed by many as fundamentally unfair. An employee could complain that he got into trouble because he was trying to help the company and, even though he has not been formally accused, the company is refusing to back him up. On the other hand, there may be circumstances where refusal to pay attorneys' fees is appropriate. For example, if it seems clear even at the outset that the employee is guilty and if the employee has violated company rules or policy designed to prevent the company from getting into criminal trouble, then the company may understandably determine not to pay for his representation.

With respect to witnesses, it is normally appropriate that a company pay for their representation by outside counsel. The one factor important to emphasize is that, in this circumstance, it must be clear to the witness and to the attorney that the attorney is representing the witness and not the company. A company that is a target may have interests that conflict with the interests of employees who are witnesses. If an employee decides that he does not wish his attorney to report to the company about the information or testimony the employee has provided the government, the attorney must honor that wish and the company must understand it. An attorney who represents the company as well as the witness will ordinarily not want to accept such a condition.

Separate Counsel for Targets and Subjects

When a criminal investigation has a number of subjects or targets, as will frequently be the case where a criminal investigation has been commenced as a result of accounting irregularities, those involved will often be tempted to seek common representation. The temptation is understandable. Lawyers are expensive. More than that, inefficiencies in communication and work can seemingly be limited when one lawyer is doing the work for several executives at the same time.

Nonetheless, separate counsel for each executive who is the focus of an investigation is often the better course. A lawyer who represents two or more targets or subjects, including a lawyer who represents an individual target and a corporate target, may have an inherent conflict of interest, and the simultaneous representation of such potential defendants is fraught with danger. For example, it may be in the interest of one of the lawyer's clients to cooperate and testify against the other, but the lawyer cannot recommend that course to his client without violating the interests of the other. Moreover, even if the lawyer should withdraw from the representation of the client in whose interest it is to cooperate, the lawyer may put himself in a situation where at trial he has to cross-examine a former client from whom he has received confidential and privileged information. The lawyer cannot do so and his only course may be to withdraw from the representation of both clients.

Nor does a client "waiver" of a conflict necessarily solve the problem. Recent court opinions allow judges to disqualify lawyers who represent more than one person even if both clients waive any conflict. This means that if a lawyer represents more than one person and a conflict develops, a judge may disqualify the lawyer from representing either person even if both provide a waiver.

Even beyond the dangers posed by the potential for conflicts of interest, a hazard arising from the simultaneous representation of several executives in a criminal investigation results from the possibility of allegations of obstruction of justice. When one lawyer represents several individuals, he is fully aware of what each of the targets or subjects is doing and saying with respect to the investigation and he is able to alert someone in the event that a target or subject begins to implicate others. It is unethical, and indeed potentially illegal, for a lawyer to do so, and when one lawyer represents several targets or subjects and the government is making no headway in the investigation, a frustrated prosecutor may look at the lawyer and the company and the possibility of obstruction-of-justice charges. Indeed, there are times when the government is unable to prove the actual offense it is investigating but manages to bring an indictment nonetheless because the target of the investigation has either committed perjury or obstructed the investigation in some way.

Plea Discussions and Sentencing Considerations

In many conspiratorial offenses, the government makes a deal with one of the conspirators and offers him leniency for his testimony against others, including the company. Sometimes this leniency may be immunity from prosecution; at other times it may be a plea bargain to reduced charges, structured in such way as to lessen the risk of incarceration or, at least, the length of any incarceration. A lawyer who seeks to negotiate with the government on behalf of a subject or target hopes his client will be treated as a witness and not a defendant. Preferably, in exchange for testimony, an executive would receive some form of immunity along the lines discussed above.

If, however, the government is unwilling to offer the executive immunity and the case against the executive is strong, the executive may have no choice but to enter a plea agreement. This also is an arrangement with the prosecutor that is a matter of contract and the terms may vary. A typical plea agreement would be one in which the executive pleads guilty to fewer crimes than the government can readily prove and may include an agreement to cooperate fully with the government. Such a plea agreement is not available in every case. In some instances, the executive will be the ultimate target and there will be no one of significance for him to testify against.

The ability of an executive to obtain formal immunity, a non-prosecution agreement, or a plea bargain varies with the strength of the government's case, the executive's perceived culpability, the government's need for his testimony, and the executive's qualities as a witness. Therefore, a lawyer faced with the task of getting the best possible terms for his client will have one important objective in mind: convincing the government that to pursue whatever it is seeking to prove against others, the government absolutely must have this particular executive's testimony.

The process by which the lawyer tries to so persuade the government is known as a *proffer*. The lawyer generally finds out from the prosecutor in what areas the prosecutor is looking for testimony and attempts to obtain a promise that if the executive can provide that testimony, then he will be immunized or some other deal struck. The lawyer then makes representations about what the executive can testify to, but the lawyer tries to be as general or hypothetical as possible so as not to give the prosecutor anything specific enough as a lead. Throughout the process, the lawyer is walking a tightrope. The lawyer must try to give the prosecutor enough to keep him interested, but not so much that the prosecutor can obtain the evidence without the executive's assistance.

Sometimes this is not enough and the prosecutor will want to talk to the executive personally. Before this is done, the executive will request informal immunity by means of the letter agreement described earlier. This is frequently referred to as an *off-the-record discussion* or *proffer discussion*. If these discussions prove fruitful and the prosecutor finds the executive to be a valuable and credible witness, then the prosecutor may offer the executive immunity or a plea agreement.

In the federal system, plea discussions will focus extensively on possible sentences under the Federal Sentencing Guidelines. For most defendants found guilty of a crime (whether by plea or verdict after trial) under these guidelines, the judge has exceedingly limited discretion in imposing sentence. A sentencing range is computed by starting with the *offense level* (a number assigned to each federal offense), to which one adds *points* reflecting the defendant's criminal history, certain aggravating factors particular to the offense (including, for example, enhancements for "more than minimal planning" or "breach of trust") and, for offenses involving fraud (such as accounting irregularities), the points corresponding to the amount of loss. For example, a typical corporate executive convicted of a single count of mail fraud in a scheme resulting in an aggregate loss to shareholders of $2.5 million will, in most cases, be sentenced in the range of 37 to 46 months of imprisonment. If the loss were $10 million, that defendant's sentence would be increased to a range of 46 to 57 months. A corporation convicted of the same offense (assuming it has 200 employees and a member of senior management participated in the scheme) will receive a base fine of $2.5 million, subject to multipliers, resulting in a fine range of $4 million to $8 million. The company may also be ordered to pay restitution and a remedial order may be entered as a condition of the company's probation to address the harm caused by the offense or prevent its recurrence. The sentencing judge can mitigate the sentence by crediting the defendant with points, but only in a narrowly circumscribed manner. For example, a defendant's sentence can be reduced up to three levels for "acceptance of responsibility" by a guilty plea.

For a corporate defendant, the potential sentence can be mitigated by up to three levels if, prior to the offense, the corporation had an effective compliance program (Exhibit 10–4). Using the earlier example, the fine could be reduced to a range of $2.5 million to $5 million. According to the Federal Sentencing Guidelines:

> An "effective program to prevent and detect violations of law" means a program that has been reasonably designed, implemented, and enforced so that it generally will be effective in preventing and detecting criminal conduct. Failure to prevent or detect the instant offense, by itself, does not mean that the program was not effective.

Exhibit 10–4. Federal Sentencing Guidelines: An Effective Program to Prevent and Detect Violations of Law

The precise actions necessary for an effective program to prevent and detect violations of law will depend upon a number of factors. Among the relevant factors are:

1. *Size of the organization*—The requisite degree of formality of a program to prevent and detect violations of law will vary with the size of the organization: the larger the organization, the more formal the program typically should be. A larger organization generally should have established written policies defining the standards and procedures to be followed by its employees and other agents.

2. *Likelihood that certain offenses may occur because of the nature of its business*—If because of the nature of an organization's business there is a substantial risk that certain types of offenses may occur, management must have taken steps to prevent and detect those types of offenses. For example, if an organization handles toxic substances, it must have established standards and procedures designed to ensure that those substances are properly handled at all times. If an organization employs sales personnel who have flexibility in setting prices, it must have established standards and procedures designed to prevent and detect price-fixing. If an organization employs sales personnel who have flexibility to represent the material characteristics of a product, it must have established standards and procedures designed to prevent fraud.

3. *Prior history of the organization*—An organization's prior history may indicate types of offenses that it should have taken actions to prevent. Recurrence of misconduct similar to that which an organization has previously committed casts doubt on whether it took all reasonable steps to prevent such misconduct.

An organization's failure to incorporate and follow applicable industry practice or the standards called for by any applicable governmental regulation weighs against a finding of an effective program to prevent and detect violations of law.

The hallmark of an effective program to prevent and detect violations of law is that the organization exercised due diligence in seeking to prevent and detect criminal conduct by its employees and other agents. Due diligence requires at a minimum that the organization must have taken the following types of steps:

1. The organization must have established compliance standards and procedures to be followed by its employees and other agents that are reasonably capable of reducing the prospect of criminal conduct.

2. Specific individual(s) within high-level personnel of the organization must have been assigned overall responsibility to oversee compliance with such standards and procedures.

3. The organization must have used due care not to delegate substantial discretionary authority to individuals whom the organization knew, or should have known through the exercise of due diligence, had a propensity to engage in illegal activities.

4. The organization must have taken steps to communicate effectively its standards and procedures to all employees and other agents, e.g., by requiring participation in training programs or by disseminating publications that explain in a practical manner what is required.

5. The organization must have taken reasonable steps to achieve compliance with its standards, e.g., by utilizing monitoring and auditing systems reasonably designed to detect criminal conduct by its employees and other agents and by having in place and publicizing a reporting system whereby employees and other agents could report criminal conduct by others within the organization without fear of retribution.

6. The standards must have been consistently enforced through appropriate disciplinary mechanisms, including, as appropriate, discipline of individuals responsible for the failure to detect an offense. Adequate discipline of individuals responsible for an offense is a necessary component of enforcement; however, the form of discipline that will be appropriate will be case specific.

7. After an offense has been detected, the organization must have taken all reasonable steps to respond appropriately to the offense and to prevent further similar offenses—including any necessary modifications to its program to prevent and detect violations of law.

A federal sentencing judge has no discretion to impose a sentence below the guidelines-sentencing range. Any such sentence can be challenged by the government in an appellate court and such sentences have been routinely corrected. The only permitted exception occurs when the defendant renders significant cooperation to the government, which permits the government (and only the government) to apply to the court for an order allowing a downward departure from the guidelines range. For most defendants this is a critical juncture in the process, because it is the only practical way to avoid a sentencing range that requires the imposition of a jail sentence. And because possible sentencing outcomes in the federal system have been narrowed and are often reasonably predictable, that critical juncture can arrive early and become dominant in discussions between counsel and the prosecutor.

Other Responsibilities of Counsel for a Target Company

As a criminal investigation progresses, the company's attorney must continue to monitor its progress, primarily by interviewing witnesses called before the grand jury. Witnesses should be promptly and thoroughly debriefed by counsel after their testimony. Debriefing should be done immediately after the testimony is completed—even a few hours delay can result in significant memory loss. Efforts should be made to learn from counsel for other witnesses, pursuant to the joint-privilege doctrine, the nature of their testimony. Debriefing should include questions about the number of jurors present and the conduct of the proceedings, both to prepare future witnesses and to discover any improprieties that may undermine the validity of any indictments.

In many cases, information about an ongoing investigation is leaked to the press by witnesses or by the government. Counsel must coordinate responses to press inquiries so that any statements are consistent with its defense strategy. This is often a tricky problem because the company and its employees will be tempted to respond to all inquiries, but by doing so, they may say something that discloses strategy secrets or that constitutes an admission that the government can use as evidence.

Counsel may also have to respond to additional subpoenas for documents. As the outline of the government's case becomes clear, he must put together a defense case. Except in the most hopeless of cases, the lawyer's goal will be to persuade the government to decline an indictment. In most instances, the lawyer will make written and oral presentations to the prosecutors and, where necessary, to the prosecutors' superiors. It is almost always possible to get a hearing within the Department of Justice or the U.S. Attorney's office at supervisory levels, and it is sometimes possible to meet with the Assistant Attorney General or U.S. Attorney ultimately responsible for the case.

Many cases are successfully resolved by persuading the government that its case is not likely to succeed at trial or that it should exercise prosecutorial discretion not to seek an indictment. The prosecutor obviously recognizes that no indictment should be recommended unless the prosecutor is personally convinced that the defendant's guilt can be proven beyond a reasonable doubt. In the context of a prosecution of the company arising out of its accounting irregularities, at this late stage the inaccuracy of the financial statements may be assumed and all of the discussions may be centered on whether any single employee acted with the willfulness required for a criminal charge. Obviously, if no single employee can be charged because of a failure of evidence, the company's position in opposition to an indictment is strengthened.

But even if an executive is likely to be charged, the company may still have arguments available against indictment. If the conduct at issue can credibly be characterized as aberrational or if it involved extraordinary efforts to circumvent sound internal controls and compliance procedures, the company may present itself as a victim. The company's early cooperation may be pointed to as evidence of its decision to disassociate itself from the errant executive and as the best argument to avoid indictment. Indeed, there have been many apparently hopeless cases in which, because cooperation was begun early—sometimes even before the criminal investigation was commenced by the company's voluntary disclosure—indictment was avoided.

Other factors may influence a prosecutor's charging decision. For example, it may be that by this stage all related litigation has been resolved and the victims of the company's accounting fraud have been made whole by settlement or otherwise. Since one of the purposes of a criminal conviction of the company in the federal system—restitution to victims—has already been accomplished, arguably an additional financial penalty in the form of a criminal fine will be borne by innocent shareholders. In other cases, discussion may center on whether there is a strong prosecutorial interest at stake, such as whether a prosecution of the company serves the goals of specific or general deterrence, or whether other mechanisms, such as enforcement by the SEC or private litigation, are sufficient.

Only if all these efforts prove fruitless and the case cannot be disposed of, does a trial become necessary.

Parallel Proceedings

A company caught up in a federal criminal investigation arising out of accounting irregularities must always be alert to the existence of parallel proceedings. These might include state criminal investigations, administrative proceedings, civil damage or injunctive suits, tax investigations, or even congressional hearings. The existence of such parallel proceedings adds still more complexity to the company's problems.

Because of the dual-sovereignty doctrine, it is possible for the federal government and a state to prosecute separately an executive or the company for exactly the same conduct. Double jeopardy prevents the federal government from trying a person twice for the same conduct, but the federal government can try a defendant for the same conduct for which he has been previously tried by a state. Thus, for example, an employee of a public company who causes the dissemination of false and misleading financial statements might be charged by the state with violations of the state laws against the creation of fraudulent business records and might also be charged by the federal government under similar statutes that apply to interstate communication facilities, the mails, or the purchase or sale of securities.

The Department of Justice has a rule that, in normal cases, it will not prosecute a defendant for conduct for which he has previously been prosecuted by a state. But there are exceptions. Moreover, the rule does not apply to state prosecutors. And state prosecutors, who frequently are elected political officials, may feel impelled to bring a parallel prosecution, particularly if it is a case that is likely to generate favorable publicity. Therefore, a lawyer who negotiates with a federal prosecutor on behalf of his client must bear in mind the possibility that he may have a problem with the state prosecutor and must make sure that any agreements that he enters with the federal government do not come back to haunt him in negotiating with the state.

Of considerable concern to the company and its officers and directors will also be the civil class action litigations. The existence of this parallel litigation is particularly troublesome during the pendency of a criminal investigation insofar as the defense of one may compromise the defense of the other. For example, it may be important to the defense of the criminal proceeding for a particular executive to assert his Fifth Amendment right against self-incrimination. However, unlike in a criminal proceeding, the assertion of that Fifth Amendment right in a civil proceeding may be used as the basis for a negative inference against the defendant. More than that, a civil jury of normal temperament may be expected to have a severely negative reaction to an executive who so declines to testify before it. As a practical matter, an optimum defense to both the civil and the criminal actions may be essentially impossible.

In a ranking of difficult choices, the company will likely conclude that preserving defenses to criminal charges by having innocent executives assert their Fifth Amendment rights is far preferable, even at the risk of a weakened position in civil litigation. Hence, a settlement of the class action litigation becomes all the more desirable. It may be of some consolation that, while settlement of such litigation in the wake of accounting irregularities is frequently painful, restitution to shareholders may operate to the advantage of those involved in the criminal investigation in negotiations with the prosecutor.

CHAPTER 11

WHAT'S AN AUDIT COMMITTEE TO DO?

Michael R. Young

Cleopatra: Horrible villain! or I'll spurn thine eyes
Like balls before me; I'll unhair thy head:
Thou shalt be whipp'd with wire, and stew'd in brine,
Smarting in lingering pickle.

Messenger: Gracious madam,
I that do bring the news made not the match.

Cleopatra: Though it be honest,
it is never good to bring bad news.

—Antony and Cleopatra, Act 2, Scene v.

Begin with a proposition: An ounce of prevention is worth a pound of cure. In few other business contexts is that as true as in the context of accounting irregularities. The costs arising out of the discovery of accounting irregularities are extraordinary. Once irregularities have surfaced, a Securities and Exchange Commission (SEC) investigation is all but inevitable. A multi-million dollar settlement of the class action litigation is a given. Delisting by the National Association of Securities Dealers (NASD) or the New York Stock Exchange (NYSE) is foreseeable if not likely. The costs include the possibility of a criminal investigation and, in serious cases, senior corporate executives going to prison. According to one report, once accounting irregularities have surfaced, it is more likely than not that the company will soon be undergoing a bankruptcy or other major structural change.

There are, therefore, compelling reasons for a board of directors to take every reasonable measure to prevent accounting irregularities from occurring in the first place. Here's another one. At its most basic level, the installation of a system to prevent accounting irregularities involves the enhancement of the organization's systems of communication, its flow of information, and its institutional level of integrity. Such improvements will do more than help prevent accounting irregularities. They will also help the bottom line.

Chapter 11 explores the development of a system of corporate governance and financial reporting directed to the prevention and early detection of accounting irregularities. In other words, it explores primarily the configuration and operation of the audit committee. The topics addressed are these: First, the chapter reviews briefly the role of the audit committee in overseeing the integrity of financial reporting systems. Second, the chapter proposes a somewhat new approach to audit committee oversight including, in particular, the identification of just a handful of key objectives. Third, the chapter goes on to discuss the configuration of an audit committee; systems to provide for the flow of information to the audit committee; and, in particular, the audit committee's interaction with senior management, the outside auditor, and internal audit. Finally, the chapter gives some practical advice on maximizing the effectiveness of audit committee oversight.

Financial Reporting and the Audit Committee

The audit committee has not always been viewed as a keystone to a successful financial reporting system. Thirty years ago, the notion of an active audit committee was referred to as not much more than a "concept" worthy of debate. Responsibility for financial reporting, much like every other aspect of corporate conduct, was viewed as falling primarily on senior management.

More recently, however, perceptions of corporate governance have taken into account the following. No matter how good its intentions, senior management will always be subject to pressure for performance. The pressure will come from shareholders. It will come from creditors. It will come from financial analysts. A viable system of financial reporting has to accept the reality that such pressure will exist.

While it is incumbent upon senior management to strive to the utmost for integrity in financial reporting, the evolving view is that senior management therefore needs support. That support is to come from the board of directors. It is increasingly the view that it is a board function to see that the fundamentals of a working financial reporting system are in place and that those fundamentals will act as a check and balance on management to keep the pressure from getting out of hand.

An entire board of directors, of course, is too clumsy effectively to fulfill this objective. It is thus that serious responsibility for integrity in financial reporting is being placed upon a committee of the board—the audit committee. Hence the increasing attention given to the audit committee's responsibility in overseeing management's installation of a financial reporting system that minimizes the risk that accounting irregularities will occur. As summarized by SEC Chairman Arthur Levitt in his seminal September 28, 1998, speech, "qualified, committed, independent and tough-minded audit committees represent the most reliable guardians of the public interest."

Checklists, Checklists, Checklists

For an audit committee seeking to fulfill this objective, one thing is for sure. It will find no shortage of checklists of tasks for the audit committee to undertake. Checklists for audit committees have been published by virtually all the national accounting firms in their audit committee how-to books. Checklists have been published by the AICPA. Checklists regularly appear in newsletters, articles, and committee recommendations. Checklists are seemingly everywhere.

There is just one problem. If audit committee members were genuinely to undertake all of the tasks listed on the checklists, they would have little time for anything else—like their day jobs. One representative audit committee checklist lists 36 different time-consuming tasks.

Checklists are certainly a handy reference tool, but they carry with them dangers even beyond the need of individual audit committee members to hold a full-time job. One is the danger of what might be referred to as a "checklist mentality"—a mindset that dutifully marching through a checklist will necessarily lead to a successful financial reporting system. The audit profession periodically has to remind itself that a checklist mentality simply does not work. There's no reason to think that such an approach would work any better for an audit committee.

Another weakness with excessive fidelity to a checklist is the danger that, when marching through the checklist, an inclination will exist to give everything equal time. That is to say that a checklist of 36 separate items contributes little to an understanding of those two or three that are critical as compared to others that may be merely important or not really important at all. The critical, the important, and the unimportant all tend to get equal treatment.

Still another problem with a focus on checklists stems from their unhelpfulness in establishing the correct allocation of responsibility between the oversight function of the audit committee and the hands-on responsibilities of those whom the audit committee is to oversee—such as the internal audit department and the outside auditor. For example, one checklist establishes as a supposed duty of the audit committee to "review filings with the SEC and other published documents containing the company's financial statements and consider whether the information contained in these documents is consistent with the information contained in the financial statements." Can we realistically expect an audit committee to do that?

An Approach to Audit Committee Oversight

Let us consider a slightly different approach. It starts with the premise that an audit committee, in seeking to develop a system directed to the prevention and early detection of fraudulent financial reporting, should at the outset establish no more than a handful of key objectives. The audit committee should then—through the use of company employees and outside professionals—put in place a system so that those key objectives are fulfilled. The audit committee should then—again through the use of company employees and outside professionals—monitor the financial reporting system so that the fulfillment of the key objectives is maintained.

A good set of key objectives with which to start might be the following:

- Seek to establish the proper tone at the top
- Be satisfied as to the logistical capabilities of the financial reporting system
- Put in place a system for the immediate detection of financial misreporting

Let's spend a moment on each.

The Tone at the Top

If the audit committee is to accomplish nothing else, it should first and foremost strive to establish the right tone at the top. If the appropriate tone at the top is established and communicated, every division, department, and individual within the organization will be pulling in the same direction. Without the appropriate tone at the top, you haven't got a chance.

What is the appropriate tone at the top? It involves an unrelenting insistence upon accuracy in financial reporting. It involves an unrelenting insistence that numbers are not to be massaged. It involves an unrelenting insistence upon truthfulness as the foremost objective of the corporate enterprise. It is a tone that makes financial misreporting unthinkable.

How does such a tone get established? The obvious place to start is with management. Senior executives must be vividly aware of the unacceptability of massaged financial results. This is a battle for a certain type of corporate culture, and therefore both big and small things mean a lot. Among the big things, the audit committee chairman should emphasize unequivocally and often the dual predicates of truth and transparency as the bases for financial reporting. It is a message that has to be explicitly or implicitly omnipresent in every matter to be addressed.

It is also a message that must be reinforced, and that takes us to small things. Remember that financial misreporting starts out small and in those hazy areas where individuals think they are still being honest. Accordingly, when dealing with senior management, audit committee members must be attentive to any indication of a desire to improperly influence reported results in order to attain performance objectives. Unrelenting vigilance is key. Any senior executive who slips into one of the telltale signs of managed earnings—contrived revenue enhancement, unjustified modification of reserves, even obsessive fidelity to the attainment of quarterly analyst expectations—must be corrected swiftly and unequivocally. Battles for corporate culture are the toughest battles to win.

That effort does not, however, stop with the senior executives. The audit committee must then seek a vehicle for communication of that message down the ranks through the lower levels of the enterprise. For example, those within the sales department must be given to understand that contrived methods to increase reported sales—side letters, quarter-end telephone calls to friendly customers, last-minute discounting that is not revealed to the accounting department—will not be tolerated. Analogous contrivances, such as quarter-end accelerated shipping or, worse, a failure to close the quarter-end books, are to be viewed as forbidden. At all levels of the enterprise, both egregious and subtle manipulations of the numbers are to be perceived as unacceptable.

One obvious vehicle of communication is a written code of conduct or mission statement, but let us candidly admit that such a written document can be almost useless at best and counterproductive at worst. It can be almost useless because a written document doesn't stand a chance against a corporate culture that goes the other way. It can be counterproductive when the chasm between the written document and the corporate culture becomes so wide that it suggests that the document's authors are somewhere between out of touch and evil.

How to get the word out? There really is little choice but to rely on the senior executives. They have the day-to-day contact with the lower levels, and they have to be the ones to see that an appropriate tone is communicated and reinforced. That objective, therefore, should be plainly understood. Where infractions occur—and they will—the audit committee should satisfy itself that the response was swift and unequivocal.

Key to maintaining the tone at the top will be sensitivity to pressure. Again, financial misreporting doesn't start with dishonesty—it starts with pressure. The audit committee, therefore, should try to be sensitive to the enormous pressures to which senior executives may be subject. Where necessary, the audit committee should be prepared to act as a counterbalance to that pressure and support senior management in the face of outsiders who would place numerical performance objectives above everything else. That does not mean that management's numerical performance does not matter. It means that the only numerical performance that matters is numerical performance that captures the truth.

More than that, the audit committee will want to be on its guard to keep the board of directors from inadvertently adding to the pressure. The audit committee should keep in mind that compensation systems may inadvertently create undue pressure for ostensibly splendid but substanceless performance. The audit committee should stay on guard for indications of overly aggressive budgets and sales targets. The board will get what it measures, so it has to make sure it measures what it wants. If the board measures only reported earnings, it will get reported earnings. But it may get them at the expense of truth.

Logistical Capability

Desire is one thing, attainment another. Establishment of an appropriate tone at the top, therefore, does not by itself ensure reliability in financial reporting—though it is probably 80% of the battle. The next step is to strive for a financial reporting system that is logistically capable of doing what everybody in the company now wants.

This is not a battle for corporate culture but a battle for staffing and computer systems and, therefore, infinitely easier to deal with. The obvious starting place is to look into whether the accounting department is adequately staffed and supervised. Inquiry should be made as to the adequacy of management information systems. In this area, useful information should not be too difficult to get. If staffing or systems are not adequate, the CFO would probably be pleased to have the opportunity to let the audit committee know.

A system that is adequate in one month, though, may not be adequate in the next. That is particularly so where the corporate enterprise is changing—for example, if it is growing through acquisition. The audit committee of a company that is in transformation, particularly where it is growing through the acquisition of others, should therefore remain sensitive to the effects of change on accounting capabilities and personnel. Frequently, the accounting systems of acquired companies will not be compatible with the accounting system of the acquirer, but the problem will be put off due to the press of events as the next acquisition candidate appears. A conglomerate of newly acquired accounting systems that together function as a Tower of Babel is a recipe for disaster—without even getting to the corporate cultures of the new personnel who have been acquired in the process. Asking about the accounting systems of acquired companies should not be too far down on the audit committee's to-do list.

Immediate Detection of Financial Misreporting

It is a mistake to think that things will always work the way they should. That doesn't mean the audit committee isn't doing its job. It just means that no financial reporting system will ever be completely free from defects. Therefore, it is not enough to establish an appropriate tone at the top and to ensure logistical support consistent with that tone. The audit committee has to assume that, from time to time, things will go wrong. It has to assume that, from time to time, the organization will slip into some level of financial misreporting.

The key is to find out quickly when it happens. The audit committee therefore needs a system that will enable it to be the first, rather than the last, to know. (More about that in a moment.)

A Properly Configured Audit Committee

The attainment of these corporate governance and financial reporting objectives will present significant challenges. If an audit committee is to have any hope of surmounting these challenges, it must have the underlying capability of doing so. That is to say, the audit committee itself must be properly configured. Indeed, proper configuration of the audit committee is not simply a matter of sound corporate governance. Today, it is also a matter of law.

Historically, the configuration of a company's audit committee has been left largely to the discretion of the particular company's board of directors. Thus, the SEC, while becoming increasingly interested in the effectiveness of audit committees, for years declined to enact detailed rules on the matter, deferring almost entirely to the rules of the exchange where the company's stock happened to be listed. The NYSE, for its part, specified that companies were to establish and maintain audit committees comprised solely of independent directors but specified little else. The NASD, while requiring companies to "establish and maintain" an audit committee, did not go as far as the NYSE in requiring all members to be independent: independence was required by only a majority of the audit committee members. The rules of the NASD went on to provide that the audit committee in substance should discuss aspects of the annual audit with the outside auditor.

In December 1999, the SEC approved a new series of rules that are substantially more rigorous. Pursuant to the recommendations of the Blue Ribbon Committee on Improving the Effectiveness of Corporate Audit Committees, the new rules establish enhanced requirements for audit committee membership, independence, sophistication, diligence, and disclosure. For companies whose securities are listed on the NYSE or quoted on Nasdaq, the new rules, which are to be phased in over a period of 18 months following their approval, require the following. First, an audit committee is to include at least three members (Exhibits 11–1, 11–2). Second, with very limited exception, each member of the committee is to be independent (Exhibits 11–3, 11–4). Third, each member is to possess (at the time he joins the audit committee or within a reasonable time thereafter) some degree of financial literacy, with at least one member having an accounting or finance background (Exhibits 11–1, 11–2). Fourth, the audit committee members are to have in place a written charter which is to be filed with the SEC every three years (Exhibits 11–5, 11–6). Fifth, the audit committee is to file with the SEC a written report that specifies, among other things, whether the

---

Exhibit 11–1. New NYSE Rules: Audit Committee Composition

- Each audit committee shall consist of at least three directors, all of whom have no relationship to the company that may interfere with the exercise of their independence from management and the company;

- Each member of the audit committee shall be financially literate, or must become financially literate within a reasonable period of time after his or her appointment to the audit committee; and

- At least one member of the audit committee must have accounting or related financial management expertise.

---

committee recommended to the board of directors that the audited financial statements be filed with the SEC (Exhibit 11–7).

In some respects, the rules are highly detailed and precise. For example, the "independence" requirements of the NASD specify that the independence prerequisite is not met by a director who was an employee of the corporation or any affiliate for the current year or any of the past three years; by a director who accepts compensation in excess of $60,000 from the corporation or any of its affiliates during the previous fiscal year (other than compensation for board service, benefits under a tax-qualified retirement plan, or nondiscretionary compensation); by a director who is an immediate family member of an individual who is, or has been in any of the past three years, an executive officer of the corporation or any of its affiliates; by a director who is a partner, controlling shareholder, or executive officer of a for-profit firm that received certain types of fees or other payments from the company in excess of a specified level; or by a director who is employed as an executive of another entity where any of the company's executives serve on that entity's compensation committee (Exhibit 11–4). The NYSE has its own set of comparably detailed "independence" requirements (Exhibit 11–3).

Viewed more broadly, though, the rules collectively strive for three overall objectives that are fundamental to audit committee effectiveness. These three objectives are:

- Independence

Exhibit 11–2. New NASD Rules: Audit Committee Composition

Each issuer must have and certify that:

- It has and will continue to have an audit committee of at least three members, comprised solely of independent directors, each of whom is able to read and understand fundamental financial statements, or will become able to do so within a reasonable period of time after his or her appointment to the audit committee; and

- It has and will continue to have at least one member of the audit committee that has past employment experience in finance or accounting, requisite professional certification in accounting, or any other comparable experience or background which results in the individual's financial sophistication.

One director who is not independent and is not a current employee or an immediate family member of such employee may be appointed to the audit committee, if:

- The board, under exceptional and limited circumstances, determines that membership on the committee by the individual is required by the best interests of the corporation and its shareholders; and

- The board discloses, in the next annual proxy statement subsequent to such determination, the nature of the relationship and the reasons for that determination.

- Financial sophistication
- Willingness to work

Each is a worthy objective and warrants some discussion.

Independence

Foremost, an audit committee should be independent from the senior executives of the company. The reason is obvious. It is a fundamental function of the audit committee to lean against the wind. It is, in other words, a fundamental function of the audit committee to offer reasoned resistance against the desires of management where those desires may compromise integrity in financial reporting.

The task is not for the fainthearted. During difficult times, management itself may be under horrific pressure for bottom-line results. Absent some degree of independence, a natural inclination to sympathize with those in the hot seat might prove almost irresistible. During particularly difficult times, resistance to management's ostensible needs may be perceived as the betrayal of prior favors bestowed. At a minimum, resistance could make board meetings exceedingly awkward.

What is meant by *independence*? As mentioned above, the new rules are highly detailed and complex (see Exhibits 11–3, 11–4). The underlying concept, though, involves the exclusion of individuals who, for whatever reason, are not in a position to stand up to the tenacious desires of determined management. Excluded from among those possessing independence, therefore, are family members of executives—it probably being no small coincidence that, where accounting irregularities have surfaced, family relationships on the board of directors have been by no means rare. Also excluded from among those possessing independence are outside professionals whose judgment may be influenced due to business relationships with the company. Also excluded are directors whose compensation at another company may be determined by executives the director is theoretically overseeing. Audit committee members should be prepared to tell management what it doesn't want to hear. Relationships that may compromise the committee's willingness to do so may impair its effectiveness.

How many members should be independent? This has been a somewhat controversial issue. The new rules of both the NYSE and the NASD generally require that all audit committee members be independent (see Exhibits 11–1, 11–2). However, in implicit recognition that sometimes a non-independent director is in the position to offer unique benefits to an audit committee, both the NYSE and the NASD include a limited exception permitting the inclusion of a non-independent director under specified circumstances (see Exhibits 11–2, 11–3). The rules make clear, however, that the inclusion of non-independent directors is intended to be a rarity. Both the NYSE and the NASD rules, for example, provide for the inclusion of a non-independent director only under "exceptional and limited circumstances." Under both the NYSE and the NASD rules, proxy statement disclosure of the non-independent director's participation is required.

Exhibit 11–3. New NYSE Rules: Audit Committee Independence

The following restrictions shall apply to every audit committee member:

- A director who is an employee (including non-employee executive officers) of the company or any of its affiliates may not serve on the audit committee until three years following the termination of his or her employment;

- A director (i) who is a partner, controlling shareholder, or executive officer of an organization that has a business relationship (including commercial, industrial, banking, consulting, legal, accounting and other relationships) with the company, or (ii) who has a direct business relationship with the company may serve on the audit committee only if the company's board of directors determines that the relationship does not interfere with the director's exercise of independent judgment. The board of directors should consider, among other things, the materiality of the relationship to the company, to the director, and, if applicable, to the organization with which the director is affiliated;

- A director who is employed as an executive of another corporation where any of the company's executives serves on that corporation's compensation committee may not serve on the audit committee; and

- A director who is an immediate family member of an individual who is an executive officer of the company or any of its affiliates cannot serve on the audit committee until three years following the termination of such employment relationship.

One director who is no longer an employee or who is an immediate family member of a former executive officer of the company or its affiliates, but is not considered independent pursuant to these provisions due to the three-year restriction period, may be appointed, under exceptional and limited circumstances, to the audit committee if:

- The company's board of directors determines that membership on the committee by the individual is required by the best interests of the corporation and its shareholders, and

• The company discloses, in the next annual proxy statement subsequent to such determination, the nature of the relationship and the reasons for that determination.

Exhibit 11–4. New NASD Rules: Audit Committee Independence

"Independent director" means a person other than an officer or employee of the company or its subsidiaries or any other individual having a relationship which, in the opinion of the company's board of directors, would interfere with the exercise of independent judgment in carrying out the responsibilities of a director.

The following persons shall not be considered independent:

• A director who is an employee of the corporation or any of its affiliates for the current year or any of the past three years;

• A director who accepts any compensation in excess of $60,000 from the corporation or any of its affiliates during the previous fiscal year, other than compensation for board service, benefits under a tax-qualified retirement plan, or non-discretionary compensation;

• A director who is an immediate family member of an individual who is, or has been in any of the past three years, an executive officer of the corporation or any of its affiliates;

• A director who is a partner in or a controlling shareholder or an executive officer of any for-profit business organization to which the corporation made, or from which the corporation received, payments that exceed 5% of the corporation's or business organization's consolidated gross revenues for that year, or $200,000, whichever is more, in any of the past three years; and

• A director who is employed as an executive of another entity where any of the company's executives serve on that entity's compensation committee.

At the risk of incurring the wrath of those whose commitment to integrity in financial reporting is unimpeachable, let us pause momentarily on the possibility that, in striving to preclude the participation of non-independent directors, the new rules may have gone too far. Certainly most of the members should be independent. However, an argument could be made that the inclusion of one non-independent member could enhance committee effectiveness. While the committee must be prepared to stand against the desires of management, it must also constitute an integral part of the board and of the company's corporate governance system. The inclusion of a non-independent (i.e., management) member may give the committee important insight into the cultural underpinnings or business rationale for a particular management objective. At the same time, a committee comprised entirely of independent members might correctly or incorrectly be perceived as an inflexible naysayer, giving rise to an ultimately self-destructive mindset of "us v. them." The inclusion of a management representative—as long as he can be squarely outvoted by those possessing genuine independence—may provide management the comfort that its views are being properly considered and that, on balance, the audit committee's conclusions are for the good of the corporate whole. That is particularly so where an unpalatable decision by an audit committee possessing one management member is, nonetheless, unanimous.

Still, the configuration of the audit committee should obviously conform to the rules. Those companies whose securities are listed on the NYSE or quoted on Nasdaq will therefore generally need audit committees comprised solely of independent directors. Perhaps the input of a management representative can then be obtained by including the representative in some audit committee meetings even without formal membership.

Financial Sophistication

Even audit committee members whose hearts are in the right place need to know what they are doing. Therefore, a second fundamental prerequisite of audit committee membership should be some level of financial sophistication.

What kind of sophistication? Here, the rules are particularly vague. The NYSE rules specify only that, "Each member of the audit committee shall be financially literate, as such qualification is interpreted by the company's Board of Directors in its business judgment." The NASD rules are only slightly more informative. They specify that each of the audit committee members must be "able to read and understand financial statements, including a company's balance sheet, income statement, and cash flow statement." (See Exhibits 11–1, 11–2.)

Broadly speaking, though, experience suggests that audit committee members should possess financial sophistication in two areas. First, audit committee members should possess some working familiarity with the rudiments of generally accepted accounting principles (GAAP) and financial reporting. That's not to say that each member must be a CPA, though at least one CPA is probably a good idea. Rather, the members should possess a basic understanding of such things as the accrual system of accounting, the extent to which (for example) operating cash flow may diverge from reported earnings, and the rudiments of SEC reporting requirements. To say it another way, the members should probably know enough to appreciate that reported earnings does not always mean cash in the bank.

But financial literacy is only the first type of financial sophistication. The second is that members should possess an understanding of corporate governance systems and, in particular, the extent to which non-optimal systems can compromise truthfulness in financial reporting. One of the key functions of the audit committee members will be to keep a sharp lookout for the telltale signs of corruption. The individual members will have to know enough to recognize them when they appear.

Willingness to Work

Audit committee members should not be expected to quit their day jobs, but they have to be willing to work. Obviously they can leverage their talents through the use of employees and outside professionals, but audit committee membership—particularly in a start-up phase, where a viable audit committee has been lacking—will require significant effort and commitment. The willingness to make the effort has got to be there.

The new rules seek to encourage audit committee willingness to make the effort in several ways, one of which is through the requirement of an audit committee "charter" (Exhibits 11–5, 11–6). Already in use at a number of public companies, the charter—which must be in writing—is to broadly outline the audit committee's responsibility for oversight of financial reporting. Thus, the new rules of both the NYSE and the NASD provide that a company's charter must specify the scope of the audit

Exhibit 11–5. New NYSE Rules: Audit Committee Charter

Each audit committee must adopt a formal written charter that is approved by the board of directors. The audit committee must review and reassess the adequacy of the audit committee charter on an annual basis.

The charter must specify the following:

- The scope of the audit committee's responsibilities and how it carries out those responsibilities

- That the outside auditor for the company is ultimately accountable to the board of directors and audit committee of the company

- That the audit committee and board of directors have the ultimate authority and responsibility to select, evaluate, and, where appropriate, replace the outside auditor

- That the audit committee is responsible for ensuring that the outside auditor submits to the audit committee a formal written statement delineating all relationships between the auditor and the company

- That the audit committee is responsible for actively engaging in a dialogue with the outside auditor with respect to any disclosed relationships or services that may affect the objectivity and independence of the outside auditor and for recommending that the board of directors take appropriate action to ensure the independence of the outside auditor

committee's responsibilities and how those responsibilities are carried out; the outside auditor's ultimate accountability to the audit committee and the board of directors; the responsibility of the audit committee and the board of directors to select, evaluate, and replace the auditor; the audit committee's responsibility for ensuring the auditor's submission of a formal written statement delineating all relationships between the auditor and the company; and the audit committee's responsibility for engaging in a dialogue with the auditor as to any relationships that may adversely affect independence. A

Exhibit 11–6. New NASD Rules: Audit Committee Charter

Each Issuer must certify that it has adopted a formal written audit committee charter. Each Issuer must certify that the audit committee has reviewed and reassessed the adequacy of the formal written charter on an annual basis.

The charter must specify the following:

- The scope of the audit committee's responsibilities, and how it carries out those responsibilities

- The audit committee's responsibility for ensuring its receipt from the outside auditor of a formal written statement delineating all relationships between the auditor and the company

- The company and the audit committee's responsibility for actively engaging in a dialogue with the auditor with respect to any disclosed relationships or services that may affect the objectivity and independence of the auditor and for taking, or recommending that the full board take, appropriate action to ensure the independence of the outside auditor

- The outside auditor's ultimate accountability to the board of directors and the audit committee, as representatives of shareholders, and these shareholder representatives' ultimate authority and responsibility to select, evaluate, and, where appropriate, replace the outside auditor

---

separate SEC rule, which requires public filing of the audit committee charter every three years, ensures that the charter's contents will be adequate to withstand public scrutiny.

Beyond the charter, the other main vehicle to encourage audit committee diligence is a written report to be filed once a year as part of the company's proxy statement (Exhibit 11–7). No specific format for the report is specified. However, the rules are clear that the substance of the report must include several things. First, the report is to state whether the audit committee has reviewed and discussed the audited financial statements with manage-

---

Exhibit 11–7. New SEC Rules to Implement the Recommendations of the Blue Ribbon Committee

- Require that companies' independent auditors review the financial information included in the companies' Form 10-Q prior to filing

- Require that companies include reports of their audit committees in their proxy statements, stating whether the audit committee has:

  — Reviewed and discussed the audited financial statements with management

  — Discussed with the independent auditors the matters required to be discussed by SAS-61 (Communication with Audit Committees)

  — Received certain disclosures from the auditors regarding the auditors' independence as required by Independence Standards Board Standard No. 1 and discussed with the auditors the auditors' independence

- Require that the report of the audit committee include a statement by the audit committee whether the audit committee recommended to the board of directors that the audited financial statements be included in the company's Form 10-K

- Require that companies disclose in their proxy statements whether their audit committee has adopted a written charter and include a copy of the charter as an appendix to the proxy statement at least once every three years

- Require that companies disclose in their proxy statements information regarding the independence of audit committee members

---

ment. Second, the report is to state whether the audit committee has discussed with the outside auditor matters specified in Statement on Auditing Standards No. 61 (Communication with Audit Committees), which is described below. Third, the report is to state whether the audit committee has addressed with the outside auditor the issue of independence in accordance with the applicable rules. Fourth, the report is to state whether the audit committee recommended to the board that the audited financial statements be included in the company's Form 10-K as filed with the SEC. Apparently for the *in terrorem* effect, the rules provide that the names of the individual audit committee members are to appear below the required disclosures. To the extent that these requirements operate to enhance audit committee diligence, they are thus consistent with the common law which, according to one articulation, requires a board of directors to seek in good faith an adequate corporate information and reporting system (Exhibit 11–8).

Compliance with all of these requirements is going to take time, and a final note on the issue of audit committee diligence is that audit committee members should be adequately compensated for their efforts. No legitimate question exists that, at whatever the appropriate level of compensation, the company will be getting a bargain. The company's best protection against corruption of its financial reporting system is an optimally functioning audit committee. The benefits will overwhelm the costs.

Ironically, though, the board of directors should probably be on its guard against paying the audit committee members too much. At some level of compensation, audit committee membership would theoretically become an attractive perk to be held onto—thereby giving rise to a potential loss of independence. As in most compensation decisions, there thus exists a need to balance benefits and costs. In that balance, though, the actual expenditure

Exhibit 11–8. Delaware Law

A board of directors' duty of care "includes a duty to attempt in good faith to assure that a corporate information and reporting system, which the board concludes is adequate, exists."

The information and reporting system should "in concept and design [be] adequate to assure the board that appropriate information will come to its attention in a timely manner as a matter of ordinary operations."

(*In re Caremark International Inc.*, 698 A.2d 959, 970 (Del. Ch. 1996))

out of the corporate coffers should not be an issue. An effective audit committee is worth it.

The Biggest Challenge: Information

Let's say that, so far, a board of directors has done everything right. Its audit committee is independent. Its audit committee is financially sophisticated. Its audit committee is ready to work, with a perfectly drafted charter firmly in place.

Such an audit committee is now perfectly positioned—to fail. That is, it is perfectly positioned to fail unless it can successfully overcome the biggest challenge. That challenge is lack of access to reliable information.

The reason may be simply stated. It is that, in a normal corporate enterprise, bad news tends not to flow up. Ever since Cleopatra struck her hapless messenger, the self-preservation instincts of even loyal subordinates have cautioned them to selectively keep bad news to themselves. The consequences of reporting bad news can be harsh and the rewards are few. Rarely does one receive stock options for reporting disaster.

The danger of the resulting "Cleopatra syndrome" is potentially the biggest hurdle an audit committee will face. At root, the problem is that the audit committee will remain in perilous danger of functioning in total ignorance. Financial reporting problems will be allowed to fester as executives seek to correct them before the audit committee is in a position to notice. Executives will not appreciate the extent to which, for the reasons described in Chapter 1, temporary bandages may only operate to make the problem worse. Gradually, the problem will grow. And the audit committee will not have a clue.

What makes this breakdown in the information flow to the audit committee ironic is that a normal corporation, no matter how infirm its systems, will ordinarily have any number of well-meaning employees who would be grateful for the chance to describe system corruption if given a non-threatening opportunity. The challenge facing the audit committee, then, is to find a way to tap into that reservoir of candid information and to install a pipeline so that it may flow upward unimpeded. Three potential sources for such information exist. They are senior management, the outside auditor, and internal audit. Not coincidentally, the "guiding principles" of the Blue Ribbon Committee focused attention on precisely these three potential information sources.

Getting Information from Senior Management

Unfortunately, a viable financial reporting system should probably accept that reliable information about system inadequacies will not be regularly made available to the audit committee by senior management. That is not to denigrate the virtue of senior executives or to suggest widespread managerial inadequacy. It is simply a recognition of human nature. Each of us has an understandable reluctance to be completely candid about our own innumerable flaws.

Some—perhaps many—senior executives would be able to rise above that. Senior executives secure with their own abilities and possessed of supreme confidence may be perfectly comfortable undertaking the laudable task of reporting to the audit committee the problems that are growing on their watch. A system that assumes such laudable candor in senior executives, though, is probably assuming too much. It is better to accept that, while striving for virtue, not everyone will achieve it.

Moreover, even secure and candid senior executives may suffer from the same problem that would plague a normal audit committee: No guarantee exists that bad news will flow up to them. A well-meaning senior executive, therefore, may be perfectly willing to share with the audit committee system inadequacies to the extent he is familiar with them. The problem may be that he doesn't fully know what they are.

The potential for managerial unfamiliarity with organizational problems is particularly acute when it comes to one of the most important aspects of the financial reporting system: the environment in which that system is to function. Management is faced with the excruciatingly difficult challenge of placing on subordinates precisely the right amount of pressure for performance: not enough, and the organization does not achieve maximum profitability; too much, and the organization is at risk that massaged numbers will slip into the reporting system. Procurement of reliable information identifying the point at which the pressure has moved from optimal to counterproductive can be difficult. Too numerous to mention are instances in which the underlying cause of financial misreporting was the pressure placed on subordinates by a CEO who would later claim total ignorance about the destructive impact his performance edicts were having.

None of this is to suggest that the audit committee should not be striving to increase senior management's candor. Nothing is ever perfect, and senior executives should be encouraged and admonished to reach into the depths of the organization and to find and report system inadequacies. Still, an audit committee has to accept that even the strongest encouragement or even the sternest admonitions will not completely overcome human nature. A financial reporting system that assumes otherwise is probably destined to fail in the long run.

Getting Information from the Outside Auditor

No financial reporting system relies exclusively on senior management. A second means of access to information about the financial reporting system exists: the outside auditor.

No doubt there are significant impediments to reliance upon the outside auditor for the prevention and early detection of deliberate financial misreporting. As discussed in Chapter 1, accounting irregularities typically start out small and well beneath the radar screen of the materiality thresholds of a typical audit. They frequently involve the allocation of earnings among quarters, and therefore start in an area that will not normally be the subject of intense year-end audit scrutiny. They start with a particular type of corporate environment, and it is a type of environment to which a normal once-a-year auditor cannot gain ready access. They start in a hazy area of financial reporting in which much depends on the judgment of management. And, as the accounting irregularities grow over time, a preoccupation of the participants becomes the deliberate deception of the outside auditor.

The impediments to outside auditor detection of fraudulent financial reporting, though, are not entirely the result of the way fraud starts and grows. The impediments are also a consequence of the competitive environment of the audit profession and the corresponding desire by auditors to deliver what management has historically seemed to want: an unqualified audit report at the lowest possible cost. Auditors are ultimately professionals who will seek to be responsive to the desires of their clients. Where the client has placed cost minimization above all else, the auditors have felt pressure to oblige.

Omnipresent among all of these problems, moreover, is the fundamental reality that, no matter how hard an auditor tries, determined executives will always be able to get away with some level of deception. However deep the auditor seeks to probe, those within the accounting department can always take the fraud one level deeper. If the business community were to find such a situation unacceptable, it could always encourage the audit profession to abandon the audit-sampling and professional-skepticism approaches that constitute the hallmarks of a modern GAAS audit. In other words, a new system of audits could be installed along the lines of a fraud investigation or forensic investigation in which the auditors essentially don't believe anything anybody within the reporting entity says. That is, basically, the approach taken where accounting irregularities have surfaced, as discussed in Chapter 5. One problem with such an approach, though, would be timeliness—an "audit" conducted along such lines would almost have to be perpetual. The other problem would be cost. The forensic investigation of the books and records of one troubled public company, for example, required more than 1,000 auditors and cost more than $3 million per day.

In seeking reliable information from the outside auditor, some of these impediments an audit committee can do something about, and some it cannot. Ultimately, though, one thing will be true. The auditor, as an outside professional, will ultimately be responsive to the desires of its client. In the end, therefore, if the audit committee makes clear to the outside auditor its desire for an enhanced audit function and improved systems information, good auditors will find a way to provide the desired level of service. That is particularly so if the audit committee is willing to pay for it.

So what kinds of information should the audit committee ask the outside auditor for? Here are some possibilities:

Environmental Information

Foremost, the audit committee will want to encourage the outside auditor to do its best to seek, find, and candidly report information about the financial reporting environment. Are people under too much pressure? Are they reluctant to report bad news? Is there a danger they are camouflaging results? These are the types of questions that auditors hate to be asked. But they are also the types of questions that are fundamental to the prevention and early detection of financial fraud.

Logistical Capabilities of the Financial Reporting System

An easier issue to explore with the outside auditor will be the logistical capabilities of the financial reporting system. Both the law (Exhibits 11–9 and 11–10) and good business sense require the company to maintain its books and records in such a way that they fairly reflect corporate transactions and

Exhibit 11–9. Foreign Corrupt Practices Act

"Every issuer which has a class of securities registered pursuant to section 781 of [the Securities Exchange Act of 1934] shall:

(A) make and keep books, records, and accounts, which, in reasonable detail, accurately and fairly reflect the transactions and dispositions of the assets of the issuer; and

(B) devise and maintain a system of internal accounting controls sufficient to provide reasonable assurances that:

    (i) transactions are executed in accordance with management's general or specific authorization;

    (ii) transactions are recorded as necessary (I) to permit preparation of financial statements in conformity with generally accepted accounting principles or any other criteria applicable to such statements and (II) to maintain accountability for assets;

    (iii) access to assets is permitted only in accordance with management's general or specific authorization; and

    (iv) the recorded accountability for assets is compared with the existing assets at reasonable intervals and appropriate action is taken with respect to any differences."

(15 U.S.C. § 78m(b)(2))

Exhibit 11–10. SEC Rule: Book and Records

"No person shall, directly or indirectly, falsify or cause to be falsified, any book, record or account subject to Section 13(b)(2)(A) of the Securities Exchange Act."

(17 C.F.R. § 240.13b2-1)

events. Staffing, sophistication, computerization, software inadequacies—all aspects of the system's logistical capabilities may accordingly warrant inquiry. On this subject, the auditor's candid views should be easier to obtain. Logistical inadequacies in the accounting system only make an audit more difficult.

Managerial Bias in the Application of GAAP

Another topic that may yield useful information involves the bias of management in the application of GAAP. Is management overly aggressive? Overly conservative? Is it trying to get it right? By their nature, GAAP will probably always depend to a meaningful extent on the judgment of management in their application. A decent auditor will come to a view as to how that judgment is being exercised. The auditor should be encouraged to share it.

On this issue, the audit committee will be assisted by new amendments to GAAS that will likely operate to increase auditor candor (Exhibits 11–11, 11–12). Intended to cultivate an "open and frank discussion" between the audit committee and the outside auditor, the new amendments require the auditor to discuss with the audit committee "the auditor's judgments about the quality, not just the acceptability, of the entity's accounting principles as applied in its financial reporting." Under the amendments, this discussion is to include such matters as the consistency of the company's accounting policies and the clarity and completeness of the company's financial statements. In order to further foster open and frank discussion, the auditor's judgments need not be communicated in writing. The amendments also require the auditor, where appropriate, to seek to discuss such matters with the audit committee not only in the context of the annual financial statements, but on a quarterly basis as well (Exhibit 11–12).

The Level of Cooperation and Difficulties Encountered

At bottom, the audit committee is trying to smell a rat. It is trying to get reliable, candid information about the environment or culture in which financial reporting takes place, the institution's logistical capabilities to fulfill its objectives, and where things might have gone astray.

Exhibit 11–11. New Amendments to Statement on Auditing Standards No. 61 (Communication with Audit Committees)

- Requires the outside auditor to discuss with the audit committee information relating to the auditor's judgment about the quality, not just the acceptability, of the company's accounting principles, including:

  — Consistency of the entity's accounting policies and their application

  — Clarity and completeness of the entity's financial statements

  — Items that have a significant impact on the representational faithfulness, verifiability, and neutrality of the accounting information included in the financial statements

- Encourages the participation of management in the discussion

- Suggests that the discussion be "open and frank"

- Does not require that written documentation of the discussion be provided to the audit committee or management

---

It therefore makes sense to ask the outside auditor about the company's level of cooperation during the course of the audit and the extent to which any difficult issues were encountered. Frequently, a lack of cooperation and the encountering of difficult issues will go hand in hand. Either individually or together they can be a telltale sign of a broader problem. In particular, they can suggest an attitude toward financial reporting that is not consistent with a healthy overall environment.

Unusual Revenue or Reserve Activity

Part of asking the auditor to do more than the bare minimum may involve encouraging the auditor to explore unusual patterns in revenues or reserves.

Exhibit 11–12. New Amendments to Statement on Auditing Standards No. 71 (Interim Financial Information)

- Clarifies that an auditor should communicate to the audit committee matters described in SAS-61 (Communication with Audit Committees) when they have been identified in the conduct of interim financial reporting

- Requires that an auditor should attempt to discuss the matters described in SAS-61 with the audit committee (or its chairman) and someone from financial management prior to:

  — The filing of the Form 10-Q, or

  — As soon as practicable if such communication cannot be made before filing

---

The reason for looking at revenues is that revenue manipulation is frequently where widespread financial fraud will get its start. In particular, the auditor can be asked to look out for instances in which revenue recognition patterns do not appear to match the ebb and flow of the company's normal cycle of business activity. Revenue spikes toward the end of a quarter or other financial reporting period may be a warning that something untoward is afoot.

Much the same is true of changes in company reserves. Here, the auditor might be encouraged to scrutinize the level of reserves not only at year-end but during the course of the year to look for unjustified or inexplicable reserve level changes. Unusual reserve activity that does not seem explainable by virtue of business developments here, too, should be explored. Reserves that are established or modified almost entirely based upon the judgment of management may warrant particular scrutiny.

Beyond issues of revenue recognition and the adjustment of reserves, the auditor might be asked about other aspects of the application of GAAP in which management judgment plays an important role. The audit committee should do its best to satisfy itself that adjustments are the natural consequence of business activity and not the manifestation of a desire to attain preestablished financial reporting targets.

Nonmaterial PAJEs

A recent addition to the list of issues for the outside auditor is the topic of *nonmaterial PAJEs*. This addition is the result of a somewhat controversial bulletin by the staff of the SEC.

First, a word about nomenclature. A *PAJE* is a proposed adjusting journal entry—that is to say, an adjusting journal entry that has been proposed by the auditor as a result of audit testing. If the adjustment is made, it becomes known simply as an *adjusting journal entry*. If the adjustment is not made, it remains a *proposed adjusting journal entry* (some might call it a *passed adjusting journal entry*) or a *PAJE*.

Historically, it has generally been within the discretion of management to decline to make adjusting journal entries as long as they collectively were not material. There were exceptions to that, but generally management could decline to record PAJEs collectively falling below a materiality threshold— say 5% to 10%—without running the risk that the financial statements would be viewed as *materially* misstated.

In Staff Accounting Bulletin No. 99 (Exhibit 11–13), the SEC has tried to change that. Apparently premised on the view that executives at some public companies were abusing the concept of materiality by declining to make "nonmaterial" adjusting journal entries to increase reported earnings, the SEC staff has taken the position that it will no longer accept purely numerical materiality analysis in assessing the fairness of financial statement presentation. In particular, the staff has taken the position that even adjustments falling below traditional numerical thresholds may nonetheless be viewed as material if, for example, failure to make the adjustment disguised a failure to meet analyst expectations, turned a loss into a profit, masked an important trend, or affected a company's compliance with regulatory requirements. In addition, the staff has suggested that a failure to make even ostensibly minor adjustments to the company's books and records may be improper when undertaken "as part of an ongoing effort directed by or known to senior management for the purposes of 'managing' earnings."

Exhibit 11–13. SEC Staff Accounting Bulletin No. 99 (Materiality)

"The staff is aware that certain registrants, over time, have developed quantitative thresholds as 'rules of thumb' to assist in the preparation of their financial statements, and that auditors also have used these thresholds in their evaluation of whether items might be considered material to users of a registrant's financial statements. One rule of thumb in particular suggests that the misstatement or omission of an item that falls under a 5% threshold is not material in the absence of particularly egregious circumstances, such as self-dealing or misappropriation by senior management. The staff reminds registrants and the auditors of their financial statements that exclusive reliance on this or any percentage or numerical threshold has no basis in the accounting literature or the law.

* * *

Among the considerations that may well render material a quantitatively small misstatement of a financial statement item are—

- whether the misstatement arises from an item capable of precise measurement or whether it arises from an estimate and, if so, the degree of imprecision inherent in the estimate

- whether the misstatement masks a change in earnings or other trends

- whether the misstatement hides a failure to meet analysts' consensus expectations for the enterprise

- whether the misstatement changes a loss into income or vice versa

- whether the misstatement concerns a segment or other portion of the registrant's business that has been identified as playing a significant role in the registrant's operations or profitability

- whether the misstatement affects the registrant's compliance with regulatory requirements

- whether the misstatement affects the registrant's compliance with loan covenants or other contractual requirements

- whether the misstatement has the effect of increasing management's compensation—for example, by satisfying requirements for the award of bonuses or other forms of incentive compensation

- whether the misstatement involves concealment of an unlawful transaction."

No longer, therefore, can an audit committee take complete comfort that financial statement inaccuracies falling below numerical materiality thresholds need not be worried about. Now they must be. Moreover, they must be worried about in a context in which the propriety of a failure to make adjustments turns on such qualitative criteria as the perceived effect of the failure and, to some extent, the motive of management.

For the time being, therefore, the audit committee may want to ask the outside auditor about any proposed adjustments that have not been made. In the event that such adjustments surface, the audit committee may face the fairly unpleasant task of inquiring into the reason and the extent to which the failure to make the adjustment would be second-guessed by the SEC or others. To avoid potential trouble, some audit committees may see fit simply to put in place a policy that, regardless of materiality, all proposed adjusting journal entries should be made.

Quarterly Information

Pursuant to the new rules, companies are now to have the financial statements included as part of their quarterly Forms 10-Q reviewed by their outside auditor before being filed (Exhibit 11–7). That review is to be undertaken pursuant to SAS-71 (Interim Financial Information), which establishes a level of auditor scrutiny of quarterly information beyond the quick once-over that historically has been the convention. In conducting a SAS-71 review, the auditor will inquire into such things as significant changes in the internal control structure, items that appear to be unusual, changes in accounting practices, and changes in business activities. A SAS-

71 review is far less than a full-fledged audit. But it is much more than many companies are asking their outside auditors to do today.

Meaningful auditor involvement with quarterly financial information is probably an idea whose time has come. The principal reason stems from the way that accounting irregularities get their start: typically through the exploitation of ambiguities in the accounting rules in the context of quarterly timing. For that reason, even before adoption of the new rules, the large accounting firms had already started making SAS-71 reviews a requirement for their audit clients.

The need for the outside auditor to conduct interim reviews thus gives the audit committee the opportunity to inquire into financial reporting issues that arose during the quarterly review process, and there is every reason for the audit committee to take advantage of that opportunity. Meaningful auditor involvement in quarterly information gives the audit committee not only access to improved information, but more of an opportunity to nip financial misreporting in the bud.

Thoroughness of the Audit

Not all audits are created equal. True, every conscientious auditor will conduct the audit tests that GAAS require. But why would the audit committee want to stop there? The audit committee might want to explore with the auditor the extent to which the auditor has done more than meet the standard professional requirements. In particular, the audit committee might ask the auditor about those devices used to gain extra insight into the corporate environment and to root out potential causes of financial misreporting. If the committee is going to go through the trouble of hiring the auditor, it may as well encourage the auditor to do an extra good job. Useful information is so precious, it seems a shame to let the auditor get away with making a minimal effort.

Auditor Independence

Probably no discussion of the audit committee's interaction with the outside auditor would be complete without at least some acknowledgment of the issue of auditor independence. Auditor independence right now is an exceedingly controversial topic. On the one hand, the accounting firms are being drawn by the desires of their clients into ever-increasing involvement with outsourced management consulting projects—such as the installment and upgrade of financial information systems—further dwarfing the significance of the audit as a profit center and, at the same time, giving rise to a web of interconnections between the accounting firm and its client that regulators fear will eviscerate independence both in appearance and in fact. On the other hand, the accounting firms insist that meaningful independence can nonetheless be preserved, that they are making an invaluable contribution to the enhancement of financial reporting and management information systems, that the audit function can be enhanced through more expansive auditor involvement with systems development, and that, in any event, they are responding to the needs of the market as well as to their own institutional needs to survive and prosper. These institutional needs, the accounting firms seem to suggest, cannot be fulfilled if the firms are to be boxed into the corner of performing only a periodic audit.

The issue of auditor independence may be one of the most difficult with which the financial community is forced to wrestle. Both sides seem to be making legitimate points. The thankless task of reconciling these seemingly legitimate but conflicting considerations has been given to the newly formed Independence Standards Board (ISB) under the able stewardship of its new chairman William Allen. The most notable of the ISB's initial efforts was the promulgation in 1999 of Independence Standards Board Standard No. 1 (Exhibit 11–14). In substance, ISB No. 1 requires the auditor to apprise the audit committee of all relationships that may bear on independence. The new rules require proxy statement disclosure of whether the dialogue has actually taken place (Exhibit 11–7).

The reason the audit committee cares about any of this is that, as illustrated by ISB No. 1 and the new disclosure requirements, all eyes seem to be turning to the audit committee to make an informed judgment as to whether, in the context of a particular audit, the independence of the outside auditor has been adequately preserved. This, too, is a thankless task. Nonetheless, in all likelihood some level of assessment of auditor independence will increasingly become a fundamental part of audit committee responsibilities.

Making the task particularly frustrating is that nobody can really agree on just what *auditor independence* should mean. At the moment, the existence of auditor independence is defined by a disparate collection of ad hoc rules embodied in GAAS, in the AICPA's Code of Professional Conduct, and in SEC regulations, centered principally around economic ties but largely lacking any entirely consistent theme or intellectual foundation. Nor

---

Exhibit 11–14. Independence Standards Board Standard No. 1 (Independence Discussions with Audit Committees)

- Applies to any auditor intending to be considered an independent accountant with respect to a specific entity administered by the SEC

- Requires that, at least annually, such an auditor shall:

  — Disclose to the audit committee of the company, in writing, all relationships between the auditor and its related entities and the company and its related entities that in the auditor's professional judgment may reasonably be thought to bear on independence

  — Confirm that, in the auditor's professional judgment, it is independent of the company within the meaning of the Securities Acts

  — Discuss the auditor's independence with the audit committee

---

is there universal agreement as to whether the concept of independence should continue to focus both on independence in fact and in appearance, as it has historically (Exhibit 11–15), or more on the former and less on the latter. At this juncture, probably the best guide to the audit committee that must evaluate auditor independence is for the committee to use its own good judgment in the context of the applicable rules. The key question should be whether the outside auditor—taking into account the totality of the circumstances—is prepared to tell it like it is. Aspects of the auditor relationship that may impede the auditor's willingness to do so—whether they be significant consulting agreements or simply a long history of close social ties with the CEO—are factors that the audit committee will probably want to take into consideration.

All the while, though, the audit committee should keep in mind this: Pure auditor independence is probably not attainable. As long as the company retains and pays the auditor, the auditor will maintain some level of sensitivity to the company's wants and needs. The key to an effective audit function,

---

Exhibit 11–15. Auditor Independence

"It is of utmost importance to the profession that the general public maintain confidence in the independence of independent auditors. Public confidence would be impaired by evidence that independence was actually lacking, and it might also be impaired by the existence of circumstances which reasonable people might believe likely to influence independence. To *be* independent, the auditor must be intellectually honest; to be *recognized* as independent, he must be free from any obligation to or interest in the client, its management, or its owners. For example, an independent auditor auditing a company of which he was also a director might be intellectually honest, but it is unlikely that the public would accept him as independent since he would be in effect auditing decisions which he had a part in making. Likewise, an auditor with a substantial financial interest in a company might be unbiased in expressing his opinion on the financial statements of the company, but the public would be reluctant to believe that he was unbiased. Independent auditors should not only be independent in fact; they should avoid situations that may lead outsiders to doubt their independence."

(AICPA Professional Standards § 220.03)

---

therefore, is not to focus on the artificial ideal of pure independence. It is, rather, to use the auditor's inevitable inclination to accommodate the desires of its client to enhance, rather than to impede, the outside audit function. In other words, it should be made clear to the auditor that thoroughness, candor, and zeal are the criteria by which performance will be measured—not the minimal requirements of GAAS and the dutiful issuance of an annual audit report. The crux of the audit relationship should evolve into one in which the auditor becomes an integral part of the system pursuant to which the audit committee gains access to useful systems information.

An underlying premise of such a relationship is that it should be the audit committee, and not senior executives, that selects and engages the auditor and determines the audit fee. For the same reasons that human nature impedes senior management's desire to convey bad news about itself, human nature similarly impedes management's desire for an auditor that will expose its own inadequacies. That is not to fault management or, for that matter, human nature. It is simply to acknowledge the way it is.

As the audit committee strives for a more complete and interconnected relationship with its outside auditor, the committee should probably keep in mind the extent to which an expansion of the auditor's role will work against the auditor's culture and traditions, which have been inclined in the direction of standardized and numerically focused reports. The level of responsiveness to an expanded audit role will likely vary not only among CPA firms, but among individual practitioners within firms. Ultimately, though, auditors should come to recognize the extent to which broader auditor involvement in financial reporting information and systems will operate to the audit profession's distinct advantage. Among other things, it will reduce if not eliminate the extent to which the audit is perceived as a mere commodity, and give opportunity to individual practitioners to demonstrate the uniqueness of their own professional excellence.

SAS-61 Items

In order to conform to the new rules, the audit committee will want to make sure it has appropriately discussed with the auditor items listed in SAS-61, referred to briefly above. Neither the new rules nor SAS-61 actually *require* the audit committee to discuss with the auditor the specified items. SAS-61 actually places the burden on the auditor to undertake the communication, and the new rules only require the audit committee to disclose whether discussion of the specified items has taken place (Exhibit 11–7). Nonetheless, given the awkwardness of a public disclosure that for some reason the specified items have not been discussed, the audit committee will want to make sure that the discussion has occurred.

The actual list of items to be discussed pursuant to SAS-61 is extensive. It includes the auditor's responsibility under GAAS; significant accounting policies; management judgments about accounting estimates; significant audit adjustments; other information in documents containing audited financial statements; disagreements with management; consultations by management with other accountants; major issues discussed with management prior to auditor retention; difficulties encountered in performing the audit; and (under the new amendments to SAS-61 discussed above) the quality, and not just the acceptability, of the company's accounting principles. Moreover, the new amendments to GAAS require appropriate discussion of SAS-61 items in conjunction with the auditor's quarterly review—not just at year end (Exhibit 11–12).

As a practical matter, to the extent that the audit committee has already delved into the areas described above, it will likely find that it has already more than adequately addressed all or virtually all of these SAS-61 items. Nonetheless, to the extent it has not, the audit committee will want to make sure that any remaining items are appropriately considered.

Getting Information from Internal Audit

Unfortunately, even the most splendid outside auditor will suffer from one fundamental impediment to its effectiveness: By definition, the auditor is an outsider. Whether the auditor undertakes fieldwork once a year, once a quarter, or even more frequently, the outside auditor will still be conducting examinations only periodically. There is one thing, therefore, that the outside auditor may not be able to accomplish. The outside auditor may not be able to sufficiently integrate itself so that it becomes part of the fiber of the enterprise and thereby gains complete access to the all-important environment or culture where accounting irregularities have their start.

To fill the gap, the audit committee may want to consider installation of an internal audit department. In general, it would make sense to ask the internal auditors to evaluate many of the areas listed above while taking advantage of the one characteristic that gives internal audit an edge: internal auditors are there all the time.

Unlike the outside auditor, therefore, the internal auditor is in a position to participate in hallway gossip; to plug itself into the processes of forecasting, budgeting, sales, and shipping; and to develop important relationships whereby it can attain a genuine feel for the pulse of the organization. While fellow employees may never let down their guard completely, certainly there is greater opportunity for internal auditors to gain access into the workings of the enterprise than for somebody whose principal function is to remain as an outsider.

A hot topic of debate is whether an audit committee should "outsource" internal audit—that is, turn over the internal audit function to the outside auditor. There are both pros and cons, but one question is whether an outsider can effectively plug himself into the culture of the organization in the same way as an employee. It may be that creative and zealous outsourced internal auditors would be able to overcome that impediment. It is a subject of legitimate debate.

Installation of an effective internal audit function, whether outsourced or not, will not necessarily be easy. One reason is that here, too, the audit committee—insofar as it seeks touchy-feely information about the corporate environment rather than crisp statistics on the reliability of numerical data—will to some extent be working against the traditions of the audit profession insofar as internal auditors are, after all, still auditors. Even internal auditors who are admonished to seek and report candidly both statistically derived and gut-level information about the workings of the financial reporting system may find themselves inclined to prefer the former at the expense of the latter.

A single anecdote will illustrate the challenge. One audit committee of a public company was fortunate to have as its chairman an individual who had not only served as CEO of several companies but who possessed extraordinary expertise in corporate governance and, in particular, in the ways that financial reporting systems can break down. This audit committee chairman undertook, as one of his top priorities, the installation of an effective internal audit capability. The structure of the reporting relationship was exactly right: the internal auditors were encouraged and admonished to look for problems. They were directed to report all problems to the audit committee directly.

Over time, the chairman got a sense that the environment was not quite right and might be conducive to problems. He shared his concerns with the internal auditors, who were admonished to look harder. Alas, the internal auditors reported that they didn't see a thing. To them, everything looked just fine.

As it turned out, things were not fine. The company did indeed suffer from an environmental problem, and the internal auditors had either not been sufficiently skilled or sufficiently zealous to plug themselves into it. The true depth of the problem became known only after a significant change in the senior management ranks.

The point of this anecdote is this. In today's world of financial reporting, audit committees are facing an extraordinary challenge. They are being asked not only to assume significant oversight responsibility for the prevention and early detection of fraudulent financial reporting. They are being asked to do so through the use of tools, such as the outside auditor and internal audit, that will themselves have to undergo some degree of cultural evolution before they are in a position to provide the kind of information a modern audit committee will want to have. Even sophisticated and diligent audit committee members will no doubt find the task exceedingly frustrating, and probably few, if any, audit committees so far have managed to install an optimum system. At root, the challenge is to reconfigure the way people think about corporate governance and financial reporting. Theoretically, the tools are there. But some modifications will be necessary before they can be made to work.

Making the Tools Work

How can the audit committee maximize the effectiveness of the tools at its disposal? In other words, how can the audit committee most effectively use the outside auditor and internal audit to trigger a cascade of information and, in particular, to enable bad news to flow up? Here are some ideas.

More on the Tone at the Top

To get the tools to work, it will be critical for the audit committee to set the right tone. If one wants to encourage the flow of bad news, then the flow of bad news must be rewarded. At the same time, the audit committee should zealously guard against the natural inclination of human nature to recoil and punish bad news. It didn't work for Cleopatra. There's no reason to think it will work any better for a modern audit committee.

As a practical matter, this translates into insistence on complete cooperation by employees and executives with both the internal and the outside audit functions. Officers and employees must be made keenly aware that truthfulness and candor are the orders of the day and, correspondingly, that attempts to obfuscate, disguise, or dissemble are absolutely forbidden. Once again, it is a battle for the culture of the organization.

At the same time, the audit committee should appreciate that the auditors must not be too heavy-handed. The auditors' mission is a delicate one and must be approached with an appreciation for the subtleties of human nature and the completely understandable reluctance of others to report bad news. At some point, the task becomes less an exercise in the application of GAAP and more an exercise in the sociology of organizations and the foibles of human nature. Auditors who appear to go about their task with any level of arrogance, swaggering boastfulness, or lack of appreciation for the sensitivity of their positions must either be admonished to change or, more likely, moved to another position. The audit function is not one in which heavy-handedness will get results.

One particularly difficult issue the audit committee will likely face, moreover, is senior-executive insecurity arising out of enhanced and expanded internal and outside auditor functions. Senior executives will no doubt appreciate that they are supposed to know what's going on within the company they are running. An understandable reaction on their part would be a level of insecurity verging on paranoia. At a minimum, the installation of enhanced internal and outside audit functions would seem to do nothing to foster a sense of trust in senior executives or their integrity.

For reasons so eloquently explained by John O. Whitney in his management text *The Economics of Trust*, a sense of mistrust must not be permitted to creep into the relationship between the audit committee and senior management. Trust is critical, and without it the installation of enhanced audit functions could end up proving counterproductive. That sense of trust must be maintained through the recognition, explicitly shared with senior executives, that nobody is perfect, no enterprise is perfect, and that, simply by virtue of its position, the audit committee may have access to information that even the most well-meaning and effective senior executives may not. That information will not be used against the executives, but, rather, will give them a heretofore unavailable opportunity to gain new insights into their company and enhance its operations. The information is not being obtained to be used against anyone. It is being obtained so that everyone may benefit from its revelation.

Will some senior executives nonetheless try to exact revenge from an employee who has spilled the beans? It is almost inevitable that the ranks of senior management will include executives who would so foolishly react. That is, therefore, still another thing for which the audit committee will want to keep its eyes open. If it learns of an executive seeking to so stifle truthful information, the committee's reaction in most instances should probably be unequivocal and swift. Such an executive in all likelihood does not know how to get information or how to use it when it's available. Who knows what's been happening in his department? He inevitably doesn't. A direct communication with the executive is probably in order. Also in order may be his removal.

Minimize Reliance on Paper

For some reason, almost anyone within an organization is drawn to demonstrate his or her diligence through the generation of paper. That is particularly so when people are not quite sure what they're supposed to be doing. As an audit committee undertakes to improve financial reporting, therefore, an inclination may exist for those involved to generate written reports—inspection reports, exception reports, reports consolidating reports—all accompanied by the normal barrage of memoranda, correspondence, and (today) e-mails.

In many areas of corporate endeavor, the mindless generation of paper merely wastes time. In the context of corporate governance and financial reporting, it can actually be counterproductive. The reason probably stems from the underlying reluctance of individuals to write with the same candor that they speak—particularly when the topic is criticism of the organization or, more frightening, their own superiors. A resulting loss of candor would be particularly unfortunate in the transmittal of information to the audit committee insofar as some of the most important information involves subtle aspects of the corporate environment and tone. Such information can be difficult to quantify and document, and exclusive reliance on written reports may cause such information to be lost completely. Human resource directors are familiar with a phenomenon in which the performance evaluations of individual employees tend to improve when, having been presented orally, they must then be reduced to writing. There's no reason to think that the phenomenon will not occur where the evaluations are of corporate rather than individual performance.

To the full extent possible, therefore, the better approach may be to minimize the use of paper and to gain access to information through direct face-to-face meetings. In that way, the true richness of feedback can be explored and the participants can be made to feel more at liberty to convey potential problems before they would seem to warrant documentation. Feelings, concerns, gut-level instincts—all of these would likely be more forthcoming if they could be presented orally rather than on paper. Presumably for such reasons, the new amendments to GAAS decline to require the auditor's written communication of certain kinds of information (Exhibit 11–11).

An additional reason exists to minimize the generation of paper, though one is loathe to acknowledge it. The reason stems from the disadvantage of unnecessary documentation in the event of litigation. While written reports might be used affirmatively in litigation to demonstrate the diligence of audit committee members, the reports might also be taken out of context to show supposedly unpardonable flaws in the financial reporting system. The minimization of written reports reduces the risk.

It is probably too much to ask that an effective communication system be entirely paper-free. After all, there will be a lot to keep track of. Nonetheless, even under the best of circumstances, the efficiency of an organization is probably inversely proportional to the amount of paper it generates. That may be particularly so when it comes to perpetual evaluation of the corporation's financial reporting system and, in particular, the corporate environment.

Learn the Business

To "learn the business" does not mean to study the most recent Form 10-K. Nor does it mean rote memorization of product lines, divisions, or facility locations. What the audit committee really wants to understand is how the organizations runs—what is the system by which the company conceives, creates, sells, and publicly reports. A significant underlying objective in understanding the system is development of an appreciation for those aspects of the system (e.g., budgeting, sales, shipping) in which vulnerabilities leading to potential breakdowns in financial reporting are most likely to occur.

That kind of information is not available from audited financial statements. It is more readily unearthed, rather, through one-to-one contact with executives and operating personnel. At one public construction company, for example, the audit committee chairman arranged for a series of half-day meetings with executives in five separate areas (finance, construction, human resources, bidding, and estimates) to develop a meaningful understanding of just how the company worked.

Public companies are, at bottom, simply collections of human beings trying to get along as best they can. An understanding of how individuals interact—the motivations, the pressures, the problems—can contribute mightily to an understanding of underlying vulnerabilities.

Meet with Others and Alone

The audit committee's function poses something of a dilemma. On the one hand, the audit committee consists of outsiders who, by definition, are at least once-removed from the company. On the other hand, the audit committee wants to develop an overall sense of the company's financial reporting weaknesses that is more objective and more vivid than that of almost anyone else.

A consequence is that the audit committee should have two types of meetings. One type is meetings with others. "Others" would include the CEO, the CFO, at times key operating personnel, the outside auditor, and internal audit. The purpose of such meetings (and their effectiveness may be enhanced if they are done separately) is to capture the full texture of each individual's experience and views as to what is going on and, more important, where problems may be developing.

The other type of meeting consists of meetings in which the audit committee members confer by themselves. Only in isolation can they candidly express their views as to the strengths and weaknesses of individuals, company systems, and the company as a whole. That is not to say that each meeting must adhere to a rigid agenda—first the CEO, then the CFO, then the internal auditor, then ten minutes for private discussion. Rather, it means that, as the audit committee seeks to explore potential vulnerabilities in financial reporting, a full spectrum of meeting configurations may be useful.

Meet When Necessary

One issue that seems to have attracted more than its share of regulatory attention is the frequency with which audit committee meetings should be held. Should they be held once a year? Once a quarter? Once a month? Before each board meeting? On an ad hoc basis?

No rule or regulation definitively answers the question, though SEC Chairman Arthur Levitt has made clear his disdain for an audit committee that presumed to fulfill its functions while meeting "only twice a year before the regular board meeting for fifteen minutes." At the other end of the spectrum, Arthur Levitt has presented to the business community his Platonic ideal of an audit committee that "meets twelve times a year."

Here is a common sense suggestion. While it sounds almost too obvious to mention, a good approach would be to hold audit committee meetings as often as necessary. For example, an audit committee just getting started or at a company whose financial reporting system suffers from a history of problems might want to meet as often as every two or three weeks. As appropriate systems are put in place, once a month or, later still, once a quarter may be just fine. The point is that the frequency of meetings should be driven by the needs of the company—not by self-imposed edict or by the desire to create an appearance of diligence. Good judgment is probably the best guide.

Use Good Judgment

The importance of good judgment brings to mind one final point. All organizations are different. They have different histories. They operate in different industries. They have different cultures. What works for one company may not work for another. It is hard to conceive of a single set of guidelines for effective audit committee oversight that would work optimally at all companies across the board.

Perhaps the most important guideline an audit committee might use to accomplish its objectives, therefore, is simply the good judgment of its individual members. In the end, the audit committee is trying to measure the pulse of the enterprise throughout the trials and tribulations of its corporate life. The overriding goal is to isolate the financial reporting system from the inevitable pressures that result when things don't go exactly as desired. No regulation, charter, checklist, mission statement, or corporate resolution can effectively guide the audit committee as it seeks to fulfill that goal. The best tool, rather, is the informed good judgment of the individual committee members.

CHAPTER 12

ACCOUNTING IRREGULARITIES AND THE FUTURE OF FINANCIAL REPORTING

Michael R. Young

We have at this point looked at the topic of accounting irregularities from almost every conceivable angle. We've looked at their origin. We've looked at the immediate aftermath of detection. We've looked at the procurement of new audited financial statements, the mechanics of an investigation, dealing with class actions, responding to regulators, and criminal implications. We've looked at prevention. Seemingly, the entirety of the subject has been thoroughly explored.

Except for one question: Why? Why now, as we begin the twenty-first century, are we seeing such an increase in fraudulently reported financial results—particularly given the seemingly contrary trend of corporations seeking to behave like good corporate citizens? What is going on in the world of financial reporting that is giving rise to almost an epidemic of misreported financial results?

As mentioned at the outset, the underlying cause is not dishonesty. Nor is it immorality. Beyond the experience of any individual company, the cause is rooted in the fact that we are at a historic moment in the evolution of financial reporting. In particular, we are at a moment where financial market demands for information are not being met by the financial reporting system that happens to be in place. On the one hand, financial markets are demanding instantaneous, non-stop financial information. On the other hand, our financial reporting system is designed to provide information only periodically—once a quarter at best. The consequence is misreported financial results.

Identification of an underlying cause of accounting irregularities is an important first step. The second step is to assess the direction in which the financial reporting system seems to be evolving and the extent to which the mismatch between financial market needs and financial reporting system capability will worsen, get better, or stay pretty much the same. Here the news is good. There is every indication that the financial reporting system is evolving in a way that will eventually cause the underlying pressures giving rise to fraudulent financial reporting to dissipate. There is much reason to hope, therefore, that the present upsurge in accounting irregularities will ultimately prove to be a temporary problem rather than a long-term feature of financial reporting by public companies.

A Real-Time World

Let us first spend a moment on the demands of today's financial markets. In particular, let us first address the insatiable thirst of financial markets for nonstop information.

In substance, financial markets today are functioning in a real-time world. Innovators such as Bloomberg, Dow Jones, and any number of entrepreneurial upstarts flash financial and business information around the world the instant it's available. One such company advertises the delivery of "global financial news to 16,000 places every minute." Traveling executives increasingly find themselves transporting miniaturized communications centers— cellular phones, pagers, beepers, even fax machines—so that they may instantaneously receive, and act upon, the latest events. Anyone with access to the Internet—which is, increasingly, everyone—has ready access to financial information that, in another era, would have been available to just a highly select few.

The extent of this information revolution has infiltrated the very fiber of our culture. Standing in line at New York's Penn Station, it seems perfectly natural to see the latest financial statistics flashed across a giant screen. It seems completely normal that, while heading for a Broadway theater in Times Square, stock prices courtesy of Dow Jones are never more than a glance away. It hardly seems surprising that the telephones on airplanes (no longer are we cut off while flying) give us second-by-second financial market updates. Even more traditional businesses are transforming themselves. CBS, through its newly created MarketWatch.com, now advertises "the hottest financial stories" and "market data in real-time" to let all of us "stay ahead of the market."

The impact of this onslaught of information on financial markets is nothing less than extraordinary. If something happens at the Bundesbank in Germany with the potential to influence United States financial markets, we might expect no more than 10 to 15 minutes to elapse before trading on the New York Stock Exchange is affected. Indeed, it seems that almost no corner of civilization, no matter how ostensibly isolated in locale or tradition, can escape the insatiable thirst for information of a real-time world. Even the courts, with their explicit exclusion of electronic communications devices from their hallowed halls, are not immune. When an important court decision is rendered, strategically placed individuals, through a carefully designed system of hand signals, find a way to get the information within seconds to the outside world so the information can be electronically transmitted and put to use.

A 1930s Financial Reporting System

Our financial reporting system, of course, was not designed with any of this in mind. The basics of today's system were, after all, designed in the 1930s during the Great Depression. It was a time when carbon paper was viewed as a technological innovation. The dominant concern at the time was not the speed of transmission of reliable financial information but the objective that reliable financial information be available to begin with. It was natural to assume that the information itself would be transmitted almost entirely on paper.

At the core of this Depression-era system, moreover, was the concept that financial information need be available only periodically. That is to say, no one had reason to think that some day technological innovation would collapse the time needed to assemble and report financial information to days or even minutes. The underlying concept of the 1930s, rather, was built upon the notion that the financial results of operations were to be assembled by a heavily-populated accounting staff, packaged for management, and ultimately—every so often—provided to the public. The public, in turn, could make its investment decisions accordingly.

Hence, the original public reporting requirements of the Securities Exchange Act of 1934 contemplated the filing of financial information only annually. Over time, the laudable objective of encouraging efficiency in financial markets caused this requirement to be changed to semi-annually and quarterly. At root, though, the system remained a periodic one. In other words, the underlying premise of the system continued to be that financial information would be made available only periodically. Today's system is thus an anachronistic remnant of the technology—i.e., carbon paper and the printing press—that existed when the system was designed.

True to its historical underpinnings, moreover, the core of today's financial reporting system continues to be a financial report that comes out once a year. That report, of course, is the set of annual financial statements that is audited by an outside accounting firm and included with the company's annual Form 10-K.

And let's pause a moment to look at how those financial statements are put together. First, we wait for the year to end. Then we wait for another twelve weeks or more while the auditor combs through the company's books and records. Then we wait while the data is assembled, typed, delivered to a printer, and, then, given to the United States Postal Service, which ends up delivering the information on foot. By the time users of the financial information receive it, the most recent information is ordinarily three months old. It took less time for Columbus to discover America.

It is true that, under encouragement from the SEC, the financial community is trying to take big strides forward. Thus, we have the development of the Edgar system of electronic SEC filing and, increasingly, companies placing their Forms 10-K and Forms 10-Q—as well as press releases, product information, and background data—on their Web sites. Although this is a big step in the right direction, it continues to be intellectually hindered by the periodic concept of the 1930s. That is, basically all we are doing is taking periodic information from paper and placing it on the computer.

Thus, a vacuum in financial reporting exists. It is a vacuum between the real-time financial information that financial markets demand and the inability of our creaky, sputtering financial reporting system to deliver information more frequently than once a quarter.

So Enter the Analysts

It is the miracle of a capitalist system that such a vacuum does not last for long. Here, an entire population of entrepreneurs has rushed in to provide to financial markets the updated financial information they so earnestly desire. Those entrepreneurs are the community of Wall Street financial analysts.

For it is not, in fact, the case that a user of financial information only has access to financial performance once a quarter. Instead, a user has available the more up-to-date information provided by financial analysts—in the form of readily published earnings expectations. This analyst information may be right or it may be wrong, but it possesses one virtue that the official financial data does not. It is available.

It is thus that we find ourselves in the peculiar position of having in place a carefully structured and painstakingly built formal financial reporting system that is being largely ignored by everybody. And a fair argument can be made that today's system is indeed being largely ignored. The annual filing of a Form 10-K does not move financial markets. By the time the 10-K comes out, the information at best is ancient history and has been factored into the stock price for months. Many have probably heard the story of a food manufacturer which, as a test of the usefulness of its annual financial statements, offered shareholders a choice: a glossy copy of the company's annual report or a free pound of cookies. Most shareholders went for the cookies.

Although unaudited quarterly statements play a more important role, rarely do even quarterly statements move markets. That is to say, rarely do quarterly statements move markets when they are consistent with already existing analyst expectations. When they are not consistent with expectations, they can move markets quite a lot.

That takes us to the crux of the matter. What moves financial markets is not an annual 10-K or even a quarterly 10-Q. What moves financial markets is the published expectations of Wall Street analysts. In substance, the published expectations of Wall Street analysts are perceived to establish, within a very narrow margin, the parameters for the upcoming actual financial results. Analyst expectations have become, in effect, a company's reported earnings.

A Consequence Is Accounting Irregularities

What does all this have to do with accounting irregularities? The elevated importance to financial markets of analyst expectations has resulted in a financial reporting environment in which, for a number of public companies, the preoccupation of financial reporting is not accurately depicting the financial performance of the enterprise. Rather, the preoccupation of financial reporting is seeing to it that analyst expectations—one way or another—are fulfilled.

For public companies faced with this preoccupation, its fulfillment can be a nightmare insofar as no legally satisfactory way exists by which the accuracy of analyst expectations can be controlled. That is not for lack of trying on the part of analysts. Analysts earn their living, and if they're lucky get famous, providing reliable estimates of future financial performance. The best way to get reliable information is to ask a company's CFO what he or she expects. The result is a periodic ritual in which outside analysts will telephone inside CFOs for the latest glimpse into the company's financial future.

This would seem like a golden opportunity for a CFO to get accurate information out on the street and to keep analyst expectations from varying from the truth. Unfortunately, the law, as a result of its understandable paranoia about the leakage of inside information, tries to keep precisely that from happening.

So here's what ends up taking place. The analyst needs to get updated financial information. He telephones the CFO. He gives the CFO, say, his latest guess as to how the quarter is going to come out. And he asks the CFO, "Am I right or wrong?"

There is no completely satisfactory way for the CFO to answer that question. Basically, the CFO has two choices. First, he can try to "steer" the analyst into a more accurate prediction or simply tell the analyst he is right or wrong. However, the CFO himself may not have a firm sense of how the quarter is going to come out and may end up inadvertently creating an expectation that can neither be fulfilled nor easily corrected. Worse than that, providing up-to-date financial results to a single analyst creates a risk of giving out inside information. If the information is material, and it probably will be, that sets up the CFO for a subsequent charge of being a participant in insider trading, which potentially exposes the CFO and his company to severe civil and regulatory penalties. It is also a felony.

The second alternative is for the CFO to keep his mouth shut. Here, the problem is a different one. If the CFO keeps his mouth shut, and the analyst goes forward with the publication of incorrect expectations, then the actual quarterly results, when they come out (by preannouncement or otherwise), will potentially wreak havoc. If actual results exceed analyst expectations, then shareholders are all the happier and no real harm results (beyond extraordinary inefficiency in information dissemination). If, however, actual results are significantly below street expectations, the result for the stock price can be significant. So-called "momentum" investors may flee the stock. The stock price may collapse. And the company—as well as the CFO, the CEO, and any number of inside and outside directors—may very well end up defendants in class action litigation.

Either way, our hapless CFO is at substantial risk that an incorrect earnings estimate will create a street expectation that cannot be fulfilled or painlessly corrected. If an incorrect estimate takes hold, then, as quarter-end approaches—and with it the inevitable day of reckoning—the pressure mounts. And so does the incentive to exploit those hazy areas of generally accepted accounting principles (GAAP) which would allow the company ostensibly to make up for the earnings shortfall. (See Chapter 1.)

It is, therefore, the vacuum resulting from what financial markets want, which is immediate financial information, and what the present structure of financial reporting systems enable companies to deliver, which is quarterly and annual reports, that has contributed so handily to the financial reporting environment that lies at the core of the recent increase in accounting irregularities. The vacuum is filled by analysts, and analyst expectations, in turn, create enormous pressure on a company to see that they are fulfilled. Accounting irregularities, of course, don't start with dishonesty. They start with pressure.

Other Capital Market Inefficiencies

Still additional problems result from the vacuum created by the real-time demands of financial markets and today's periodic system of financial reporting.

One such problem is the resulting volatility both in individual stock market prices and in the market as a whole. The underlying causes of that volatility, of course, are numerous. A big cause, though, stems from the market gyrations that come about during "earnings season" when companies announce or preannounce quarterly results. For an individual company, the fallout can include a collapsing stock price, a demoralized work force (whose stock options may now be under water), anxious lenders, and class action litigation (even in the absence of an accounting irregularity problem). An October 1999 announcement of a weak outlook by IBM resulted in a one-day loss of market value of $39 billion. Three months later, Lucent

Technologies' announcement of an anticipated failure to attain analyst expectations (it said it expected to miss them by about 15 cents) translated into a market capital loss almost twice as large—$64 billion.

But the fallout is not limited to the management and the shareholders of the particular company that happens to disappoint. When Intel preannounced disappointing earnings for the first quarter of 1998, it reportedly triggered a collapse in securities markets around the world. Unpredictable volatility in the securities markets—in particular in the high-tech sector, where capital arguably makes the largest contribution to economic growth—is something that investors have just learned to live with.

But they don't live with it for free. Volatility means risk. And risk means investors want a higher return on their capital investment. An important consequence of the volatility that necessarily results from our periodic financial reporting system, therefore, is the additional premium investors require from the securities markets to compensate for the increased risk. Here, again, the cost is not limited to the company or investors of a particular company that happens to disappoint. To some extent, it is shared by the stock market as a whole.

Operational inefficiencies from a periodic reporting system follow as well. Manufacturing companies, on going public, have perceived a change in the buying patterns of their customers, owing to their customers' awareness of the manufacturers' need to attain a certain level of quarterly revenue. One such company, for example, found that, after going public, purchases by distributors tended to become clustered in the third month of each quarter. As the company went into each third month, its nervousness over a prospective failure to make its quarterly numbers led to increasing levels of discounting, which only increased the incentives for the company's customers to hold off their purchases as long as they could. After several years, the company found its assembly lines less active in the first month of each quarter and then working overtime in the third. Shipping problems developed as the physical limitations of the loading docks could not accommodate quarter-end peak demand. The problem was exacerbated insofar as other manufacturing companies in the geographic vicinity seemed to be going through the same thing and all were simultaneously seeking to line up available trucking. On top of everything else, quarter-end also presented a shortage of trucks.

Such logistical problems can lead to breakdowns in accounting systems. One representative of the SEC's Division of Enforcement encountered a public company which, he suspected, had turned back its computer clock as a result of a logistical failure to ship all merchandise during a quarter-end peak. Faced with seemingly corroborative documentation from the independent trucker which showed that shipment had in fact taken place before quarter-end, the SEC official on a hunch telephoned the trucker only to learn that the trucker, at the request of the manufacturer, had back-dated the shipping documentation. Nor was the request that the trucker do so apparently at all unusual. The trucker went on to explain that, at the end of each quarter, he received literally hundreds of similar requests from other companies.

The problems do not stop there. Still another results from almost extraordinary inefficiency in the way that critical financial information ends up being transmitted to the public through the intermediary of financial analysts. Mechanically, the present system works something like this: The typical CFO at a public company has sitting on his desk a computer. That computer is plugged into the company's management information system, which provides information that is sufficiently reliable for the fundamental operational and financial decisions of the enterprise. It tells the CFO, and for that matter anybody who's plugged into it, financial performance to date and, by inference, to some extent where the company will be at the end of the quarter.

Now let's consider a Wall Street analyst whose office happens to be, say, in a building across the street. He has sitting on his desk a computer. It is the analyst's fundamental mission in life to find out what's on the CFO's computer and to get it into *his* computer. He'll take whatever information he can get, put it into his own computer, and thereby generate an earnings forecast.

To find out what's on the CFO's computer, the analyst uses one of the most up-to-date of technological devices—the telephone. He telephones the CFO to extricate whatever clues and insights he can gain about the company's financial performance.

For reasons already discussed, the law heavily discourages the CFO from candidly providing direct information. So the two end up speaking in code. The analyst may say something like, "I'm predicting EPS of $.32 for the quarter—how comfortable are you in that area?" The CFO, having been cautioned against expressing a view on analyst expectations, at most will limit himself to talking about the past. He accordingly might respond with something like, "How can you be at $.32 when this quarter last year we came in at $.25, as we have, in fact, for the previous 17 quarters." At some point, our analyst gets the message and, sure enough, puts out his new earnings forecast: $.25. Although both possess the most efficient means of electronic communication in the history of civilization, our CFO and Wall Street analyst have digressed into a communication system of winks and nods over which cuneiform would be an improvement.

And that's without even getting to company incentives to "talk down" analyst expectations to less than actually foreseen, or to the potential incentive by analysts to issue favorable reports owing to preexisting relationships between the company and the analyst's investment bank. All of these amount to extraordinary inefficiencies in the dissemination of financial information to the investing public.

Our Depression-era periodic system of financial reporting even creates inefficiencies from the perspective of financial management. The chairman of one high-tech company once observed that his internal financial reporting systems were sufficiently sophisticated that every day he, like other senior executives, received on his e-mail a report of revenue on the previous day's shipments. It so happened that the nature of the company's business was such that its margins were fairly consistent. Thus, receipt of shipping information in terms of revenues yielded in substance daily information of earnings and, by inference, earnings per share. The information was reliable and always up to date. Unfortunately, such was the terror instilled in the chairman by virtue of the federal securities laws, that the chairman (who wanted periodically to sell a portion of his very substantial stock holdings) became paranoid about having access to such timely information when the public did not. He accordingly had himself disconnected from the company's e-mail.

There's Another Way

So that's where we are at the moment. Our periodic system of financial reporting creates enormous pressure for fundamentally honest people to perpetrate accounting fraud. It creates unnecessary volatility in the stock market. It requires rational investors to demand a premium for securities investments. It gives rise to operational inefficiencies. It results in enormous inefficiency in the transmission of information from public companies to financial markets. It even creates an incentive for corporate managers to disconnect themselves from up-to-date information.

There's got to be a better way. And, in fact, there is. Members of the financial community are increasingly acknowledging the need for an evolution beyond the financial reporting system of the 1930s into an era of non-stop information of the sort financial markets want. In other words, there was an alternative available to our chairman who disconnected himself from the company e-mail, though we can hardly blame him for not thinking of it. He could have stayed connected to his e-mail. And, in fact, he could have let the e-mail go out to the analysts and the financial community at large. That is to say, he could have reported his company's financial results on a real-time basis.

Now an understandable reaction on the part of CFOs might be unmitigated terror. Anyone familiar with the agony of putting out a quarterly press release has reason to flee from the concept of fundamentally doing so at least once a day. How would the information be checked? What controls would there be on reliability? What happens if there's an honest mistake? How can we protect ourselves from the class action plaintiffs?

Those are all good questions, and not all of them have perfect answers. But the accelerating pace of innovation in technology and financial reporting systems will make increasingly apparent the need to move beyond the periodic system rooted in the technology of the 1930s. Already the AICPA is hard at work on the development of real-time auditor "assurance services" so that users may be satisfied as to the reliability of real-time financial information without waiting for the comfort of a year-end audit. At the same time, scholars are embracing the potential for innovations in financial reporting potentially made available by the concept of computer-to-computer interaction. Experts on legal liability are fashioning new ways to manage the risk of exposure to litigation arising out of real-time financial information, including the possibility of contractual limitations to liability entered through the use of "electronic signatures" transmitted by computer.

At the very least, moreover, the opportunity for dramatic advances in capital market efficiency will be lost on no one. Among other things, real-time financial reporting would free corporate America from its economically nonsensical preoccupation with quarterly results. There is absolutely no economic justification for focusing upon a quarter as the economic unit in which to take stock of financial performance beyond the fact that that's what's written in the law. Making available financial information on a real-time basis would almost require users of financial information to discard the quarter as a unit of measurement and to adopt a unit that made sense for each particular business and industry. For some companies and industries, that unit might be a week, a month, a quarter, semi-annually, or a year. The point is that users would have the freedom to adopt a time period that actually made sense rather than the "one size fits all" period decreed by federal law.

A more fundamental advantage, moreover, would be the opportunity for increased efficiency in financial markets as investment would be allocated not according to quarterly results or the "best guess" estimates of financial analysts, but by reliable financial information provided directly by the company all the time. A collateral but equally significant benefit would be the decrease in stock market volatility insofar as discrepancies between market expectations and actual results would never develop or, having developed, would be corrected in modest amounts every day rather than in one large correction at the end of each quarter.

Still another advantage would be the practical elimination of the principal incentive for—and perhaps the mechanical ability to perpetrate—financial misreporting in the form of accounting irregularities. Gone would be the brooding omnipresence of quarterly analyst expectations and, accordingly, the pressure to manipulate results in order to meet them. More than that, also largely eliminated would be the mechanical ability to perpetrate accounting sleights of hand, insofar as financial information would be publicly available automatically before any of the (at least traditional) manipulations could be put in place. That is not to suggest, of course, that real-time financial reporting would eliminate financial fraud for all time. We all know better than that. But it would take us a giant step in the right direction.

None of this is to suggest that anyone is proposing that the totality of a company's internal reporting system be opened up to the outside world. Public companies will inevitably want to limit access to information that is reliable and that can reasonably be transmitted on a regular basis. In addition, the transmittal of any such information would presumably be accompanied by appropriate caveats and warnings directed to the extent of the information's reliability. Before any of this can happen, moreover, financial reporting systems would have to be improved to the point where the real-time transmission of key information were possible. Companies would have to follow the example of companies such as Microsoft, which is collapsing the time it takes to assemble and report financial results to achieve a "continuous close" where information is accurate and current every day of the month.

Nevertheless, the real-time needs of financial markets are dragging today's financial reporting system in the direction of increased frequency of financial reporting without anyone really focusing on the broader implications. An increasingly common example is the advent of earnings "preannouncements" when actual results are diverging significantly from analyst expectations. According to a recent survey, 72% of Fortune 500 CFOs have decided to preannounce or provide early guidance on earnings, presumably as a consequence of the downside of waiting for the end of the legally mandated quarter. Other examples of more frequent data being made available without waiting for quarter-end include retailers who post on their Web sites updated sales figures, hotel chains whose Web sites include updated occupancy rates, and newspapers whose Web sites include updated circulation figures.

The good news, therefore, is that, although fraudulent financial reporting will never be eliminated, the pressures giving rise to the present-day epidemic of accounting irregularities will foreseeably cease. Change rarely comes easily, and we can expect earnest debate and startling innovation as financial reporting proceeds through the twenty-first century. Some will inevitably long for the days of carbon paper. But for others, a new era of financial reporting may be, at least to some extent, exhilarating.

SECURITIES AND EXCHANGE COMMISSION INITIATIVES AGAINST ACCOUNTING IRREGULARITIES AND MANAGED EARNINGS

Appendix A	New Rules of the Securities and Exchange Commission Regarding Audit Committee Disclosure	270
Appendix B	New Rules of the New York Stock Exchange Regarding Corporate Governance and Audit Committees	296
Appendix C	New Rules of the National Association of Securities Dealers Regarding Corporate Governance and Audit Committees	308
Appendix D	SEC Staff Accounting Bulletin No. 99—Materiality	320
Appendix E	SEC Staff Accounting Bulletin No. 100—Restructuring and Impairment Charges	331
Appendix F	SEC Staff Accounting Bulletin No. 101—Revenue Recognition in Financial Statements	348

Final Rule: Audit Committee Disclosure

SECURITIES AND EXCHANGE COMMISSION
17 CFR Parts 210, 228, 229, and 240
[Release No. 34-42266; File No. S7-22-99]
RIN 3235-AH83
Audit Committee Disclosure

Agency: Securities and Exchange Commission

Action: Final rule

Summary: The Securities and Exchange Commission is adopting new rules and amendments to its current rules to require that companies' independent auditors review the companies' financial information prior to the companies filing their Quarterly Reports on Form 10-Q or Form 10-QSB with the Commission, and to require that companies include in their proxy statements certain disclosures about their audit committees and reports from their audit committees containing certain disclosures. The rules are designed to improve disclosure related to the functioning of corporate audit committees and to enhance the reliability and credibility of financial statements of public companies.

Dates: Effective Date: [Insert date 30 days after publication in the Federal Register.] Compliance Dates:: Registrants must obtain reviews of interim financial information by their independent auditors starting with their Forms 10-Q or 10-QSB to be filed for fiscal quarters ending on or after March 15, 2000. Registrants must comply with the new proxy and information disclosure requirements (e.g., the requirement to include a report of their audit committee in their proxy statements, provide disclosures regarding the independence of their audit committee members, and attach a copy of the audit committee's charter) for all proxy and information statements relating to votes of shareholders occurring after December 15, 2000. Companies who become subject to Item 302(a) of Regulation S-K as a result of today's amendments must comply with its requirements after December 15, 2000. Registrants voluntarily may comply with any of the new requirements prior to the compliance dates.

For Further Information Contact: Mark Borges, Attorney-Adviser, Division of Corporation Finance (202-942-2900), Meridith Mitchell, Senior Counselor, Office of the General Counsel (202-942-0900), or W. Scott Bayless, Associate Chief Accountant, or Robert E. Burns, Chief Counsel, Office of the Chief Accountant (202-942-4400).

Supplementary Information: The Commission is adopting amendments to Rule 10-01 of Regulation S-X,[1] Item 310 of Regulation S-B,[2] Item 7 of Schedule 14A[3] under the Securities Exchange Act of 1934 (the "Exchange Act"),[4] and Item 302 of Regulation S-K.[5] Additionally, the Commission is adopting new Item 306 of Regulation S-K[6] and Item 306 of Regulation S-B.[7]

I. Executive Summary

We are adopting new rules and amendments to current rules to improve disclosure relating to the functioning of corporate audit committees and to enhance the reliability and credibility of financial statements of public companies.[8] As more fully described in the Proposing Release, the new rules and amendments are based in large measure on recommendations made by the Blue Ribbon Committee on Improving the Effectiveness of Corporate Audit Committees (the "Blue Ribbon Committee").[9] The new rules and amendments have been adopted in most respects as proposed, with modifications discussed below.

Audit committees play a critical role in the financial reporting system by overseeing and monitoring management's and the independent auditors' participation in the financial reporting process. We have seen a number of significant changes in our markets, such as technological developments and increasing pressure on companies to meet earnings expectations,[10] that make it ever more important for the financial reporting process to remain disciplined and credible.[11] We believe that additional disclosures about a company's audit committee and its interaction with the company's auditors and management will promote investor confidence in the integrity of the financial reporting process. In addition, increasing the level of scrutiny by independent auditors of companies' quarterly financial statements should lead to fewer year-end adjustments, and, therefore, more reliable financial information about companies throughout the reporting year.

Accordingly, the new rules and amendments:

- require that companies' independent auditors review the financial information included in the companies' Quarterly Reports on Form 10-Q or 10-QSB prior to the companies filing such reports with the Commission (see Section III.A below);

- extend the requirements of Item 302(a) of Regulation S-K (requiring at fiscal year end appropriate reconciliations and descriptions of any adjustments to the quarterly information previously reported in a Form 10-Q for any quarter)[12] to a wider range of companies (see Section III.A below);

- require that companies include reports of their audit committees in their proxy statements;[13] in the report, the audit committee must state whether the audit committee has: (i) reviewed and discussed the audited financial statements with management; (ii) discussed with the independent auditors the matters required to be discussed by Statement on Auditing Standards No. 61,[14] as may be modified or supplemented; and (iii) received from the auditors disclosures regarding the auditors' independence required by Independence Standards Board Standard No. 1,[15] as may be modified or supplemented, and discussed with the auditors the auditors' independence (see Section III.B below);

- require that the report of the audit committee also include a statement by the audit committee whether, based on the review and discussions noted above, the audit committee recommended to the Board of Directors that the audited financial statements be included in the company's Annual Report on Form 10-K or 10-KSB (as applicable) for the last fiscal year for filing with the Commission (see Section III.B below);

- require that companies disclose in their proxy statements whether their Board of Directors has adopted a written charter for the audit committee, and if so, include a copy of the charter as an appendix to the company's proxy statements at least once every three years (see Section III.C below);

- require that companies, including small business issuers,[16] whose securities are quoted on Nasdaq or listed on the American Stock Exchange ("AMEX") or New York Stock Exchange ("NYSE"), disclose in their proxy statements whether the audit committee members are "independent" as defined in the applicable listing standards,[17] and disclose certain information regarding any director on the audit committee who is not "independent"(see Section III.D below); require that companies, including small business issuers, whose securities are not quoted on Nasdaq or listed on the AMEX or NYSE disclose in their proxy statements whether, if they have an audit committee, the members are "independent," as defined in the NASD's, AMEX's or NYSE's listing standards, and which definition was used (see Section III.D below); and

- provide "safe harbors" for the new proxy statement disclosures to protect companies and their directors from certain liabilities under the federal securities laws (see Section III.E below).

To provide companies with the opportunity to evaluate their compliance with the revised listing standards of the NASD, AMEX, and NYSE and to prepare for the new disclosure requirements, we are providing transition periods for compliance with the new requirements (see Section V below).

II. Background

As discussed in the Proposing Release, given the changes in our markets, such as the increasing number of investors entering our markets and changes in the way and speed with which investors receive information, it is vitally important for investors to remain confident that they are receiving the highest quality financial reporting. The demand for reliable financial information appears to be at an all time high, as technology makes information available to more people more quickly. The new dynamics of our capital markets have presented companies with an increasingly complex set of challenges. One challenge is that companies are under increasing pressure to meet earnings expectations.[18] We have become increasingly concerned about inappropriate "earnings management," the practice of distorting the true financial performance of the company.[19]

The changes in our markets and the increasing pressures on companies to maintain positive earnings trends have highlighted the importance of strong and effective audit committees. Effective oversight of the financial reporting process is fundamental to preserving the integrity of our markets. Audit committees play a critical role in the financial reporting system by overseeing and monitoring management's and the independent auditors' participation in the financial reporting process. Audit committees can, and should, be the corporate participant best able to perform that oversight function.

As discussed more fully in the Proposing Release, since the early 1940s, the Commission, along with the auditing and corporate communities, has had a continuing interest in promoting effective and independent audit committees. Most recently, the NYSE and NASD sponsored the Blue Ribbon Committee in response to "an increasing sense of urgency surrounding the need for responsible financial reporting given the market's increasing focus on corporate earnings and a long and powerful bull market."[20] The new rules and amendments affirm what have long been considered sound practice and good policy within the accounting and corporate communities.[21]

While almost all of the commenters that provided comment letters on the Proposing Release[22] supported our goals of improving disclosure about audit committees and enhancing the reliability and credibility of financial statements, many commenters suggested alternative approaches to achieving those goals. Some commenters believed that we should impose more rigorous requirements.[23] Other commenters recommended that we not adopt certain aspects of the proposals. In this regard, the concern most frequently expressed was that as a result of the new requirements to provide certain disclosures in a report, audit committees may be exposed to additional liability, and that consequently it may be difficult for companies to find qualified people to serve on audit committees.[24]

It is not our intention to subject audit committee members to increased liability. We addressed concerns about liability by modifying our initial proposals from the Blue Ribbon Committee's recommendations and by providing safe harbor protections. Nevertheless, we appreciate that many commenters continue to be concerned about the audit committee report generally, and specifically the requirement that the audit committee state whether anything has come to the attention of the members of the audit committee that caused the audit committee to believe that the audited financial statements included in the company's Annual Report on Form 10-K or 10-KSB contain an untrue statement of material fact or omit to state a material fact necessary to make the statements made, in light of the circumstances under which they were made, not misleading.

In response, we have modified that disclosure item, which was the subject of most of the commentary. We are adopting, instead, one of the other alternatives proposed – the audit committee must state whether, based on the review and discussion of the audited financial statements with management and discussions with the independent auditors, the audit committee recommended to the Board that the audited financial statements be included in the company's Annual Report on Form 10-K or 10-KSB (as applicable) for the last fiscal year for filing with the Commission. As we discussed in the Proposing Release, we do not believe that improved disclosure about the audit committee and increased involvement by the audit committee should result in increased exposure to liability. Consequently, we believe that this modification, together with the safe harbors, should further alleviate concerns about increased liability exposure, while promoting our goal of improving the financial reporting process.

Some commenters expressed concern about applying the new requirements to small businesses, particularly the interim financial review requirement. We have considered those comments carefully. We think that improvements in the financial reporting process for companies of all sizes is important for promoting investor confidence in our markets.[25] In this regard, because we have seen instances of financial fraud at small companies as well as at large companies, [26] we think that improving disclosures about the audit committees of small and large companies is important. As discussed in the Proposing Release, interim financial information generally may include more estimates than annual financial statements, but interim financial statements have never been subject to the discipline provided by having auditors associated with these statements on a timely basis. Investors, however, rely on and react quickly to quarterly results of companies, large and small. Accordingly, we believe that it is appropriate to require small business issuers to obtain reviews of interim financial information. As discussed below, however, small business issuers are not included in the expanded group of issuers subject to Item 302(a) disclosure requirements. In addition, we think that the transition period should help small businesses prepare for and adapt to the new requirements.

The Blue Ribbon Committee also made recommendations that call for action by the NASD, the NYSE, and the AICPA. In response, the NASD and NYSE proposed, and the Commission approved, changes to their listing standards,[27] and the Auditing Standards Board ("ASB") recently proposed amendments[28] to SAS 61[29] and SAS 71.[30]

III. Discussion of New Rules and Amendments

A. Pre-Filing Review of Quarterly Financial Statements; Item 302(a)

We are adopting, as proposed, amendments to Rule 10-01(d) of Regulation S-X and Item 310(b) of Regulation S-B to require that a company's interim financial statements be reviewed by an independent public accountant prior to the company filing its Form 10-Q or 10-QSB with the Commission.[31] The amendments would require that independent auditors follow "professional standards and procedures for conducting such reviews, as established by generally accepted auditing standards, as may be modified or supplemented by the Commission." Under current auditing standards, this means that the auditors would be required to follow the procedures set forth in SAS 71, or such other auditing standards that may in time modify, supplement, or replace SAS 71.

As noted above, we believe that more discipline is needed for the quarterly financial reporting process.[32] We believe that the reviews required will facilitate early identification and resolution of material accounting and reporting issues because the auditors will be involved earlier in the year. Early involvement of the auditors should reduce the likelihood of restatements or other year-end adjustments and enhance the reliability of financial information. In addition, as a result of changes in the markets, companies may be experiencing increasing pressure to "manage" interim financial results. Inappropriate earnings management could be deterred by imposing more discipline on the process of preparing interim financial information before filing such information with the Commission.

Many commenters supported the interim review requirement.[33] Several commenters expressed concern, however, about the cost of obtaining interim reviews, particularly for small business issuers.[34] As discussed above, we believe that improving the interim reporting process is important for companies of all sizes. As noted in the Proposing Release, we understand that the five largest U.S. accounting firms and other firms have policies to require that their clients have reviews of quarterly financial statements as a condition to acceptance of the audit.[35] Consequently, those firms already have implemented the new requirement for the companies that are audited by those firms.

In the Proposing Release, we solicited comment on whether, in light of the proposal to require interim reviews, we should require all companies to comply with Item 302(a) of Regulation S-K. Currently, under Item 302(a) of Regulation S-K, larger, more widely-held companies[36] supplement their annual financial information with disclosures of selected quarterly financial data. Item 302(a) requires appropriate reconciliations and descriptions of any adjustments to the quarterly information previously reported in a Form 10-Q for any quarter. The selected financial data must be reviewed by the independent auditors in accordance with SAS 71, but the review can occur at the end of the year and as part of the audit of the annual financial statements. We are amending Item 302(a) to extend the requirements to all companies[37] (except small business issuers filing on small business forms) that have securities registered under Sections 12(b)[38] or 12(g)[39] of the Exchange Act regardless of the size of the company or public float.[40]

Regulation S-B does not require small business issuers to provide Item 302(a) type disclosures. Today's amendments continue to exclude small business issuers filing under Regulation S-B from those disclosure requirements,[41] but we will continue to consider whether and how such requirements should apply to small business issuers.

We believe that the amendments to Item 302(a) are consistent with the new requirement to obtain interim reviews. Both new measures should add discipline to the process of preparing and reporting quarterly financial information. Both should also encourage early identification of accounting issues and resolution of those issues before they must be subject to an auditor's review or a "reconciling" disclosure under Item 302(a)(2). Because the information to be disclosed should be readily available from each company's Form 10-Q filings, no additional audit or review costs will be imposed by the amendments to Item 302(a).

B. The Audit Committee Report

We are adopting new Item 306 of Regulations S-K and S-B and Item 7(e)(3) of Schedule 14A that require the audit committee to provide a report in the company's proxy statement. The required disclosure will help inform shareholders of the audit committee's oversight with respect to financial reporting, and underscore the importance of that role.

Many commenters were concerned that a report by the audit committee that indicates whether various discussions have occurred would expose the audit committee members to increased scrutiny and liability.[42] We do not believe that will be the case. Under state corporation law, the more informed the audit committee becomes through its discussions with management and the auditors, the more likely that the "business judgment rule" will apply and provide broad protection.[43] Those discussions should serve to strengthen the "information and reporting system" that should be in place.[44] Adherence to a sound process should result in less, not more, exposure to liability.[45]

Accordingly, we are adopting, as proposed, the requirement that the audit committee disclose whether the audit committee has reviewed and discussed the audited financial statements with management and discussed certain matters with the independent auditors.[46] Under paragraphs (a)(1), (a)(2), and (a)(3) of Item 306 (paragraph (a)(4) is discussed separately, below), audit committees must state whether:

(1) the audit committee has reviewed[47] and discussed the audited financial statements with management;

(2) the audit committee has discussed with the independent auditors the matters required to be discussed by SAS 61, as may be modified or supplemented;[48] and

(3) the audit committee has received the written disclosures and the letter from the independent auditors required by ISB Standard No. 1, as may be modified or supplemented, and has discussed with the auditors the auditors' independence.

If the company does not have an audit committee, the board committee tasked with similar responsibilities, or the full board of directors, would be responsible for the disclosure.

The disclosure required by paragraph (a)(3) relates to written disclosures, a letter from the independent auditors, and discussions between the audit committee and the independent auditors required by ISB Standard No. 1. The Commission has long recognized the importance of auditors being independent from their audit clients.[49] Public confidence in the reliability of a company's financial statements depends on investors perceiving the company's auditors as being independent from the company.

As noted above, paragraph (a)(4) was the subject of the most criticism. Commenters expressed concern about increased liability exposure, which they believed may result in qualified audit committee members resigning or companies having difficulty recruiting qualified members.[50] Some commenters, on the other hand, were skeptical that there would be increased liability exposure.[51]

Because of concerns about liability, we did not propose the disclosure requirement recommended by the Blue Ribbon Committee,[52] but instead proposed that the audit committee indicate whether, based on its discussions with management and the auditors, its members became aware of material misstatements or omissions in the financial statements. As discussed in the Proposing Release, we did not intend, nor do we believe, that the proposed disclosure about the audit committee and increased involvement by the audit committee would result in increased exposure to liability. Because commenters continued to be concerned, however, we are adopting an alternative contained in the Proposing Release. We believe that the revised language, together with the safe harbors, addresses those concerns.

As adopted, new paragraph (a)(4) requires the audit committee to state whether, based on the review and discussions referred to in paragraphs (a)(1) through (a)(3), it recommended to the Board of Directors that the financial statements be included in the Annual Report on Form 10-K or 10-KSB for the last fiscal year for filing with the Commission.[53] Because the new language in paragraph (a)(4) focuses on the annual audited financial statements and the filing of those financial statements with the Commission, we believe that this requirement will provide investors with a better understanding of the audit committee's oversight role in the financial reporting process. The audit committee's recommendation that the financial statements be used in Commission filings already is implicit in, and is consistent with, board members signing the company's Annual Report on Form 10-K or 10-KSB.[54] Further, several commenters preferred this alternative.[55]

In addition, in performing its oversight function, the audit committee likely will be relying on advice and information that it receives in its discussions with management and the independent auditors. Accordingly, the text of the new requirement acknowledges that the audit committee had such discussions with management and the auditors, and, based on those discussions, made decisions about the financial statements and the filing of the company's Form 10-K or 10-KSB. This approach is consistent with state corporation law that permits board members to rely on the representations of management and the opinions of experts retained by the corporation when reaching business judgments.[56] The Blue Ribbon Committee noted the "impracticability of having the audit committee do more than rely upon the information it receives, questions, and assesses in making this disclosure."[57]

We are adopting, as proposed, the requirement that the new disclosure appear over the printed names of each member of the audit committee.[58] This requirement will emphasize for shareholders the importance of the audit committee's oversight role in the financial reporting process.

The disclosures are required in the company's proxy statement because they could have a direct bearing on shareholders' voting decisions, and because the proxy statement is actually delivered to shareholders and is accessible on the SEC's web site. Companies must provide the disclosure only in a proxy statement relating to an annual meeting of shareholders at which directors are to be elected (or special meeting or written consents in lieu of such meeting). The disclosure needs to be provided only one time during the year (e.g., in a proxy statement for an annual meeting at which directors are to be elected, but not in proxy solicitation material used in a subsequent election contest during that same year).

C. Audit Committee Charters

We are adopting, as proposed, the requirement that companies disclose in their proxy statements whether their audit committee is governed by a charter, and if so, include a copy of the charter as an appendix to the proxy statement at least once every three years. The requirement appears in new paragraph (e)(3) under Item 7 of Schedule 14A. The new disclosure regarding audit committees' charters should help shareholders assess the role and responsibilities of the audit committee.

We believe that audit committees that have their responsibilities set forth in a written charter are more likely to play an effective role in overseeing the company's financial reports. The amendments, however, will not require companies to adopt audit committee charters, or dictate the content of the charter if one is adopted.[59]

Several commenters expressed concern that the requirement to attach the charter would result in boilerplate charters.[60] We believe that it is useful for shareholders to know about the responsibilities and the duties of audit committees,[61] and while it is inevitable that some of the same provisions will appear in charters of different audit committees, we encourage companies to tailor the charters to their specific circumstances.

Consistent with some of the comments regarding the audit committee report, some commenters recommended that the charter be attached to the Form 10-K instead of the proxy statement because of concerns about expanding the length of the proxy statement.[62] We believe that information about the responsibilities and the duties of audit committees is most relevant to shareholders when they are electing directors and reviewing their performance. Accordingly, we have determined to require, as proposed, that the charter be attached to the proxy statement every three years.

D. Disclosure About "Independence" of Audit Committee Members

As early as 1940, the Commission encouraged the use of audit committees composed of independent directors. As the Commission staff stated in a report to Congress in 1978, "[i]f the [audit] committee has members with vested interests related to those of management, the audit committee probably cannot function effectively. In some instances this may be worse than having no audit committee at all by creating the appearance of an effective body while lacking the substance."[63] Further, as the Blue Ribbon Committee noted, ". . . common sense dictates that a director without any financial, family, or other material personal ties to management is more likely to be able to evaluate objectively the propriety of management's accounting, internal control and reporting practices."[64]

As noted in the Proposing Release, because of the importance of having an audit committee that is comprised of independent directors,[65] we believe that shareholders should know about the independence of the members. We believe that the new disclosures will accomplish that goal.

Under the revised listing standards of the NYSE, AMEX, and NASD, under exceptional and limited circumstances, companies may appoint to their audit committee one director who is not independent if the Board determines that membership on the committee by the individual is required by the best interests of the corporation and its shareholders, and the Board discloses, in the next annual proxy statement subsequent to such determination, the nature of the relationship and the reasons for that determination. We are adopting, as proposed, the requirement that companies whose securities are listed on the NYSE or AMEX or quoted on Nasdaq that have a non-independent audit committee member disclose the nature of the relationship that makes that individual not independent and the reasons for the Board's determination to appoint the director to the audit committee. Small business issuers are not required to comply with this requirement.

In addition, companies, including small business issuers, whose securities are listed on the NYSE or AMEX or quoted on Nasdaq, must disclose whether the audit committee members are independent, as defined in the applicable listing standards.[66] While companies are required to provide in their proxy statements certain disclosures that relate to the independence of directors,[67] we thought that it was important to make the disclosure about all of the audit committee members' independence explicit and clear for shareholders. For example, if we required disclosure about only those audit committee members who are not independent, there would have been an implication that all of the other members are independent. Because of the importance of having independent directors on the audit committee, shareholders should be informed explicitly, rather than implicitly, of each member's status.

While we recognize that the new requirements of the NYSE, AMEX, and NASD regarding independence of audit committees need not be complied with for 18 months, we think that companies will be able to provide the new disclosures in the first proxy season after year 2000 because, as a practical matter, to meet the 18-month deadline, most companies will elect new directors during the year 2000. For other companies, this will show their progress in moving toward compliance with the listing requirements.

We are also adopting, as proposed, the requirement that companies, including small business issuers, whose securities are not listed on the NYSE or AMEX or quoted on Nasdaq, disclose in their proxy statements whether, if they have an audit committee, the members are independent as defined in the NYSE's, AMEX's, or NASD's listing standards, and which definition was used. These companies would be able to choose which definition of "independence" to apply to the audit committee members in making the disclosure. Whichever definition is chosen must be applied consistently to all members of the audit committee.

E. Safe Harbors

We are adopting, as proposed, "safe harbors" for the new disclosures.[68] The "safe harbors" would track the treatment of compensation committee reports under Item 402 of Regulation S-K.[69] The safe harbors are in paragraph (c) in new Item 306 of Regulations S-K and S-B and paragraph (e)(v) of Schedule 14A. Under the "safe harbors," the additional disclosure would not be considered "soliciting material," "filed" with the Commission, subject to Regulation 14A or 14C (and, therefore, not subject to the antifraud provisions of Rules 14a-9 or 14c-6)[70] or to the liabilities of Section 18 of the Exchange Act, except to the extent that the company specifically requests that it be treated as soliciting material, or specifically incorporates it by reference into a document filed under the Securities Act or the Exchange Act.

Several commenters recommended that the Commission also provide a safe harbor from private litigation.[71] After careful consideration, we do not believe an additional safe harbor is necessary or appropriate. As discussed more fully above, in adopting the new rules and amendments, we do not intend to subject companies or their directors to increased exposure to liability under the federal securities laws, or to create new standards for directors to fulfill their duties under state corporation law. We do not believe that the disclosure requirements will result in increased exposure to liability or create new standards. We have modified the disclosure required in Item 306 in response to commenters' concerns. To the extent the disclosure requirements would result in more clearly defined procedures for, and disclosure of, the operation of the audit committee, liability claims alleging breach of fiduciary duties under state law actually may be reduced. Accordingly, we believe that the safe harbors adopted are appropriate and sufficient.

IV. Applicability to Foreign Private Issuers and Section 15(d) Reporting Companies

A. Foreign Private Issuers

We proposed to exclude from the new requirements foreign private issuers with a class of securities registered under Section 12 of the Exchange Act or that file reports under Section 15(d) of the Exchange Act.[72] Foreign private issuers currently are exempt from the proxy rules, are not required to file Quarterly Reports on Form 10-Q or 10-QSB,[73] and are subject to different corporate governance regimes in their home countries. Accordingly, we do not believe it is appropriate to extend the new requirements to foreign private issuers at this time. The Commission, however, is continuing to consider how the periodic reporting requirements for domestic companies should apply to foreign private issuers.

B. Section 15(d) Reporting Companies

As noted in the Proposing Release, companies whose reporting obligations arise solely under Section 15(d) of the Exchange Act are not required to file proxy statements with the Commission. We solicited comment on whether we should require those companies to provide the new disclosures in their Form 10-Ks or some other filing. Because we believe that the disclosures are most relevant to voting decisions on the basis of disclosure in proxy statements, and because of the nature of the market for the securities of such companies, we are not adopting such a scheme. Accordingly, at this time we are not extending the proxy statement disclosure requirements to Section 15(d) companies.

V. Compliance Dates

Several commenters requested that we provide a transition period to allow companies time to consider the rules and to revise, if necessary, any of their procedures.[74] We agree, and have provided a transition period for compliance with the new requirements. Registrants must obtain reviews of interim financial information by their independent auditors starting with their Forms 10-Q or 10-QSB to be filed for fiscal quarters ending on or after March 15, 2000. Registrants must comply with the new proxy and information disclosure requirements (e.g., the requirement to include a report of their audit committee in their proxy statements, provide disclosures regarding the independence of their audit committee members, and attach a copy of their audit committee's charter) for all proxy and information statements relating to votes of shareholders occurring after December 15, 2000. Companies who become subject to Item 302(a) as a result of today's amendments must comply with its requirements after December 15, 2000. Registrants voluntarily may comply with any of the new requirements prior to the compliance dates.

VI. Paperwork Reduction Act

Earlier this year, the staff submitted the proposed amendments to Regulations 14A and 14C to the Office of Management and Budget ("OMB") for review in accordance with 44 U.S.C. § 3507(d) and 5 CFR 1320.11. Regulations 14A and 14C contain "collection of information" requirements within the meaning of the Paperwork Reduction Act of 1995 (44 U.S.C. § 3501 et seq.). The titles for the collections of information are: (1) Proxy Statements – Regulation 14A (Commission Rules 14a-1 through 14a-15) and Schedule 14A; and (2) Information Statements – Regulation 14C (Commission Rules 14c-1 through 14c-7) and Schedule 14C. Also, in accordance with the Paperwork Reduction Act, we solicited comments on the accuracy of our burden estimates for Regulations 14A and 14C. We did not receive any comments that address specifically the estimated paperwork burdens associated with those collections of information. The comments we received primarily addressed the costs and benefits of the proposals in general terms, and liability concerns, rather than issues relating to the collection of information. Commenters' more generalized concerns about costs and benefits of the amendments are addressed more fully in the cost-benefit and other sections of this release.

We proposed and are adopting amendments that will require a company to include additional disclosures in Schedules 14A and 14C, including certain information about the company's audit committee. The audit committee will have to disclose whether it had certain discussions with management and the company's independent auditors. The substance of the discussions would not be required to be disclosed. Companies will also have to disclosure information regarding the independence of audit committee members. The amendments would also require companies that have adopted a written charter for their audit committee to include a copy of the charter as an appendix to Schedules 14A and 14C at least once every three years. The amendments do not require companies to prepare charters.

An agency may not conduct or sponsor, and a person is not required to respond to, a collection of information unless it displays a currently valid control number. Schedule 14A (OMB Control No. 3235-0059)[75] and Schedule 14C (OMB Control No. 3235-0057)[76] were adopted pursuant to Sections 14(a) and 14(c) of the Exchange Act. Schedule 14A prescribes information that a company must include in its proxy statement to ensure that shareholders are provided material information relating to voting decisions. Schedule 14C prescribes information that a company must include in its information statement to shareholders where votes are solicited by means other than proxies.

We solicited comments on whether we should require all companies to comply with Item 302(a) of Regulation S-K. As discussed in previous sections of the release, Item 302(a) of Regulation S-K currently requires larger, more widely-held companies to supplement their annual financial information with disclosures of selected quarterly financial data. We are amending Item 302(a) to extend the requirements to all companies (but not small business issuers filing on small business forms and foreign private issuers) that have securities registered under Section 12(b) or 12(g) of the Exchange Act. The Item 302(a) information will continue to appear as a table in the Form 10-K.

Form 10-K under the Exchange Act (OMB Control Number 3235-0063)[77] is used by registrants to file annual reports. The title for this collection of information is Form 10-K. Form 10-K provides a comprehensive overview of the registrant's business and financial condition. The Commission estimates that Form 10-K currently results in a total annual compliance burden of approximately 17,886,463 hours. The burden was calculated by multiplying the estimated number of entities filing Form 10-K (approximately 10,381) by the estimated average number of hours each entity spends completing the Form (approximately 1723 hours). The Commission based the number of entities that complete and file Form 10-K on the actual number of filers during the 1998 fiscal year. The staff estimated the average number of hours an entity spends completing Form 10-K by contacting a number of law firms and other persons regularly involved in completing the forms.

We estimate that the incremental burden of extending Item 302(a) to all companies with securities registered under Sections 12(b) or 12(g) of the Exchange Act (except small business issuers filing on small business forms) will increase the total by approximately 2000 hours. This burden was calculated by multiplying the estimated number of entities that do not currently provide Item 302(a) information by the number of additional hours it would take to provide the additional information. The staff estimates that approximately 8000 Form 10-K filers do not currently provide Item 302(a) information, and that it would take a total of approximately .25 hours to include the new disclosure in a Form 10-K. The Commission based the number of Form 10-K filers not currently providing Item 302(a) information on the approximate number of companies in the Compustat database that currently are required to file Item 302(a) information based on the criteria set forth in Item 302(a) of Regulation S-K.

We believe that the amendments will promote investor confidence in the securities markets by informing investors about the important role that audit committees play in the financial reporting process and will enhance the reliability and credibility of financial statements of public companies.

Compliance with the disclosure requirements is mandatory. There will be no mandatory retention period for the information disclosed, and responses to the disclosure requirements will not be kept confidential.

Pursuant to 44 U.S.C. § 3506(c)(2)(B), the Commission solicits comments to: (i) evaluate whether the revised rule is necessary for the proper performance of the functions of the agency, including whether the information will have practical utility; (ii) evaluate the accuracy of the Commission's estimate of the burden of the proposed collection of information; (iii) determine whether there are ways to enhance the quality, utility, and clarity of the information to be collected; and (iv) evaluate whether there are ways to minimize the burden of the collection of information on those who are to respond, including through the use of automated collection techniques or other forms of information technology.

Persons submitting comments on the collection of information requirements for Form 10-K should direct the comments to the Office of Management and Budget, Attention: Desk Officer for the Securities and Exchange Commission, Office of Information and Regulatory Affairs, Washington, D.C. 20503, and should send a copy to Jonathan G. Katz, Secretary, Securities and Exchange Commission, 450 Fifth Street, N.W., Washington, D.C. 20549-0609, with reference to File No. S7-22-99. Requests for materials submitted to OMB by the Commission with regard to these collections of information should be in writing, refer to File No. S7-22-99, and be submitted to the Securities and Exchange Commission, Records Management, Office of Filings and Information Services. OMB is required to make a decision concerning the collection of information between 30 and 60 days after publication of this release. Consequently, a comment to OMB is assured of having its full effect if OMB receives it within 30 days of publication.

VII. Cost-Benefit Analysis

The amendments are expected to improve disclosure related to the functioning of the corporate audit committees and to enhance the reliability and credibility of financial statements of public companies. We believe that the amendments will promote investor confidence in the securities markets by informing investors about the important role that audit committees play in the financial reporting process. As the Blue Ribbon Committee summarized:

> Improving oversight of the financial reporting process necessarily involves the imposition of certain burdens and costs on public companies. Despite these costs, the Committee believes that a more transparent and reliable financial reporting process ultimately results in a more efficient allocation of and lower cost of capital. To the extent that instances of outright fraud, as well as other practices that result in lower quality financial reporting, are reduced with improved oversight, the benefits clearly justify these expenditures of resources.[78]

As noted above, the amendments are part of a larger, coordinated series of actions by the NYSE, NASD, AMEX, and the accounting profession that were recommended by the Blue Ribbon Committee to improve the financial reporting process. The Commission's rule amendments and new rules complement and strengthen the efforts of the NYSE, NASD, AMEX and the accounting profession. This cost-benefit analysis concentrates only on the effect of the Commission's rules. The benefits of the new requirements cannot be readily quantified.[79] However, these measures should mitigate inappropriate earnings management, enhance the reliability of financial information, improve disclosure to investors, and could improve securities pricing efficiency by encouraging the distribution of higher quality earnings numbers on a more timely basis.

Reviews of Quarterly Financial Statements

We are requiring interim reviews of quarterly financial statements filed on Form 10-Q or 10-QSB.[80] Under the amendments, a company's quarterly financial statements must be reviewed by independent auditors using "professional standards and procedures for conducting such reviews, as established by generally accepted auditing standards, as may be modified or supplemented by the Commission." Currently, that means that the review would follow the procedures established by SAS 71. The amendments apply only to the financial information contained in the company's Quarterly Reports on Form 10-Q or 10-QSB. Accordingly, the amendments do not require any review of quarterly financial information released to the public before the filing of the Form 10-Q or 10-QSB, such as the so-called quarterly "earnings release."

We believe that companies are under increasing pressure to meet financial analysts' expectations, and that pressure can be even more acute in the context of reports on quarterly earnings. We believe that the participation of auditors in the financial reporting process at interim dates will help to counterbalance that pressure and impose increased discipline on the process of preparing interim financial information.[81] Auditor involvement in the financial reporting process earlier in the year should facilitate timely identification and resolution of significant and sensitive issues and result in fewer year-end adjustments, which should reduce the cost of annual audits.[82] The increased focus and discipline imposed on the preparation of interim financial statements should enhance the efficiency of the capital markets by improving the reliability of quarterly financial statements, although these benefits are difficult to quantify.

We have prepared our best estimate of the incremental costs of preparing a SAS 71 review for those companies not currently having them performed. Our estimate of those incremental costs is based on data provided to the staff by the SEC Practice Section of the AICPA ("SECPS"), discussions with experienced practitioners, the experiences of current SEC staff members, and data provided by commenters.

Firms providing information to the SECPS indicated that the procedures they currently use are similar, if not the same, as those described in SAS 71. Most indicated that review reports are seldom issued. The firms also indicated that they are not aware of (and do not expect) clients switching auditing firms because of their new policies.

The firms providing information to the SECPS identified several unquantifiable benefits that they believe would result from the reviews, including better interim reporting, earlier identification and resolution of accounting issues, improvement in the quality of accounting estimates, and improved communications between clients and auditors. These benefits could also improve pricing efficiency of the issuer's securities. Several comment letters from accounting firms supported this view.[83] Medium and smaller sized accounting firms, however, indicated to the SECPS that SAS 71 reviews of small companies' interim financial statements may cause delays in filing Forms 10-Q or 10-QSB, be relatively more costly for small companies, be hampered by inadequate financial reporting processes, and would result in small companies shifting work from the company to the CPA firm. One small business commenter expressed concern that increased pressure to meet the filing deadlines would require hiring another employee.[84] Based on staff experience and discussions with practitioners, we believe many of the required review procedures can be performed simultaneously with the preparation of the quarterly financial statements, and accordingly, should not delay these filings. In addition, we believe that the same management personnel who work with the auditors at year end should be able to assist with the quarterly reviews.

The firms responding to the SECPS generally indicated that the costs of reviews of quarterly financial statements vary depending on several factors, including: (i) the sophistication of the client's accounting and reporting system; (ii) the quality of the client's accounting personnel; (iii) the identification of "fraud risk factors;" (iv) the client's industry; (v) the number and location of the client's subsidiaries; (vi) the seasonality of the client's business; (vii) the existence of contentious accounting issues; and (viii) whether there will be a staffing "crunch" at the firm to handle the reviews each quarter.

The five largest U.S. accounting firms, the so-called "Big 5," and some other firms, currently have in place policies that require their clients to have interim reviews as a condition to acceptance of an audit. Based on the Compustat database and information from the SECPS and from commenters, we estimate that approximately 8,934 companies for calendar year 1998 retained auditors that require SAS 71 reviews. Based on a total of approximately 12,972 Forms 10-K and 10-KSB filed in 1998, we therefore estimate that approximately 4,038 companies are not currently subject to SAS 71 reviews.

Based on the data provided to staff by the SECPS, our experience, and information from commenters, we estimate the incremental cost to conduct a SAS 71 review will be nominal for those companies currently audited by the Big 5 firms and for the remaining companies would range from approximately $1,000 to about $4,000[85] per quarter. Multiplying $7,500 (the mid-point of the average cost per firm of $3,000 to $12,000 per year) by 4038 produces an estimated $30 million a year cost for SAS 71 reviews.[86] Obviously, if more companies are currently subject to SAS 71 reviews, or if the cost of the reviews is offset by a reduction in annual fees, the cost estimate would be smaller.

Disclosure Related to the Functioning of the Audit Committee

The principal benefits of the proposals are improved disclosure relating to the functioning of corporate audit committees and enhanced reliability and credibility of financial statements. The benefits of improved disclosure regarding the audit committee's communications with management and the independent auditors are not readily quantifiable. We believe, however, that they would include increased market efficiency due to improved information and investor confidence in the reliability of companies' financial disclosures. As discussed above, most of the commenters supported the goals of improving disclosure about audit committees, although some suggested alternative disclosure requirements. Commenters' principal concern was that audit committees may be exposed to additional liability, with the result that they would find it more difficult to recruit qualified audit committee members; others disagreed with that view. As discussed above, we modified the Item 306 audit committee report requirement to respond to commenters' concerns about liability.

We believe the costs associated with these amendments would derive principally from the disclosure obligations – we are not placing any substantive requirements on audit committees or their members. At the proposing stage, we estimated that the additional disclosure contemplated by the amendments would, on average, require less than three-fourths of a page in a company's proxy statement, based on the staff's experience with proxy statements, and analogous cost estimates. A financial printing company informed the staff that this disclosure would not likely increase the printing cost because up to three-fourths of a page can normally be incorporated without increasing the page length by reformatting the document. The printer reported that adding one more page could increase costs by about $1,500 for an average sized company.

Only a few commenters mentioned printing costs, with one stating that the costs of printing the charter in the proxy statement "could be significant," but did not quantify the amount.[87] We continue to believe that the printing costs of the disclosures and charter[88] would not be significant. The charter, for example, needs to be printed only once every three years, so the cost has been averaged over three years. We estimate the total average disclosure per year – the average annual burden of printing the charter and the other disclosures – would be one printed proxy statement page. Consequently, the annual aggregate cost would be approximately $15 million.[89]

This amount, however, does not include possible "start up" costs for some companies. First, some companies may have to set up procedures to monitor the activities of their audit committee in order to collect and record the information required by the amendments. In our view, such monitoring costs are most likely to result from disclosing the fact of the audit committee's discussions with management and the independent auditors and receiving from the independent auditors certain required disclosures and a letter from the independent auditors. We believe such monitoring costs will be insignificant.

Second, some companies may seek the help of outside experts, particularly outside legal counsel, in formulating responses to the new requirements.[90] In some circumstances, for instance, the audit committee may seek the advice of legal counsel before making the required disclosure about the audited financial statements. Commenters provided no cost data. We understand that many audit committees already use outside experts, but do not know what, if any, incremental cost there will be. As we modified our proposals to reflect better the oversight role of audit committees and address liability concerns, we anticipate that any costs attributable to the increased use of outside experts to respond to the new disclosure requirements will be negligible.

For purposes of the Paperwork Reduction Act, we estimated that our required disclosures would, on average, impose one additional burden hour, exclusive of printing costs, on each filer of Schedule 14A or 14C, or an aggregate annual total of 10,145 additional burden hours. This estimate reflects the time companies would spend preparing the additional disclosures in the proxy statement.[91] The total annual costs accordingly would be approximately $1 million.

These amendments are not intended to increase companies' or directors' exposure to liability under federal or state law. A number of commenters indicated that, in their assessment, the proposals would have the effect of increasing the companies' and/or directors' exposure to liability, with attendant costs, but provided no economic data. For the reasons discussed in previous sections of this release, we believe that the amendments will likely result in better and more reliable financial reporting, but should not increase liability exposure. In particular, we modified requirements to address this liability concern. In addition, the amendments include liability "safe harbors" similar to those that apply to compensation committee reports under current rules.[92]

Item 302(a) of Regulation S-K

The Commission is requiring more companies to provide the supplemental financial information described in Item 302 of Regulation S-K. That information consists of selected quarterly financial data, such as net sales and gross profit, for the prior two years. We recognize that requiring all public companies (except Form S-B filers, Section 15(d) reporting companies, and foreign private issuers) to provide supplemental financial information under Item 302(a) of Regulation S-K may have some incremental cost. Currently only certain large, widely-held companies that meet certain tests (involving, among other things, the number of security holders, stock price, and market capitalization) must file supplemental financial information. Taking into account that auditors will be performing SAS 71 reviews for these companies, the incremental cost of preparing and presenting the supplementary financial information is small.

Based on the staff's experience, we do not believe that it will take company employees much time to pull the data from their prior quarterly reports to prepare the supplementary financial information for the Form 10-K. While the information will take up part of an additional page in the Form 10-K, there are no printing costs attributable to disclosure of this information since it is not typically contained in the annual report that is printed and distributed to investors.

We believe the supplementary financial information is a useful resource for investors and justifies the cost of its collection and filing. By tying the regulatory threshold to an existing, widely used test (e.g., the definition of small business issuer in Regulation S-B), the Commission is simplifying the regulatory scheme. Such simplification is an additional benefit of the amendments.

VIII. Consideration of Impact on the Economy, Burden on Competition, and Promotion of Efficiency, Competition, and Capital Formation

Section 3(f) of the Exchange Act requires the Commission, when engaging in rulemaking that requires it to consider or determine whether an action is necessary or appropriate in the public interest, also to consider whether the action will promote efficiency, competition, and capital formation. We believe that the proposals will promote investor confidence in the securities markets by improving the transparency of the role of corporate audit committees and enhancing the reliability and credibility of financial statements of public companies. More reliable financial statements should help to lower the costs of capital. Accordingly, the proposals should promote capital formation and market efficiency.

Section 23(a) of the Exchange Act requires the Commission, when adopting rules under the Exchange Act, to consider the impact on competition of any rule it adopts. We do not believe that the proposals would have any anti-competitive effects since the proposals should improve the transparency, reliability, and credibility of companies' financial statements. We requested comment on any anti-competitive effects of the proposals. For the reasons discussed above, we have decided to exclude foreign private issuers from these disclosure requirements. Any competitive effect that may occur by requiring domestic public companies to comply with these additional disclosure requirements, compared to foreign private issuers, is necessary and appropriate for the protection of investors.

IX. Final Regulatory Flexibility Analysis

This Final Regulatory Flexibility Analysis has been prepared in accordance with the Regulatory Flexibility Act ("RFA"). It relates to amendments to Rule 10-01 of Regulation S-X, Item 310 of Regulation S-B, Item 302(a) of Regulation S-K, Item 7 of Schedule 14A under the Exchange Act, and new Item 306 of Regulations S-B and S-K.

A. Need for the Rules and Rule Amendments

The new rules and amendments to current rules are designed to improve disclosure relating to the functioning of corporate audit committees and to enhance the reliability and credibility of financial statements of public companies. The required disclosure will help inform shareholders of the audit committee's role in overseeing the preparation of the financial statements and underscore the importance of the audit committee's participation in the financial reporting process.

The required reviews of interim financial information should facilitate early identification and resolution of material accounting and reporting issues because the auditors will be involved earlier in the year. More reliable interim financial information will be available to investors, and early involvement of the auditors should reduce the number of restatements or other year-end adjustments. We believe that the disclosures will reinforce the audit committee's awareness of its responsibilities, and make visible for shareholders the audit committee's role in promoting reliable and transparent financial reporting.

B. Significant Issues Raised by Public Comment

Many commenters were concerned that the proposed rules would expose audit committee members to increased scrutiny and liability. As a result, those commenters suggested that we amend certain disclosure requirements and provide an additional safe harbor from private litigation. We modified the required audit committee report to address the liability concerns, and consequently, as discussed in previous sections of this release, we do not believe additional safe harbors are necessary or appropriate. We are adopting, as proposed, the same report requirements and safe harbors for companies of all sizes.

The Commission requested comment on whether the scope of the proposed rules should be narrowed to exclude companies under a certain size. Some commenters questioned the need for interim reviews for small entities,[93] particularly in light of the additional costs. However, we continue to believe that improving the interim reporting process is important for small companies. Investors rely on and react quickly to quarterly results of companies, large and small. Moreover, the COSO Report found that the incidence of financial fraud was greater at small companies.[94] The COSO Report specifically noted that the "concentration of fraud among companies with under $50 million in revenues and with generally weak audit committees highlights the importance of rigorous audit committee practices, even for smaller organizations."[95] In light of the COSO Report, we believe it would be inconsistent with the purposes of the rule to exempt small business issuers from the proposed requirement for interim reviews.

We also solicited comment on whether we should require all companies to comply with Item 302(a) of Regulation S-K. Commenters generally agreed that we should extend the requirements to other companies, but questioned the need to include small companies. We are adopting the Item 302(a) requirement for all Section 12(b) and 12(g) registered companies (except small business issuers reporting on small business forms) to maintain the more simplified reporting format of the regulatory scheme for small business issuers.

C. Small Entities Subject to the Rule

For purposes of the RFA, Exchange Act Rule 0-10 defines "small business" as a company whose total assets on the last day of its most recent fiscal year were $5 million or less.[96] The rules will affect small businesses that are required to file proxy materials on Schedule 14A or 14C and Quarterly Reports on Form 10-Q or 10-QSB under the Exchange Act. We estimate that there are approximately 830 reporting companies (that are not investment companies) with assets of $5 million or less. The Commission bases its estimate on information from the Insight database from Compustat, a division of Standard and Poors.

D. Projected Reporting, Recordkeeping, and Other Compliance Requirements

1. Reviews of Quarterly Financial Statements

The rules will require companies to engage their independent auditors to conduct interim reviews of their quarterly financial statements prior to the company filing its Forms 10-Q or 10-QSB. Based on information provided to the Commission by the SECPS,[97] it appears that most companies already engage their independent auditors to undertake some level of review of their quarterly financial statements.

Medium and smaller sized accounting firms indicated to the SECPS that SAS 71 reviews of small companies' interim financial statements may cause delays in filing Forms 10-Q or 10-QSB, be relatively more costly for all companies, be hampered by inadequate financial reporting processes, and would result in small companies shifting financial responsibilities from the company to the CPA firm.

However, based on the SECPS survey, we believe that the costs of compliance would be partially offset by a reduction in year-end audit fees and would lead to earlier identification of accounting and auditing issues and an improvement in the quality of the process used for preparing interim financial reports.

2. Disclosure Related to the Functioning of the Audit Committee

Issuers, both large and small, will be required to provide certain additional disclosure in their proxy statements regarding the company's audit committee, including attaching every three years a copy of the audit committee's charter, if they have one. Companies will be required to include reports of their audit committees in which the audit committee provides disclosure about whether certain discussions between the audit committee and management and the auditors took place. No disclosure of the substance of the discussions is required. The increased disclosure will require all entities, large and small, to spend additional time and incur additional costs in preparing disclosures. In particular, smaller companies may incur additional costs to set up procedures in order to respond to the new disclosure requirements. Smaller companies may also incur additional costs in seeking the help of outside experts, particularly outside legal counsel, in formulating responses to the new requirements.

3. Disclosure Related to Independence

We are requiring that companies whose securities are listed on the NYSE, AMEX, or traded on Nasdaq make certain disclosures about any member of the audit committee who is not independent (small business issuers are not subject to that requirement) and whether the audit committee members are independent. Companies, including small business issuers, whose securities are not listed on the NYSE or AMEX or quoted on Nasdaq are required to disclose whether their members are independent, but may choose which definition of independence to use and must disclose which definition was used.

E. Agency Action to Minimize Effect on Small Entities

As required by Section 603 of the RFA, the Commission has considered the following alternatives to minimize the economic impact of the rules on small entities: (a) the establishment of differing compliance or reporting requirements or timetables that take into account the resources available to small entities; (b) the clarification, consolidation, or simplification of compliance and reporting requirements under the rules for small entities; (c) the use of performance rather than design standards; and (d) an exemption from coverage of the rules, or any part thereof, for small entities.

We continue to believe investors in smaller companies would want and benefit from the disclosures about the audit committee and the advantages of interim reviews just as much as investors in larger companies. We have made some adjustments to the rules to decrease their impact on small businesses. For example, we did not extend Item 302(a) to small business issuers filing on small business forms.

In addition, small businesses not subject to the NASD's, AMEX's or NYSE's listing standards can choose which definition of independence to use, as long as it is used consistently. Further, small business issuers are not required to state the reasons for including a non-independent audit committee member, since under the listing standards, they are not required to have all independent members on their audit committees.

Finally, to provide companies with the opportunity to evaluate their compliance with the revised listing standards of the NASD, AMEX, and NYSE and to prepare for the new disclosure requirements, we are providing transition periods for compliance with the new requirements, which should benefit all companies, large and small.

X. Statutory Bases and Text of Amendments

We are adopting amendments to Rules 10-01 of Regulation S-X and 14a-101 (Schedule 14A), Item 310 of Regulation S-B, and Item 302(a) of Regulation S-K, and adopting new Item 306 of Regulations S-K and S-B, under the authority set forth in Sections 2, 13, 14, and 23 of the Exchange Act.

List of Subjects

17 CFR Part 210 Accountant, Accounting, Reporting and recordkeeping requirements, Securities.

17 CFR Part 228 Reporting and recordkeeping requirements, Securities, Small businesses.

17 CFR Parts 229 and 240 Reporting and recordkeeping requirements, Securities.

Text of Amendments

In accordance with the foregoing, Title 17, Chapter II of the Code of Federal Regulations is amended as follows:

PART 210 - FORM AND CONTENT OF AND REQUIREMENTS FOR FINANCIAL STATEMENTS, SECURITIES ACT OF 1933, SECURITIES EXCHANGE ACT OF 1934, PUBLIC UTILITY HOLDING COMPANY ACT OF 1935, INVESTMENT COMPANY ACT OF 1940, AND ENERGY POLICY AND CONSERVATION ACT OF 1975

1. The authority citation for Part 210 continues to read as follows:

Authority: 15 U.S.C. 77f, 77g, 77h, 77j, 77s, 77z-2, 77aa(25), 77aa(26), 78j-1, 78l, 78m, 78n, 78o(d), 78u-5, 78w(a), 78ll(d), 79e(b), 79j(a), 79n, 79t(a), 80a-8, 80a-20, 80a-29, 80a-30, 80a-37(a), unless otherwise noted.

2. By amending § 210.10-01 by revising paragraph (d) to read as follows:

§ 210.10-01 Interim financial statements.

* * * * *

(d) Interim review by independent public accountant. Prior to filing, interim financial statements included in quarterly reports on Form 10-Q (17 CFR 249.308(a)) must be reviewed by an independent public accountant using professional standards and procedures for conducting such reviews, as established by generally accepted auditing standards, as may be modified or supplemented by the Commission. If, in any filing, the company states that interim financial statements have been reviewed by an independent public accountant, a report of the accountant on the review must be filed with the interim financial statements.

* * * * *

PART 228 - INTEGRATED DISCLOSURE SYSTEM FOR SMALL BUSINESS ISSUERS

3. The authority citation for Part 228 continues to read as follows:

Authority: 15 U.S.C. 77e, 77f, 77g, 77h, 77j, 77k, 77s, 77z-2, 77aa(25), 77aa(26), 77ddd, 77eee, 77ggg, 77hhh, 77jjj, 77nnn, 77sss, 78l, 78m, 78n, 78o, 78u-5, 78w, 78ll, 80a-8, 80a-29, 80a-30, 80a-37, 80b-ll, unless otherwise noted.

4. Section 228.305 is added and reserved and § 228.306 is added to read as follows:

§ 228.305 [RESERVED]

§ 228.306 (Item 306) Audit Committee Report .

(a) The audit committee must state whether:

(1) The audit committee has reviewed and discussed the audited financial statements with management;

(2) The audit committee has discussed with the independent auditors the matters required to be discussed by SAS 61, as may be modified or supplemented;

(3) The audit committee has received the written disclosures and the letter from the independent accountants required by Independence Standards Board Standard No. 1 (Independence Standards Board Standard No. 1, Independence Discussions with Audit Committees), as may be modified or supplemented, and has discussed with the independent accountant the independent accountant's independence; and

(4) Based on the review and discussions referred to in paragraphs (a)(1) through (a)(3) of this Item, the audit committee recommended to the Board of Directors that the audited financial statements be included in the company's Annual Report on Form 10-KSB (17 CFR 249.310b) for the last fiscal year for filing with the Commission.

(b) The name of each member of the company's audit committee (or, in the absence of an audit committee, the board committee performing equivalent functions or the entire board of directors) must appear below the disclosure required by this Item.

(c) The information required by paragraphs (a) and (b) of this Item shall not be deemed to be "soliciting material," or to be "filed" with the Commission or subject to Regulation 14A or 14C (17 CFR 240.14a-1 et seq. or 240.14c-1 et seq.), other than as provided in this Item, or to the liabilities of section 18 of the Exchange Act (15 U.S.C. 78r), except to the extent that the company specifically requests that the information be treated as soliciting material or specifically incorporates it by reference into a document filed under the Securities Act or the Exchange Act.

(d) The information required by paragraphs (a) and (b) of this Item need not be provided in any filings other than a registrant proxy or information statement relating to an annual meeting of security holders at which directors are to be elected (or special meeting or written consents in lieu of such meeting). Such information will not be deemed to be incorporated by reference into any filing under the Securities Act or the Exchange Act, except to the extent that the registrant specifically incorporates it by reference.

5. By amending § 228.310 by revising the introductory text of paragraph (b) to read as follows:

§ 228.310 (Item 310) Financial Statements.

* * * * *

(b) Interim Financial Statements. Interim financial statements may be unaudited; however, prior to filing, interim financial statements included in quarterly reports on Form 10-QSB (17 CFR 249.308b) must be reviewed by an independent public accountant using professional standards and procedures for conducting such reviews, as established by generally accepted auditing standards, as may be modified or supplemented by the Commission. If, in any filing, the issuer states that interim financial statements have been reviewed by an independent public accountant, a report of the accountant on the review must be filed with the interim financial statements. Interim financial statements shall include a balance sheet as of the end of the issuer's most recent fiscal quarter and income statements and statements of cash flows for the interim period up to the date of such balance sheet and the comparable period of the preceding fiscal year.

* * * * *

PART 229 - STANDARD INSTRUCTIONS FOR FILING FORMS UNDER SECURITIES ACT OF 1933, SECURITIES EXCHANGE ACT OF 1934 AND ENERGY POLICY AND CONSERVATION ACT OF 1975 - REGULATION S-K 6. The authority citation for Part 229 continues to read in part as follows:

Authority: 15 U.S.C. 77e, 77f, 77g, 77h, 77j, 77k, 77s, 77z-2, 77aa(25), 77aa(26), 77ddd, 77eee, 77ggg, 77hhh, 77iii, 77jjj, 77nnn, 77sss, 78c, 78i, 78j, 78l, 78m, 78n, 78o, 78u-5, 78w, 78ll(d), 79e, 79n, 79t, 80a-8, 80a-29, 80a-30, 80a-37, 80b-11, unless otherwise noted.

* * * * *

7. By amending § 229.302 by revising paragraph (a)(5) to read as follows:

§ 229.302 (Item 302) Supplementary financial information.

(a) Selected quarterly financial data. * * *

(5) This paragraph (a) applies to any registrant, except a foreign private issuer, that has securities registered pursuant to sections 12(b) (15 U.S.C. § 78l(b)) (other than mutual life insurance companies) or 12(g) of the Exchange Act (15 U.S.C. § 78l(g)).

* * * * *

8. By adding § 229.306 to read as follows:

§ 229.306 (Item 306) Audit committee report.

(a) The audit committee must state whether:

(1) The audit committee has reviewed and discussed the audited financial statements with management;

(2) The audit committee has discussed with the independent auditors the matters required to be discussed by SAS 61 (Codification of Statements on Auditing Standards, AU § 380), as may be modified or supplemented;

(3) The audit committee has received the written disclosures and the letter from the independent accountants required by Independence Standards Board Standard No. 1 (Independence Standards Board Standard No. 1, Independence Discussions with Audit Committees), as may be modified or supplemented, and has discussed with the independent accountant the independent accountant's independence; and

(4) Based on the review and discussions referred to in paragraphs (a)(1) through (a)(3) of this Item, the audit committee recommended to the Board of Directors that the audited financial statements be included in the company's Annual Report on Form 10-K (17 CFR 249.310) (or, for closed-end investment companies registered under the Investment Company Act of 1940 (15 U.S.C. § 80a-1 et seq.), the annual report to shareholders required by Section 30(e) of the Investment Company Act of 1940 (15 U.S.C. § 80a-29(e)) and Rule 30d-1 (17 CFR 270.30d-1) thereunder) for the last fiscal year for filing with the Commission.

(b) The name of each member of the company's audit committee (or, in the absence of an audit committee, the board committee performing equivalent functions or the entire board of directors) must appear below the disclosure required by this Item.

(c) The information required by paragraphs (a) and (b) of this Item shall not be deemed to be "soliciting material," or to be "filed" with the Commission or subject to Regulation 14A or 14C (17 CFR 240.14a-1 et seq. or 240.14c-1 et seq.), other than as provided in this Item, or to the liabilities of section 18 of the Exchange Act (15 U.S.C. § 78r), except to the extent that the company specifically requests that the information be treated as soliciting material or specifically incorporates it by reference into a document filed under the Securities Act or the Exchange Act.

(d) The information required by paragraphs (a) and (b) of this Item need not be provided in any filings other than a company proxy or information statement relating to an annual meeting of security holders at which directors are to be elected (or special meeting or written consents in lieu of such meeting). Such information will not be deemed to be incorporated by reference into any filing under the Securities Act or the Exchange Act, except to the extent that the company specifically incorporates it by reference.

* * * * *

PART 240 - GENERAL RULES AND REGULATIONS, SECURITIES EXCHANGE ACT OF 1934

9. The authority citation for Part 240 continues to read, in part, as follows:

Authority: 15 U.S.C. 77c, 77d, 77g, 77j, 77s, 77z-2, 77eee, 77ggg, 77nnn, 77sss, 77ttt, 78c, 78d, 78f, 78i, 78j, 78j-1, 78k, 78k-1, 78l, 78m, 78n, 78o, 78p, 78q, 78s, 78u-5, 78w, 78x, 78ll(d), 78mm, 79q, 79t, 80a-20, 80a-23, 80a-29, 80a-37, 80b-3, 80b-4 and 80b-11, unless otherwise noted.

* * * * *

10. By amending § 240.14a-101 by adding paragraph (e)(3) to Item 7 to read as follows:

§ 240.14a-101 Schedule 14A. Information required in proxy statement.

* * * * *

Item 7. Directors and executive officers. * * *

(e) * * *

(3) If the registrant has an audit committee:

(i) Provide the information required by Item 306 of Regulation S-K (17 CFR 229.306).

(ii) State whether the registrant's Board of Directors has adopted a written charter for the audit committee.

(iii) Include a copy of the written charter, if any, as an appendix to the registrant's proxy statement, unless a copy has been included as an appendix to the registrant's proxy statement within the registrant's past three fiscal years.

(iv)(A) For registrants whose securities are listed on the New York Stock Exchange ("NYSE") or American Stock Exchange ("AMEX") or quoted on Nasdaq:

(1) Disclose whether the members of the audit committee are independent (as independence is defined in Sections 303.01(B)(2)(a) and (3) of the NYSE's listing standards, Section 121(A) of the AMEX's listing standards, or Rule 4200(a)(15) of the National Association of Securities Dealers' ("NASD") listing standards, as applicable and as may be modified or supplemented); and

(2) If the registrant's Board of Directors determines in accordance with the requirements of Section 303.02(D) of the NYSE's listing standards, Section 121(B)(b)(ii) of the AMEX's listing standards, or Section 4310(c)(26)(B)(ii) or 4460(d)(2)(B) of the NASD's listing standards, as applicable and as may be modified or supplemented, to appoint one director to the audit committee who is not independent, disclose the nature of the relationship that makes that individual not independent and the reasons for the Board's determination. Small business issuers (17 CFR 228.10(a)(1)) need not provide the information required by this paragraph (e)(3)(iv)(A)(2).

(B) For registrants, including small business issuers, whose securities are not listed on the NYSE or AMEX or quoted on Nasdaq, disclose whether, if the registrant has an audit committee, the members are independent. In determining whether a member is independent, registrants must use the definition of independence in Sections 303.01(B)(2)(a) and (3) of the NYSE's listing standards, Section 121(A) of the AMEX's listing standards, or Rule 4200(a)(15) of the NASD's listing standards, as such sections may be modified or supplemented, and state which of these definitions was used. Whichever definition is chosen must be applied consistently to all members of the audit committee.

(v) The information required by paragraph (e)(3) of this Item shall not be deemed to be "soliciting material," or to be "filed" with the Commission or subject to Regulation 14A or 14C (17 CFR 240.14a-1 et seq. or 240.14c-1 et seq.), other than as provided in this Item, or to the liabilities of section 18 of the Exchange Act (15 U.S.C. § 78r), except to the extent that the registrant specifically requests that the information be treated as soliciting material or specifically incorporates it by reference into a document filed under the Securities Act or the Exchange Act. Such information will not be deemed to be incorporated by reference into any filing under the Securities Act or the Exchange Act, except to the extent that the registrant specifically incorporates it by reference.

(vi) The disclosure required by this paragraph (e)(3) need only be provided one time during any fiscal year.

(vii) Investment companies registered under the Investment Company Act of 1940 (15 U.S.C. § 80a-1 et seq.), other than closed-end investment companies, need not provide the information required by this paragraph (e)(3).

* * * * *

By the Commission.

Jonathan G. Katz
Secretary

Dated: December 22, 1999

Footnotes

1. 17 CFR 210.10-01.
2. 17 CFR 228.310.
3. 17 CFR 240.14a-101.
4. 15 U.S.C. § 78a et seq.
5. 17 CFR 229.302.
6. 17 CFR 229.306.
7. 17 CFR 228.306.
8. The new rules and amendments were proposed in Exchange Act Release No. 41987 (Oct. 7, 1999) [64 FR 55648] (the "Proposing Release").
9. See Report and Recommendations of the Blue Ribbon Committee on Improving the Effectiveness of Corporate Audit Committees (1999) (the "Blue Ribbon Report"). The Blue Ribbon Report is available [Webmaster note: in PDF format] on the internet at http://www.nasd.com and http://www.nyse.com.
10. See, e.g., Jack Ciesielski, Editorial, *More Second-Guessing: Markets Need Better Disclosure of Earnings Management*, Barrons, Aug. 24, 1998, at 47.
11. The Commission recently filed 30 enforcement actions against 68 individuals and companies for fraud and related misconduct in the accounting, reporting, and disclosure of financial results by 15 different public companies. See SEC Press Release 99-124 (Sept. 28, 1999).
12. 17 CFR 229.302(a).
13. References in this release to proxy statements also include information statements.
14. See Codification of Statements on Auditing Standards, AU § 380 ("SAS 61").
15. Independence Standards Board Standard No. 1, Independence Discussions with Audit Committees ("ISB Standard No. 1"). A copy of ISB Standard No. 1 can be obtained at www.cpaindependence.org.
16. "Small business issuer" is defined in Item 10(a)(1) of Regulation S-B, 17 CFR 228.10(a)(1), as a company with less than $25 million in revenues and market capitalization.

17. The listing standards of the National Association of Securities Dealers ("NASD"), AMEX and NYSE are available on their websites at: http://www.nasd.com, http://www.amex.com, and http://www.nyse.com, respectively. See infra note 27 regarding recent changes to the listing standards of the NASD, AMEX, and NYSE.

18. See, e.g., Carol J. Loomis et al., *Lies, Damned Lies, and Managed Earnings*, Fortune, Aug. 2, 1999, at 74; Thor Valdmanis, *Accounting Abracadabra*, USA Today, Aug. 11, 1998, at 1B; Bernard Condon, *Pick a Number, Any Number*, Forbes, Mar. 23, 1998, at 124; Justin Fox & Rajiv Rao, *Learn to Play the Earnings Game*, Fortune, Mar. 31, 1997, at 76.

19. See, e.g., Arthur Levitt, Chairman, SEC, Address to the NYU Center for Law and Business (Sept. 28, 1998). A copy of this speech is available on the SEC's website at www.sec.gov.

20. Blue Ribbon Report, supra note 9, at 17.

21. See Advisory Panel on Auditor Independence ("Kirk Panel"), *Strengthening the Professionalism of the Independent Auditor*, Report by the Oversight Board of the SEC Practice Section, American Institute of Certified Public Accountants ("AICPA") (Sept. 13, 1994) (the "Kirk Panel Report"); see also Report of the National Commission on Fraudulent Financial Reporting (Oct. 1987) (the "Treadway Report").

22. You may read and copy the comment letters in our Public Reference Room at 450 Fifth Street, N.W., Washington, D.C. 20549. Ask for File No. S7-22-99. You may view the comment letters that were submitted by electronic mail at the Commission's web site: www.sec.gov.

23. See, e.g., Letter dated November 8, 1999 from Sarah A.B. Teslik, Executive Director, Council of Institutional Investors; Letter dated October 14, 1999 from Robert B. Hodes, Willkie Farr & Gallagher.

24. See, e.g., Letter dated November 29, 1999 from Stephanie B. Mudick, General Counsel -Corporate Law, Citigroup Inc. ("Citigroup Letter"); Letter dated November 22, 1999 from Michael L. Conley, Executive Vice President and CFO, McDonald's Corporation.

25. See, e.g., Letter dated November 19, 1999 from the New York State Bar Association, Committee on Securities Regulation ("NYS Bar Letter") and Letter dated November 17, 1999 from KPMG LLP ("KPMG Letter") supporting application of the amendments and new rules to companies of all sizes.

26. See supra note 11; see also Beasley, Carcello, and Hermanson, Fraudulent Financial Reporting: 1987-1997, An Analysis of U.S. Public Companies (Mar. 1999) (study commissioned by the Committee of Sponsoring Organizations of the Treadway Commission) (the "COSO Report").

27. See Order Approving Proposed Rule Change by the NASD, Exchange Act Release No. 42231, File No. SR-NASD-99-48; Order Approving Proposed Rule Change by the NYSE, Exchange Act Release No. 42233, File No. SR-NYSE-99-39. While the Blue Ribbon Committee's recommendations were directed to the NYSE and the NASD, the AMEX proposed, and the Commission approved, rule changes to AMEX's listing standards. See Order Approving Proposed Rule Change by the AMEX, Exchange Act Release No. 42232, File No. SR-Amex-99-38.

28. See Exposure Draft for Proposed Statement on Auditing Standards: Amendments to Statements on Auditing Standard No. 61, Communication with Audit Committees and Statements on Auditing Standard No. 71, Interim Financial Information (Oct. 1, 1999) ("ASB Exposure Draft"). A copy of the ASB Exposure Draft can be obtained at www.aicpa.org/members/div/auditstd/drafts.htm.

29. SAS 61 requires independent auditors to communicate certain matters related to the conduct of an audit to those who have responsibility for oversight of the financial reporting process, specifically the audit committee. Among the matters to be communicated to the audit committee are: (1) methods used to account for significant unusual transactions; (2) the effect of significant accounting policies in controversial or emerging areas for which there is a lack of authoritative guidance or consensus; (3)

the process used by management in formulating particularly sensitive accounting estimates and the basis for the auditor's conclusions regarding the reasonableness of those estimates; and (4) disagreements with management over the application of accounting principles, the basis for management's accounting estimates, and the disclosures in the financial statements.

30. See Codification of Statements on Auditing Standards, AU § 722. SAS 71 provides guidance to independent accountants on performing reviews of interim financial information.

31. In the Proposing Release, we solicited comment on whether to require companies to disclose whether their quarterly financial statements have been reviewed by independent auditors. We are not adopting that requirement, but are retaining the current requirement of Rule 10-01(d) of Regulation S-X, 17 CFR 210.10-01(d), that if a company discloses that an independent auditor has performed a review of interim financial information, it must file a copy of the auditor's report. A conforming change to Item 310(b) has been made as proposed.

32. In 1989, the Commission issued a concept release on whether it should propose amendments to its rules to require more involvement of the independent accountant in the preparation of interim financial information. See Exchange Act Release No. 26949 (June 20, 1989) [54 FR 27023]. The Treadway Commission recommended that the SEC require independent public accountants to review quarterly financial data before a company releases it to the public. Treadway Report, supra note 21, at 53.

33. See, e.g., Letter dated November 29, 1999 from The Business Roundtable ("We believe that a requirement for such a review would not impose a substantial burden and would help to improve the investor's comfort with interim statements"); Letter dated November 23, 1999 from Mark Wovsaniker, Vice President - Accounting Policy, America Online Incorporated ("To promote the accuracy and the high quality of the quarterly results, the auditor's regular involvement throughout the year, not just once at the end of each year, is necessary"); Letter dated November 22, 1999 from the Association for Investment Management and Research -Advocacy Advisory Committee ("AIMR Letter") ("[The proposal] will require auditor involvement throughout the year, which should help mitigate earnings management, as well as reduce the likelihood of restatements or other year-end adjustments").

34. See, e.g., Letter dated December 3, 1999 from the American Bar Association - Section of Business Law ("ABA Letter").

35. One firm's policy apparently applies only to clients filing selected quarterly financial data under Item 302(a) of Regulation S-K, 17 CFR 229.302(a).

36. Prior to today's amendments, Item 302(a) required registrants to provide Item 302(a) information if the registrant met certain tests, including but not limited to: (1) two of the three following requirements: (a) shares outstanding have a market value of at least $2.5 million; (b) the minimum bid price is at least $5 per share; or (c) the registrant has at least $2.5 million of capital, surplus, and undivided profits; and (2) the registrant and its subsidiaries: (a) have had net income after taxes but before extraordinary items and the cumulative effect of a change in accounting of at least $250,000 for each of the last three fiscal years; or (b) had total assets of at least $200 million for the last fiscal year end.

37. See, e.g., KPMG Letter, supra note 25, supporting this amendment.

38. 15 U.S.C. § 78l(b).

39. 15 U.S.C. § 78l(g)

40. We are eliminating the requirement for large, widely-traded insurance companies, which file periodic reports solely pursuant to Section 15(d) of the Exchange Act, to provide Item 302(a) information. It is noted in this regard that other types of issuers reporting solely pursuant to Section 15(d) are not required to provide Item 302(a) information. The Item 302(a) amendments will accord insurance companies the same treatment under Item 302(a) as other issuers that report solely pursuant to Section 15(d).

41. See Letter dated November 29, 1999 from Ernst & Young recommending that the criteria for Item 302(a) compliance be based on a company's market capitalization, such as above $25 million.

42. See, e.g., Letter dated November 24, 1999 from Tommy Chisholm, Secretary, Southern Company; Citigroup Letter, supra note 24. But see Letter dated November 26, 1999 from Peter C. Clapman, Senior Vice President and Chief Counsel, Investments, Teachers Insurance and Annuity Association College Retirement Equities Fund ("TIAA-CREF Letter").

43. See 1 American Law Institute, *Principles of Corporate Governance: Analysis and Recommendations* 134-98 (1994); In re Caremark Int'l Inc. Derivative Litig., 698 A.2d 959, 967-70 (Del. Ch. 1996).

44. Caremark, 698 A.2d at 970 (boards must assure "themselves that information and reporting systems exist in the organization that are reasonably designed to provide to senior management and to the board itself timely, accurate information sufficient to allow management and the board, each within its scope, to reach informed judgments concerning both the corporation's compliance with law and its business performance").

45. See generally Report of the Public Oversight Board ("POB"), "Directors, Management, and Auditors: Allies in Protecting Shareholder Interests," in which the POB discusses, among other things, a recommendation of the Kirk Panel to require audit committees to discuss with management and the auditors the quality of the accounting principles and judgments used in preparing financial statements. The POB notes its belief that compliance with that recommendation would not increase the exposure of board members to litigation because, among other things, the procedures will reduce the possibility that the financial statements are in fact misleading, thereby reducing the danger of finding directors at fault, and the additional steps taken should be persuasive in convincing courts and juries that the financial statements were prepared with care.

46. At least in some measure, these discussions are already prescribed by the auditing literature. See SAS 61. See, e.g., Letter dated November 29, 1999 from America's Community Bankers and Letter dated November 22, 1999 from the Massachusetts Financial Services Company supporting the requirements of paragraphs (a)(1), (2) and (3).

47. We recognize that the auditing literature defines the term "review" to include a particular set of required procedures. See SAS 71. In using the term "reviewed" in the new disclosure requirement, we are not suggesting that the audit committee members can or should follow the procedures required of auditors performing reviews of interim financial statements.

48. See ASB Exposure Draft, supra note 28.

49. The federal securities laws recognize the importance of independent auditors. See, e.g., Items 25 and 26 of Schedule A of the Securities Act and Sections 12(b)(1)(J) and 13(a)(2) of the Exchange Act, 15 U.S.C. §§ 78l(b)(1)(J) and 78m(a)(2).

50. See supra note 24.

51. See, e.g., TIAA-CREF Letter, supra note 42.

52. The Blue Ribbon Committee recommended that the audit committee state that, in reliance on the review and discussions with management and the auditors, the audit committee "believes that the company's financial statements are fairly presented in conformity with Generally Accepted Accounting Principles (GAAP) in all material respects." Blue Ribbon Report, supra note 9, at 35.

53. For closed-end investment companies, paragraph (a)(4) clarifies that this requirement applies to financial statements included in a fund's annual report to shareholders required by Section 30(e) of the Investment Company Act of 1940 and Rule 30d-1. These reports must be filed with the Commission pursuant to Rule 30b2-1, 17 CFR 270.30b2-1, under the Investment Company Act of 1940. Commenters disagreed about whether closed-end funds be excluded altogether from the new proxy statement

disclosure requirements. See, e.g., ABA Letter, supra note 34; Letter dated November 29, 1999 from Stuart M. Strauss, Morgan Stanley Dean Witter; Letter dated November 29, 1999 from Arthur Andersen LLP; Letter dated November 3, 1999 from the Investment Company Institute. We have concluded, however, that the application of these requirements to closed-end funds is warranted because of the critical role that audit committees play in overseeing the financial reporting process.

54. The signature requirement is described in General Instruction D of Form 10-K and General Instruction C of Form 10-KSB. The Commission amended the signature requirements for Form 10-K in 1980 in order to "enhance director awareness of and participation in the preparation of the Form 10-K information." See Securities Act Release No. 6176 (Jan. 15, 1980) [45 FR 5972].

55. See, e.g., Letter dated December 1, 1999 from Ira M. Millstein, Weil Gotshal & Manges LLP, and John C. Whitehead. Messrs. Millstein and Whitehead were co-chairmen of the Blue Ribbon Committee; Letter dated November 29, 1999 from Deloitte & Touche LLP; Letter dated November 29, 1999 from James E. Kelly, General Counsel, Dime Bancorp, Inc.; Letter dated November 23, 1999 from Michael A. Rocca, Senior Vice President, Chief Financial Officer, Mallinckrodt Inc. ("This type of report better describes the audit committee's oversight role. . . . Moreover, in our view this alternative language would create a less significant litigation risk to audit committees"); NYS Bar Letter, supra note 25; Letter dated November 16, 1999 from Ernst & Young LLP. See also Letter dated August 20, 1999 from Ernst & Young LLP to Harvey J. Goldschmid, General Counsel, and Lynn E. Turner, Chief Accountant, SEC, commenting on the recommendations of the Blue Ribbon Committee and recommending a variation of this alternative.

56. Delaware General Corporation Law, for example, states that board members are "fully protected in relying in good faith upon the records of the corporation X. Statutory Bases and Text of Amendments

57. See Blue Ribbon Report, supra note 9, at 34.

58. This approach is consistent with the current treatment of the report from the company's compensation committee. See Instruction 9 to Item 402(a)(3) of Regulation S-K, 17 CFR 229.402(a)(3).

59. We note, however, that the revised listing standards of the NYSE, NASD, and AMEX require the audit committee to: (1) adopt a formal written charter that is approved by the full board of directors and that specifies the scope of the committee's responsibilities, and how it carries out those responsibilities, including structure, processes, and membership requirements; and (2) review and reassess the adequacy of the audit committee's charter on an annual basis. See supra note 27.

60. See, e.g., Letter dated November 29, 1999 from William E. Eason, Jr., Senior Vice President and General Counsel, Scientific-Atlanta, Inc.; Letter dated November 29, 1999 from Paul V. Stahlin, Senior Vice President and Comptroller, Summit Bancorp.

61. See, e.g., TIAA-CREF Letter, supra note 42.

62. See, e.g., Letter dated November 29, 1999 from David K. Owens, Edison Electric Institute.

63. Staff of the SEC, 95th Cong., 2d Sess., Report to Congress on the Accounting Profession and the Commission's Oversight Role, Subcommittee on Governmental Efficiency and the District of Columbia of the Senate Committee on Governmental Affairs, at 97 (Comm. Print July 1978). See also Blue Ribbon Report, supra note 9, at 22-23; Treadway Report, supra note 21, at 40-41; In the Matter of McKesson & Robbins, Accounting Series Release No. 19, Exchange Act Release No. 2707 (Dec. 5, 1940).

64. Blue Ribbon Report, supra note 9, at 22.

65. See, e.g., TIAA-CREF Letter, supra note 42.

66. The revised listing standards of the NASD and AMEX require that small business issuers have at least two members of their audit committee, a majority of whom must be independent. In responding to the new disclosure requirement, small business is-

suers, of course, can disclose that the listing standards of the NASD or AMEX do not require that all members of their audit committee be independent. See supra note 27.

67.   Item 7 of Schedule 14A requires companies to provide the disclosures required by Items 401 and 404(a) and (c) of Regulation S-K.

68.   See Blue Ribbon Report, supra note 9, at 35, recommending a safe harbor.

69.   See Instruction 9 to Item 402(a)(3) of Regulation S-K, 17 CFR 229.402(a)(3).

70.   The other antifraud provisions of the Exchange Act and Securities Act of 1933 (the "Securities Act"), however, would continue to apply.

71.   See, e.g., Letter dated November 29, 1999 from Katherine K. Combs, Deputy General Counsel and Corporate Secretary, PECO Energy Company; Letter dated November 30, 1999 from the American Society of Corporate Secretaries (the "ASCS Letter").

72.   15 U.S.C. § 78o(d).

73.   A "foreign private issuer" must file reports on Form 6-K promptly after the information required by the Form is made public in accordance with the laws of its home country or a foreign securities exchange. See 17 CFR 240.13a-16(b).

74.   See, e.g., ASCS Letter, supra note 71.

75.   17 CFR 240.14a-101.

76.   17 CFR 240.14c-101.

77.   17 CFR 249.310.

78.   Blue Ribbon Report, supra note 9, at 19.

79.   OMB, *Report to Congress on the Costs and Benefits of Federal Regulation* 21 (1998) (OMB has recognized that while it may be difficult to quantify the benefits of disclosure requirements, there is a strong consensus among economists that, in general, disclosure-based regulatory schemes can improve the functioning of markets and produce significant benefits for consumers).

80.   See Section III.A above.

81.   COSO Report, supra note 26, at 34 ("Close scrutiny of quarterly financial information and a move toward continuous auditing strategies may increase opportunities for earlier detection of financial statement improprieties").

82.   See, e.g., AIMR Letter, supra note 33.

83.   See, e.g., KPMG Letter, supra note 25 ("In our experience that policy [of conducting SAS 71 reviews] has resulted in the earlier identification of accounting and reporting issues and has therefore enhanced the quality of interim financial reporting").

84.   Letter dated November 22, 1999 from Michael Dee.

85.   One non-Big 5 accounting firm indicated in its comment letter that the upper end of the range (i.e., about $4,000 per quarter) comported with its experience for small to medium size companies. Letter dated October 14, 1999 from Edward W. O'Connell, Wiss & Company, LLP.

86.   At the proposing stage, we used 2,150 companies to reach an estimate of $16 million.

87.   See NYS Bar Letter, supra note 25.

88.   Preparation of the charter is required by the NYSE, NASD, and AMEX and not the Commission's rules.

89.   The $15 million figure derives from one page at $1,500 per page for approximately 10,145 companies.

90.   See, e.g., Letter dated November 19, 1999 from Patricia Gallup, Chairman of the Board, PC Connection, Inc.

91.   The estimate does not include the amount of time the audit committee would spend conducting the discussions with the independent accountants and management to which new Item 306 of Regulations S-K and S-B and the amendments to Item 7 of

Schedule 14A refer. The amendments would not require that the audit committee hold the discussions, but merely that it disclose whether the discussions have taken place.

92. See Section III.E above.

93. See ABA Letter, supra note 34.

94. See generally COSO Report, supra note 26. In fact, the COSO Report specifically found that a "regulatory focus on companies with market capitalization in excess of $200 million may fail to target companies with greater risk for financial statement fraud activities." Id. at 4.

95. COSO Report, supra note 26, at 5.

96. A "small business issuer" under Regulation S-B, however, is a company with less than $25 million in revenues and market capitalization.

97. See Section VII above.

NYSE Rulemaking: Order Approving Proposed Rule Change Amending the Audit Committee Requirements and Notice of Filing and Order Granting Accelerated Approval of Amendments No. 1 and No. 2 Thereto

SECURITIES AND EXCHANGE COMMISSION

(Release No. 34-42233; File No. SR-NYSE-99-39)

December 14, 1999

Self-Regulatory Organizations; Order Approving Proposed Rule Change by the New York Stock Exchange, Inc. Amending the Exchange's Audit Committee Requirements and Notice of Filing and Order Granting Accelerated Approval of Amendments No. 1 and No. 2 Thereto

I. Introduction

On September 20, 1999, the New York Stock Exchange, Inc. ("NYSE" or "Exchange") submitted to the Securities and Exchange Commission ("SEC" or "Commission"), pursuant to Section 19(b)(1) of the Securities Exchange Act of 1934 ("Act")[1] and Rule 19b-4 thereunder,[2] a proposed rule change amending the Exchange's audit committee requirements.

The Federal Register published the proposed rule change for comment on October 13, 1999.[3] In response, the Commission received 25 comment letters.[4] On October 15, 1999 and December 8, 1999, the Exchange submitted Amendments No. 1[5] and No. 2,[6] respectively, to the proposed rule change. This order approves the proposed rule change and grants accelerated approval to Amendments No. 1 and No. 2. The Commission is also soliciting comment on Amendments No. 1 and No. 2 to the proposed rule change.

II. Description of the Proposed Rule Change

A. Background

In February 1999, the Blue Ribbon Committee on Improving the Effectiveness of Corporate Audit Committees ("Blue Ribbon Committee") issued a report containing recommendations aimed at strengthening the independence of the audit committee, making the audit committee more effective, and addressing mechanisms for accountability among the audit committee, the outside auditors, and management.[7]

The Exchange distributed to its listed companies the Exchange staff's suggestions for rule changes in response to the Blue Ribbon Committee's report. The comments from the Exchange's listed companies were generally supportive of the suggestions put forth by the Exchange, with some commenters expressing concerns about "financial literacy" requirement.

In response to the Blue Ribbon Committee's recommendations, the Exchange proposes to revise its listing standards regarding audit committees. The proposed rule change specifies four requirements for a qualified audit committee and defines the terms "Immediate Family" and "Affiliate" for purposes of the proposed audit committee requirements.

The text of the proposed rule change, as amended by Amendments No. 1 and No. 2, is as follows. Language deleted by Amendments No. 1 and No. 2 is in brackets. Language added by Amendments No. 1 and No. 2 is in italics.

NYSE Listed Company Manual

* * *

Section 3

Corporate Responsibility

303.00 Corporate Governance Standards

In addition to the numerical listing standards, the Exchange has adopted certain corporate governance listing standards. These standards apply to all companies listing common stock on the Exchange. However, the Exchange does not apply a particular standard to a non-U.S. company if the company provides the Exchange with a written certification from independent counsel of the company's country of domicile stating that the company's corporate governance practices comply with home country law and the rules of the principal securities market for the company's stock outside the United States.

303.01 Audit Committee

(A) Audit Committee Policy. Each company must have a qualified audit committee.

(B) Requirements for a Qualified Audit Committee.

(1) Formal Charter. [Each audit committee must adopt a formal written charter that is approved by the Board of Directors.] The Board of Directors must adopt and approve a formal written charter for the audit committee. The audit committee must review and reassess the adequacy of the audit committee charter on an annual basis. The charter must specify the following:

 (a) the scope of the audit committee's responsibilities and how it carries out those responsibilities, including structure, processes and membership requirements;

 (b) that the outside auditor for the company is ultimately accountable to the Board of Directors and audit committee of the company, that the audit committee and Board of Directors have the ultimate authority and responsibility to select, evaluate and, where appropriate, replace the outside auditor (or to nominate the outside auditor to be proposed for shareholder approval in any proxy statement); and

 (c) that the audit committee is responsible for ensuring that the outside auditor submits on a periodic basis to the audit committee a formal written statement delineating all relationships between the auditor and the company and that the audit committee is responsible for actively engaging in a dialogue with the outside auditor with respect to any disclosed relationships or services that may impact the objectivity and independence of the outside auditor and for recommending that the Board of Directors take appropriate action [to ensure the independence of the outside auditor] in response to the outside auditors' report to satisfy itself of the outside auditors' independence.

(2) Composition/Expertise Requirement of Audit Committee Members.

 (a) Each audit committee shall consist of at least three directors, all of whom have no relationship to the company that may interfere with the exercise of their independence from management and the company ("Independent");

 (b) Each member of the audit committee shall be financially literate, as such qualification is interpreted by the company's Board of Directors in its business judgment, or must become financially literate within a reasonable period of time after his or her appointment to the audit committee; and

 (c) At least one member of the audit committee must have accounting or related financial management expertise, as the Board of Directors interprets such qualification in its business judgment.

(3) Independence Requirement of Audit Committee Members. In addition to the definition of Independent provided above in (2)(a), the following restrictions shall apply to every audit committee member:

(a) Employees. A director who is an employee (including non-employee executive officers) of the company or any of its affiliates may not serve on the audit committee until three years following the termination of his or her employment. In the event the employment relationship is with a former parent or predecessor of the company, the director could serve on the audit committee after three years following the termination of the relationship between the company and the former parent or predecessor.

(b) Business Relationship. A director (i) who is a partner, controlling shareholder, or executive officer of an organization that has a business relationship with the company, or (ii) who has a direct business relationship with the company (e.g., a consultant) may serve on the audit committee only if the company's Board of Directors determines in its business judgment that the relationship does not interfere with the director's exercise of independent judgment. In making a determination regarding the independence of a director pursuant to this paragraph, the Board of Directors should consider, among other things, the materiality of the relationship to the company, to the director, and, if applicable, to the organization with which the director is affiliated.

"Business relationships" can include commercial, industrial, banking, consulting, legal, accounting and other relationships. A director can have this relationship directly with the company, or the director can be a partner, officer or employee of an organization that has such a relationship. The director may serve on the audit committee without the above-referenced Board of Directors' determination after three years following the termination of, as applicable, either (1) the relationship between the organization with which the director is affiliated and the company, (2) the relationship between the director and his or her partnership status, shareholder interest or executive officer position, or (3) the direct business relationship between the director and the company.

(c) Cross Compensation Committee Link. A director who is employed as an executive of another corporation where any of the company's executives serves on that corporation's compensation committee may not serve on the audit committee.

(d) Immediate Family. A director who is an Immediate Family member of an individual who is an executive officer of the company or any of its affiliates cannot serve on the audit committee until three years following the termination of such employment relationship. See para. 303.02 for definition of "Immediate Family."

303.02 Application of Standards

(A) "Immediate Family" includes a person's spouse, parents, children, siblings, mothers-in-law and fathers-in-law, sons and daughters-in-law, brothers and sisters-in-law, and anyone (other than employees) who shares such person's home.

(B) "Affiliate" includes a subsidiary, sibling company, predecessor, parent company, or former parent company.

(C) Written Affirmation. As part of the initial listing process, and with respect to any subsequent changes to the composition of the audit committee, and otherwise approximately once each year, each company should provide the Exchange written confirmation regarding:

(1) any determination that the company's Board of Directors has made regarding the independence of directors pursuant to any of the subparagraphs above;

(2) the financial literacy of the audit committee members;

(3) the determination that at least one of the audit committee members has accounting or related financial management expertise; and

(4) the annual review and reassessment of the adequacy of the audit committee charter.

(D) Independence Requirement of Audit Committee Members. Notwithstanding the requirements of subparagraphs (3)(a) and (3)(d) of para. 303.01, one director who is no longer an employee or who is an Immediate Family member of a former executive officer of the company or its affiliates, but is not considered independent pursuant to these provisions due to the three-year restriction period, may be appointed, under exceptional and limited circumstances, to the audit committee if the company's board of directors determines in its business judgment that membership on the committee by the individual is required by the best interests of the corporation and its shareholders, and the company discloses, in the next annual proxy statement subsequent to such determination, the nature of the relationship and the reasons for that determination.

(E) "Officer" shall have the meaning specified in Rule 16a-1(f) under the Securities Exchange Act of 1934, or any successor rule.

(F) Initial Public Offering. Companies listing in conjunction with their initial public offering (including spin-offs and carve outs) will be required to have two qualified audit committee members in place within three months of listing and a third qualified member in place within twelve months of listing.

B. Charter

The Exchange proposes to require audit committees to adopt a formal written charter that is approved by the company's board and to review and reassess annually the adequacy of the charter. The charter must specify: (i) the scope of the audit committee's responsibilities and how they are being carried out; (ii) the ultimate accountability of the outside auditor to the board and audit committee; (iii) the responsibility of the audit committee and board for selection, evaluation and replacement of the outside auditor; and (iv) the responsibility of the audit committee for ensuring the independence of the outside auditor by reviewing, and discussing with the board if necessary, any relationships between the auditor and the company or any other relationships that may adversely affect the independence of the auditor.

C. Structure and Membership of the Audit Committee

The Exchange also proposes to change the structure and membership qualifications of the audit committee. Under the proposed rule change, each audit committee must have at least three independent directors, subject to a board override for one director. The board may override the three-year bar for one audit committee member after finding that an override is required in the best interests of the company and its shareholders. If it exercises the override, the company must disclose in its next annual proxy statement the nature of the relationship and the reasons for that determination. Potential candidates that are not considered independent because of a business relationship with the company or a cross compensation committee link may not be the subject of a board override.

As a result of the audit committee's responsibility for a company's accounting and financial reporting, the Exchange believes that audit committee members should have a basic understanding of financial statements. Therefore, the proposed rule change requires each audit committee member to be financially literate, or to become financially literate within a reasonable period of time after his or her appointment to the audit committee, as such qualification is interpreted by the company's board in its business judgment. Furthermore, in order to further enhance the effectiveness of the audit committee, the proposal requires at least one member of each audit committee to have accounting or related financial management expertise, as the company's board interprets such qualification in its business judgment.

D. Independence

The proposed rule change places four restrictions on audit committee members for purposes of determining each member's independence. First, employees (including non-employee executive officers) of the company or its affiliates may not serve on the audit committee until three years following the termination of employment. However, if the relationship is with a former parent or predecessor of the company (see definition of "Affiliate" described in Subsection F below), the three-year bar applies to the time period following the severance of the relationship between the company and the former parent or predecessor.

Second, a director: (i) who is a partner, controlling shareholder, or executive officer of an organization that has a business relationship with the company, or (ii) who has a direct business relationship with the company (e.g., a consultant), may serve on the audit committee only if the company's board determines in its business judgment that the relationship does not interfere with the director's exercise of independent judgment. Business relationships can include commercial, industrial, banking, consulting, legal, accounting and other relationships. A director can have this relationship directly with the company, or the director can be a partner, officer or employee of an organization that has the business relationship.

Third, a director who is employed as an executive of another corporation where any of the company's executives serves on that corporation's compensation committee may not serve on the audit committee.

Fourth, a director who is "Immediate Family" (as that term is defined by proposed Exchange Rule 303.01(B)(3)(d)) of an individual who is an executive officer of the company or any of its affiliates cannot serve on the audit committee until three years following the termination of such employment relationship.

E. Written Affirmation

To monitor compliance with the proposed rule change, the Exchange proposes to incorporate an ongoing written affirmation requirement. In this regard, as part of the initial listing process, and with respect to any subsequent changes to the composition of the audit committee, and otherwise approximately once each year, each company must provide the Exchange written confirmation regarding:

   i)   any determination that the company's board has made regarding the independence of directors;

   ii)   the financial literacy of the audit committee members;

   iii)   the determination that at least one of the audit committee members has accounting or related financial management expertise; and

   iv)   the annual review and reassessment of the adequacy of the audit committee charter.

F. Definitions

The Exchange proposes to codify two long-standing interpretations under the current audit committee requirements as follows:

   i)   "Immediate Family" includes a person's spouse, parents, children, siblings, mothers-in-law and fathers-in-law, sons and daughters-in-law, brothers and sisters-in-law, and anyone (other than employees) who shares such person's home; and

   ii)   "Affiliate" includes a subsidiary, sibling company, predecessor, parent company, or former parent company.

G. Implementation

The Exchange proposes to implement a transition period to provide its issuers with sufficient time to comply with the proposed rule change. Specifically, the Exchange proposes to: (i) "grandfather" all public company audit committee members qualified under current NYSE rules until they are re-elected or replaced; and (ii) give companies that have less than three members on their audit committees eighteen months from the date of Commission approval of this rule filing to recruit the requisite members. Issuers listed on the Exchange as of the effective date of the proposed rule change will have six months to adopt a formal written audit committee charter.[8]

III. Comments

As of December 9, 1999, the Commission received 25 comment letters on the proposed rule change.[9] In general, most commenters favored the proposed rule change but recommended certain modifications. Three commenters opposed the proposed rule change.[10]

In particular, the CII supports the new requirements, but stated that the proposed board override provision, which allows a company's board to include a non-independent director on an audit committee, is not appropriate because companies should not have a problem finding financially literate, truly independent directors.[11] In addition, the AFL-CIO stated that the restriction period for former employees, or relatives of former employees, should be three years instead of five years.[12] MFSC stated that audit committees should not be required to describe in their charters how they carry out their responsibilities.[13]

Many of the commenters pointed to differences between the proposed rule change, on the one hand, and the Amex Proposal and Nasdaq Proposal, on the other. Specifically, several commenters stated that the Exchange should adopt the Amex's and Nasdaq's definitions of financial literacy and expertise.[14] These commenters noted that allowing individual companies to define these terms will lead to inconsistencies. In addition, several commenters stated that the proposed rule change will discourage qualified candidates from serving on audit committees.[15] Moreover, one commenter stated that the restriction that prohibits an individual who is an immediate family member of an executive officer of the company or any of its affiliates from serving on the audit committee should not be limited to executive officers.[16] Finally, three commenters stated that the Exchange should adopt a bright line test for identifying when a director has a significant business relationship with the company, as in the Amex Proposal and Nasdaq Proposal.[17] On the other hand, another commenter opposed a bright line test and stated that the Exchange should not revise its current test to determine if a significant business relationship exists.[18]

In addition, one commenter stated that past non-executive employment should be treated as a significant business relationship.[19] This commenter also stated that consultants who receive from the company more than a de minimis amount of compensation should be treated as employees, while consultants who do not should be treated as having a business relationship with the company.[20] According to the commenter, the company's board should be permitted to determine that the compensation does not impair the director's objectivity.[21] Moreover, the commenter objected to the financial expertise requirement and stated that no director will want to be designated the financial expert because of the added exposure to liability.[22]

APTC stated that the proposed rule change will be counter productive to the goal of better audit committees.[23] In addition, APTC stated that the proposed rule change will disadvantage smaller companies more than larger companies, but concluded that it is appropriate to apply the proposed rule change to all companies, regardless of size.[24] Moreover, APTC is opposed to the proposal's financial literacy requirement.[25] APTC believes that the financial literacy requirement may deprive audit committees of the service of individuals with "exceptional character and/or operational experience."[26] The commenter suggested that the Exchange replace this requirement with a requirement that the committee as a whole possess a certain level of financial acumen.[27]

TI stated that to reduce unrealistic expectations, the proposed rule change should require or permit a disclaimer in the audit committee charter stating that the committee does not provide any special assurances with regard to the company's financial statements, nor does the audit committee give a professional evaluation of the quality of the audits performed by the independent public accountants.[28] Exxon and NYSBA stated that the company's board, not the audit committee, should be required to adopt the audit committee charter because audit committees are created by the board in its discretion and under authority granted by state law.[29]

Exxon also stated that proposed Rule 303.01(B)(2)(a), which requires audit committees to have at least three directors, all of whom must be independent, should provide a business judgment standard for independence, as subparts (b) and (c) of this Rule do with respect to financial literary and expertise.[30] Exxon also stated that proposed Rule 303.01(B)(1) should not give both the board and the audit committee ultimate responsibility to select, evaluate, and replace the outside auditor.[31] Exxon stated that only one body can have ultimate authority.[32] McDonald's stated that a yearly written confirmation regarding financial literacy, financial expertise, independence of directors, and adequacy of the audit committee's charter is unnecessary.[33]

Deloitte and PWC each stated that requiring a company's board or audit committee to "ensure" the independence of the outside auditor goes beyond what can reasonably be expected of the board and the audit committee in their oversight role.[34] Deloitte suggested that the Exchange replace the word "ensure" with "monitor" or "actively oversee."[35] E&Y supports the proposed rule change overall, but stated that Small Business Filers should not be exempt from the financial literacy and expertise requirements and that the Exchange should expand its definition of immediate family member to include sons-in-law and daughters-in-law.[36] Airlease stated that smaller companies should not be required to have three independent auditors on their audit committees.[37]

In addition, the NVCA stated that the proposed rule change should exclude venture capital investors from the independence qualifications.[38] The NVCA also stated that the proposed rule change should give companies that have just completed an initial public offering ("IPO") eighteen months to comply with the new requirements.[39]

Three commenters stated that the proposed rule change should not apply to closed-end investment companies.[40] ICI and MSDW noted that closed-end investment companies are adequately regulated under the 1940 Act.[41] These two commenters also stated that the potential abuses that the proposed rule change is designed to address do not exist with respect to closed-end investment funds because the assets of closed-end funds, consist exclusively of investment securities and thus there is no opportunity to "manage" earnings or results through the selective application of accounting policies.[42]

IV. Discussion

The Commission finds that the proposed rule change is consistent with the requirements of the Act and the rules and regulations thereunder applicable to a national securities exchange,[43] and, in particular, the requirements of Section 6(b)(5) of the Act.[44] The Commission believes that the proposed rule change will protect investors by improving the effectiveness of audit committees of companies listed on the Exchange. The Commission also believes that the new requirements will enhance the reliability and credibility of financial statements of companies listed on the Exchange by making it more difficult for companies to inappropriately distort their true financial performance.

Specifically, the Commission believes that the proposed definition of independence will promote the quality and reliability of a company's financial statements. The Commission believes that directors without financial, familial, or other material personal ties to management will be more likely to objectively evaluate the propriety of management's accounting, internal control, and financial reporting practices. The Commission also believes that the proposal's prohibition against employees serving on the audit committee is appropriate and that the Exchange should not be required to distinguish between executive and non-executive employees.[45] In addition, the Commission considers that the proposed provision permitting a company to appoint one non-independent director to its audit committee, if the board determines that membership on the committee by the individual is required by the best interests of the corporation and its shareholders, adequately balances the need for objective, independent directors with the company's need for flexibility in exceptional and unusual circumstances. The Commission believes that the proposal's requirement that the company disclose in its next annual proxy statement the nature of the relationship and the board's reasons for determining that the appointment was in the best interests of the corporation will adequately guard against abuse of the proposed exception to the independence requirement.[46]

The Commission does not believe that venture capital investors should be excluded from the Exchange's definition of independence. The Commission does not view the proposed rule change as posing an undue hardship on venture capital firms or companies listed on the NYSE. The Commission notes that the proposed rule change will only prohibit venture capital investors from sitting on a company's audit committee if the investor does not fall within the Exchange's definition of independence. The proposed rule change will not prohibit previously eligible investors from serving on the company's board.

In addition, the Commission believes that requiring boards of directors of listed companies to adopt formal written charters specifying the audit committee's responsibilities, and how it carries out those responsibilities, will help the audit committee, management, investors, and the company's auditors recognize, and understand the function of the audit committee and the relationship among the parties. Moreover, the Commission believes that the proposal's requirement that companies provide yearly written confirmation regarding the independence, financial literacy, and financial expertise of directors, as well as the adequacy of the audit committee charter, will help the Exchange to ensure that listed companies are complying with the proposed rule change.

The Commission believes that the proposed rule change's requirement that each issuer have an audit committee composed of three independent directors who are able to read and understand fundamental financial statements will enhance the effectiveness of the audit committee and help to ensure that audit committee members are able to adequately fulfill their responsibilities. The Commission believes that requiring each audit committee member to satisfy this standard will help to ensure that the committee as a whole is financially literate.[47] Moreover, the Commission believes that requiring one member of the audit committee to have past employment experience in finance or accounting, requisite professional certification in accounting, or any other comparable experience or background that indicates the individual's financial sophistication, will further enhance the effectiveness of the audit committee in carrying out its financial oversight responsibilities. The Commission does not believe that these requirements will discourage qualified candidates from serving on audit committees. Rather, the Commission believes that these requirements will better enable companies to identify and select qualified directors. In addition, the Commission does not believe that companies will experience undue difficulty recruiting an audit committee member that satisfies the financial expertise requirements.

Moreover, the Commission considers the Exchange's decision to exempt Small Business Filers as appropriate.[48] The Commission notes that relatively few companies that qualify for listing on the Exchange would also qualify as Small Business Filers under SEC Regulation S-B.[49]

Furthermore, the Commission does not believe that the Exchange should be required to adopt the Amex and Nasdaq proposed definitions of financial literacy and expertise or the test to determine when a potential director has a significant business relationship with the company. The Commission notes that the proposed rule change is not inconsistent with the Act.

Moreover, the Commission has concluded that the Exchange's decision to include investment companies in the proposed rule change is warranted. While the Commission recognizes that the opportunity for some types of financial reporting abuses may be limited by the nature of fund assets,[50] it believes that audit committees do play an important role in overseeing the financial reporting process for investment companies.

Finally, the Commission does not view the proposed rule change as circumventing state law.[51] The Commission notes that the Exchange is amending its own listing standards, which is a function within the Exchange's discretion, as long as those changes are consistent with the Act.

The Commission finds good cause for approving Amendments No. 1 and No. 2 to the proposed rule change prior to the thirtieth day after publication in the Federal Register. The Commission notes that Amendment No. 1 revises the implementation time periods for the proposed rule change solely to provide greater clarity to issuers and to investors. The Commission believes that Amendment No. 1 will enable issuers to determine when they must comply with the new requirements and will enable investors to determine when to rely on the protections afforded by the proposed rule change. The Commission notes that Amendment No. 2 simply codifies the Exchange's existing policy on the timing of audit committee requirements for IPOs; clarifies that the company's board must take appropriate action to satisfy itself of the outside auditor's independence, and is not intended to provide an absolute guarantee of independence; and requires the board to adopt the audit committee charter, rather than approving the charter adopted by the audit committee. The Commission believes that accelerated approval will allow the Exchange to simultaneously make all relevant modifications to its Listed Company Manual and will avoid potential confusion. Accordingly, the Commission finds good cause to accelerate approval of Amendments No. 1 and No. 2 to the proposed rule change, consistent with Sections 6(b)(5)[52] and 19(b)[53] of the Act.

V. Solicitation of Comments

Interested persons are invited to submit written data, views and arguments concerning the foregoing, including whether the proposed rule change is consistent with the Act. Persons making written submissions should file six copies thereof with the Secretary, Securities and Exchange

Commission, 450 Fifth Street, N.W., Washington, D.C. 20549-0609. Copies of the submission, all subsequent amendments, all written statements with respect to the proposed rule change that are filed with the Commission, and all written communications relating to the proposed rule change between the Commission and any person, other than those that may be withheld from the public in accordance with the provisions of 5 U.S.C. 552, will be available for inspection and copying in the Commission's Public Reference Room. Copies of such filing will also be available for inspection and copying at the principal office of the Exchange. All submissions should refer to the File No. SR-NYSE-99-39 and should be submitted by [insert date 21 days from the date of publication].

VI. Conclusion

For the foregoing reasons, the Commission finds that the Exchange's proposal to amend its audit committee requirements is consistent with the requirements of the Act and the rules and regulations thereunder.

It is therefore ordered, pursuant to Section 19(b)(2) of the Act,[54] that the amended proposed rule change (SR-NYSE-99-39) is approved.

For the Commission, by the Division of Market Regulation, pursuant to delegated authority.[55]

Jonathan G. Katz Secretary

Footnotes

1. 15 U.S.C. 78s(b)(1).
2. 17 CFR 240.19b-4.
3. Securities Exchange Act Release No. 41980 (Oct. 6, 1999), 64 FR 55514 (Oct. 13, 1999). The Nasdaq Stock Market, Inc. and The American Stock Exchange LLC have proposed rule changes relating to audit committees. See Securities Exchange Act Release No. 41982 (Oct. 6, 1999), 64 FR 55510 (Oct. 13, 1999)("Nasdaq Proposal"), and Securities Exchange Act Release No. 41981 (Oct. 6, 1999), 64 FR 55505 (Oct. 13, 1999) ("Amex Proposal").
4. The comment letters are discussed in Section III of this order.
5. Letter from James E. Buck, Senior Vice President and Secretary, NYSE, to Richard Strasser, Assistant Director, Division of Market Regulation ("Division"), Commission, dated October 14, 1999 ("Amendment No. 1"). The Exchange submitted Amendment No. 1 to require issuers to adopt a formal written audit committee charter within six months of the effective date of the proposed rule change. As originally filed, the proposed rule change required issuers to adopt the charter within eighteen months of the effective date of the proposed rule change. Amendment No. 1 also extends the definition of "officer" in Rule 16a-1(f) under the Act to Paragraph 303 of the Exchange's *Listed Company Manual*. Previously, the Exchange permitted each company's by-laws and charter to define this term.
6. Letter from James E. Buck, Senior Vice President and Secretary, NYSE, to Richard Strasser, Assistant Director, Division, Commission, dated December 6, 1999 ("Amendment No. 2"). Amendment No. 2 revises proposed rule 303.01(B)(1) to require the board to adopt the audit committee charter. Under the original proposal, the audit committee adopted the charter, subject to board approval. Amendment No. 2 also revises proposed Rule 303.01(B)(1)(c) to replace the provision that required the board to take appropriate steps to ensure the independence of the outside auditors. The revised provision requires the board "to take appropriate action in response to the outside auditors report to satisfy itself of the outside auditor's independence." Finally, Amendment No. 2 revises proposed Rule 303.02 to require companies listing on the Exchange in conjunction with an initial public offering to have two qualified audit committee members in place within three months of listing, and a third qualified member within twelve months of listing.

7. *Report and Recommendations of the Blue Ribbon Committee on Improving the Effectiveness of Corporate Audit Committees* (1999). A copy of this Report [Webmaster note: in PDF format] can be found on-line at www.nasdaqnews.com.

8. See Amendment No. 1, supra n.5.

9. See letters from: Ernst & Young LLP ("E&Y") dated November 1, 1999; Deloitte & Touche LLP ("Deloitte") dated November 3, 1999; Council of Institutional Investors ("CII") dated November 8, 1999; Brian T. Borders (on behalf of the National Venture Capital Association ("NVCA")) dated November 12, 1999; Investment Company Institute ("ICI") dated November 3, 1999; PricewaterhouseCoopers LLP ("PWC") dated November 1, 1999; Gary P. Kreider ("Kreider") dated November 5, 1999; Emerson Electric Co. ("Emerson") dated November 1, 1999; Exxon Corporation ("Exxon") dated November 3, 1999; McDonald's Corporation (McDonald's) dated November 1, 1999; Connectiv ("Connectiv") dated November 2, 1999; Texas Instruments ("TI") dated November 2, 1999; Dime Bancorp, Inc. ("Dime") dated November 3, 1999; Airlease Management Services, Inc. ("Airlease") dated November 3, 1999; The Dun & Bradstreet Corporation ("D&B") dated November 3, 1999; EMC Corporation ("EMC") dated November 1, 1999; Dorsey & Whitney LLP ("Dorsey") (on behalf of nine closed-end investment management companies whose stock is listed on the Exchange) dated October 28, 1999; Massachusetts Financial Services Company ("MFSC") (on behalf of six closed-end funds advised by MFSC) dated November 22, 1999; Meritor Automotive, Inc. ("Meritor") dated November 24, 1999; American Federation of Labor and Congress of Industrial Organizations ("AFL-CIO") dated November 29, 1999; Mayer, Brown & Platt on behalf of Morgan Stanley Dean Witter ("MSDW") dated November 29, 1999; Arthur Andersen LLP ("Arthur Andersen") dated December 3, 1999; Association of Publicly Traded Companies ("APTC") dated December 6, 1999; Robert A. Profusek ("Profusek") dated December 3, 1999; Stanley Keller and Richard Rowe ("Keller and Rowe") dated December 7, 1999; and The Committee on Securities Regulation of the Business Law Section of the New York State Bar Association ("NYSBA") dated December 1, 1999.

10. See Kreider Letter at 2; EMC Letter at 2; APTC Letter at 2. Kreider stated his belief that the proposed rule change circumvents state corporate law. EMC stated that the proposed rule change substitutes over-generalized restrictions for the more flexible, traditional standards of good faith, candor, care and loyalty that underlie the business judgment rule under state law. EMC also stated that the independence standards may deprive audit committees of valuable financially-expert directors.

11. CII Letter at 2; see also AFL-CIO Letter at 2.

12. AFL-CIO Letter at 2.

13. MFSC Letter at 1.

14. Dorsey Letter at 7, 9; E&Y Letter at 3; Connectiv Letter at 2; D&B Letter at 2; Emerson Letter at 2; NYSBA Letter at 5. In addition, two commenters stated that the terms financial literacy and expertise are too subjective and should be further defined, but did not state the Amex/Nasdaq versions should be adopted. See McDonald's Letter at 1; MFSC Letter at 2. MFSC also stated that it is not reasonable to expect a company's board to request agreement from a potential audit committee candidate that he will become financially literate because there are no accreditation criteria or specific timeframes for completing this undertaking. MFSC Letter at 2.

15. Dime Letter at 2; NVCA Letter at 2; D&B Letter at 2; MFSC at 2.

16. Keller and Rowe Letter at 2.

17. E&Y Letter at 2; Emerson at 2; Arthur Andersen Letter at 1. In addition, the AFL-CIO stated that the NYSE should adopt a bright line test, but does not think the $60,000 threshold adopted by the Amex and Nasdaq is stringent enough. AFL-CIO Letter at 3.

18. Profusek Letter at 2

19. Keller and Rowe Letter at 2.

20. Id. at 3.

21. Id.

22. Id.; see also NYSBA Letter at 6.

23. APTC Letter at 2.

24. Id. at 3.

25. Id. at 4-5.

26. Id.

27. Id. at 5.

28. TI Letter at 1.

29. Exxon Letter at 1; NYSBA Letter at 2.

30. Exxon Letter at 2. The Commission notes that proposed Rule 303.01(B)(2)(b) and (c) require each company's board to interpret the terms "financial literary" and "financial expertise." The business judgment standard therefore applies to the board's interpretation of these terms. Subpart (a) of the rule does not require the board to interpret the term "independence" and, thus, there is no need for a business judgment standard.

31. Exxon Letter at 1.

32. Id.

33. McDonald's Letter at 2.

34. Deloitte Letter at 1; PWC Letter at 1; Meritor Letter at 2.

35. Id. at 2.

36. E&Y Letter at 4. In addition, the NVCA stated that the exemption for Small Business Filers should be expanded to apply to companies with less than $50 million in revenue. NVCA Letter at 4. The Commission notes, unlike the Nasdaq Proposal and the Amex Proposal, there is no exemption for Small Business Filers under the NYSE's proposed rule change.

37. Airlease Letter at 1.

38. NVCA Letter at 5.

39. Id. at 4.

40. ICI Letter at 2; MSDW Letter at 1; Keller and Rowe Letter at 3. In addition, Keller and Rowe stated that the proposed rule change should exempt all investment companies because their audit committee members are already required not to be "interested persons" as that term is defined in Section 2(a)(9) of the Investment Company Act of 1940 ("1940 Act"). Keller and Rowe Letter at 5. Moreover, Dorsey supported the application of the proposed rule change to investment companies. Dorsey Letter at 3.

41. ICI Letter at 3-4; MSDW Letter at 2.

42. ICI Letter at 3; MSDW Letter at 1. ICI and MSDW also noted that the independent accountants of investment funds are selected by the independent directors of the fund.

43. In approving the proposal, the Commission has considered its impact on efficiency, competition, and capital formation. 15 U.S.C. 78c(f).

44. 15 U.S.C. 78f(b)(5).

45. See Keller and Rowe Letter at 2.

46. The Commission does not believe that the Exchange should require its listed companies to adopt a separate provision on consultants. See Keller and Rowe Letter at 3.

47. See APTC Letter at 5.

48. See NVCA and Airlease Letters.

49. Small Business Filer is defined by Regulation S-B as an issuer that: (i) has revenue of less than $25,000,000; (ii) is a U.S. or Canadian issuer; and (iii) if a majority owned subsidiary, the parent corporation is a small business issuer. 17 CFR 228.10(a)(1).

50. See Keller and Rowe Letter at 5; ICI Letter at 3; MSDW Letter at 1.

51. Kreider Letter at 2.
52. 15 U.S.C. 78f(b)(5).
53. 15 U.S.C. 78s(b).
54. 15. U.S.C. 78s(b)(2).
55. 17 CFR 200.30-3(a)(12).

NASD Rulemaking: Order Approving Proposed Rule Change Amending the Audit Committee Requirements and Notice of Filing and Order Granting Accelerated Approval of Amendments No. 1 and No. 2 Thereto

SECURITIES AND EXCHANGE COMMISSION

(Release No. 34-42231; File No. SR-NASD-99-48)

December 14, 1999

Self-Regulatory Organizations; Order Approving Proposed Rule Change by the National Association of Securities Dealers, Inc. Amending Its Audit Committee Requirements and Notice of Filing and Order Granting Accelerated Approval of Amendments No. 1 and No. 2 Thereto

I. Introduction

On September 20, 1999, the National Association of Securities Dealers, Inc. ("NASD" or "Association"), through its wholly owned subsidiary, The Nasdaq Stock Market, Inc. ("Nasdaq"), submitted to the Securities and Exchange Commission ("SEC" or "Commission"), pursuant to Section 19(b)(1) of the Securities Exchange Act of 1934 ("Act")[1] and Rule 19b-4 thereunder,[2] a proposed rule change amending Nasdaq's audit committee requirements.

The Federal Register published the proposed rule change for comment on October 13, 1999.[3] In response, the Commission received fourteen comment letters. On November 15, 1999 and December 9, 1999, the Association submitted Amendments No. 1[4] and No. 2,[5] respectively, to the proposed rule change. This order approves the proposed rule change and grants accelerated approval to Amendments No. 1 and No. 2. The Commission is also soliciting comment on Amendments No. 1 and No. 2 to the proposed rule change.

II. Description of the Proposed Rule Change

A. Background

In February 1999, the Blue Ribbon Committee on Improving the Effectiveness of Corporate Audit Committees ("Blue Ribbon Committee") issued a report containing recommendations aimed at strengthening the independence of the audit committee; making the audit committee more effective; and addressing mechanisms for accountability among the audit committee, the outside auditors, and management.[6] In response to the Blue Ribbon Committee's recommendations, Nasdaq proposes to amend its listing standards regarding audit committee requirements. The proposed changes cover three general areas: 1) the definition of independence; 2) the structure and membership of the audit committee; and 3) the audit committee charter.

The text of the proposed rule change, as amended by Amendments No. 1 and No. 2, is as follows. Language deleted by Amendments No. 1 and No. 2 is in brackets. Language added by Amendments No. 1 and No. 2 is in italics.

Rule 4200. Definitions

(a) For purposes of the Rule 4000 Series, unless the context requires otherwise:

(1) - (14) No change

(15) "Independent director" means a person other than an officer or employee of the company or its subsidiaries or any other individual having a relationship which, in the opinion of the company's board of directors, would interfere with the exercise of independent judgment in carrying out the responsibilities of a director. The following persons shall not be considered independent:

(a) a director who is employed by the corporation or any of its affiliates for the current year or any of the past three years;

(b) a director who accepts any compensation from the corporation or any of its affiliates in excess of $60,000 during the previous fiscal year, other than compensation for board service, benefits under a tax-qualified retirement plan, or non-discretionary compensation;

(c) a director who is a member of the immediate family of an individual who is, or has been in any of the past three years, employed by the corporation or any of its affiliates as an executive officer. Immediate family includes a person's spouse, parents, children, siblings, mother-in-law, father-in-law, brother-in-law, sister-in-law, son-in-law, daughter-in-law, and anyone who resides in such person's home;

(d) a director who is a partner in, or a controlling shareholder or an executive officer of, any for-profit business organization to which the corporation made, or from which the corporation received, payments (other than those arising solely from investments in the corporation's securities) that exceed 5% of the corporation's or business organization's consolidated gross revenues for that year, or $200,000, whichever is more, in any of the past three years;

(e) a director who is employed as an executive of another entity where any of the company's executives serve on that entity's compensation committee.

(15) - (36) renumbered as (16) - (37)

(b) No change

Rule 4310. Qualification Requirements for Domestic and Canadian Securities

To qualify for inclusion in Nasdaq, a security of a domestic or Canadian issuer shall satisfy all applicable requirements contained in paragraphs (a) or (b), and (c) hereof.

(a) - (b) No change

(c) In addition to the requirements contained in paragraph (a) or (b) above, and unless otherwise indicated, a security shall satisfy the following criteria for inclusion in Nasdaq:

(1) - (24) No change

(25) Corporate Governance Requirements

* * * * * *

(A) No change

(B) Independent Directors

Each issuer shall maintain a sufficient number of independent directors on its board of directors to satisfy the audit committee requirement set forth in Rule 4310(c)(26)(B).

(D) - (H) renumbered as (C) - (G)

(26) Audit Committee

(A) Audit Committee Charter

Each Issuer must certify that it has adopted a formal written audit committee charter and that the Audit Committee has reviewed and reassessed the adequacy of the formal written charter on an annual basis. The charter must specify the following:

(i) the scope of the audit committee's responsibilities, and how it carries out those responsibilities, including structure, processes, and membership requirements;

(ii) the audit committee's responsibility for ensuring its receipt from the outside auditors of a formal written statement delineating all relationships between the auditor and the company, consistent with Independence Standards Board Standard 1, and the audit committee's responsibility for actively engaging in a dialogue with the auditor with respect to any disclosed relationships or services that may impact the objectivity and independence of the auditor and for taking, or recommending that the full board take, appropriate action to [ensure] oversee the independence of the outside auditor; and

(iii) the outside auditor's ultimate accountability to the board of directors and the audit committee, as representatives of shareholders, and these shareholder representatives' ultimate authority and responsibility to select, evaluate, and, where appropriate, replace the outside auditor (or to nominate the outside auditor to be proposed for shareholder approval in any proxy statement).

(B) Audit Committee Composition

(i) Each issuer must have, and certify that it has and will continue to have, an audit committee of at least three members, comprised solely of independent directors, each of whom is able to read and understand fundamental financial statements, including a company's balance sheet, income statement, and cash flow statement or will become able to do so within a reasonable period of time after his or her appointment to the audit committee. Additionally, each issuer must certify that it has, and will continue to have, at least one member of the audit committee that has past employment experience in finance or accounting, requisite professional certification in accounting, or any other comparable experience or background which results in the individual's financial sophistication, including being or having been a chief executive officer, chief financial officer or other senior officer with financial oversight responsibilities.

(ii) Notwithstanding paragraph (i), one director who is not independent as defined in Rule 4200, and is not a current employee or an immediate family member of such employee, may be appointed to the audit committee, if the board, under exceptional and limited circumstances, determines that membership on the committee by the individual is required by the best interests of the corporation and its shareholders, and the board discloses, in the next annual proxy statement subsequent to such determination, the nature of the relationship and the reasons for that determination.

(iii) Exception for Small Business Filers -- Paragraphs (B)(i) and (B)(ii) do not apply to issuers that file reports under SEC Regulation S-B. Such issuers must establish and maintain an Audit Committee of at least two members, a majority of the members of which shall be independent directors.

(26) - (28) renumbered as (27) - (29)

(d) No change

Rule 4320. Qualification Requirements for Non-Canadian Foreign Securities and American Depositary Receipts

To qualify for inclusion in Nasdaq, a security of a non-Canadian foreign issuer, an American Depositary Receipt (ADR) or similar security issued in respect of a security of a foreign issuer shall satisfy the requirements of paragraphs (a), (b) or (c), and (d) and (e) of this Rule.

(a) - (d) No change

(e) In addition to the requirements contained in paragraphs (a), (b) or (c), and (d), the security shall satisfy the following criteria for inclusion in Nasdaq:

(1) - (20) No change

(21) Corporate Governance Requirements -- No provisions of this subparagraph or of subparagraph (24) shall be construed to require any foreign issuer to do any act that is contrary to a law, rule or regulation of any public authority exercising jurisdiction over such issuer or that is contrary to generally accepted business practices in the issuer's country of domicile. Nasdaq shall have the ability to provide exemptions from the applicability of these provisions as may be necessary or appropriate to carry out this intent.

Nasdaq shall review the issuer's past corporate governance activities. This review may include activities taking place while the issuer is listed on Nasdaq or an exchange that imposes corporate governance requirements, as well as activities taking place after the issuer is no longer listed on Nasdaq or an exchange that imposes corporate governance requirements. Based on such review, Nasdaq may take any appropriate action, including placing of restrictions on or additional requirements for listing, or the denial of listing of a security if Nasdaq determines that there have been violations or evasions of such corporate governance standards. Determinations under this subparagraph shall be made on a case-by-case basis as necessary to protect investors and the public interest.

(A) No change

(B) Independent Directors

Each issuer shall maintain a sufficient number of independent directors on its board of directors to satisfy the audit committee requirement set forth in Rule 4320(e)(22)(B).

(D) - (H) renumbered as (C) - (G)

(22) Audit Committee

(A) Audit Committee Charter

Each Issuer must certify that it has adopted a formal written audit committee charter and that the Audit Committee has reviewed and reassessed the adequacy of the formal written charter on an annual basis. The charter must specify the following:

(i) the scope of the audit committee's responsibilities, and how it carries out those responsibilities, including structure, processes, and membership requirements;

(ii) the audit committee's responsibility for ensuring its receipt from the outside auditors of a formal written statement delineating all relationships between the auditor and the company, consistent with Independence Standards Board Standard 1, and the audit committee's responsibility for actively engaging in a dialogue with the auditor with respect to any disclosed relationships or services that may impact the objectivity and independence of the auditor and for taking, or recommending that the full board take, appropriate action to [ensure] oversee the independence of the outside auditor; and

(iii) the outside auditor's ultimate accountability to the board of directors and the audit committee, as representatives of shareholders, and these shareholder representatives' ultimate authority and responsibility to select, evaluate, and, where appropriate, replace the outside auditor (or to nominate the outside auditor to be proposed for shareholder approval in any proxy statement).

(B) Audit Committee Composition

(i) Each issuer must have, and certify that it has and will continue to have, an audit committee of at least three members, comprised solely of independent directors, each of whom is able to read and understand fundamental financial statements, including a company's balance sheet, income statement, and cash flow statement or will become able to do so within a reasonable period of time after his or her appointment to the audit committee. Additionally, each issuer must certify that it has, and will continue to have, at least one member of the audit committee that has past employment experience in finance or accounting, requisite professional certification in accounting, or any other comparable experience or background which results in the individual's financial sophistication, including being or having been a chief executive officer, chief financial officer or other senior officer with financial oversight responsibilities.

(ii) Notwithstanding paragraph (i), one director who is not independent as defined in Rule 4200, and is not a current employee or an immediate family member of such employee, may be appointed to the audit committee, if the board, under exceptional and limited circumstances, determines that membership on the committee by the individual is required by the best interests of the corporation and its shareholders, and the board discloses, in the next annual proxy statement subsequent to such determination, the nature of the relationship and the reasons for that determination.

(iii) Exception for Small Business Filers -- Paragraphs (B)(i) and (B)(ii) do not apply to issuers that file reports under SEC Regulation S-B. Such issuers must establish and maintain an Audit Committee of at least two members, a majority of the members of which shall be independent directors.

(22) - (24) renumbered as (23) - (25)

(f) No change

Rule 4460. Non-Quantitative Designation Criteria for Issuers Excepting Limited Partnerships

(a) - (b) No change

(c) Independent Directors

Each NNM issuer shall maintain a sufficient number of independent directors on its board of directors to satisfy the audit committee requirement set forth in Rule 4460(d)(2).

(d) Audit Committee

(1) Audit Committee Charter

Each Issuer must certify that it has adopted a formal written audit committee charter and that the Audit Committee has reviewed and reassessed the adequacy of the formal written charter on an annual basis. The charter must specify the following:

(A) the scope of the audit committee's responsibilities, and how it carries out those responsibilities, including structure, processes, and membership requirements;

(B) the audit committee's responsibility for ensuring its receipt from the outside auditors of a formal written statement delineating all relationships between the auditor and the company, consistent with Independence Standards Board Standard 1, and the audit committee's responsibility for actively engaging in a dialogue with the auditor with respect to any disclosed relationships or services that may impact the objectivity and independence of the auditor and for taking, or recommending that the full board take, appropriate action to [ensure] oversee the independence of the outside auditor; and

(C) the outside auditor's ultimate accountability to the board of directors and the audit committee, as representatives of shareholders, and these shareholder representatives' ultimate authority and responsibility to select, evaluate, and, where appropriate, replace the outside auditor (or to nominate the outside auditor to be proposed for shareholder approval in any proxy statement).

(2) Audit Committee Composition

(A) Each issuer must have, and certify that it has and will continue to have, an audit committee of at least three members, comprised solely of independent directors, each of whom is able to read and understand fundamental financial statements, including a company's balance sheet, income statement, and cash flow statement or will become able to do so within a reasonable period of time after his or her appointment to the audit committee. Additionally, each issuer must certify that it has, and will continue to have, at least one member of the audit committee that has past employment experience in finance or accounting, requisite professional certification in accounting, or any other comparable experience or background which results in the individual's financial sophistication, including being or having been a chief executive officer, chief financial officer or other senior officer with financial oversight responsibilities.

(B) Notwithstanding paragraph (i), one director who is not independent as defined in Rule 4200, and is not a current employee or an immediate family member of such employee, may be appointed to the audit committee, if the board, under exceptional and limited circumstances, determines that membership on the committee by the individual is required by the best interests of the corporation and its shareholders, and the board discloses, in the next annual proxy statement subsequent to such determination, the nature of the relationship and the reasons for that determination.

(C) Exception for Small Business Filers -- Paragraphs (2)(A) and (2)(B) do not apply to issuers that file reports under SEC Regulation S-B. Such issuers must establish and maintain an Audit Committee of at least two members, a majority of the members of which shall be independent directors.

(e) - (n) No change

B. Independence

Nasdaq proposes to narrow its current definition of "independent director" by specifying five new relationships that could impair a director's independent judgment as a result of financial, familial, or other material ties to management or the corporation. The proposed definition will apply to all directors, not just those serving on audit committees. Under the proposed rule change, directors with any of the following five relationships will not be considered independent: (1) employment by the corporation or any of its affiliates for the current year or any of the past three years; (2) acceptance of any compensation from the corporation or any of its affiliates in excess of $60,000 during the previous fiscal year, other than compensation for board service, benefits under a tax-qualified retirement plan, or non-discretionary compensation; (3) member of the immediate family of an individual who is, or has been in any of the past three years, employed by the corporation or any of its affiliates as an executive officer; (4) partnership in, or a controlling shareholder or an executive officer of, any for-profit business organization to which the corporation made, or from which the corporation received, payments (other than those arising solely from investments in the corporation's securities) that exceed five percent of the corporation's or business organization's consolidated gross revenues for that year, or $200,000, whichever is more, in any of the past three years; or (5) employment as an executive of another entity where any of the company's executives serve on that entity's compensation committee.

C. Structure and Membership of the Audit Committee

Nasdaq also proposes to change the structure and membership qualifications of the audit committee. Specifically, Nasdaq proposes to change the required composition of the audit committee from at least two to at least three members. Furthermore, the audit committee must be comprised solely of independent directors rather than a majority of independent directors. Nasdaq is conscious of the fact that in exceptional circumstances, issuers may appropriately conclude that it would be in the best interests of the corporation for a non-independent director to serve on the audit committee. In such exceptional and limited circumstances, a non-independent director can serve on the audit committee, provided that the board determines that it is required by the best interests of the corporation and its shareholders, and the board discloses its reasons for the determination in the next annual proxy statement. Due to the nature of this exception, however, a corporation could have no more than one non-independent director serving on its audit committee. Also, current employees or officers, or their immediate family members, may not serve on the audit committee under this exception.

As a result of the audit committee's responsibility for a corporation's accounting and financial reporting, Nasdaq believes that audit committee members should have a basic understanding of financial statements. Therefore, the proposed rule change requires each member of the audit committee to be able to read and understand fundamental financial statements, including a company's balance sheet, income statement, and cash flow statement, or become able to do so within a reasonable period of time after his or her appointment to the audit committee. Furthermore, in order to further enhance the effectiveness of the audit committee, at least one member of the audit committee must have past employment experience in finance or accounting, requisite professional certification in accounting, or any other comparable experience or background which results in the individual's financial sophistication, including being or having been a chief executive officer, chief financial officer, or other senior officer with financial oversight responsibilities.

Nasdaq is sensitive to the potential burden that the proposed changes to the audit committee composition requirements may place on small companies. Therefore, Nasdaq proposes to exempt those corporations that file under SEC Regulation S-B ("Small Business Filers").[7] Small Business Filers will be held to Nasdaq's existing requirements with respect to audit committee composition. That is, they must maintain an audit committee of at least two members, a majority of whom are independent.

D. Charter

Nasdaq believes that a written charter will help the audit committee as well as management and the corporation's auditors recognize the function of the audit committee and the relationship among these parties. The proposed rule change requires each issuer to adopt a formal written charter. This charter must specify the scope of the audit committee's responsibilities, and how it carries out those responsibilities, including structure, processes, and membership requirements. In addition, the charter must specify the audit committee's responsibility for ensuring its receipt from the outside auditors of a formal written statement delineating all relationships between the auditor and the company, consistent with Independence Standards Board Standard 1.[8] The charter must also specify the audit committee's responsibility for actively engaging in a dialogue with the auditor with respect to any disclosed relationships or services that may impact the objectivity and independence of the auditor and for taking, or recommending that the full board take, appropriate action to oversee the independence of the outside auditor. Finally, it must specify the outside auditor's ultimate accountability to the board of directors and the audit committee, as representatives of shareholders, and these shareholder representatives' ultimate authority and responsibility to select, evaluate, and, where appropriate, replace the outside auditor (or to nominate an outside auditor for shareholder approval in any proxy statement). The proposed rule change requires issuers to review their charter on an annual basis.

E. Implementation

In order to minimize disruption to existing issuer audit committees, to permit current audit committee members to serve out their terms, and to allow adequate time to recruit the requisite members, Nasdaq proposes to provide its issuers listed as of the effective date of the proposed rule change eighteen months after the proposed rule change is approved by the Commission to meet the audit committee structure and membership requirements.

Additionally, Nasdaq proposes that issuers listed as of the effective date of the rule change be provided six months following the date of Commission approval of the proposed rule change to adopt a formal written audit committee charter in compliance with proposed Rules 4310(c)(26)(A), 4320(e)(22)(A), or 4460(d)(1).

Further, for issuers that applied for listing prior to the effective date of the proposed rule change, Nasdaq proposes that they be able to qualify for listing under the listing standards in force at the time of their application, and to receive the same grace periods provided to currently listed issuers, as described above. Also, in order to avoid prejudicing issuers that transfer to Nasdaq from the American Stock Exchange and the New York Stock Exchange, Nasdaq proposed that these issuers be afforded the same grace periods they would have received under their previous market's implementation schedule.

III. Comments

As of December 9, 1999, the Commission received 14 comment letters on the proposed rule change.[9] In general, the commenters favored the proposed rule change but recommended certain modifications. Two commenters opposed the proposed rule change.[10]

In particular, the CII supports the new requirements, but stated that the proposed override provision, which allows a company's board to include a non-independent director on the audit committee is not appropriate because companies should not have a problem finding financially literate, truly independent directors.[11] In addition, the AFL-CIO stated that the restriction period for former employees, or relatives of former employees, should be five years instead of three years.[12] The AFL-CIO also stated that the $60,000 threshold to disqualify a candidate because of a significant business relationship is not stringent enough.[13] Another commenter, on the other hand, stated that a quantitative test is too inflexible.[14] Keller and Rowe stated that former non-executive employment should be treated as a significant business relationship.[15] This commenter also stated that consultants who receive from the company more than a de minimis amount of compensation should be treated as employees, while consultants who do not should be treated as having a business relationship with the company.[16] According to this comment letter, the company's board should be permitted to determine that the compensation does not impair the director's objectivity.[17] Keller and Rowe also objected to the financial expertise requirement and stated that no director will want to be designated the financial expert because of the added exposure to liability.[18]

Deloitte and Price each stated that requiring a company's board or audit committee to "ensure" the independence of the outside auditor goes beyond what can reasonably be expected of the board and the audit committee in their oversight role.[19] Deloitte suggested that Nasdaq replace the word "ensure" with "monitor" or "actively oversee."[20] E&Y supported the proposed rule change, but stated that Nasdaq should not exempt Small Business Filers from the financial literacy and expertise requirements and also should expand its definition of immediate family member to include sons-in-law and daughters-in-law.[21] NYSBA stated that the company's board should be required to adopt the audit committee charter, rather than the audit committee adopting the charter subject to board approval.[22]

In addition, the NVCA stated that the proposed rule change should exclude venture capital investors from the independence qualifications.[23] The NVCA also stated that the proposed rule change should give companies that have just completed an initial public offering eighteen months to comply with the new requirements and that the exemption for Small Business Filers should be expanded to apply to companies with less than $50 million in revenue.[24]

APTC stated that the proposed rule change will be counter productive to the goal of better audit committees.[25] In addition, APTC stated that the proposed rule change will disadvantage smaller companies more than larger companies, but concluded that it is appropriate to apply the proposed rule change to all companies, regardless of size.[26] Moreover, APTC is opposed to the proposal's financial literacy requirement.[27] APTC believes that the financial literacy requirement may deprive audit committees of the service of individuals with "exceptional character and/or operational experience."[28] The commenter suggested that the Exchange replace this requirement with a requirement that the committee as a whole possess a certain level of financial acumen.[29]

Finally, two commenters stated that the proposed rule change should not apply to closed-end investment companies.[30] These commenters noted that closed-end investment companies are adequately regulated under the 1940 Act.[31] The commenters also stated that the potential abuses that the proposed rule change is designed to address do not exist with closed-end investment funds.[32] Finally, the commenters noted that because the assets of these funds consist exclusively of investment securities, there is no opportunity to "manage" earnings or results through selective application of accounting policies.[33]

IV. Discussion

The Commission finds that the proposed rule change is consistent with the requirements of the Act and the rules and regulations thereunder applicable to a national securities association,[34] and, in particular, the requirements of Section 15A(b)(6) of the Act.[35] The Commission believes that the proposed rule change will protect investors by improving the effectiveness of audit committees of companies listed on Nasdaq. The Commission also believes that the new requirements will enhance the reliability and credibility of financial statements of companies listed on Nasdaq by making it more difficult for companies to inappropriately distort their true financial performance.

Specifically, the Commission believes that the proposed definition of independence will promote the quality and reliability of a company's financial statements. The Commission believes that directors without financial, familial, or other material personal ties to management will be more likely to objectively evaluate the propriety of management's accounting, internal control, and financial reporting practices. The Commission believes that the proposal's prohibition against employees serving on the audit committee is appropriate and that the Exchange should not be required to distinguish between executive and non-executive employees.[36] The Commission also believes that the proposed provision that permits a company to appoint one director to its audit committee who is not independent, if the board determines that membership on the committee by the individual is required by the best interests of the corporation and its shareholders, adequately balances the need for objective, independent directors with the company's need for flexibility in exceptional and unusual circumstances. The Commission believes that the requirement that the company disclose in its next annual proxy statement the nature of the director's relationship with the company and the board's reasons for determining the appointment was in the best interests of the corporation will adequately guard against abuse of the proposed exception to the independence requirement. Moreover, the Commission believes that the $60,000 threshold to determine if a potential audit committee director has a significant business relationship with the company is a reasonable measure to balance the company's need to recruit audit committee members with the independence requirement.

The Commission does not believe that venture capital investors should be excluded from Nasdaq's definition of independence. The Commission does not believe that the proposed rule change will pose an undue hardship on venture capital firms or companies listed on Nasdaq. The Commission notes that the proposed rule change will only prohibit venture capital investors from sitting on a company's audit committee if the investor does not fall within Nasdaq's definition of independent. The proposed rule change will not prohibit previously eligible investors from serving on the company's board. The Commission also notes that a venture capital investor that is not considered independent may serve on the company's audit committee, if the board determines it is in the best interests of the corporation and its shareholders and the company discloses its reasons for the determination and the nature of the director's relationship to the company in its next annual proxy statement.

In addition, the Commission believes that requiring companies to adopt formal written charters specifying the audit committee's responsibilities, and how the committee carries out those responsibilities, will help the audit committee, management, investors, and the company's auditors recognize the function of the audit committee and the relationship among the parties. Moreover, the Commission believes that requiring the charter to specify that the audit committee is responsible for taking, or recommending that the company's full board take, appropriate action to oversee the independence of the outside auditor will make it more likely that companies will select objective, unbiased auditors.

The Commission believes that the proposed rule change's compositional requirement that each issuer have an audit committee composed of three independent directors who are able to read and understand fundamental financial statements will enhance the effectiveness of the audit committee and help to ensure that audit committee members are able to adequately fulfill their responsibilities. The Commission believes that requiring each audit committee member to satisfy this standard will help to ensure that the committee as a whole is financially literate.[37] Moreover, the Commission considers that requiring one member of the audit committee to have past employment experience in finance or accounting, requisite professional certification in accounting, or any other comparable experience or background that indicates the individual's financial sophistication, will further enhance the effectiveness of the audit committee in carrying out its financial oversight responsibilities. In addition, the Commission does not believe that companies will experience undue difficulty recruiting an audit committee member that satisfies the financial expertise requirements. Moreover, the Commission believes that the proposed rule change appropriately exempts Small Business Filers from the proposed composition requirements because these companies may experience more difficulty meeting these enhanced requirements. The Commission notes that these companies will remain subject to Nasdaq's existing rules on audit committees, which require an audit committee to have at least two members, a majority of whom are independent.

Moreover, the Commission does not believe that the proposed rule change circumvents state law.[38] The Commission notes that Nasdaq is amending its own qualification requirements governing an issuer's listing on Nasdaq, which is an appropriate function for Nasdaq as long as those requirements are consistent with the Act.

Moreover, the Commission has concluded that Nasdaq's decision to include investment companies in the proposed rule change is warranted. While the Commission recognizes that the opportunity for some types of financial reporting abuses may be limited by the nature of fund assets,[39] it believes that audit committees do play an important role in overseeing the financial reporting process for investment companies

The Commission finds good cause for approving Amendments No. 1 and No. 2 to the proposed rule change prior to the thirtieth day after publication in the Federal Register. The Commission notes that Amendment No. 1 merely revises the implementation time periods for the proposed rule change to provide greater clarity to issuers and to investors. The Commission believes that Amendment No. 1 will enable issuers to determine when they must comply with the new requirements and will enable investors to determine when to rely on the protections afforded by the proposed rule change. The Commission notes that Amendment No. 2 simply clarifies that the audit committee is required to oversee, rather than ensure, the independence of the company's outside auditors, and expands Nasdaq's definition of "immediate family." The Commission believes that accelerated approval will allow Nasdaq to simultaneously make all relevant modifications to its Rules and will avoid potential confusion. Accordingly, the Commission finds good cause to accelerate approval of Amendments No. 1 and No. 2 to the proposed rule change, consistent with Sections 6(b)(5)[40] and 19(b)[41] of the Act.

V. Solicitation of Comments

Interested persons are invited to submit written data, views, and arguments concerning the foregoing, including whether the proposed rule change is consistent with the Act. Persons making written submissions should file six copies thereof with the Secretary, Securities and Exchange Commission, 450 Fifth Street, N.W., Washington, D.C. 20549-0609. Copies of the submission, all subsequent amendments, all written statements with respect to the proposed rule change that are filed with the Commission, and all written communications relating to the proposed rule change between the Commission and any person, other than those that may be withheld from the public in accordance with the provisions of 5 U.S.C. 552, will be available for inspection and copying in the Commission's Public Reference Room. Copies of such filing will also be available for inspection and copying at the principal office of the NASD. All submissions should refer to the File No. SR-NASD-99-48 and should be submitted by [insert date 21 days from the date of publication].

VI. Conclusion

For the foregoing reasons, the Commission finds that Nasdaq's proposal to amend its audit committee requirements is consistent with the requirements of the Act and the rules and regulations thereunder.

It is therefore ordered, pursuant to Section 19(b)(2) of the Act,[42] that the amended proposed rule change (SR-NASD-99-48) is approved.

For the Commission, by the Division of Market Regulation, pursuant to delegated authority.[43]

Jonathan G. Katz
Secretary

Footnotes

1.   15 U.S.C. 78s(b)(1).

2.   17 CFR 240.19b-4.

3.   Securities Exchange Act Release No. 41982 (Oct. 6, 1999), 64 FR 55510. The American Stock Exchange LLC and The New York Stock Exchange, Inc. have proposed

rule changes relating to audit committees. See Securities Exchange Act Release No. 41981 (Oct. 6, 1999), 64 FR 55505 (Oct. 13, 1999) ("Amex Proposal"), and Securities Exchange Act Release No. 41980 (Oct. 6, 1999), 64 FR 55514 (Oct. 13, 1999) ("NYSE Proposal").

4.   Letter from Robert E. Aber, Senior Vice President and General Counsel, Nasdaq-Amex Market Group, to Richard Strasser, Assistant Director, Division of Market Regulation, Commission, dated November 12, 1999 ("Amendment No. 1"). The Association submitted Amendment No. 1 to require issuers listed as of the effective date of Commission approval of the proposed rule change to adopt a formal written audit committee charter within six months of the effective date of the proposed rule change. As originally filed, the proposed rule change required issuers to adopt the charter within eighteen months of the effective date of the proposed rule change. Amendment No. 1 also states that issuers that applied for listing prior to the effective date of the proposed rule change would qualify for listing under the listing standards in force at the time of their application, and receive the same grace periods provided to currently listed issuers. Finally, Amendment No. 1 modifies proposed Rule 4320(e)(21) to provide that the requirement that each issuer execute a listing agreement will not be construed to require any foreign issuer to do any act that is contrary to a law of any public authority exercising jurisdiction over the foreign issuer.

5.   Letter from Sara Nelson Bloom, Associate General Counsel, Nasdaq-Amex Market Group, to Richard Strasser, Assistant Director, Division, Commission, dated December 8, 1999 ("Amendment No. 2"). The Association submitted Amendment No. 2 to revise proposed Rules 4310(c)(26)(A)(ii), 4320(e)(22)(A)(ii), and 4460(d)(1)(B) to provide that the audit committee is required to oversee the independence of the outside auditor, rather than ensure the independence of the outside auditor. Amendment No. 2 also revises Nasdaq's definition of immediate family found in Rule 4200(a)(15)(c) to include sons-in-law and daughters-in-law.

6.   *Report and Recommendations of the Blue Ribbon Committee on Improving the Effectiveness of Corporate Audit Committees* (1999). A copy of this Report [Webmaster note: in PDF format] can be found on-line at www.nasdaqnews.com.

7.   Small Business Filer is defined by Regulation S-B as an issuer that: (i) has revenue of less than $25,000,000; (ii) is a U.S. or Canadian issuer; and (iii) if a majority owned subsidiary, the parent corporation is a small business issuer. 17 CFR 228.10(a)(1).

8.   Independence Standard No. 1, Independence Discussions with Audit Committees (January 1999), which can be found on-line at www.cpaindependence.org.

9.   See letters from: Ernst & Young LLP ("E&Y") dated November 1, 1999; Deloitte & Touche LLP ("Deloitte") dated November 3, 1999; Council of Institutional Investors ("CII") dated November 8, 1999; Brian T. Borders on behalf of the National Venture Capital Association ("NVCA") dated November 12, 1999; PricewaterhouseCoopers LLP ("Price") dated November 1, 1999; Gary P. Kreider ("Kreider") dated November 5, 1999; American Federation of Labor and Congress of Industrial Organizations ("AFL-CIO") dated November 29, 1999; Mayer, Brown & Platt on behalf of Morgan Stanley Dean Witter ("MSDW") dated November 29, 1999; Investment Company Institute ("ICI") dated November 3, 1999; Arthur Andersen LLP ("Arthur Andersen") dated December 3, 1999; Association of Publicly Traded Companies ("APTC") dated December 6, 1999; Robert A. Profusek ("Profusek") dated December 3, 1999; Stanley Keller and Richard Rowe ("Keller and Rowe") dated December 7, 1999; and The Committee on Securities Regulation of the Business Law Section of the New York State Bar Association ("NYSBA") dated December 1, 1999.

10.   See Kreider Letter; APTC Letter at 2. Kreider stated that the proposed rule change "represent[s] an awkward attempt to circumvent state corporate law and micro-manage the functions of audit committees." Id. at 2.

11.   CII Letter, at 2; see also AFL-CIO Letter at 2.

12.   AFL-CIO Letter at 2.

13.   Id.

14. Profusek Letter at 2. In addition, Keller and Rowe stated that this provision might preclude a number of highly qualified candidates from serving on audit committees. Keller and Rowe Letter at 3.

15. Keller and Rowe Letter at 2.

16. Id. at 3.

17. Id.

18. Id.

19. Deloitte Letter at 1; Price Letter at 1.

20. Id. at 2.

21. E&Y Letter at 4.

22. NYSBA Letter at 2.

23. NVCA Letter at 5.

24. Id. at 4.

25. APTC Letter at 2.

26. Id. at 3.

27. Id. at 4-5.

28. Id.

29. Id. at 5.

30. ICI Letter at 2; MSDW Letter at 1. In addition, Keller and Rowe stated that the proposed rule change should exempt all investment companies because their audit committee members are already required not to be "interested persons" as that term is defined in Section 2(a)(9) of the Investment Company Act of 1940 ("1940 Act"). Keller and Rowe Letter at 5.

31. ICI Letter at 3-4; MSDW Letter at 2.

32. ICI Letter at 3; MSDW Letter at 1. ICI and MSDW also noted that the independent accountants of investment funds are selected by the independent directors of the fund.

33. ICI Letter at 3; MSDW Letter at 1.

34. In approving the proposal, the Commission has considered its impact on efficiency, competition, and capital formation. 15 U.S.C. 78c(f).

35. 15 U.S.C. 78o-3(b)(6).

36. See Keller and Rowe Letter at 2.

37. See APTC Letter at 5.

38. Kreider Letter at 2.

39. See Keller and Rowe Letter at 5; ICI Letter at 3; MSDW Letter at 1.

40. 15 U.S.C. 78f(b)(5).

41. 15 U.S.C. 78s(b).

42. 15. U.S.C. 78s(b)(2).

43. 17 CFR 200.30-3(a)(12).

SEC Staff Accounting Bulletin:
No. 99 – Materiality

Securities and Exchange Commission
17 CFR Part 211
[Release No. SAB 99]
Staff Accounting Bulletin No. 99

AGENCY: Securities and Exchange Commission

ACTION: Publication of Staff Accounting Bulletin

SUMMARY: This staff accounting bulletin expresses the views of the staff that exclusive reliance on certain quantitative benchmarks to assess materiality in preparing financial statements and performing audits of those financial statements is inappropriate; misstatements are not immaterial simply because they fall beneath a numerical threshold.

DATE: August 12, 1999

FOR FURTHER INFORMATION CONTACT: W. Scott Bayless, Associate Chief Accountant, or Robert E. Burns, Chief Counsel, Office of the Chief Accountant (202-942-4400), or David R. Fredrickson, Office of General Counsel (202-942-0900), Securities and Exchange Commission, 450 Fifth Street, N.W., Washington, D.C. 20549-1103; electronic addresses: BaylessWS@sec.gov; BurnsR@sec.gov; FredricksonD@sec.gov.

SUPPLEMENTARY INFORMATION: The statements in the staff accounting bulletins are not rules or interpretations of the Commission, nor are they published as bearing the Commission's official approval. They represent interpretations and practices followed by the Division of Corporation Finance and the Office of the Chief Accountant in administering the disclosure requirements of the Federal securities laws.

Jonathan G. Katz
Secretary
Date: August 12, 1999

Part 211 - (AMEND) Accordingly, Part 211 of Title 17 of the Code of Federal Regulations is amended by adding Staff Accounting Bulletin No. 99 to the table found in Subpart B.

STAFF ACCOUNTING BULLETIN NO. 99

The staff hereby adds Section M to Topic 1 of the Staff Accounting Bulletin Series. Section M, entitled "Materiality," provides guidance in applying materiality thresholds to the preparation of financial statements filed with the Commission and the performance of audits of those financial statements.

STAFF ACCOUNTING BULLETINS
TOPIC 1: FINANCIAL STATEMENTS

M. Materiality

1. Assessing Materiality

Facts: During the course of preparing or auditing year-end financial statements, financial management or the registrant's independent auditor becomes aware of misstatements in a registrant's financial statements. When combined, the misstatements result in a 4% overstatement of net income and a $.02 (4%) overstatement of earnings per share. Because no item in the registrant's consolidated financial statements is misstated by more than 5%, management and the independent auditor conclude that the deviation from generally accepted accounting principles ("GAAP") is immaterial and that the accounting is permissible.[1]

Question: Each Statement of Financial Accounting Standards adopted by the Financial Accounting Standards Board ("FASB") states, "The provisions of this Statement need not be applied to immaterial items." In the staff's view, may a registrant or the auditor of its financial statements assume the immateriality of items that fall below a percentage threshold set by management or the auditor to determine whether amounts and items are material to the financial statements?

Interpretive Response: No. The staff is aware that certain registrants, over time, have developed quantitative thresholds as "rules of thumb" to assist in the preparation of their financial statements, and that auditors also have used these thresholds in their evaluation of whether items might be considered material to users of a registrant's financial statements. One rule of thumb in particular suggests that the misstatement or omission[2] of an item that falls under a 5% threshold is not material in the absence of particularly egregious circumstances, such as self-dealing or misappropriation by senior management. The staff reminds registrants and the auditors of their financial statements that exclusive reliance on this or any percentage or numerical threshold has no basis in the accounting literature or the law.

The use of a percentage as a numerical threshold, such as 5%, may provide the basis for a preliminary assumption that – without considering all relevant circumstances – a deviation of less than the specified percentage with respect to a particular item on the registrant's financial statements is unlikely to be material. The staff has no objection to such a "rule of thumb" as an initial step in assessing materiality. But quantifying, in percentage terms, the magnitude of a misstatement is only the beginning of an analysis of materiality; it cannot appropriately be used as a substitute for a full analysis of all relevant considerations. Materiality concerns the significance of an item to users of a registrant's financial statements. A matter is "material" if there is a substantial likelihood that a reasonable person would consider it important. In its Statement of Financial Accounting Concepts No. 2, the FASB stated the essence of the concept of materiality as follows:

> The omission or misstatement of an item in a financial report is material if, in the light of surrounding circumstances, the magnitude of the item is such that it is probable that the judgment of a reasonable person relying upon the report would have been changed or influenced by the inclusion or correction of the item.[3]

This formulation in the accounting literature is in substance identical to the formulation used by the courts in interpreting the federal securities laws. The Supreme Court has held that a fact is material if there is –

> a substantial likelihood that the . . . fact would have been viewed by the reasonable investor as having significantly altered the "total mix" of information made available. [4]

Under the governing principles, an assessment of materiality requires that one views the facts in the context of the "surrounding circumstances," as the accounting literature puts it, or the "total mix" of information, in the words of the Supreme Court. In the context of a misstatement of a financial statement item, while the "total mix" includes the size in numerical or percentage terms of the misstatement, it also includes the factual context in which the user of financial statements would view the financial statement item. The shorthand in the accounting and auditing literature for this analysis is that financial management and the auditor must consider both "quantitative" and "qualitative" factors in assessing an item's materiality.[5] Court decisions, Commission rules and enforcement actions, and accounting and auditing literature[6] have all considered "qualitative" factors in various contexts.

The FASB has long emphasized that materiality cannot be reduced to a numerical formula. In its Concepts Statement No. 2, the FASB noted that some had urged it to promulgate quantitative materiality guides for use in a variety of situations. The FASB rejected such an approach as representing only a "minority view," stating –

> The predominant view is that materiality judgments can properly be made only by those who have all the facts. The Board's present position is that no general standards of materiality could be formulated to take into account all the considerations that enter into an experienced human judgment. [7]

The FASB noted that, in certain limited circumstances, the Commission and other authoritative bodies had issued quantitative materiality guidance, citing as examples guidelines ranging from one to ten percent with respect to a variety of disclosures.[8] And it took account of contradictory studies, one showing a lack of uniformity among auditors on materiality judgments, and another suggesting widespread use of a "rule of thumb" of five to ten percent of net income.[9] The FASB also considered whether an evaluation of materiality could be based solely on anticipating the market's reaction to accounting information.[10]

The FASB rejected a formulaic approach to discharging "the onerous duty of making materiality decisions"[11] in favor of an approach that takes into account all the relevant considerations. In so doing, it made clear that –

> [M]agnitude by itself, without regard to the nature of the item and the circumstances in which the judgment has to be made, will not generally be a sufficient basis for a materiality judgment.[12]

Evaluation of materiality requires a registrant and its auditor to consider allthe relevant circumstances, and the staff believes that there are numerous circumstances in which misstatements below 5% could well be material. Qualitative factors may cause misstatements of quantitatively small amounts to be material; as stated in the auditing literature:

> As a result of the interaction of quantitative and qualitative considerations in materiality judgments, misstatements of relatively small amounts that come to the auditor's attention could have a material effect on the financial statements.[13]

Among the considerations that may well render material a quantitatively small misstatement of a financial statement item are –

- whether the misstatement arises from an item capable of precise measurement or whether it arises from an estimate and, if so, the degree of imprecision inherent in the estimate[14]
- whether the misstatement masks a change in earnings or other trends
- whether the misstatement hides a failure to meet analysts' consensus expectations for the enterprise
- whether the misstatement changes a loss into income or vice versa
- whether the misstatement concerns a segment or other portion of the registrant's business that has been identified as playing a significant role in the registrant's operations or profitability
- whether the misstatement affects the registrant's compliance with regulatory requirements
- whether the misstatement affects the registrant's compliance with loan covenants or other contractual requirements
- whether the misstatement has the effect of increasing management's compensation – for example, by satisfying requirements for the award of bonuses or other forms of incentive compensation
- whether the misstatement involves concealment of an unlawful transaction.

This is not an exhaustive list of the circumstances that may affect the materiality of a quantitatively small misstatement.[15] Among other factors, the demonstrated volatility of the price of a registrant's securities in response to certain types of disclosures may provide guidance as to whether investors regard quantitatively small misstatements as material. Consideration of potential market reaction to disclosure of a misstatement is by itself "too blunt an instrument to be depended on" in considering whether a fact is material.[16] When, however, management or the independent auditor expects (based, for example, on a pattern of market performance) that a known misstatement may result in a significant positive or negative market reaction, that expected reaction should be taken into account when considering whether a misstatement is material.[17]

For the reasons noted above, the staff believes that a registrant and the auditors of its financial statements should not assume that even small intentional misstatements in financial statements, for example those pursuant to actions to "manage" earnings, are immaterial.[18] While the intent of management does not render a misstatement material, it may provide significant evidence of materiality. The evidence may be particularly compelling where management has intentionally misstated items in the financial statements to "manage" reported earnings. In that instance, it presumably has done so believing that the resulting amounts and trends would be significant to users of the registrant's financial statements.[19] The staff believes that investors generally would regard as significant a management practice to over- or under-state earnings up to an amount just short of a percentage threshold in order to "manage" earnings. Investors presumably also would regard as significant an accounting practice that, in essence, rendered all earnings figures subject to a management-directed margin of misstatement.

The materiality of a misstatement may turn on where it appears in the financial statements. For example, a misstatement may involve a segment of the registrant's operations. In that instance, in assessing materiality of a misstatement to the financial statements taken as a whole, registrants and their auditors should consider not only the size of the misstatement but also the significance of the segment information to the financial statements taken as a whole.[20] "A misstatement of the revenue and operating profit of a relatively small segment that is represented by management to be important to the future profitability of the entity"[21] is more likely to be material to investors than a misstatement in a segment that management has not identified as especially important. In assessing the materiality of misstatements in segment information - as with materiality generally -

> situations may arise in practice where the auditor will conclude that a matter relating to segment information is qualitatively material even though, in his or her judgment, it is quantitatively immaterial to the financial statements taken as a whole.[22]

Aggregating and Netting Misstatements

In determining whether multiple misstatements cause the financial statements to be materially misstated, registrants and the auditors of their financial statements should consider each misstatement separately and the aggregate effect of all misstatements.[23] A registrant and its auditor should evaluate misstatements in light of quantitative and qualitative factors and "consider whether, in relation to individual line item amounts, subtotals, or totals in the financial statements, they materially misstate the financial statements taken as a whole."[24] This requires consideration of -

> the significance of an item to a particular entity (for example, inventories to a manufacturing company), the pervasiveness of the misstatement (such as whether it affects the presentation of numerous financial statement items), and the effect of the misstatement on the financial statements taken as a whole ....[25]

Registrants and their auditors first should consider whether each misstatement is material, irrespective of its effect when combined with other misstatements. The literature notes that the analysis should consider whether the misstatement of "individual amounts" causes a material misstatement of the financial statements taken as a whole. As with materiality generally, this analysis requires consideration of both quantitative and qualitative factors.

If the misstatement of an individual amount causes the financial statements as a whole to be materially misstated, that effect cannot be eliminated by other misstatements whose effect may be to diminish the impact of the misstatement on other financial statement items. To take an obvious example, if a registrant's revenues are a material financial statement item and if they are materially overstated, the financial statements taken as a whole will be materially misleading even if the effect on earnings is completely offset by an equivalent overstatement of expenses.

Even though a misstatement of an individual amount may not cause the financial statements taken as a whole to be materially misstated, it may nonetheless, when aggregated with other misstatements, render the financial statements taken as a whole to be materially misleading. Registrants and the auditors of their financial statements accordingly should consider the effect of the misstatement on subtotals or totals. The auditor should aggregate all misstatements that affect each subtotal or total and consider whether the misstatements in the aggregate affect the subtotal or total in a way that causes the registrant's financial statements taken as a whole to be materially misleading.[26]

The staff believes that, in considering the aggregate effect of multiple misstatements on a subtotal or total, registrants and the auditors of their financial statements should exercise particular care when considering whether to offset (or the appropriateness of offsetting) a misstatement of an estimated amount with a misstatement of an item capable of precise measurement. As noted above, assessments of materiality should never be purely mechanical; given the imprecision inherent in estimates, there is by definition a corresponding imprecision in the aggregation of misstatements involving estimates with those that do not involve an estimate.

Registrants and auditors also should consider the effect of misstatements from prior periods on the current financial statements. For example, the auditing literature states,

> Matters underlying adjustments proposed by the auditor but not recorded by the entity could potentially cause future financial statements to be materially misstated, even though the auditor has concluded that the adjustments are not material to the current financial statements.[27]

This may be particularly the case where immaterial misstatements recur in several years and the cumulative effect becomes material in the current year.

2. Immaterial Misstatements That are Intentional

Facts: A registrant's management intentionally has made adjustments to various financial statement items in a manner inconsistent with GAAP. In each accounting period in which such actions were taken, none of the individual adjustments is by itself material, nor is the aggregate effect on the financial statements taken as a whole material for the period. The registrant's earnings "management" has been effected at the direction or acquiescence of management in the belief that any deviations from GAAP have been immaterial and that accordingly the accounting is permissible.

Question: In the staff's view, may a registrant make intentional immaterial misstatements in its financial statements?

Interpretive Response: No. In certain circumstances, intentional immaterial misstatements are unlawful.

Considerations of the Books and Records Provisions Under the Exchange Act

Even if misstatements are immaterial,[28] registrants must comply with Sections 13(b)(2) - (7) of the Securities Exchange Act of 1934 (the "Exchange Act").[29] Under these provisions, each registrant with securities registered pursuant to Section 12 of the Exchange Act,[30] or required to file reports pursuant to Section 15(d),[31] must make and keep books, records, and accounts, which, in reasonable detail, accurately and fairly reflect the transactions and dispositions of assets of the registrant and must maintain internal accounting controls that are sufficient to provide reasonable assurances that, among other things, transactions are recorded as necessary to permit the preparation of financial statements in conformity with GAAP.[32] In this context, determinations of what constitutes "reasonable assurance" and "reasonable detail" are based not on a "materiality" analysis but on the level of detail and degree of assurance that would satisfy prudent officials in the conduct of their own affairs.[33] Accordingly, failure to record accurately immaterial items, in some instances, may result in violations of the securities laws.

The staff recognizes that there is limited authoritative guidance[34] regarding the "reasonableness" standard in Section 13(b)(2) of the Exchange Act. A principal statement of the Commission's policy in this area is set forth in an address given in 1981 by then Chairman

Harold M. Williams.[35] In his address, Chairman Williams noted that, like materiality, "reasonableness" is not an "absolute standard of exactitude for corporate records."[36] Unlike materiality, however, "reasonableness" is not solely a measure of the significance of a financial statement item to investors. "Reasonableness," in this context, reflects a judgment as to whether an issuer's failure to correct a known misstatement implicates the purposes underlying the accounting provisions of Sections 13(b)(2) - (7) of the Exchange Act.[37]

In assessing whether a misstatement results in a violation of a registrant's obligation to keep books and records that are accurate "in reasonable detail," registrants and their auditors should consider, in addition to the factors discussed above concerning an evaluation of a misstatement's potential materiality, the factors set forth below.

- **The significance of the misstatement.** Though the staff does not believe that registrants need to make finely calibrated determinations of significance with respect to immaterial items, plainly it is "reasonable" to treat misstatements whose effects are clearly inconsequential differently than more significant ones.

- **How the misstatement arose.** It is unlikely that it is ever "reasonable" for registrants to record misstatements or not to correct known misstatements – even immaterial ones – as part of an ongoing effort directed by or known to senior management for the purposes of "managing" earnings. On the other hand, insignificant misstatements that arise from the operation of systems or recurring processes in the normal course of business generally will not cause a registrant's books to be inaccurate "in reasonable detail."[38]

- **The cost of correcting the misstatement.** The books and records provisions of the Exchange Act do not require registrants to make major expenditures to correct small misstatements.[39] Conversely, where there is little cost or delay involved in correcting a misstatement, failing to do so is unlikely to be "reasonable."

- **The clarity of authoritative accounting guidance with respect to the misstatement.** Where reasonable minds may differ about the appropriate accounting treatment of a financial statement item, a failure to correct it may not render the registrant's financial statements inaccurate "in reasonable detail." Where, however, there is little ground for reasonable disagreement, the case for leaving a misstatement uncorrected is correspondingly weaker.

There may be other indicators of "reasonableness" that registrants and their auditors may ordinarily consider. Because the judgment is not mechanical, the staff will be inclined to continue to defer to judgments that "allow a business, acting in good faith, to comply with the Act's accounting provisions in an innovative and cost-effective way."[40]

The Auditor's Response to Intentional Misstatements

Section 10A(b) of the Exchange Act requires auditors to take certain actions upon discovery of an "illegal act."[41] The statute specifies that these obligations are triggered "whether or not [the illegal acts are] perceived to have a material effect on the financial statements of the issuer . . . ." Among other things, Section 10A(b)(1) requires the auditor to inform the appropriate level of management of an illegal act (unless clearly inconsequential) and assure that the registrant's audit committee is "adequately informed" with respect to the illegal act.

As noted, an intentional misstatement of immaterial items in a registrant's financial statements may violate Section 13(b)(2) of the Exchange Act and thus be an illegal act. When such a violation occurs, an auditor must take steps to see that the registrant's audit committee is "adequately informed" about the illegal act. Because Section 10A(b)(1) is triggered regardless of whether an illegal act has a material effect on the registrant's financial statements, where the illegal act consists of a misstatement in the registrant's financial statements, the auditor will be required to report that illegal act to the audit committee irrespective of any "netting" of the misstatements with other financial statement items.

The requirements of Section 10A echo the auditing literature. See, for example, Statement on Auditing Standards No. ("SAS") 54, "Illegal Acts by Clients," and SAS 82, "Consideration of Fraud in a Financial Statement Audit." Pursuant to paragraph 38 of SAS 82, if the auditor determines there is evidence that fraud may exist, the auditor must discuss the matter with the appropriate level of management. The auditor must report directly to the audit committee fraud involving senior management and fraud that causes a material misstatement of the financial statements. Paragraph 4 of SAS 82 states that "misstatements arising from fraudulent financial reporting are intentional misstatements or omissions of amounts or disclosures in financial statements to deceive financial statement users."[42] SAS 82 further states that fraudulent financial reporting may involve falsification or alteration of accounting records; misrepresenting or omitting events, transactions or other information in the financial statements; and the intentional misapplication of accounting principles relating to amounts, classifications, the manner of presentation, or disclosures in the financial statements.[43] The clear implication of SAS 82 is that immaterial misstatements may be fraudulent financial reporting. [44]

Auditors that learn of intentional misstatements may also be required to (1) re-evaluate the degree of audit risk involved in the audit engagement, (2) determine whether to revise the nature, timing, and extent of audit procedures accordingly, and (3) consider whether to resign.[45]

Intentional misstatements also may signal the existence of reportable conditions or material weaknesses in the registrant's system of internal accounting control designed to detect and deter improper accounting and financial reporting.[46] As stated by the National Commission on Fraudulent Financial Reporting, also known as the Treadway Commission, in its 1987 report,

> The tone set by top management - the corporate environment or culture within which financial reporting occurs - is the most important factor contributing to the integrity of the financial reporting process. Notwithstanding an impressive set of written rules and procedures, if the tone set by management is lax, fraudulent financial reporting is more likely to occur.[47]

An auditor is required to report to a registrant's audit committee any reportable conditions or material weaknesses in a registrant's system of internal accounting control that the auditor discovers in the course of the examination of the registrant's financial statements. [48]

GAAP Precedence Over Industry Practice

Some have argued to the staff that registrants should be permitted to follow an industry accounting practice even though that practice is inconsistent with authoritative accounting literature. This situation might occur if a practice is developed when there are few transactions and the accounting results are clearly inconsequential, and that practice never changes despite a subsequent growth in the number or materiality of such transactions. The staff disagrees with this argument. Authoritative literature takes precedence over industry practice that is contrary to GAAP.[49]

General Comments

This SAB is not intended to change current law or guidance in the accounting or auditing literature.[50] This SAB and the authoritative accounting literature cannot specifically address all of the novel and complex business transactions and events that may occur. Accordingly, registrants may account for, and make disclosures about, these transactions and events based on analogies to similar situations or other factors. The staff may not, however, always be persuaded that a registrant's determination is the most appropriate under the circumstances. When disagreements occur after a transaction or an event has been reported, the consequences may be severe for registrants, auditors, and, most importantly, the users of financial statements who have a right to expect consistent accounting and reporting for, and disclosure of, similar transactions and events. The staff, therefore, encourages registrants and auditors to discuss on a timely basis with the staff proposed accounting treatments for, or disclosures about, transactions or events that are not specifically covered by the existing accounting literature.

Footnotes

1. American Institute of Certified Public Accountants ("AICPA"), Codification of Statements on Auditing Standards ("AU") § 312, "Audit Risk and Materiality in Conducting an Audit," states that the auditor should consider audit risk and materiality both in (a) planning and setting the scope for the audit and (b) evaluating whether the financial statements taken as a whole are fairly presented in all material respects in conformity with generally accepted accounting principles. The purpose of this Staff

Accounting Bulletin ("SAB") is to provide guidance to financial management and independent auditors with respect to the evaluation of the materiality of misstatements that are identified in the audit process or preparation of the financial statements (i.e., (b) above). This SAB is not intended to provide definitive guidance for assessing "materiality" in other contexts, such as evaluations of auditor independence, as other factors may apply. There may be other rules that address financial presentation. See, e.g., Rule 2a-4, 17 CFR 270.2a-4, under the Investment Company Act of 1940.

2. As used in this SAB, "misstatement" or "omission" refers to a financial statement assertion that would not be in conformity with GAAP.

3. FASB, Statement of Financial Accounting Concepts No. 2, Qualitative Characteristics of Accounting Information ("Concepts Statement No. 2"), 132 (1980). See also Concepts Statement No. 2, Glossary of Terms - Materiality.

4. TSC Industries v. Northway, Inc., 426 U.S. 438, 449 (1976). See also Basic, Inc. v. Levinson, 485 U.S. 224 (1988). As the Supreme Court has noted, determinations of materiality require "delicate assessments of the inferences a 'reasonable shareholder' would draw from a given set of facts and the significance of those inferences to him . . . ." TSC Industries, 426 U.S. at 450.

5. See, e.g., Concepts Statement No. 2, 123-124; AU § 312.[10] (" . . . materiality judgments are made in light of surrounding circumstances and necessarily involve both quantitative and qualitative considerations."); AU § 312.34 ("Qualitative considerations also influence the auditor in reaching a conclusion as to whether misstatements are material."). As used in the accounting literature and in this SAB, "qualitative" materiality refers to the surrounding circumstances that inform an investor's evaluation of financial statement entries. Whether events may be material to investors for non-financial reasons is a matter not addressed by this SAB.

6. See, e.g., Rule 1-02(o) of Regulation S-X, 17 CFR 210.1-02(o), Rule 405 of Regulation C, 17 CFR 230.405, and Rule 12b-2, 17 CFR 240.12b-2; AU §§ 312.10 - .11, 317.13, 411.04 n. 1, and 508.36; In re Kidder Peabody Securities Litigation, 10 F. Supp. 2d 398 (S.D.N.Y. 1998); Parnes v. Gateway 2000, Inc., 122 F.3d 539 (8th Cir. 1997); In re Westinghouse Securities Litigation, 90 F.3d 696 (3d Cir. 1996); In the Matter of W.R. Grace & Co., Accounting and Auditing Enforcement Release No. ("AAER") 1140 (June 30, 1999); In the Matter of Eugene Gaughan, AAER 1141 (June 30, 1999); In the Matter of Thomas Scanlon, AAER 1142 (June 30, 1999); and In re Sensormatic Electronics Corporation, Sec. Act Rel. No. 7518 (March 25, 1998).

7. Concepts Statement No. 2, 131 (1980).

8. Concepts Statement No. 2, 131 and 166.

9. Concepts Statement No. 2, 167.

10. Concepts Statement No. 2, 168-69.

11. Concepts Statement No. 2, 170.

12. Concepts Statement No. 2, 125.

13. AU § 312.11.

14. As stated in Concepts Statement No. 2, 130:

Another factor in materiality judgments is the degree of precision that is attainable in estimating the judgment item. The amount of deviation that is considered immaterial may increase as the attainable degree of precision decreases. For example, accounts payable usually can be estimated more accurately than can contingent liabilities arising from litigation or threats of it, and a deviation considered to be material in the first case may be quite trivial in the second.

This SAB is not intended to change current law or guidance in the accounting literature regarding accounting estimates. See, e.g., Accounting Principles Board Opinion No. 20, Accounting Changes 10, 11, 31-33 (July 1971).

15. The staff understands that the Big Five Audit Materiality Task Force ("Task Force") was convened in March of 1998 and has made recommendations to the Auditing Standards Board including suggestions regarding communications with audit com-

mittees about unadjusted misstatements. See generally Big Five Audit Materiality Task Force, "Materiality in a Financial Statement Audit – Considering Qualitative Factors When Evaluating Audit Findings" (August 1998). The Task Force memorandum is available at www.aicpa.org.

16. See Concepts Statement No. 2, 169.

17. If management does not expect a significant market reaction, a misstatement still may be material and should be evaluated under the criteria discussed in this SAB.

18. Intentional management of earnings and intentional misstatements, as used in this SAB, do not include insignificant errors and omissions that may occur in systems and recurring processes in the normal course of business. See notes 38 and 50 infra.

19. Assessments of materiality should occur not only at year-end, but also during the preparation of each quarterly or interim financial statement. See, e.g., In the Matter of Venator Group, Inc., AAER 1049 (June 29, 1998).

20. See, e.g., In the Matter of W.R. Grace & Co., AAER 1140 (June 30, 1999).

21. AUI § 326.33.

22. Id.

23. The auditing literature notes that the "concept of materiality recognizes that some matters, either individually or in the aggregate, are important for fair presentation of financial statements in conformity with generally accepted accounting principles." AU § 312.03. See also AU § 312.04.

24. AU § 312.34. Quantitative materiality assessments often are made by comparing adjustments to revenues, gross profit, pretax and net income, total assets, stockholders' equity, or individual line items in the financial statements. The particular items in the financial statements to be considered as a basis for the materiality determination depend on the proposed adjustment to be made and other factors, such as those identified in this SAB. For example, an adjustment to inventory that is immaterial to pretax income or net income may be material to the financial statements because it may affect a working capital ratio or cause the registrant to be in default of loan covenants.

25. AU § 508.36.

26. AU § 312.34

27. AU § 380.09.

28. FASB Statements of Financial Accounting Standards ("Standards" or "Statements") generally provide that "[t]he provisions of this Statement need not be applied to immaterial items." This SAB is consistent with that provision of the Statements. In theory, this language is subject to the interpretation that the registrant is free intentionally to set forth immaterial items in financial statements in a manner that plainly would be contrary to GAAP if the misstatement were material. The staff believes that the FASB did not intend this result.

29. 15 U.S.C. §§ 78m(b)(2) - (7).

30. 15 U.S.C. § 78l.

31. 15 U.S.C. § 78o(d).

32. Criminal liability may be imposed if a person knowingly circumvents or knowingly fails to implement a system of internal accounting controls or knowingly falsifies books, records or accounts. 15 U.S.C. §§ 78m(4) and (5). See also Rule 13b2-1 under the Exchange Act, 17 CFR 240.13b2-1, which states, "No person shall, directly or indirectly, falsify or cause to be falsified, any book, record or account subject to Section 13(b)(2)(A) of the Securities Exchange Act."

33. 15 U.S.C. § 78m(b)(7). The books and records provisions of section 13(b) of the Exchange Act originally were passed as part of the Foreign Corrupt Practices Act ("FCPA"). In the conference committee report regarding the 1988 amendments to the FCPA, the committee stated,

The conference committee adopted the prudent man qualification in order to clarify that the current standard does not connote an unrealistic degree of exactitude or precision. The concept of reasonableness of necessity contemplates the weighing of a number of relevant factors, including the costs of compliance.

Cong. Rec. H2116 (daily ed. April 20, 1988).

34. So far as the staff is aware, there is only one judicial decision that discusses Section 13(b)(2) of the Exchange Act in any detail, SEC v. World-Wide Coin Investments, Ltd., 567 F. Supp. 724 (N.D. Ga. 1983), and the courts generally have found that no private right of action exists under the accounting and books and records provisions of the Exchange Act. See e.g., Lamb v. Phillip Morris Inc., 915 F.2d 1024 (6th Cir. 1990) and JS Service Center Corporation v. General Electric Technical Services Company, 937 F. Supp. 216 (S.D.N.Y. 1996).

35. The Commission adopted the address as a formal statement of policy in Securities Exchange Act Release No. 17500 (January 29, 1981), 46 FR 11544 (February 9, 1981), 21 SEC Docket 1466 (February 10, 1981).

36. Id. at 46 FR 11546.

37. Id.

38. For example, the conference report regarding the 1988 amendments to the FCPA stated, The Conferees intend to codify current Securities and Exchange Commission (SEC) enforcement policy that penalties not be imposed for insignificant or technical infractions or inadvertent conduct. The amendment adopted by the Conferees [Section 13(b)(4)] accomplishes this by providing that criminal penalties shall not be imposed for failing to comply with the FCPA's books and records or accounting provisions. This provision [Section 13(b)(5)] is meant to ensure that criminal penalties would be imposed where acts of commission or omission in keeping books or records or administering accounting controls have the purpose of falsifying books, records or accounts, or of circumventing the accounting controls set forth in the Act. This would include the deliberate falsification of books and records and other conduct calculated to evade the internal accounting controls requirement.

Cong. Rec. H2115 (daily ed. April 20, 1988).

39. As Chairman Williams noted with respect to the internal control provisions of the FCPA, "[t]housands of dollars ordinarily should not be spent conserving hundreds." 46 FR 11546.

40. Id., at 11547.

41. Section 10A(f) defines, for purposes of Section 10A, an "illegal act" as "an act or omission that violates any law, or any rule or regulation having the force of law." This is broader than the definition of an "illegal act" in AU § 317.02, which states, "Illegal acts by clients do not include personal misconduct by the entity's personnel unrelated to their business activities."

42. AU § 316.04. See also AU § 316.03. An unintentional illegal act triggers the same procedures and considerations by the auditor as a fraudulent misstatement if the illegal act has a direct and material effect on the financial statements. See AU §§ 110 n. 1, 316 n. 1, 317.05 and 317.07. Although distinguishing between intentional and unintentional misstatements is often difficult, the auditor must plan and perform the audit to obtain reasonable assurance that the financial statements are free of material misstatements in either case. See AU § 316 note 3.

43. AU § 316.04. Although the auditor is not required to plan or perform the audit to detect misstatements that are immaterial to the financial statements, SAS 82 requires the auditor to evaluate several fraud "risk factors" that may bring such misstatements to his or her attention. For example, an analysis of fraud risk factors under SAS 82 must include, among other things, consideration of management's interest in maintaining or increasing the registrant's stock price or earnings trend through the use of unusually aggressive accounting practices, whether management has a practice of committing to analysts or others that it will achieve unduly aggressive or clearly unrealistic forecasts, and the existence of assets, liabilities, revenues, or expenses based on significant estimates that involve unusually subjective judgments or uncertainties. See AU §§ 316.17a and .17c.

44. AU §§ 316.34 and 316.35, in requiring the auditor to consider whether fraudulent misstatements are material, and in requiring differing responses depending on whether the misstatement is material, make clear that fraud can involve immaterial misstatements. Indeed, a misstatement can be "inconsequential" and still involve fraud.

Under SAS 82, assessing whether misstatements due to fraud are material to the financial statements is a "cumulative process" that should occur both during and at the completion of the audit. SAS 82 further states that this accumulation is primarily a "qualitative matter" based on the auditor's judgment. AU § 316.33. The staff believes that in making these assessments, management and auditors should refer to the discussion in Part 1 of this SAB.

45. AU §§ 316.34 and 316.36. Auditors should document their determinations in accordance with AU §§ 316.37, 319.57, 339, and other appropriate sections.

46. See, e.g., AU § 316.39.

47. Report of the National Commission on Fraudulent Financial Reporting at 32 (October 1987). See also Report and Recommendations of the Blue Ribbon Committee on Improving the Effectiveness of Corporate Audit Committees (February 8, 1999).

48. AU § 325.02. See also AU § 380.09, which, in discussing matters to be communicated by the auditor to the audit committee, states,

The auditor should inform the audit committee about adjustments arising from the audit that could, in his judgment, either individually or in the aggregate, have a significant effect on the entity's financial reporting process. For purposes of this section, an audit adjustment, whether or not recorded by the entity, is a proposed correction of the financial statements....

49. See AU § 411.05.

50. The FASB Discussion Memorandum, Criteria for Determining Materiality, states that the financial accounting and reporting process considers that "a great deal of the time might be spent during the accounting process considering insignificant matters . . . . If presentations of financial information are to be prepared economically on a timely basis and presented in a concise intelligible form, the concept of materiality is crucial." This SAB is not intended to require that misstatements arising from insignificant errors and omissions (individually and in the aggregate) arising from the normal recurring accounting close processes, such as a clerical error or an adjustment for a missed accounts payable invoice, always be corrected, even if the error is identified in the audit process and known to management. Management and the auditor would need to consider the various factors described elsewhere in this SAB in assessing whether such misstatements are material, need to be corrected to comply with the FCPA, or trigger procedures under Section 10A of the Exchange Act. Because this SAB does not change current law or guidance in the accounting or auditing literature, adherence to the principles described in this SAB should not raise the costs associated with recordkeeping or with audits of financial statements.

SEC Staff Accounting Bulletin: No. 100 – Restructuring and Impairment Charges

Securities and Exchange Commission
17 CFR Part 211
[Release No. SAB 100]
Staff Accounting Bulletin No. 100

Agency: Securities and Exchange Commission

Action: Publication of Staff Accounting Bulletin

Summary: This staff accounting bulletin expresses views of the staff regarding the accounting for and disclosure of certain expenses commonly reported in connection with exit activities and business combinations. This includes accrual of exit and employee termination costs pursuant to Emerging Issues Task Force (EITF) Issues No. 94-3, Liability Recognition for Certain Employee Termination Benefits and Other Costs to Exit an Activity (Including Certain Costs Incurred in a Restructuring), and No. 95-3, Recognition of Liabilities in Connection with a Purchase Business Combination, and the recognition of impairment charges pursuant to Accounting Principles Board (APB) Opinion No. 17, Intangible Assets, and Statement of Financial Accounting Standards (SFAS) No. 121, Accounting for the Impairment of Long-Lived Assets and for Long-Lived Assets to be Disposed Of .

Date: November 24, 1999

For Further Information Contact: Eric Jacobsen, Paul Kepple, or Eric Casey, Office of the Chief Accountant (202-942-4400), Robert Bayless, Division of Corporation Finance (202-942-2960), Securities and Exchange Commission, 450 Fifth Street, N.W., Washington, D.C., 20549; electronic addresses: jacobsene@sec.gov; kepplep@sec.gov; caseye@sec.gov; baylessr@sec.gov.

Supplementary Information: The statements in staff accounting bulletins are not rules or interpretations of the Commission, nor are they published as bearing the Commission's official approval. They represent interpretations and practices followed by the Division of Corporation Finance and the Office of the Chief Accountant in administering the disclosure requirements of the Federal securities laws.

Jonathan G. Katz
Secretary
Date: November 24, 1999

Part 211 - (AMEND)

Accordingly, Part 211 of Title 17 of the Code of Federal Regulations is amended by adding Staff Accounting Bulletin No. 100 to the table found in Subpart B.

Staff Accounting Bulletin No. 100

1. Amend Section A of Topic 2 of the Staff Accounting Bulletin Series to add new subsection 9. Liabilities Assumed in a Purchase Business Combination. Revise the title of Section P of Topic 5 to Restructuring Charges , designate the current section P as subsection 3 of Section P of Topic 5, Income Statement Presentation of Restructuring Charges , deleting the first paragraph under that subsection, and renumbering Questions 1, 2, and 3 in that subsection to be

Questions 13, 14, and 15. Add new subsection 1. Characteristics of an Exit Plan to Section P of Topic 5. Add new subsection 2. Characteristics of an Exit Cost to Section P of Topic 5. Add new subsection 4. Disclosures . to Section P of Topic 5 Furthermore, add new Sections BB. Inventory Valuation Allowances and CC. Impairments to Topic 5.

Topic 2: Business Combinations

A. Purchase Method

* * * * *

8. Business Combinations Prior to an Initial Public Offering

* * * * *

9. Liabilities Assumed in a Purchase Business Combination

Facts: Company A acquires Company Z in a business combination accounted for as a purchase. Company Z has recorded liabilities for contingencies such as product warranties and environmental costs.

Question: Are there circumstances in which it is appropriate for Company A to adjust Company Z's carrying value for these liabilities in the purchase price allocation?

Interpretive Response: Yes. Accounting Principles Board Opinion No. 16, Business Combinations, requires that receivables, liabilities, and accruals be recorded in the purchase price allocation at their fair value, typically the present value of amounts to be received or paid, determined using appropriate current market interest rates. In some cases, fair value is readily determinable from contemporaneous arms-length transactions involving substantially identical assets or liabilities, or from amounts quoted by a third party to purchase the assets or assume the liabilities. More frequently, fair values are based on estimations of the underlying cash flows to be received or paid, discounted to their present value using appropriate current market interest rates.

The historical accounting by Company Z for receivables or liabilities may often be premised on estimates of the amounts to be received or paid. Amounts recorded by Company A in its purchase price allocation may be expected to differ from Company Z's historical carrying values due, at least, to the effects of the acquirer's discounting, including differences in interest rates. Estimation of probable losses and future cash flows involves judgment, and companies A and Z may differ in their systematic approaches to such estimation. Nevertheless, assuming that both companies employ a methodology that appropriately considers all relevant facts and circumstances affecting cash flows, the staff believes that the two estimates of undiscounted cash inflows and outflows should not differ by an amount that is material to the financial statements of Company Z, unless Company A will settle the liability in a manner demonstrably different from the manner in which Company Z had planned to do so (for example, settlement of the warranty obligation through outsourcing versus an internal service department). But the source of other differences in the estimates of the undiscounted cash flows to be received or paid should be investigated and reconciled. If those estimates of undiscounted cash flows are materially different, an accounting error in Company Z's historical financial statements may be present, or Company A may be unaware of important information underlying Company Z's estimates that also is relevant to an estimate of fair value.

The staff is not suggesting that an acquiring company should record assumed liabilities at amounts that reflect an unreasonable estimate. If Company Z's financial statements as of the acquisition date are not fairly stated in accordance with generally accepted accounting principles (GAAP) because of an improperly recorded liability, that liability should not serve as a basis for recording assumed amounts. That is, the correction of a seller's erroneous application of GAAP should not occur through the purchase price allocation. Rather, Company Z's financial statements should be restated to reflect an appropriate amount, with the resultant adjustment being applied to the historical income statement of Company Z for the period(s) in which the trends, events, or changes in operations and conditions that gave rise to the needed change in the liability occurred. It would also be inappropriate for Company Z to report the amount of any necessary adjustment in the period just prior to the acquisition, unless that is the period in which the trends, events, or changes in operations and conditions occurred. The staff would expect that such trends, events, and changes would be disclosed in Management's Discussion and Analysis in the appropriate period(s) if their effect was material to a company's financial position, results of operations or cash flows.

In summary, the staff believes that purchase price adjustments necessary to record liabilities and loss accruals at fair value typically are required, while merely adding an additional "cushion" of 10 or 20 or 30 percent to such account balances is not appropriate. To arrive at those fair values, the undiscounted cash flows must be projected, period by period, based on historical experience and discounted at the appropriate current market discount rate.

* * * * *

Topic 5: Miscellaneous Accounting

* * * * *

P. Restructuring Charges

The term "restructuring charge" is not defined in the existing authoritative literature. While the events or transactions triggering the recognition[1] of what are often identified as restructuring charges vary, these charges typically result from the consolidation and/or relocation of operations, or the disposition or abandonment of operations or productive assets. Restructuring charges may be incurred in connection with a business combination, a change in an enterprise's strategic plan, or a managerial response to declines in demand, increasing costs, or other environmental factors.

Some types of restructuring charges, such as "exit costs," as defined in Emerging Issues Task Force[2] (EITF) Issue No. 94-3, Liability Recognition for Certain Employee Termination Benefits and Other Costs to Exit an Activity (including Certain Costs Incurred in a Restructuring) (EITF 94-3), are recognized as liabilities and charged to operations when management commits to a restructuring plan, while other types of restructuring charges contemplated by the plan may not be recognized until they are actually incurred. The circumstances in which the intended actions of management result in the recognition of a liability are identified in either EITF 94-3 or EITF Issue No. 95-3, Recognition of Liabilities in Connection with a Purchase Business Combination (EITF 95-3), collectively referred to as the "Consensuses."

1. Characteristics of an Exit Plan

Accrual of certain involuntary employee termination benefits and exit costs under the Consensuses requires a commitment by the company to a termination or exit plan (hereinafter collectively referred to as an exit plan) that specifically identifies all significant actions to be taken.[3] Not all plans qualify under the Consensuses as a basis for recognizing a liability for exit costs or involuntary employee termination benefits.

Facts: Prior to year end, senior management of a company approves a plan to exit certain activities and terminate employees involuntarily. Approval by the board of directors is required by the Company's policies to implement the exit plan, but is not obtained until after year end.

Question 1: Would it be appropriate for the company to accrue exit costs and involuntary employee termination benefits as of year end pursuant to the Consensuses?

Interpretive Response: No. The Consensuses do not permit accrual of exit costs or involuntary employee termination benefits prior to the date the company is committed to an exit plan by management having the appropriate level of authority (the commitment date). The staff believes that if the Company's policies require board of directors' approval, or management elects to seek board of directors' approval, the appropriate level of authority needed to commit the company under the Consensuses would be that of the board of directors. If board of directors' approval is neither required nor sought, the appropriate level of authority would be at a level below the board of directors (e.g., chief executive officer). The appropriate level of authority would be a division or branch manager if that manager can and will commit the enterprise to incur particular exit costs or involuntary employee termination benefits without additional ratification or budget authorization.

Facts: Corporate management is developing an exit plan which will include involuntary employee terminations, plant shutdowns, and asset dispositions associated with the consolidation and reduction of operations in several of its business units. Senior management of the company has set a target of reducing its North American distribution costs by 50 percent within two years. However, the exit plan is in the development stage, with only initial cost estimates having been developed. The corporate management team currently is developing the more detailed plans, significant actions, and related budgets for which individual business units and plant managers will be held accountable and be required to execute. The more detailed plans will set forth how, when, and by whom the cost reductions will be achieved.

Question 2: Does the staff believe that exit costs may be accrued prior to the completion of a more detailed exit plan?

Interpretive Response: No. The EITF set restrictive standards for plan specificity when it stated in EITF 94-3, "The exit plan specifically identifies all significant actions to be taken to complete the exit plan... and the period of time to complete the exit plan indicates that significant changes to the exit plan are not likely (emphasis added)." Consistent with the intent of the EITF, and to minimize the opportunities for earnings management, the staff believes that a liability for exit costs arising from a discretionary management action should be accrued only if the discretionary action is part of a comprehensive plan that has been rigorously developed and thoroughly supported.

In assessing whether an exit plan has sufficient detail, the staff would expect generally that a company's exit plan would be at least comparable in terms of the level of detail and precision of estimation to other operating and capital budgets the company prepares, such as annual business unit budgets. The absence of controls and procedures to detect, explain and, if necessary, correct variances or adjust accounting accruals would indicate that the plan lacked the authenticity and management commitment necessary for it to serve as a basis for recognizing a liability for exit costs.

The staff also believes that as a prerequisite to accruing exit costs at the commitment date, the company must be able to estimate reliably[4] the nature, timing, and amount of the exit costs associated with the significant actions it has specifically identified. Factors the staff believes should be considered when determining whether exit costs can be estimated reliably include whether:

- The estimate reflects the most likely expected outcome given all the information currently available to management;
- The exit plan identifies all significant actions expected to be taken;
- The exit plan includes an expected timetable for completing those actions;
- The plan is the one that will be used to evaluate the performance of those responsible for executing the plan and for making periodic comparisons of planned versus actual results and variances;
- All significant actions are documented in the plan in sufficient detail, including but not limited to details such as, geographic locations, estimated costs, expected cash flows, etc.;
- The components used in making the detailed calculation in the plan and arriving at the estimated liability (for example, per person costs, number of people, etc.) have a reasonably supportable basis; and
- The key assumptions used in developing the plan have a reasonably supportable basis.

Repeated material changes in the nature, timing, or amount of the estimated exit costs and involuntary termination benefits subsequent to the commitment date may also indicate an inability to make reliable estimates.

Facts: Company A operates five hundred retail outlets and has identified the specific location of 80 out of 100 stores which it intends to close pursuant to a store consolidation plan. The exit plan for the 80 stores identifies all significant actions and related costs in budget line item detail, such as lease termination costs, involuntary employee termination costs, store closure costs, subcontractor costs (where appropriate), etc. for each facility, as well as all other information specifically enumerated by the Consensuses. Management believes that the average cost to close the additional 20 stores will approximate the average cost of closing the 80 identified stores.

Question 3: Assuming that all other provisions of EITF 94-3 have been met, may Company A recognize a liability at the commitment date for the exit costs and involuntary termination benefits associated with all 100 stores?

Interpretive Response: No. While recognition of estimated exit costs and involuntary termination benefits for the 80 identified stores is appropriate, the staff believes that Company A has not met the requirements in EITF 94-3 for the 20 stores yet to be identified. The staff believes that all exit costs and involuntary termination benefits should be identified by specific property location and that no higher level of identification or aggregation (e.g., country, region, state, county, etc.) is appropriate under the guidance in EITF 94-3. If and when Company A identifies the specific locations of other stores, the involuntary termination benefits, the exit costs, and the exit plan associated with those stores should be evaluated and accounted for as a new exit plan under the Consensuses rather than a revision of the exit plan for the 80 stores.

Although Company A may be unable to specifically identify significant actions to be taken to complete some parts of the exit plan (and so recognizing a liability currently under the Consensuses is not appropriate), management should consider its disclosure obligations under the Commission's rules and regulations regarding its future plans, including those obligations relating to Management's Discussion and Analysis (MD&A).

Question 4: If Company A decides not to close one of the stores in a period following the quarter in which it recognized a liability for exit costs and involuntary employee termination benefits for the 80 identified stores, may Company A leave the accrued exit costs and involuntary employee termination benefits for that store on its balance sheet in anticipation of costs expected to be incurred when other stores are identified for closing?

Interpretive Response: No. Exit costs and involuntary employee termination benefits accrued for the store should be reversed. At each balance sheet date (annual or interim), exit cost and involuntary employee termination benefits accruals should be evaluated to ensure that any accrued amount no longer needed for its originally intended purpose is reversed in a timely manner. When an exit, termination, or other loss accrual is no longer appropriate, reversal of the liability should be recorded through the same income statement line item that was used when the liability was initially recorded. Generally accepted accounting principles (GAAP) do not permit unused or excess liability accruals to be retained as general accruals, used for purposes other than that for which the liability was established initially, or returned to earnings over time and in small amounts. Furthermore, costs actually incurred in connection with an exit plan should be charged to the exit accrual only to the extent those costs were specifically included in the original estimation of the accrual. Costs incurred in connection with an exit plan but not specifically contemplated in the original estimate of the liability for exit costs and involuntary employee termination benefits should be charged to operating expense in the period incurred, or the period that the exit cost or involuntary termination benefit qualifies for accrual under EITF 94-3, with appropriate explanation in MD&A.

Companies should have appropriate internal accounting controls with respect to exit, termination, or other loss accruals and the related expenses. These controls must ensure the company is in compliance with Section 13(b) of the Securities Exchange Act of 1934 and provide a reasonable basis for ensuring adjustments required by GAAP (increases or decreases) with respect to such liabilities are made on a timely basis.

Question 5: The Consensuses require that the exit plan begin as soon as possible after the commitment date and that the time needed to complete it indicates that significant changes in the plan (due to changing market conditions or other external factors, for example) are unlikely. What factors may indicate that an exit plan will not begin or be executed within a period of time that significant changes in the plan are unlikely?

Interpretive Response: Based on the staff's experience, a number of factors may indicate that an exit plan might not begin or be executed within a period of time that is short enough to allow a company to appropriately conclude that significant changes in the exit plan are unlikely (and consequently, that recognizing a liability pursuant to the Consensuses would not be appropriate), including:

1. Where all significant actions to be undertaken pursuant to the plan have not been identified with sufficient specificity or are not reasonably estimable,

2. Where it is likely that execution of the plan will be delayed due to events or circumstances that are reasonably likely to occur, or

3. Where a company lacks the internal controls or information needed to monitor effectively the activities being performed, compare the costs incurred to the plan, and make adjustments to the plan on a timely basis.

Facts: In the first quarter of 2000, a company develops a strategic plan to restructure four divisions during the next three years. The exit plan will be implemented one division at a time.

Question 6: May the company recognize a liability for the exit costs and involuntary employee termination benefits for all four divisions in the first quarter of 2000?

Interpretive Response: The Consensuses contemplate completion of an exit plan within a time period that indicates that significant changes in the exit plan are unlikely. In order to satisfy that condition, the staff believes that management must be able to make reasonable estimates of the exit costs and involuntary employee termination benefits, and that those estimates would not be likely to change materially within that time period. Today's dynamic and constantly changing business environment often affects a company's ability to identify exit activities to be undertaken and estimate exit costs and involuntary employee termination benefits to be incurred after the commitment date with sufficient precision and specificity to permit the accrual of those costs at the commitment date[5] under the Consensuses. Thus, the staff generally believes that the further out an exit activity is from the commitment date, the greater the risk that either all or part of the exit plan will be materially revised in response to events or circumstances that are reasonably likely to occur. Furthermore, the staff also observes that many of the illustrative examples in EITF 94-3 assume completion of significant actions within one year of the commitment date.[6] Therefore, the staff believes that a rebuttable presumption exists that the exit plan should be completed and the exit costs and involuntary employee termination benefits incurred within one year from the commitment date.

The staff recognizes, however, that an exit plan might not be completed within one year of the commitment date due to circumstances outside the company's control. Circumstances outside the company's control would include, for example, legal or contractual restrictions on the company's ability to complete the exit plan, such as existing union contracts or enacted legal restrictions concerning the length of notice required to involuntarily terminate employees. In such circumstances, management should have appropriate evidence and support for concluding that execution of its plan will not be materially affected by intervening developments and that reasonable estimates of the nature, timing, and amount of exit costs and involuntary employee termination benefits can be made so far in advance.

Facts: As of the balance sheet date, Company A's exit plan provides only that it will terminate involuntarily a certain number of employees within certain grades and classes of employees in connection with consolidation of 10 facilities in Europe. The specific grades of employees to be terminated involuntarily have not been identified at the balance sheet date. Company A has not made any announcement regarding its exit or termination plans. The involuntary termination benefits are expected to vary based on the grade and class of employee as well as the country in which the worker is employed.

Question 7: Assuming that the board of directors of Company A approves the exit and termination plans in the condition described above by year end, in the staff's view, may Company A recognize a liability at the balance sheet date for the costs it expects to incur to terminate involuntarily certain grades of employees within certain classes of employees pursuant to the Consensuses?

Interpretive Response: No. In order to recognize a liability for the cost to terminate employees involuntarily, the Consensuses require that the exit plan must specifically identify (a) the benefit formula to be used for determining individual employee involuntary termination payments, (b) the number of employees to be involuntarily terminated, and (c) the employees' job classifications or functions and locations.

Furthermore, the EITF considered notification to be an essential element obligating the employer to fulfill its commitment, giving rise to a liability. Therefore, the employees within the classifications or functions at risk of being involuntarily terminated must also be notified of the pending involuntary termination prior to the balance sheet date. The notification must include the provisions of the involuntary termination benefit formula in sufficient detail such that each employee would be able to calculate the severance benefit to be received if terminated involuntarily.

In this example, Company A has not met the notification requirements of the Consensuses, nor does it appear that Company A has finalized the information called for under (a), (b), or (c) referred to above.[7]

2. Characteristics of Exit Costs

Under the Consensuses, an exit cost is a cost that results from a plan to exit an activity pursuant to a qualified exit plan and that meets all of the following conditions:

1. The cost is not associated with or does not benefit activities that will be continued.

2. The cost is not associated with or is not incurred to generate revenues after the commitment date.

3. The cost meets one of the following criteria: a. It is incremental to other costs incurred in the company's conduct of its activities prior to the commitment date and will be incurred as a direct result of the exit plan; or b. The cost will be incurred under a contractual obligation that existed prior to the commitment date and will either continue after the exit plan is completed with no economic benefit to the company or be a penalty to cancel the contractual obligation.

FASB Concept Statement No. 6, Elements of Financial Statements (SFAC 6), paragraphs 35 to 43 and FASB Statement of Financial Accounting Standards No. 5, Accounting for Contingencies (SFAS 5) provide guidance for when to recognize liabilities in general and loss contingencies in particular. Registrants should not analogize to the Consensuses for costs that are outside the scope of the Consensuses. Moreover, to fall within the scope of the Consensuses, a cost cannot be associated with or benefit continuing activities.

Facts: For existing customers of a product line or service that is to be discontinued, a company is developing a plan to transition the customers over the next year to a new product line or service.

Question 8: May the costs the company expects to incur to complete this transition be recognized as a liability for exit costs pursuant to the Consensuses as of the date the company commits to a plan to transition these existing customers?

Interpretive Response: No. The costs are being incurred in order to benefit future periods through the retention of customers, and with the expectation of generating future revenues. The staff believes that the costs to transition the customers may not be recognized as a liability for exit costs under the Consensuses and should be recognized and expensed as incurred in operating income.

Facts: A franchiser announces a franchisee cash incentive program in order to induce its franchisees to upgrade their equipment over the next year. The franchiser is not contractually obligated to make any payments to individual franchisees until the franchisees accept the offer and incur "qualifying" costs to upgrade their equipment, which costs are reimbursable by the franchiser.

Question 9: May the franchiser accrue the estimated cost of the incentive program at the date it announces the plan pursuant to the Consensuses?

Interpretive Response: No. The franchiser is incurring the cost in order to benefit continuing activities and with the expectation of indirect future economic benefit. Therefore, the staff believes that these are not exit costs. Furthermore, considering the definition and characteristics of a liability as provided in paragraphs 35 through 43 of SFAC 6 and SFAS 5, costs such as the above should not be accrued until the franchiser becomes contractually obligated to make such payments.

Facts: Company A licenses technology from Company B on a perpetual, exclusive basis, paying an annual royalty of 10 percent of sales. Prior to the balance sheet date, the board of directors of Company A approves a plan to renegotiate terms of the royalty arrangement. In exchange for reducing the annual royalty rate from 10 percent of all sales to 5 percent of the first $20 million in annual sales, Company A will propose to pay Company B a nonrecurring, lump-sum payment of $5 million. Although internally committed to the plan, as of the balance sheet date, Company A has not yet approached Company B regarding renegotiating the royalty terms of the technology license.

Question 10: May Company A recognize a liability at the balance sheet date pursuant to the Consensuses for its estimate of the cost to modify the royalty arrangement as well as the estimated nonrecurring, lump-sum payment by the company?

Interpretive Response: No. The lump-sum payment is outside the scope of exit costs contemplated by the Consensuses because it is being incurred to modify terms of an existing and continuing relationship. The staff does not believe that the modification of an executory contract (for example, license and royalty, purchase or sales commitments, servicing, etc.) represents the "exiting" of one contract and the initiation of a new, unrelated contract.[8] In addition, the staff notes that, although the board of directors of Company A has committed to a plan, Company B has not agreed to the terms under which it would accept modification of the royalty arrangement. Under these facts and circumstances, it does not appear to the staff that Company A would have a basis upon which to reasonably estimate the costs of changing the arrangement.

Under these facts and circumstances, the staff believes that any costs to modify the contract would not fall within the scope of the Consensuses. Furthermore, GAAP would not permit recognition of liabilities for costs associated with modifying the contract prior to their being incurred.

Facts: A company, in responding to significant staffing shortages, hires an executive search firm, agreeing to pay the firm a fixed fee for each successful recruitment. In addition, the company commits to pay the relocation costs of future employees recruited by the executive search firm.

Question 11: May the company accrue the estimated fees to be paid to the executive search firm as well as the estimated cost to relocate new employees at the date the company engages the firm and commits to the plan to pay relocation costs?

Interpretive Response: No. Such costs are being incurred to benefit continuing activities, are not necessarily incremental to other costs incurred by the company in the normal course of business, and do not represent obligations of the company at the date the company engages the executive search firm. That is, the staff believes that these costs are neither exit nor integration costs that will be incurred as a result of a purchase business combination and thus, they do not fall within the scope of the Consensuses.[9] Rather, the fees to be paid to the executive search firm and the relocation costs should be recognized as liabilities as and when the services are provided.

Question 12: May the company accrue as an exit cost at the balance sheet date an asset impairment in accordance with the Consensuses for facilities it expects to close or dispose of?

Interpretive Response: No. The Consensuses address recognition of liabilities associated with exit plans and not recognition of losses associated with asset impairments. That is, the recognition of losses on asset impairments, even in connection with exit plans, does not fall within the scope of the Consensuses. The closure and disposition or abandonment of a registrant's own long-lived assets, such as manufacturing plants, not constituting a business segment in accordance with APB 30, would be accounted for in accordance with SFAS 121, with any losses on asset impairment being charged to operating income.[10]

3. Income Statement Presentation of Restructuring Charges

Facts: Because restructuring charges typically do not relate to "a single separate major line of business or class of customer,"[11] they do not qualify for presentation as losses on the disposal of a discontinued operation. Additionally, since the charges are not both unusual and infrequent[12] they are not presented in the income statement as extraordinary items.

Question 13.

* * *

Question 14.

* * *

Question 15.

* * *

4. Disclosures

Beginning with the period in which the exit plan is committed to, the Consensuses require disclosure, in all periods, including interim periods, until the exit plan is completed, of the following:

1. The amount of involuntary termination benefits accrued and charged to expense and their income statement classification.
2. The number of employees to be terminated.
3. A description of the employee group(s) to be terminated.
4. The actual amount of involuntary termination benefits paid and charged against the liability and the number of employees actually terminated pursuant to the exit plan.
5. Where the activities that will not be continued are significant to the enterprise's revenue or operating results or if the exit costs recognized at the commitment date are material:
   a. A description of the major actions comprising the exit plan, activities that will not be continued, including the method of disposition, and the anticipated date of completion.
   b. A description of the type and amount of exit costs recognized as liabilities and their income statement classification.[13]
   c. A description of the type and amount of exit costs paid and charged against the liability.
   d. The revenue and net operating income or losses from activities that will not be continued if those activities have separately identifiable operations for all periods presented.
6. The amount of any adjustment(s) to the liability account and whether the corresponding entry was recorded as an adjustment of the cost of an acquiree or included in the determination of net income for the period.
7. Where an acquirer has not finalized the plan to exit an activity or involuntarily terminate (relocate) employees of the acquiree as of the balance sheet date, a description of any unresolved issues, the types of additional liabilities that may result in a change to the purchase price allocation, and how any adjustments will be reported.[14]

Question 16: What specific disclosures about restructuring charges has the staff requested to fulfill the disclosure requirements of the Consensuses and Management's Discussion and Analysis (MD&A)?

Interpretive Response: The staff often has requested greater disaggregation and more precise labeling when exit and involuntary termination costs are grouped in a note or income statement line item with items unrelated to the exit plan.[15] For the reader's understanding, the staff has requested that discretionary, or decision-dependent, costs of a period, such as exit costs, be disclosed and explained in MD&A separately. Also to improve transparency, the staff has requested disclosure of the nature and amounts of additional types of exit costs and other types of restructuring charges[16] that appear quantitatively or qualitatively material, and requested that losses relating to asset impairments be identified separately from charges based on estimates of future cash expenditures.

The staff frequently reminds registrants that in periods subsequent to the commitment date that material changes and activity in the liability balances of each significant type of exit cost and involuntary employee termination benefits (either as a result of expenditures or changes in/reversals of estimates) should be disclosed in the footnotes to the interim and annual financial statements and discussed in MD&A. In the event a company recognized liabilities for exit costs and involuntary employee termination benefits relating to multiple exit plans, the staff believes presentation of separate information for each individual exit plan that has a material effect on the balance sheet, results of operations or cash flows generally is appropriate.

For material exit or involuntary employee termination costs related to an acquired business, the staff has requested disclosure in either MD&A or the financial statements of –

a. When the registrant began formulating exit plans for which accrual may be necessary,

b. The types and amounts of liabilities recognized for exit costs and involuntary employee termination benefits and included in the acquisition cost allocation, and

c. Any unresolved contingencies or purchase price allocation issues and the types of additional liabilities that may result in an adjustment of the acquisition cost allocation.

The staff has noted that the economic or other events that cause a registrant to consider and/or adopt an exit plan or that impair the carrying amount of assets, generally occur over time. Accordingly, the staff believes that as those events and the resulting trends and uncertainties evolve, they often will meet the requirement for disclosure pursuant to the Commission's MD&A rules prior to the period in which the exit costs and liabilities are recorded pursuant to GAAP. Whether or not currently recognizable in the financial statements, material exit or involuntary termination costs that affect a known trend, demand, commitment, event, or uncertainty to management, should be disclosed in MD&A. The staff believes that MD&A should include discussion of the events and decisions which gave rise to the exit costs and exit plan, and the likely effects of management's plans on financial position, future operating results and liquidity unless it is determined that a material effect is not reasonably likely to occur. Registrants should identify the periods in which material cash outlays are anticipated and the expected source of their funding. Registrants should also discuss material revisions to exit plans, exit costs, or the timing of the plan's execution, including the nature and reasons for the revisions.

The staff believes that the expected effects on future earnings and cash flows resulting from the exit plan (for example, reduced depreciation, reduced employee expense, etc.) should be quantified and disclosed, along with the initial period in which those effects are expected to be realized. This includes whether the cost savings are expected to be offset by anticipated increases in other expenses or reduced revenues. This discussion should clearly identify the income statement line items to be impacted (for example, cost of sales; marketing; selling, general and administrative expenses; etc.). In later periods if actual savings anticipated by the exit plan are not achieved as expected or are achieved in periods other than as expected, MD&A should discuss that outcome, its reasons, and its likely effects on future operating results and liquidity.

The staff often finds that, because of the discretionary nature of exit plans and the components thereof, presenting and analyzing material exit and involuntary termination charges in tabular form, with the related liability balances and activity (e.g., beginning balance, new charges, cash payments, other adjustments with explanations, and ending balances) from balance sheet date to balance sheet date, is necessary to explain fully the components and effects of significant restructuring charges. The staff believes that such a tabular analysis aids a financial statement user's ability to disaggregate the restructuring charge by income statement line item in which the costs would have otherwise been recognized, absent the restructuring plan, (for example, cost of sales; selling, general, and administrative; etc.).

* * * * *

A.A. * * *

B.B. Inventory Valuation Allowances

Facts: Accounting Research Bulletin No. 43 (ARB 43), Chapter 4, Statement 5, specifies that:

A departure from the cost basis of pricing the inventory is required when the utility of the goods is no longer as great as its cost. Where there is evidence that the utility of goods, in their disposal in the ordinary course of business, will be less than cost, whether due to physical obsolescence, changes in price levels, or other causes, the difference should be recognized as a loss of the current period. This is generally accomplished by stating such goods at a lower level commonly designated as market."

Footnote 2 to that same chapter indicates that "In the case of goods which have been written down below cost at the close of a fiscal period, such reduced amount is to be considered the cost for subsequent accounting purposes."

Lastly, Accounting Principles Board Opinion No. 20, Accounting Changes, provides "inventory obsolescence" as one of the items subject to estimation and changes in estimates under the guidance in paragraphs 10-11 and 31-33 of that standard.

Question: Does the write-down of inventory to the lower of cost or market, as required by ARB 43, create a new cost basis for the inventory or may a subsequent change in facts and circumstances allow for restoration of inventory value, not to exceed original historical cost?

Interpretive Response: Based on ARB 43, footnote 2, the staff believes that a write-down of inventory to the lower of cost or market at the close of a fiscal period creates a new cost basis that subsequently cannot be marked up based on changes in underlying facts and circumstances.[17]

C.C. Impairments

Standards for recognizing and measuring impairment of the carrying amount of long-lived assets, certain identifiable intangibles, and goodwill related to those assets to be held and used are found in Statement of Financial Accounting Standards No. 121, Accounting for the Impairment of Long-Lived Assets and for Long-Lived Assets to Be Disposed Of (SFAS 121). Additional guidance related to goodwill impairment is also provided in Accounting Principles Board (APB) Opinion No. 17, Intangible Assets (APB 17). The FASB currently has active projects addressing both SFAS 121 and APB 17 issues. The staff will reconsider the guidance provided below upon completion of those projects.

Facts: Company X has mainframe computers that are to be abandoned in six to nine months as replacement computers are put in place. The mainframe computers were placed in service in January 19X0 and were being depreciated on a straight-line basis over seven years. No salvage value had been projected at the end of seven years and the original cost of the computers was $8,400. The board of directors, with the appropriate authority, approved the abandonment of the computers in March 19X3 when the computers had a remaining carrying value of $4,600. No proceeds are expected upon abandonment. Abandonment cannot occur prior to the receipt and installation of replacement computers, which is expected prior to the end of 19X3. Management had begun reevaluating its mainframe computer capabilities in January 19X2 and had included in its 19X3 capital expenditures budget an estimated amount for new mainframe computers. The 19X3 capital expenditures budget had been prepared by management in August 19X2, had been discussed with the company's board of directors in September 19X2 and was formally approved by the board of directors in March 19X3. Management had also begun soliciting bids for new mainframe computers beginning in the fall of 19X2. The mainframe computers, when grouped with assets at the lowest level of identifiable cash flows, were not impaired on a "held and used" basis throughout this time period. Management had not adjusted the original estimated useful life of the computers (seven years) since 19X0.

Question 1: Company X proposes to recognize an impairment charge under SFAS 121 for the carrying value of the mainframe computers of $4,600 in March 19X3. Does Company X meet the requirements in SFAS 121 to classify the mainframe computer assets as "to be disposed of?"

Interpretive Response: No. SFAS 121, paragraph 15, provides that when management, having the authority to approve the action, has committed to a plan to dispose of the assets, whether by sale or abandonment, the assets to be disposed of should be reported at the lower of carrying amount or fair value less cost to sell. The staff believes that registrants must also consider the criteria in APB Opinion No. 30, Reporting the Results of Operations – Reporting the Effects of Disposal of a Segment of a Business, and Extraordinary, Unusual and Infrequently Occurring Events and Transactions (APB 30), paragraph 14, and Emerging Issues Task Force Issue No. 94-3, Liability Recognition for Certain Employee Termination Benefits and Other Costs to Exit an Activity (Including Certain Costs Incurred in a Restructuring) (EITF 94-3) to determine whether a plan is sufficiently robust to designate the assets as assets to be disposed of. APB 30 and EITF 94-3 require a plan to have the following characteristics:

- Prior to the date of the financial statements, management having the appropriate level of authority approves and commits the enterprise to a formal plan of disposal, whether by sale or abandonment;

- The plan specifically identifies all major assets to be disposed of, significant actions to be taken to complete the plan, including the method of disposition and location of those activities, and the expected date of completion;

- There is an active program to find a buyer if disposal is to be by sale;

- Management can estimate proceeds to be realized on disposal;

- Actions required by the plan will begin as soon as possible after the commitment date; and

- The period of time to complete the plan indicates that significant changes to the plan are not likely.

The staff believes that a necessary condition of a plan to dispose of assets in use is that management have the current ability to remove the assets from operations. For example, the staff believes that the above fact pattern would not qualify as a plan of disposal under SFAS 121 in March 19X3 because the mainframe computer assets cannot be taken out of service and abandoned prior to installing the new, but not yet available, mainframe computers. The operational requirement to continue to use the assets is indicative that the assets are still held for use. The staff does not intend this guidance to mean that assets to be sold must be removed from service in order to be designated as assets held for disposal. Rather, the company must be able to remove the assets from service upon identification of a buyer or receipt of an acceptable bid, but the assets can otherwise remain in service provided the criterion in SFAS 121 has been met. If a buyer is found and an acceptable offer is received, but the assets must be retained by the seller for some period due to ongoing operational needs, the criterion for "to be disposed of" treatment has not been met.

The staff also believes that an active program to find a buyer exists only if the marketing effort commenced promptly after the commitment date and continued unabated until the sale was accomplished.

Question 2: Would the staff accept an adjustment to write down the carrying value of the computers to reflect a "normalized depreciation" rate for the period from March 19X3 through actual abandonment (e.g., December 19X3)? Normalized depreciation would represent the amount of depreciation otherwise expected to be recognized during that period without adjustment of the asset's useful life, or $1,000 ($100/month for ten months) in the example fact pattern.

Interpretive Response: No. Whether the mainframe computers are viewed as "to be disposed of" or "held and used" at March 19X3, there is no basis under SFAS 121 to write down an asset to an amount that would subsequently result in a "normalized depreciation" charge through the disposal date. For an asset that meets the requirements to be classified as "to be disposed of" under SFAS 121, paragraph 15 of that standard requires the asset to be valued at the lower of carrying amount or fair value less cost to sell. For assets that are classified as "held and used" under SFAS 121, an assessment must first be made as to whether the asset is impaired. Paragraph 6 of SFAS 121 indicates that an impairment loss should be recognized only if the sum of the expected future cash flows (undiscounted and without interest charges) is less than the carrying amount of the asset(s) grouped at the lowest level of identifiable cash flows. If an impairment loss is to be recognized for an asset to be "held and used," it is measured as the amount by which the carrying amount of the asset exceeds the fair value of the asset. The staff would object to a write down of long-lived assets to a "normalized deprecia-tion" value as representing an acceptable alternative to the approaches required in SFAS 121.

The staff also believes that registrants must continually evaluate the appropriateness of use-ful lives assigned to long-lived assets, including identifiable intangible assets and goodwill.[18] In the above fact pattern, management had contemplated removal of the mainframe computers beginning in January 19X2 and, more formally, in August 19X2 as part of compiling the 19X3 capital expenditures budget. At those times, at a minimum, management should have reevalu-ated the original useful life assigned to the computers to determine whether a seven year amor-tization period remained appropriate given the company's current facts and circumstances, in-cluding ongoing technological changes in the market place. This reevaluation process should have continued at the time of the September 19X2 board of directors' meeting to discuss capi-tal expenditure plans and, further, as the company pursued mainframe computer bids. Given the contemporaneous evidence that management's best estimate during much of 19X2 was that the current mainframe computers would be removed from service in 19X3, the depreciable life of the computers should have been adjusted prior to 19X3 to reflect this new estimate. The staff does not view the recognition of an impairment charge to be an acceptable substitute for choosing the appropriate initial amortization or depreciation period or subsequently adjusting this period as company or industry conditions change. The staff's view applies also to selection of, and changes to, estimated residual values. Consequently, the staff may challenge impair-ment charges for which the timely evaluation of useful life and residual value cannot be dem-onstrated.

Question 3: Although the carrying amount of goodwill related to assets to be held and used must be assessed for impairment in conformity with SFAS 121, paragraph 107 of that standard observes that cost of goodwill that is not identified with impaired assets (i.e., "enterprise level") continues to be accounted for under APB 17. Companies are required by paragraph 31 of APB 17 to evaluate continually whether events and circumstances warrant revised estimates of use-ful lives or recognition of a charge-off of carrying amounts. APB 17 does not specify a par-ticular quantitative methodology for measuring the existence or extent of an impairment. What methodologies are acceptable for determining impairment of "enterprise level" goodwill under APB 17?

Interpretive Response: Several methodologies have evolved for measuring impairment of en-terprise level goodwill under APB 17. These methodologies appear to fall within three general categories: market value method, undiscounted cash flows methods, and discounted cash flows methods. A market value method compares the enterprise's net book value to the value indi-cated by the market price of its equity securities; if net book value exceeds market capitaliza-tion, the excess carrying amount of goodwill is written off. Cash flow methods employ fore-casts of the enterprise's future cash flows, with comparison of the enterprise's net book value to (a) aggregate cash flow, or (b) the present value of those cash flows. The staff has observed variations in practice with respect to when a registrant will recognize an impairment of the carrying amount of enterprise goodwill depending on which of these methods is applied, how an enterprise's capitalization will be considered in cash flow forecasts, and how the discount rate is selected.

Regardless of the method used and the diversity in application of some of those methods, the staff believes that the evaluation of enterprise level goodwill cannot occur at a level which does not include all of the operations which benefit directly from that acquired intangible. If an acquired business has been managed as a separate business unit, the business unit may be the appropriate level to evaluate the related goodwill. In contrast, if the acquired business has been fully integrated into the registrant's operations, evaluation of the purchased goodwill would be appropriate only at the level of the registrant as a whole.

Question 4: A registrant's method of assessing and measuring the impairment of enterprise level goodwill under APB 17 is an accounting policy subject to APB Opinion No. 22, Disclo-sure of Accounting Policies (APB 22).[19] What disclosures would the staff expect regarding the method selected?

Interpretive Response: Until diversity in practice is reduced, a company that reports material amounts of unamortized cost of goodwill or that recognizes material amounts of goodwill am-ortization should describe the manner in which the carrying amount of enterprise level good-will is assessed for recoverability and how and when any impairment would be measured. Materiality is to be assessed based on the relationship of the unamortized asset balance to other financial position measurements (including shareholders' equity) or of the relationship of the amortization expense to income statement measurements.

The staff believes that the policy adopted by the company, and the description of that policy included in the financial statements, should be explicit and refer to objective, rather than discretionary, factors. The staff would expect the following to be addressed:

- What conditions would trigger an impairment assessment of the carrying amount of enterprise level goodwill;

- What method – market value, discounted or undiscounted cash flows – would be used to measure an impairment;

- How the method would be implemented, including how interest charges would be considered in the assessment, how the discount rate would be selected, and other significant aspects of the policy.

When there is a change in the method used to assess the carrying value of goodwill, the Commission's rules[20] require a preferability letter from the company's auditors. The staff does not believe that it would be appropriate to rely on the guidance in SFAS 121 concerning impairments of long-lived assets to justify preferability of changes in the method of evaluating impairment of the carrying amount of enterprise level goodwill. For example, a company that previously changed from an undiscounted cash flow method to assess recoverability of enterprise level goodwill to a method that uses discounted cash flow could not justify a change back to an undiscounted cash flow method by reference to SFAS 121. The staff believes that, generally, a discounted cash flows approach is preferable to an undiscounted cash flows approach and a market value approach is preferable to using a discounted cash flows approach, assuming that market value is reliably determinable.

The staff believes that an impairment triggered by a change in accounting policy should be treated as a change in accounting principle inseparable from a change in estimate.[21] The impairment charge should be presented as a change in estimate within operating income (or loss) and not as the cumulative effect of a change in accounting principle.

Facts: Company A acquires 100 percent of Company B in a purchase business combination, with Company B becoming a wholly owned subsidiary of Company A. The acquisition cost of $1,000 is pushed down to Company B's financial records, resulting in an allocation of $300 to fixed assets, $600 to goodwill, and $100 to other net assets. The fixed assets are composed entirely of four manufacturing facilities.

Two years after the acquisition, Company A commits to a reorganization plan that calls for the relocation of Company B's manufacturing operations to facilities separately owned and operated by Company A. Company B's line of products will continue to be marketed. There will be no reduction in the level of output of Company B's products as a result of the relocation, nor will there be any diminution in expected profitability in future years. That level of profitability is expected to recover the remaining cost of the unamortized goodwill. Company A has committed to dispose of the manufacturing facilities of Company B and has met all of the criteria necessary to classify those assets as "to be disposed of" under SFAS 121. Company A expects to realize $200 in net proceeds from the sale of the four manufacturing facilities. The current carrying amounts for the facilities and goodwill are $280 and $480, respectively, which are not impaired on a "held and used" basis.

Question 5: Is it appropriate to recognize an impairment loss of $560 ($280+$480-$200) based on the excess of the carrying amount of goodwill and fixed assets over net sales proceeds?

Interpretive Response: No. An impairment loss can be recognized only for the $80 loss ($280-$200) on the sale of the facilities. Paragraph 123 of SFAS 121 indicates that goodwill related to assets to be disposed of by an entity should be accounted for under the provisions of APB 17, paragraph 32, which states:

> Ordinarily goodwill and similar intangible assets cannot be disposed of apart from the enterprise as a whole. However, a large segment or separable group of assets of an acquired company or the entire acquired company may be sold

or otherwise liquidated, and all or a portion of the unamortized cost of the goodwill recognized in the acquisition should be included in the cost of the assets sold."

In the above fact pattern, the staff believes that the operations and business of Company B, which supported the initial premium resulting in the recognition of goodwill, were not diminished by the disposition of solely physical facilities. The underlying operations, customer relationships, future revenue streams, and business outlook remained intact and, as a result, the staff believes that it is inappropriate to treat the disposition of manufacturing facilities as if the business itself had been disposed of. The staff would object to the allocation of goodwill to the disposed manufacturing facilities.

Paragraph 19 of SFAS 121 requires disclosure of the results of operations of assets held for disposal. If revenues attributable to assets to be disposed of, that remain in operation for some period of time prior to their disposal, cannot be segregated because substantially the same revenues will continue after the assets are disposed of, the amount of the benefit from suspending depreciation, in accordance with SFAS 121, paragraph 16, should be disclosed. The effect associated with assets held for disposal should be discussed in Management's Discussion and Analysis (MD&A), if material.

Facts: Assume the same fact pattern as for Question 5, except that the four manufacturing facilities will be shut down, but not disposed of or abandoned. The four manufacturing facilities do not meet the criteria necessary to be classified as "to be disposed of" under SFAS 121 but are impaired on a "held and used" basis under SFAS 121. Company A intends to retain the four facilities in case the need arises in the future for further manufacturing capacity.

Question 6: Would the staff object to the company's proposal to recognize an impairment loss based on the excess of the carrying amount of goodwill and fixed assets over fair value?

Interpretive Response: Yes. Paragraph 12 of SFAS 121 specifies:

> If an asset being tested for recoverability was acquired in a business combination accounted for using the purchase method, the goodwill that arose in that transaction shall be accounted for as part of the asset grouping ... in determining recoverability. If some but not all of the assets acquired in that transaction are being tested, goodwill shall be allocated to the assets being tested for recoverability on a pro rata basis using the relative fair values of the long-lived assets and identifiable intangibles acquired at the acquisition date unless there is evidence to suggest that some other method of associating the goodwill with those assets is more appropriate."

In the above fact pattern, the staff believes that it is inappropriate to allocate the carrying amount of the goodwill balance to the four facilities being evaluated for impairment. In this instance, the goodwill that existed at the time Company B was acquired principally was the result of a customer base, marketing activities, existing product lines and new products being developed. It did not relate to the fixed assets but, rather, the ongoing operations of the business, which have not been reduced in any way. The goodwill represents the inherent value of the going concern element of Company B and the ability of the entity to generate a return in excess of the return that could be generated on the acquired assets individually, all of which are still in place. The staff contrasts this scenario with one where facilities are eliminated in conjunction with a subsequent decision to abandon the product or business line housed in those facilitites. If the revenue producing activity and the facilities had been acquired in a business combination giving rise to recognition of goodwill, a portion of goodwill should be allocated to the facilities based on their relative fair value, unless another allocation method is more appropriate.

Question 7: Has the staff expressed any views with respect to company-determined estimates of cash flows used for assessing and measuring impairment of assets under SFAS 121?

Interpretive Response: In providing guidance on the development of cash flows for purposes of applying the provisions of SFAS 121, paragraph 9 of that standard indicates that estimates of expected future cash flows should be the best estimate based on reasonable and supportable assumptions and projections. Additionally, paragraph 9 indicates that all available evidence should be considered in developing estimates of expected future cash flows and that the weight given to the evidence should be commensurate with the extent to which the evidence can be verified objectively.

The staff recognizes that various factors, including management's judgments and assumptions about the business plans and strategies, affect the development of future cash flow projections for purposes of applying SFAS 121. The staff, however, cautions registrants that the judgments and assumptions made for purposes of applying SFAS 121 must be consistent with other financial statement calculations and disclosures and disclosures in MD&A. The staff also expects that forecasts made for purposes of applying SFAS 121 be consistent with other forward-looking information prepared by the company, such as that used for internal budgets, incentive compensation plans, discussions with lenders or third parties, and/or reporting to management or the board of directors.

For example, the staff has reviewed a fact pattern where a registrant developed cash flow projections for purposes of applying the provisions of SFAS 121 using one set of assumptions and utilized a second, more conservative set of assumptions for purposes of determining whether deferred tax valuation allowances were necessary when applying the provisions of Statement of Financial Accounting Standards No. 109, Accounting for Income Taxes . In this case, the staff objected to the use of inconsistent assumptions.

In addition to disclosure of key assumptions used in the development of cash flow projections, the staff also has required discussion in MD&A of the implications of assumptions. For example, do the projections indicate that a company is likely to violate debt covenants in the future? What are the ramifications to the cash flow projections used in the impairment analysis? If growth rates used in the impairment analysis are lower than those used by outside analysts, has the company had discussions with the analysts regarding their overly optimistic projections? Has the company appropriately informed the market and its shareholders of its reduced expectations for the future that are sufficient to cause an impairment charge? The staff believes that cash flow projections used in the impairment analysis must be both internally consistent with the company's other projections and externally consistent with financial statement and other public disclosures.

* * * *

Notes

1. The Financial Accounting Standards Board (FASB) has on its agenda currently three projects which are expected to improve existing financial reporting with regard to certain aspects of liability recognition and presentation, including the recognition or non-recognition of constructive obligations. In the interim, pending completion of the FASB's efforts to improve financial reporting in this area, the staff is providing interpretive guidance regarding the existing accounting requirements for exit costs. The staff will reconsider the guidance provided herein upon completion of the FASB's projects.

2. The Emerging Issues Task Force is a private sector body established by the FASB. The Commission's Chief Accountant participates in the body's deliberations.

3. Registrants should refer to the Consensuses for their specific requirements. Registrants are reminded that they are required at the commitment date to account for those types of costs (exit, termination, etc.) falling within the scope of the Consensuses that are incurred in connection with a qualifying exit plan in accordance with the Consensuses. That is, applying the Consensuses (being Level C GAAP per AU411.16) is not optional.

4. See FASB Concept Statement No. 2, Qualitative Characterisitics of Accounting Information and FASB Concept Statement No. 5, Recognition and Measurement in Financial Statements of Business Enterprises, paragraph 63.

5. For purposes of EITF 95-3, the date the plan is finalized, not to exceed one year from consummation.

6. A one-year period is also consistent with Accounting Principles Board Opinion (APB) No. 30, Reporting the Results of Operations – Reporting the Effects of Disposal of a Segment of a Business, and Extraordinary, Unusual and Infrequently Occurring Events

and Transactions (APB 30), SAB No. 93, Accounting and Disclosures Regarding Discontinued Operations, FASB Statement of Financial Accounting Standards No. 38, Accounting for Preacquisition Contingencies of Purchased Enterprises, EITF Issue No. 87-11, Allocation of Purchase Price to Assets to Be Sold and Statement on Auditing Standards No. 59, The Auditor's Consideration of an Entity's Ability to Continue as a Going Concern .

7. While recognizing a liability at the commitment date pursuant to the Consensuses would not be appropriate, registrants are reminded to consider the requirements of FASB Statement of Financial Accounting Standards No. 88, Employers Accounting for Settlements and Curtailments of Defined Pension Plans and for Termination Benefits and FASB Statement of Financial Accounting Standards No. 112, Employer's Accounting for Postemployment Benefits for those involuntary termination benefits that may be payable pursuant to pre-existing contractual arrangements (e.g., union contracts) or regulatory requirements (e.g., national labor laws).

8. The staff observes that not all contract terminations are exit activities within the scope of the Consensuses. The applicability of the Consensuses depends on the particular facts and circumstances surrounding the termination.

9. For employee relocation costs incurred relative to employees of a company acquired in a business combination accounted for under the purchase method, registrants are reminded to consider the requirements of EITF 95-3.

10. Where an acquirer intends, at the consummation date, to dispose of certain of an acquiree's long-lived assets, registrants are reminded to consider the requirements of APB 16, EITF Issue No. 87-11, and EITF Issue No. 90-6 in allocating the purchase price to and subsequently accounting for such assets held for disposal.

11. See APB 30, paragraph 13.

12. See APB 30, paragraph 20.

13. Registrants should refer to EITF Issue No. 96-9, Classification of Inventory Markdowns and Other Costs Associated with a Restructuring for additional comments as to income statement presentation. For example, the staff believes that inventory writedowns should be classified in the income statement as a component of cost of goods sold.

14. Registrants are reminded of the requirements in FASB Statement No. 38, paragraph 4(b) and SAB Topic 2-A (7). The staff believes that the allocation period should not extend beyond the minimum reasonable period necessary to gather the information that the registrant has arranged to obtain for purposes of the estimate, and in any event usually should not exceed one year.

15. EITF 94-3 requires that the effect of recognizing a liability for exit costs should be presented in income from continuing operations and not net of taxes. Refer to EITF 94-3 for additional guidance regarding the income statement presentation.

16. Examples of common components of exit costs and other types of restructuring charges which should be considered for separate disclosure include, but are not limited to, involuntary employee terminations and related costs, changes in valuation of current assets such as inventory writedowns, long term asset disposals, adjustments for warranties and product returns, leasehold termination payments, and other facility exit costs, among others.

17. See also disclosure requirements for inventory balances in Rule 5-02-6 of Regulation S-X.

18. See APB 17, paragraph 31, and SFAS 121, paragraph 6 and footnote 1.

19. See also APB Opinion No. 12, Omnibus Opinion - 1967, regarding disclosure requirements for depreciable assets.

20. See Rule 10-01(b)(6) of Regulation S-X.

21. See paragraph 32 of APB Opinion No. 20, Accounting Changes .

SEC Staff Accounting Bulletin: No. 101 – Revenue Recognition in Financial Statements

Securities and Exchange Commission
17 CFR Part 211
[Release No. SAB 101]
Staff Accounting Bulletin No. 101

Agency: Securities and Exchange Commission

Action: Publication of Staff Accounting Bulletin

Summary: This staff accounting bulletin summarizes certain of the staff's views in applying generally accepted accounting principles to revenue recognition in financial statements. The staff is providing this guidance due, in part, to the large number of revenue recognition issues that registrants encounter. For example, a March 1999 report entitled Fraudulent Financial Reporting: 1987-1997 An Analysis of U. S. Public Companies, sponsored by the Committee of Sponsoring Organizations (COSO) of the Treadway Commission, indicated that over half of financial reporting frauds in the study involved overstating revenue.

Date: December 3, 1999

For Further Information Contact: Richard Rodgers, Scott Taub, or Eric Jacobsen, Professional Accounting Fellows (202/942-4400) or Robert Bayless, Division of Corporation Finance (202/942-2960), Securities and Exchange Commission, 450 Fifth Street, NW, Washington, DC 20549; electronic addresses: RodgersR@sec.gov; TaubS@sec.gov; JacobsenE@sec.gov; BaylessR@sec.gov.

Supplementary Information: The statements in the staff accounting bulletins are not rules or interpretations of the Commission, nor are they published as bearing the Commission's official approval. They represent interpretations and practices followed by the Division of Corporation Finance and the Office of the Chief Accountant in administering the disclosure requirements of the Federal securities laws.

Jonathan G. Katz
Secretary
Date: December 3, 1999

Part 211 - (AMEND)

Accordingly, Part 211 of Title 17 of the Code of Federal Regulations is amended by adding Staff Accounting Bulletin No. 101 to the table found in Subpart B.

Staff Accounting Bulletin No. 101

The staff hereby adds new major Topic 13, "Revenue Recognition," and Topic 13-A, "Views on Selected Revenue Recognition Issues," to the Staff Accounting Bulletin Series. Topic 13-A provides the staff's views in applying generally accepted accounting principles to selected revenue recognition issues. In addition, the staff hereby revises Topic 8-A to conform to FASB Statement No. 13, Accounting for Leases .

Topic 13: Revenue Recognition

A. Selected Revenue Recognition Issues

1. Revenue Recognition - General

The accounting literature on revenue recognition includes both broad conceptual discussions as well as certain industry-specific guidance. Examples of existing literature on revenue recognition include Financial Accounting Standards Board (FASB) Statements of Financial Accounting Standards (SFAS) No. 13, Accounting for Leases, No. 45, Accounting for Franchise Fee Revenue, No. 48, Revenue Recognition When Right of Return Exists, No. 49, Accounting for Product Financing Arrangements, No. 50, Financial Reporting in the Record and Music Industry, No. 51, Financial Reporting by Cable Television Companies, and No. 66, Accounting for Sales of Real Estate ; Accounting Principles Board (APB) Opinion No. 10, Omnibus Opinion - 1966 ; Accounting Research Bulletin (ARB) Nos. 43 (Chapter 1a) and 45, Long-Term Construction-Type Contracts ; American Institute of Certified Public Accountants (AICPA) Statements of Position (SOP) No. 81-1, Accounting for Performance of Construction-Type and Certain Production-Type Contracts, and No. 97-2, Software Revenue Recognition ; Emerging Issues Task Force (EITF) Issue No. 88-18, Sales of Future Revenues, No. 91-9, Revenue and Expense Recognition for Freight Services in Process, No. 95-1, Revenue Recognition on Sales with a Guaranteed Minimum Resale Value, and No. 95-4, Revenue Recognition on Equipment Sold and Subsequently Repurchased Subject to an Operating Lease ; and FASB Statement of Financial Accounting Concepts (SFAC) No. 5, Recognition and Measurement in Financial Statements of Business Enterprises.[1] If a transaction is within the scope of specific authoritative literature that provides revenue recognition guidance, that literature should be applied. However, in the absence of authoritative literature addressing a specific arrangement or a specific industry, the staff will consider the existing authoritative accounting standards as well as the broad revenue recognition criteria specified in the FASB's conceptual framework that contain basic guidelines for revenue recognition.

Based on these guidelines, revenue should not be recognized until it is realized or realizable and earned.[2] SFAC No. 5, paragraph 83(b) states that "an entity's revenue-earning activities involve delivering or producing goods, rendering services, or other activities that constitute its ongoing major or central operations, and revenues are considered to have been earned when the entity has substantially accomplished what it must do to be entitled to the benefits represented by the revenues" [footnote reference omitted]. Paragraph 84(a) continues "the two conditions (being realized or realizable and being earned) are usually met by the time product or merchandise is delivered or services are rendered to customers, and revenues from manufacturing and selling activities and gains and losses from sales of other assets are commonly recognized at time of sale (usually meaning delivery)" [footnote reference omitted]. In addition, paragraph 84(d) states that "If services are rendered or rights to use assets extend continuously over time (for example, interest or rent), reliable measures based on contractual prices established in advance are commonly available, and revenues may be recognized as earned as time passes."

The staff believes that revenue generally is realized or realizable and earned when all of the following criteria are met:

- Persuasive evidence of an arrangement exists,[3]
- Delivery has occurred or services have been rendered,[4]
- The seller's price to the buyer is fixed or determinable,[5] and
- Collectibility is reasonably assured.[6]

2. Persuasive Evidence of an Arrangement

Question 1

Facts: Company A has product available to ship to customers prior to the end of its current fiscal quarter. Customer Beta places an order for the product, and Company A delivers the product prior to the end of its current fiscal quarter. Company A's normal and customary business practice for this class of customer is to enter into a written sales agreement that requires the signatures of the authorized representatives of the Company and its customer to be binding. Company A prepares a written sales agreement, and its authorized representative signs the agreement before the end of the quarter. However, Customer Beta does not sign the agreement because Customer Beta is awaiting the requisite approval by its legal department. Customer Beta's purchasing department has orally agreed to the sale and stated that it is highly likely that the contract will be approved the first week of Company A's next fiscal quarter.

Question: May Company A recognize the revenue in the current fiscal quarter for the sale of the product to Customer Beta when (1) the product is delivered by the end of its current fiscal quarter and (2) the final written sales agreement is executed by Customer Beta's authorized representative within a few days after the end of the current fiscal quarter?

Interpretive Response: No. Generally the staff believes that, in view of Company A's business practice of requiring a written sales agreement for this class of customer, persuasive evidence of an arrangement would require a final agreement that has been executed by the properly authorized personnel of the customer. In the staff's view, Customer Beta's execution of the sales agreement after the end of the quarter causes the transaction to be considered a transaction of the subsequent period.[7] Further, if an arrangement is subject to subsequent approval (e.g., by the management committee or board of directors) or execution of another agreement, revenue recognition would be inappropriate until that subsequent approval or agreement is complete.

Customary business practices and processes for documenting sales transactions vary among companies and industries. Business practices and processes may also vary within individual companies (e.g., based on the class of customer, nature of product or service, or other distinguishable factors). If a company does not have a standard or customary business practice of relying on written contracts to document a sales arrangement, it usually would be expected to have other forms of written or electronic evidence to document the transaction. For example, a company may not use written contracts but instead may rely on binding purchase orders from third parties or on-line authorizations that include the terms of the sale and that are binding on the customer. In that situation, that documentation could represent persuasive evidence of an arrangement.

The staff is aware that sometimes a customer and seller enter into "side" agreements to a master contract that effectively amend the master contract. Registrants should ensure that appropriate policies, procedures, and internal controls exist and are properly documented so as to provide reasonable assurances that sales transactions, including those affected by side agreements, are properly accounted for in accordance with generally accepted accounting principles and to ensure compliance with Section 13 of the Securities Exchange Act of 1934 (i.e., the Foreign Corrupt Practices Act). Side agreements could include cancellation, termination, or other provisions that affect revenue recognition. The existence of a subsequently executed side agreement may be an indicator that the original agreement was not final and revenue recognition was not appropriate.

Question 2

Facts: Company Z enters into an arrangement with Customer A to deliver Company Z's products to Customer A on a consignment basis. Pursuant to the terms of the arrangement, Customer A is a consignee, and title to the products does not pass from Company Z to Customer A until Customer A consumes the products in its operations. Company Z delivers product to Customer A under the terms of their arrangement.

Question: May Company Z recognize revenue upon delivery of its product to Customer A?

Interpretive Response: No. Products delivered to a consignee pursuant to a consignment arrangement are not sales and do not qualify for revenue recognition until a sale occurs. The staff believes that revenue recognition is not appropriate because the seller retains the risks and rewards of ownership of the product and title usually does not pass to the consignee.

Other situations may exist where title to delivered products passes to a buyer, but the substance of the transaction is that of a consignment or a financing. Such arrangements require a careful analysis of the facts and circumstances of the transaction, as well as an understanding of the rights and obligations of the parties, and the seller's customary business practices in such arrangements. The staff believes that the presence of one or more of the following characteristics in a transaction precludes revenue recognition even if title to the product has passed to the buyer:

1. The buyer has the right to return the product and:

   a) the buyer does not pay the seller at the time of sale, and the buyer is not obligated to pay the seller at a specified date or dates.[8]

   b) the buyer does not pay the seller at the time of sale but rather is obligated to pay at a specified date or dates, and the buyer's obligation to pay is contractually or implicitly excused until the buyer resells the product or subsequently consumes or uses the product,[9]

   c) the buyer's obligation to the seller would be changed (e.g., the seller would forgive the obligation or grant a refund) in the event of theft or physical destruction or damage of the product,[10]

   d) the buyer acquiring the product for resale does not have economic substance apart from that provided by the seller,[11] or

   e) the seller has significant obligations for future performance to directly bring about resale of the product by the buyer.[12]

2. The seller is required to repurchase the product (or a substantially identical product or processed goods of which the product is a component) at specified prices that are not subject to change except for fluctuations due to finance and holding costs,[13] and the amounts to be paid by the seller will be adjusted, as necessary, to cover substantially all fluctuations in costs incurred by the buyer in purchasing and holding the product (including interest).[14] The staff believes that indicators of the latter condition include:

   a) the seller provides interest-free or significantly below market financing to the buyer beyond the seller's customary sales terms and until the products are resold,

   b) the seller pays interest costs on behalf of the buyer under a third-party financing arrangement, or

   c) the seller has a practice of refunding (or intends to refund) a portion of the original sales price representative of interest expense for the period from when the buyer paid the seller until the buyer resells the product.

3. The transaction possesses the characteristics set forth in EITF Issue No. 95-1, Revenue Recognition on Sales with a Guaranteed Minimum Resale Value, and does not qualify for sales-type lease accounting.

4. The product is delivered for demonstration purposes.[15]

This list is not meant to be a checklist of all characteristics of a consignment or a financing arrangement, and other characteristics may exist. Accordingly, the staff believes that judgment is necessary in assessing whether the substance of a transaction is a consignment, a financing, or other arrangement for which revenue recognition is not appropriate. If title to the goods has passed but the substance of the arrangement is not a sale, the consigned inventory should be reported separately from other inventory in the consignor's financial statements as "inventory consigned to others" or another appropriate caption.

3. Delivery and Performance

Question 3

Facts: Company A receives purchase orders for products it manufactures. At the end of its fiscal quarters, customers may not yet be ready to take delivery of the products for various reasons. These reasons may include, but are not limited to, a lack of available space for inventory, having more than sufficient inventory in their distribution channel, or delays in customers' production schedules.

Questions: May Company A recognize revenue for the sale of its products once it has completed manufacturing if it segregates the inventory of the products in its own warehouse from its own products?

May Company A recognize revenue for the sale if it ships the products to a third-party warehouse but (1) Company A retains title to the product and (2) payment by the customer is dependent upon ultimate delivery to a customer-specified site?

Interpretive Response: Generally, no. The staff believes that delivery generally is not considered to have occurred unless the customer has taken title and assumed the risks and rewards of ownership of the products specified in the customer's purchase order or sales agreement. Typically this occurs when a product is delivered to the customer's delivery site (if the terms of the sale are "FOB destination") or when a product is shipped to the customer (if the terms are "FOB shipping point").

The Commission has set forth criteria to be met in order to recognize revenue when delivery has not occurred.[16] These include:

1. The risks of ownership must have passed to the buyer;

2. The customer must have made a fixed commitment to purchase the goods, preferably in written documentation;

3. The buyer, not the seller, must request that the transaction be on a bill and hold basis.[17] The buyer must have a substantial business purpose for ordering the goods on a bill and hold basis;

4. There must be a fixed schedule for delivery of the goods. The date for delivery must be reasonable and must be consistent with the buyer's business purpose (e.g., storage periods are customary in the industry);

5. The seller must not have retained any specific performance obligations such that the earning process is not complete;

6. The ordered goods must have been segregated from the seller's inventory and not be subject to being used to fill other orders; and

7. The equipment [product] must be complete and ready for shipment.

The above listed conditions are the important conceptual criteria which should be used in evaluating any purported bill and hold sale. This listing is not intended as a checklist. In some circumstances, a transaction may meet all factors listed above but not meet the requirements for revenue recognition. The Commission also has noted that in applying the above criteria to a purported bill and hold sale, the individuals responsible for the preparation and filing of financial statements also should consider the following factors:[18]

1. The date by which the seller expects payment, and whether the seller has modified its normal billing and credit terms for this buyer;[19]

2. The seller's past experiences with and pattern of bill and hold transactions;

3. Whether the buyer has the expected risk of loss in the event of a decline in the market value of goods;

4. Whether the seller's custodial risks are insurable and insured;

5. Whether extended procedures are necessary in order to assure that there are no exceptions to the buyer's commitment to accept and pay for the goods sold (i.e., that the business reasons for the bill and hold have not introduced a contingency to the buyer's commitment).

Delivery generally is not considered to have occurred unless the product has been delivered to the customer's place of business or another site specified by the customer. If the customer specifies an intermediate site but a substantial portion of the sales price is not payable until delivery is made to a final site, then revenue should not be recognized until final delivery has occurred.[20]

After delivery of a product or performance of a service, if uncertainty exists about customer acceptance, revenue should not be recognized until acceptance occurs.[21] Customer acceptance provisions may be included in a contract, among other reasons, to enforce a customer's rights to (1) test the delivered product, (2) require the seller to perform additional services subsequent to delivery of an initial product or performance of an initial service (e.g., a seller is required to install or activate delivered equipment), or (3) identify other work necessary to be done before accepting the product. The staff presumes that such contractual customer acceptance provisions are substantive, bargained-for terms of an arrangement. Accordingly, when such contractual customer acceptance provisions exist, the staff generally believes that the seller should not recognize revenue until customer acceptance occurs or the acceptance provisions lapse.

A seller should substantially complete or fulfill the terms specified in the arrangement in order for delivery or performance to have occurred.[22] When applying the substantially complete notion, the staff believes that only inconsequential or perfunctory actions may remain incomplete such that the failure to complete the actions would not result in the customer receiving a refund or rejecting the delivered products or services performed to date. In addition, the seller should have a demonstrated history of completing the remaining tasks in a timely manner and reliably estimating the remaining costs. If revenue is recognized upon substantial completion of the arrangement, all remaining costs of performance or delivery should be accrued.

If an arrangement (i.e., outside the scope of SOP 81-1) requires the delivery or performance of multiple deliverables, or "elements," the delivery of an individual element is considered not to have occurred if there are undelivered elements that are essential to the functionality of the delivered element because the customer does not have the full use of the delivered element.[23]

In licensing and similar arrangements (e.g., licenses of motion pictures, software, technology, and other intangibles), the staff believes that delivery does not occur for revenue recognition purposes until the license term begins.[24] Accordingly, if a licensed product or technology is physically delivered to the customer, but the license term has not yet begun, revenue should not be recognized prior to inception of the license term. Upon inception of the license term, revenue should be recognized in a manner consistent with the nature of the transaction and the earnings process.

Question 4

Facts: Company R is a retailer that offers "layaway" sales to its customers. Company R retains the merchandise, sets it aside in its inventory, and collects a cash deposit from the customer. Although Company R may set a time period within which the customer must finalize the purchase, Company R does not require the customer to enter into an installment note or other fixed payment commitment or agreement when the initial deposit is received. The merchandise generally is not released to the customer until the customer pays the full purchase price. In the event that the customer fails to pay the remaining purchase price, the customer forfeits its cash deposit. In the event the merchandise is lost, damaged, or destroyed, Company R either must refund the cash deposit to the customer or provide replacement merchandise.

Question: In the staff's view, when may Company R recognize revenue for merchandise sold under its layaway program?

Interpretive Response: Provided that the other criteria for revenue recognition are met, the staff believes that Company R should recognize revenue from sales made under its layaway program upon delivery of the merchandise to the customer. Until then, the amount of cash received should be recognized as a liability entitled such as "deposits received from customers for layaway sales" or a similarly descriptive caption. Because Company R retains the risks of ownership of the merchandise, receives only a deposit from the customer, and does not have an enforceable right to the remainder of the purchase price, the staff would object to Company R recognizing any revenue upon receipt of the cash deposit. This is consistent with item two (2) in the Commission's criteria for bill-and-hold transactions which states that "the customer must have made a fixed commitment to purchase the goods."

Question 5

Facts: Registrants may negotiate arrangements pursuant to which they may receive nonrefundable fees upon entering into arrangements or on certain specified dates. The fees may ostensibly be received for conveyance of a license or other intangible right or for delivery of particular products or services. Various business factors may influence how the registrant and customer structure the payment terms. For example, in exchange for a greater up-front fee for an intangible right, the registrant may be willing to receive lower unit prices for related products to be delivered in the future. In some circumstances, the right, product, or service conveyed in conjunction with the nonrefundable fee has no utility to the purchaser separate and independent of the registrant's performance of the other elements of the arrangement. Therefore, in the absence of the registrant's continuing involvement under the arrangement, the customer would not have paid the fee. Examples of this type of arrangement include the following:

- A registrant sells a lifetime membership in a health club. After paying a nonrefundable "initiation fee," the customer is permitted to use the health club indefinitely, so long as the customer also pays an additional usage fee each month. The monthly usage fees collected from all customers are adequate to cover the operating costs of the health club.

- A registrant in the biotechnology industry agrees to provide research and development activities for a customer for a specified term. The customer needs to use certain technology owned by the registrant for use in the research and development activities. The technology is not sold or licensed separately without the research and development activities. Under the terms of the arrangement, the customer is required to pay a nonrefundable "technology access fee" in addition to periodic payments for research and development activities over the term of the contract.

- A registrant requires a customer to pay a nonrefundable "activation fee" when entering into an arrangement to provide telecommunications services. The terms of the arrangement require the customer to pay a monthly usage fee that is adequate to recover the registrant's operating costs. The costs incurred to activate the telecommunications service are nominal.

Question: When should the revenue relating to nonrefundable, up-front fees in these types of arrangements be recognized?

Interpretive Response: The staff believes that registrants should consider the specific facts and circumstances to determine the appropriate accounting for nonrefundable, up-front fees. Unless the up-front fee is in exchange for products delivered or services performed that represent the culmination of a separate earnings process,[25] the deferral of revenue is appropriate.

In the situations described above, the staff does not view the activities completed by the registrants (i.e., selling the membership, signing the contract, or enrolling the customer or activating telecommunications services) as discrete earnings events.[26] The terms, conditions, and amounts of these fees typically are negotiated in conjunction with the pricing of all the elements of the arrangement, and the customer would ascribe a significantly lower, and perhaps no, value to elements ostensibly associated with the up-front fee in the absence of the registrant's performance of other contract elements. The fact that the registrants do not sell the initial rights, products, or services separately (i.e., without the registrants' continuing involvement) supports the staff's view. The staff believes that the customers are purchasing the ongoing rights, products, or services being provided through the registrants' continuing involvement. Further, the staff believes that the earnings process is completed by performing under the terms of the arrangements, not simply by originating a revenue-generating arrangement.

Supply or service transactions may involve the charge of a nonrefundable initial fee with subsequent periodic payments for future products or services. The initial fees may, in substance, be wholly or partly an advance payment for future products or services. In the examples above, the on-going rights or services being provided or products being delivered are essential to the customers receiving the expected benefit of the up-front payment. Therefore, the up-front fee and the continuing performance obligation related to the services to be provided or products to be delivered are assessed as an integrated package. In such circumstances, the staff believes that up-front fees, even if nonrefundable, are earned as the products and/or services are delivered and/or performed over the term of the arrangement or the expected period of performance[27] and generally should be deferred and recognized systematically over the periods that the fees are earned.[28]

Question 6

Facts: Company A provides its customers with activity tracking or similar services (e.g., tracking of property tax payment activity, sending delinquency letters on overdue accounts, etc.) for a ten-year period. Company A requires customers to prepay for all the services for the term specified in the arrangement. The on-going services to be provided are generally automated after the initial customer set-up. At the outset of the arrangement, Company A performs set-up procedures to facilitate delivery of its on-going services to the customers.[29] Such procedures consist primarily of establishing the necessary records and files in Company A's pre-existing computer systems in order to provide the services. Once the initial customer set-up activities are complete, Company A provides its services in accordance with the arrangement. Company A is not required to refund any portion of the fee if the customer terminates the services or does not utilize all of the services to which it is entitled. However, Company A is required to provide a refund if Company A terminates the arrangement early. Assume Company A's activities are not within the scope of SFAS No. 91.

Question: When should Company A recognize the service revenue?

Interpretive Response: The staff believes that, provided all other revenue recognition criteria are met, service revenue should be recognized on a straight-line basis, unless evidence suggests that the revenue is earned or obligations are fulfilled in a different pattern, over the contractual term of the arrangement or the expected period during which those specified services will be performed,[30] whichever is longer. In this case, the customer contracted for the on-going activity tracking service, not for the set-up activities. The staff notes that the customer could not, and would not, separately purchase the set-up services without the on-going services. The services specified in the arrangement are performed continuously over the contractual term of the arrangement (and any subsequent renewals). Therefore, the staff believes that Company A should recognize revenue on a straight-line basis, unless evidence suggests that the revenue is earned or obligations are fulfilled in a different pattern, over the contractual term of the arrangement or the expected period during which those specified services will be performed, whichever is longer.

In this situation, the staff would object to Company A recognizing revenue in proportion to the costs incurred because the set-up costs incurred bear no direct relationship to the performance of services specified in the arrangement. The staff also believes that it is inappropriate to recognize the entire amount of the prepayment as revenue at the outset of the arrangement by accruing the remaining costs because the services required by the contract have not been performed.

4. Fixed or Determinable Sales Price

A company's contracts may include customer cancellation or termination clauses. Cancellation or termination provisions may be indicative of a demonstration period or an otherwise incomplete transaction. Examples of transactions that financial management and auditors should be aware of and where such provisions may exist include "side" agreements and significant transactions with unusual terms and conditions. These contractual provisions raise questions as to whether the sales price is fixed or determinable. The sales price in arrangements that are cancelable by the customer are neither fixed nor determinable until the cancellation privileges lapse.[31] If the cancellation privileges expire ratably over a stated contractual term, the sales price is considered to become determinable ratably over the stated term.[32] Short-term rights of return, such as thirty-day money-back guarantees, and other customary rights to return products are not considered to be cancellation privileges, but should be accounted for in accordance with SFAS No. 48.[33]

Question 7

Facts: Company M is a discount retailer. It generates revenue from annual membership fees it charges customers to shop at its stores and from the sale of products at a discount price to those customers. The membership arrangements with retail customers require the customer to pay the entire membership fee (e.g., $35) at the outset of the arrangement. However, the customer has the unilateral right to cancel the arrangement at any time during its term and receive a full refund of the initial fee. Based on historical data collected over time for a large number of homogeneous transactions, Company M estimates that approximately 40% of the customers will request a refund before the end of the membership contract term. Company M's data for the past five years indicates that significant variations between actual and estimated cancellations have not occurred, and Company M does not expect significant variations to occur in the foreseeable future.

Question: May Company M recognize in earnings the revenue for the membership fees and accrue the costs to provide membership services at the outset of the arrangement?

Interpretive Response: No. In the staff's view, it would be inappropriate for Company M to recognize the membership fees as earned revenue upon billing or receipt of the initial fee with a corresponding accrual for estimated costs to provide the membership services. This conclusion is based on Company M's remaining and unfulfilled contractual obligation to perform services (i.e., make available and offer products for sale at a discounted price) throughout the membership period. Therefore, the earnings process, irrespective of whether a cancellation clause exists, is not complete.

In addition, the ability of the member to receive a full refund of the membership fee up to the last day of the membership term raises an uncertainty as to whether the fee is fixed or determinable at any point before the end of the term. Generally, the staff believes that a sales price is not fixed or determinable when a customer has the unilateral right to terminate or cancel the contract and receive a cash refund. A sales price or fee that is variable until the occurrence of future events (other than product returns that are within the scope of SFAS No. 48) generally is not fixed or determinable until the future event occurs. The revenue from such transactions should not be recognized in earnings until the sales price or fee becomes fixed or determinable. Moreover, revenue should not be recognized in earnings by assessing the probability that significant, but unfulfilled, terms of a contract will be fulfilled at some point in the future. Accordingly, the revenue from such transactions should not be recognized in earnings prior to the refund privileges expiring. The amounts received from customers or subscribers (i.e., the $35 fee mentioned above) should be credited to a monetary liability account such as "customers' refundable fees."

The staff believes that if a customer has the unilateral right to receive both (1) the seller's substantial performance under an arrangement (e.g., providing services or delivering product) and (2) a cash refund of prepaid fees, then the prepaid fees should be accounted for as a monetary liability in accordance with SFAS No. 125, Accounting for Transfers and Servicing of Financial Assets and Extinguishments of Liabilities, paragraph 16. SFAS No. 125 provides that liabilities may be derecognized only if (1) the debtor pays the creditor and is relieved of its obligation for the liability (paying the creditor includes delivery of cash, other financial assets, goods, or services or reacquisition by the debtor of its outstanding debt securities) or (2) the debtor is legally released from being the primary obligor under the liability.[34] If a customer has the unilateral right to receive both (1) the seller's substantial performance under the arrangement and (2) a cash refund of prepaid fees, then the refund obligation is not relieved upon performance of the service or delivery of the products. Rather, the seller's refund obligation is relieved only upon refunding the cash or expiration of the refund privilege.

Some have argued that there may be a limited exception to the general rule that revenue from membership or other service transaction fees should not be recognized in earnings prior to the refund privileges expiring. Despite the fact that SFAS No. 48 expressly does not apply to the accounting for service revenue if part or all of the service fee is refundable under cancellation privileges granted to the buyer,[35] they believe that in certain circumstances a potential refund of a membership fee may be seen as being similar to a right of return of products under SFAS No. 48. They argue that revenue from membership fees, net of estimated refunds, may be recognized ratably over the period the services are performed whenever pertinent conditions of SFAS No. 48 are met, namely, there is a large population of transactions that grant customers the same unilateral termination or cancellation rights and reasonable estimates can be made of how many customers likely will exercise those rights.

The staff believes that, because service arrangements are specifically excluded from the scope of SFAS No. 48, the most direct authoritative literature to be applied to the extinguishment of obligations under such contracts is SFAS No. 125. As noted above, because the refund privilege extends to the end of the contract term irrespective of the amount of the service performed, SFAS No. 125 indicates that the liability would not be extinguished (and therefore no revenue would be recognized in earnings) until the cancellation or termination and related refund privileges expire. Nonetheless, the staff recognizes that over the years the accounting for membership refunds evolved based on analogy to SFAS No. 48 and that practice did not change when SFAS No. 125 became effective. Reasonable people held, and continue to hold, different views about the application of the accounting literature. For the staff to prohibit such accounting in this SAB may result in significant change in practice that, in these particular circumstances, may be more appropriately addressed in a formal rulemaking or standards-setting project.

Pending further action in this area by the FASB, the staff will not object to the recognition of refundable membership fees, net of estimated refunds, as earned revenue over the membership term in the limited circumstances where all of the following criteria have been met:[36]

- The estimates of terminations or cancellations and refunded revenues are being made for a large pool of homogeneous items (e.g., membership or other service transactions with the same characteristics such as terms, periods, class of customers, nature of service, etc.).

- Reliable estimates of the expected refunds can be made on a timely basis.[37] Either of the following two items would be considered indicative of an inability to make reliable estimates: (1) recurring, significant differences between actual experience and estimated cancellation or termination rates (e.g., an actual cancellation rate of 40% versus an estimated rate of 25%) even if the impact of the difference on the amount of estimated refunds is not material to the consolidated financial statements[38] or (2) recurring variances between the actual and estimated amount of refunds that are material to either revenue or net income in quarterly or annual financial statements. In addition, the staff believes that an estimate, for purposes of meeting this criterion, would not be reliable unless it is remote[39] that material adjustments (both individually and in the aggregate) to previously recognized revenue would be required. The staff presumes that reliable estimates cannot be made if the customer's termination or cancellation and refund privileges exceed one year.

- There is a sufficient company-specific historical basis upon which to estimate the refunds,[40] and the company believes that such historical experience is predictive of future events. In assessing these items, the staff believes that estimates of future refunds should take into consideration, among other things, such factors as historical experience by service type and class of customer, changing trends in historical experience and the basis thereof (e.g., economic conditions), the impact or introduction of competing services or products, and changes in the customer's "accessibility" to the refund (i.e., how easy it is for customers to obtain the refund).

- The amount of the membership fee specified in the agreement at the outset of the arrangement is fixed, other than the customer's right to request a refund.

If Company M does not meet all of the foregoing criteria, the staff believes that Company M should not recognize in earnings any revenue for the membership fee until the cancellation privileges and refund rights expire.

If revenue is recognized in earnings over the membership period pursuant to the above criteria, the initial amounts received from customer or subscribers (i.e., the $35 fee mentioned above) should be allocated to two liability accounts. The amount of the fee representing estimated refunds should be credited to a monetary liability account, such as "customers' refundable fees," and the remaining amount of the fee representing unearned revenue should be credited to a nonmonetary liability account, such as "unearned revenues." For each income statement presented, registrants should disclose in the footnotes to the financial statements the amounts of (1) the unearned revenue and (2) refund obligations as of the beginning of each period, the amount of cash received from customers, the amount of revenue recognized in earnings, the amount of refunds paid, other adjustments (with an explanation thereof), and the ending balance of (1) unearned revenue and (2) refund obligations.

If revenue is recognized in earnings over the membership period pursuant to the above criteria, the staff believes that adjustments for changes in estimated refunds should be recorded using a retrospective approach whereby the unearned revenue and refund obligations are remeasured and adjusted at each balance sheet date with the offset being recorded as earned revenue.

Companies offering memberships often distribute membership packets describing and discussing the terms, conditions, and benefits of membership. Packets may include vouchers, for example, that provide new members with discounts or other benefits. The costs associated with the vouchers should be expensed when distributed. Advertising costs to solicit members should be accounted for in accordance with SOP 93-7, Reporting on Advertising Costs . Incremental direct costs incurred in connection with enrolling customers (e.g., commissions paid to agents) should be accounted for as follows: (1) if revenue is deferred until the cancellation or termination privileges expire, incremental direct costs should be either (a) charged to expense when incurred if the costs are not refundable to the company in the event the customer obtains a refund of the membership fee, or (b) if the costs are refundable to the company in the event the customer obtains a refund of the membership fee, recorded as an asset until the earlier of termination or cancellation or refund; or (2) if revenue, net of estimated refunds, is recognized in earnings over the membership period, a like percentage of incremental direct costs should be deferred and recognized in earnings in the same pattern as revenue is recognized, and the remaining portion should be either (a) charged to expense when incurred if the costs are not refundable to the company in the event the customer obtains a refund of the membership fee, or (b) if the costs are refundable to the company in the event the customer obtains a refund of the membership fee, recorded as an asset until the refund occurs.[41] All costs other than incremental direct costs (e.g., indirect costs) should be expensed as incurred.

Question 8

Facts: Company A owns and leases retail space to retailers. Company A (lessor) renews a lease with a customer (lessee) that is classified as an operating lease. The lease term is one year and provides that the lease payments are $1.2 million, payable in equal monthly installments on the first day of each month, plus one percent of the lessee's net sales in excess of $25 million if the net sales exceed $25 million during the lease term (i.e., contingent rental). The lessee has historically experienced annual net sales in excess of $25 million in the particular space being leased, and it is probable that the lessee will generate in excess of $25 million net sales during the term of the lease.

Question: In the staff's view, should the lessor recognize any rental income attributable to the one percent of the lessee's net sales exceeding $25 million before the lessee actually achieves the $25 million net sales threshold?

Interpretive Response: No. The staff believes that contingent rental income "accrues" (i.e., it should be recognized as revenue) when the changes in the factor(s) on which the contingent lease payments is (are) based actually occur.[42]

SFAS No. 13, Accounting for Leases, paragraph 19(b) states that lessors should account for operating leases as follows: "Rent shall be reported in income over the lease term as it becomes receivable according to the provisions of the lease. However, if the rentals vary from a straight-line basis, the income shall be recognized on a straight-line basis unless another systematic and rational basis is more representative of the time pattern in which use benefit from the leased property is diminished, in which case that basis shall be used."

SFAS No. 29, Determining Contingent Rentals, amended SFAS No. 13 and clarifies that "lease payments that depend on a factor that does not exist or is not measurable at the inception of the lease, such as future sales volume, would be contingent rentals in their entirety and, accordingly, would be excluded from minimum lease payments and included in the determination of income as they accrue." [Summary] Paragraph 17 of SFAS No. 29 provides the following example of determining contingent rentals:

> A lease agreement for retail store space could stipulate a monthly base rental of $200 and a monthly supplemental rental of one-fourth of one percent of monthly sales volume during the lease term. Even if the lease agreement is a renewal for store space that had averaged monthly sales of $25,000 for the past 2 years, minimum lease payments would include only the $200 monthly base rental; the supplemental rental is a contingent rental that is excluded from minimum lease payments. The future sales for the lease term do not exist at the inception of the lease, and future rentals would be limited to $200 per month if the store were subsequently closed and no sales were made thereafter.

FASB Technical Bulletin (FTB) 85-3, Accounting for Operating Leases with Scheduled Rent Increases, addresses whether it is appropriate for lessors in operating leases to recognize scheduled rent increases on a basis other than as required in SFAS No. 13, paragraph 19(b). Paragraph 2 of FTB 85-3 states "using factors such as the time value of money, anticipated inflation, or expected future revenues [emphasis added] to allocate scheduled rent increases is inappropriate because these factors do not relate to the time pattern of the physical usage of the leased property. However, such factors may affect the periodic reported rental income or expense if the lease agreement involves contingent rentals, which are excluded from minimum lease payments and accounted for separately under Statement 13, as amended by Statement 29." In developing the basis for why scheduled rent increases should be recognized on a straight-line basis, the FASB distinguishes the accounting for scheduled rent increases from contingent rentals. Paragraph 13 states "There is an important substantive difference between lease rentals that are contingent upon some specified future event and scheduled rent increases that are unaffected by future events; the accounting under Statement 13 reflects that difference. If the lessor and lessee eliminate the risk of variable payments by agreeing to scheduled rent increases, the accounting should reflect those different circumstances."

The example provided in SFAS No. 29 implies that contingent rental income in leases classified as sales-type or direct-financing leases becomes "accruable" when the changes in the factors on which the contingent lease payments are based actually occur. FTB 85-3 indicates that contingent rental income in operating leases should not be recognized in a manner consistent with scheduled rent increases (i.e., on a straight-line basis over the lease term or another systematic and rational allocation basis if it is more representative of the time pattern in which the leased property is physically employed) because the risk of variable payments inherent in contingent rentals is substantively different than scheduled rent increases. The staff believes that the reasoning in FTB 85-3 supports the conclusion that the risks inherent in variable payments associated with contingent rentals should be reflected in financial statements on a basis different than rental payments that adjust on a scheduled basis and, therefore, operating lease income associated with contingent rents would not be recognized as time passes or as the leased property is physically employed. Furthermore, prior to the lessee's achievement of the target upon which contingent rentals are based, the lessor has no legal claims on the contingent amounts. Consequently, the staff believes that it is inappropriate to anticipate changes in the factors on which contingent rental income in operating leases is based and recognize rental income prior to the resolution of the lease contingencies.

Because Company A's contingent rental income is based upon whether the customer achieves net sales of $25 million, the contingent rentals, which may not materialize, should not be recognized until the customer's net sales actually exceed $25 million. Once the $25 million threshold is met, Company A would recognize the contingent rental income as it becomes accruable, in this case, as the customer recognizes net sales. The staff does not believe that it is appropriate to recognize revenue based upon the probability of a factor being achieved. The contingent revenue should be recorded in the period in which the contingency is resolved.

Question 9

Facts: Paragraph 8 of SFAS No. 48 lists a number of factors that may impair the ability to make a reasonable estimate of product returns in sales transactions when a right of return exists.[43] The paragraph concludes by stating "other factors may preclude a reasonable estimate."

Question: What "other factors," in addition to those listed in paragraph 8 of SFAS No. 48, has the staff identified that may preclude a registrant from making a reasonable and reliable estimate of product returns?

Interpretive Response: The staff believes that the following additional factors, among others, may affect or preclude the ability to make reasonable and reliable estimates of product returns: (1) significant increases in or excess levels of inventory in a distribution channel (sometimes referred to as "channel stuffing"), (2) lack of "visibility" into or the inability to determine or observe the levels of inventory in a distribution channel and the current level of sales to end users, (3) expected introductions of new products that may result in the technological obsolescence of and larger than expected returns of current products, (4) the significance of a particular distributor to the registrant's (or a reporting segment's) business, sales and marketing, (5) the newness of a product, (6) the introduction of competitors' products with superior technology or greater expected market acceptance, and other factors that affect market demand and changing trends in that demand for the registrant's products. Registrants and their auditors should carefully analyze all factors, including trends in historical data, that may affect registrants' ability to make reasonable and reliable estimates of product returns.

The staff reminds registrants that if a transaction fails to meet all of the conditions of paragraphs 6 and 8 in SFAS No. 48, no revenue may be recognized until those conditions are subsequently met or the return privilege has substantially expired, whichever occurs first.[44] Simply deferring recognition of the gross margin on the transaction is not appropriate.

5. Income Statement Presentation

Question 10

Facts: Company A operates an internet site from which it will sell Company T's products. Customers place their orders for the product by making a product selection directly from the internet site and providing a credit card number for the payment. Company A receives the order and authorization from the credit card company, and passes the order on to Company T. Company T ships the product directly to the customer. Company A does not take title to the product and has no risk of loss or other responsibility for the product. Company T is responsible for all product returns, defects, and disputed credit card charges. The product is typically sold for $175 of which Company A receives $25. In the event a credit card transaction is rejected, Company A loses its margin on the sale (i.e., the $25).

Question: In the staff's view, should Company A report revenue on a gross basis as $175 along with costs of sales of $150 or on a net basis as $25, similar to a commission?

Interpretive Response: Company A should report the revenue from the product on a net basis. In assessing whether revenue should be reported gross with separate display of cost of sales to arrive at gross profit or on a net basis, the staff considers whether the registrant:

1. acts as principal in the transaction,
2. takes title to the products,
3. has risks and rewards of ownership, such as the risk of loss for collection, delivery, or returns, and
4. acts as an agent or broker (including performing services, in substance, as an agent or broker) with compensation on a commission or fee basis.[45]

If the company performs as an agent or broker without assuming the risks and rewards of ownership of the goods, sales should be reported on a net basis.

B. Disclosures

Question 1

Question: What disclosures are required with respect to the recognition of revenue?

Interpretive Response: A registrant should disclose its accounting policy for the recognition of revenue pursuant to APB Opinion No. 22, Disclosure of Accounting Policies . Paragraph 12 thereof states that "the disclosure should encompass important judgments as to appropriateness of principles relating to recognition of revenue...." Because revenue recognition generally involves some level of judgment, the staff believes that a registrant should always disclose its revenue recognition policy. If a company has different policies for different types of revenue transactions, including barter sales, the policy for each material type of transaction should be disclosed. If sales transactions have multiple elements, such as a product and service, the accounting policy should clearly state the accounting policy for each element as well as how multiple elements are determined and valued. In addition, the staff believes that changes in estimated returns recognized in accordance with SFAS No. 48 should be disclosed, if material (e.g., a change in estimate from two percent of sales to one percent of sales).

Regulation S-X requires that revenue from the sales of products, services, and other products each be separately disclosed on the face of the income statement.[46] The staff believes that costs relating to each type of revenue similarly should be reported separately on the face of the income statement.

Management's Discussion and Analysis (MD&A) requires a discussion of liquidity, capital resources, results of operations and other information necessary to an understanding of a registrant's financial condition, changes in financial condition and results of operations.[47] This includes unusual or infrequent transactions, known trends or uncertainties that have had, or might reasonably be expected to have, a favorable or unfavorable material effect on revenue, operating income or net income and the relationship between revenue and the costs of the revenue. Changes in revenue should not be evaluated solely in terms of volume and price changes, but should also include an analysis of the reasons and factors contributing to the increase or decrease. The Commission stated in Financial Reporting Release (FRR) 36 that MD&A should "give investors an opportunity to look at the registrant through the eyes of management by providing a historical and prospective analysis of the registrant's financial condition and results of operations, with a particular emphasis on the registrant's prospects for the future."[48] Examples of such revenue transactions or events that the staff has asked to be disclosed and discussed in accordance with FRR 36 are:

- Shipments of product at the end of a reporting period that significantly reduce customer backlog and that reasonably might be expected to result in lower shipments and revenue in the next period.

- Granting of extended payment terms that will result in a longer collection period for accounts receivable (regardless of whether revenue has been recognized) and slower cash inflows from operations, and the effect on liquidity and capital resources. (The fair value of trade receivables should be disclosed in the footnotes to the financial statements when the fair value does not approximate the carrying amount.)[49]

- Changing trends in shipments into, and sales from, a sales channel or separate class of customer that could be expected to have a significant effect on future sales or sales returns.

- An increasing trend toward sales to a different class of customer, such as a reseller distribution channel that has a lower gross profit margin than existing sales that are principally made to end users. Also, increasing service revenue that has a higher profit margin than product sales.

- Seasonal trends or variations in sales.

- A gain or loss from the sale of an asset(s).[50]

Question 2

Question: Will the staff expect retroactive changes by registrants to comply with the accounting described in this bulletin?

Interpretive Response: All registrants are expected to apply the accounting and disclosures described in this bulletin. The staff, however, will not object if registrants that have not applied this accounting do not restate prior financial statements provided they report a change in accounting principle in accordance with APB Opinion No. 20, Accounting Changes, no later than the first fiscal quarter of the fiscal year beginning after December 15, 1999. In periods subsequent to transition, registrants should disclose the amount of revenue (if material to income before income taxes) recognized in those periods that was included in the cumulative effect adjustment. If a registrant files financial statements with the Commission before applying the guidance in this bulletin, disclosures similar to those described in Staff Accounting Bulletin Topic 11-M, Disclosure of the Impact that Recently Issued Accounting Standards Will Have on the Financial Statements of a Registrant When Adopted in a Future Period, should be provided. With regard to question 10 of Topic 13-A and Topic 8-A regarding income statement presentation, the staff would normally expect retroactive application to all periods presented unless the effect of applying the guidance herein is immaterial.

However, if registrants have not previously complied with generally accepted accounting principles, for example, by recording revenue for products prior to delivery that did not comply with the applicable bill-and-hold guidance, those registrants should apply the guidance in APB Opinion No. 20 for the correction of an error.[51] In addition, registrants should be aware that the Commission may take enforcement action where a registrant in prior financial statements has violated the antifraud or disclosure provisions of the securities laws with respect to revenue recognition.

Topic 8: Retail Companies

A. Sales of Leased or Licensed Departments

Facts: Department stores and other retailers customarily include the sales of leased or licensed departments in the amount reported as "total revenues."

Question: Does the staff have any objection to this practice?

Interpretive Response: In November 1975 the staff issued staff accounting bulletin number 1 that addressed this issue. In that bulletin the staff did not object to retailers presenting sales of leased or licensed departments in the amount reported as "total revenues" because of industry practice. Subsequently, in November 1976 the FASB issued SFAS No. 13. In June 1995, the AICPA staff amended its Technical Practice Aid (TPA) section 5100.16, Rental Revenue Based on Percentage of Sales, based upon an interpretation of SFAS No. 13 that leases of departments within a retail establishment are leases of tangible assets within the scope of SFAS No. 13.[52] Consistent with the interpretation in TPA section 5100.16, the staff believes that SFAS No. 13 requires department stores and other retailers that lease or license store space to account for rental income from leased departments in accordance with SFAS No. 13. Accordingly, it would be inappropriate for a department store or other retailer to include in its revenue the sales of the leased or licensed departments. Rather, the department store or other retailer should include the rental income as part of its gross revenue. The staff would not object to disclosure in the footnotes to the financial statements of the amount of the lessee's sales from leased departments. If the arrangement is not a lease but rather a service arrangement that provides for payment of a fee or commission, the retailer should recognize the fee or commission as revenue when earned. If the retailer assumes the risk of bad debts associated with the lessee's merchandise sales, the retailer generally should present bad debt expense in accordance with Regulation S-X article 5-03 (b)(5).

B. * * * * *

This Staff Accounting Bulletin is not intended to change current guidance in the accounting literature. For this reason, adherence to the principles described in this Staff Accounting Bulletin should not raise the costs associated with record-keeping or with audits of financial statements.

1. In February 1999, the AICPA published a booklet entitled "Audit Issues in Revenue Recognition." This booklet provides an overview of the current authoritative accounting literature and auditing procedures for revenue recognition and identifies indicators of improper revenue recognition.

2. SFAC No. 5, ¶83-84; ARB No. 43, Chapter 1A, ¶1; APB Opinion No. 10, ¶12. The citations provided herein are not intended to present the complete population of citations where a particular criterion is relevant. Rather, the citations are intended to provide the reader with additional reference material.

3. SFAC No. 2, Qualitative Characteristics of Accounting Information, ¶63 states "Representational faithfulness is correspondence or agreement between a measure or description and the phenomenon it purports to represent." The staff believes that evidence of an exchange arrangement must exist to determine if the accounting treatment represents faithfully the transaction. See also SOP 97-2, ¶8. The use of the term "arrangement" in this Staff Accounting Bulletin is meant to identify the final understanding between the parties as to the specific nature and terms of the agreed-upon transaction.

4. SFAC No. 5, ¶84(a), (b), and (d). Revenue should not be recognized until the seller has substantially accomplished what it must do pursuant to the terms of the arrangement, which usually occurs upon delivery or performance of the services.

5. SFAC No. 5, ¶83(a); SFAS No. 48, ¶6(a); SOP 97-2, ¶8. SOP 97-2 defines a "fixed fee" as a "fee required to be paid at a set amount that is not subject to refund or adjustment. A fixed fee includes amounts designated as minimum royalties." Paragraphs

26-33 of SOP 97-2 discuss how to apply the fixed or determinable fee criterion in software transactions. The staff believes that the guidance in paragraphs 26 and 30-33 is appropriate for other sales transactions where authoritative guidance does not otherwise exist. The staff notes that paragraphs 27 through 29 specifically consider software transactions, however, the staff believes that guidance should be considered in other sales transactions in which the risk of technological obsolescence is high.

6. ARB No. 43, Chapter 1A, ¶1 and APB Opinion No. 10, ¶12. See also SFAC No. 5, ¶84(g) and SOP 97-2, ¶8.

7. AICPA, Codification of Statements on Auditing Standards (AU) §560.05, Subsequent Events .

8. SFAS No. 48, ¶6(b) and 22.

9. SFAS No. 48, ¶6(b) and 22. The arrangement may not specify that payment is contingent upon subsequent resale or consumption. However, if the seller has an established business practice permitting customers to defer payment beyond the specified due date(s) until the products are resold or consumed, then the staff believes that the seller's right to receive cash representing the sales price is contingent.

10. SFAS No. 48, ¶6(c).

11. SFAS No. 48, ¶6(d).

12. SFAS No. 48, ¶6(e).

13. SFAS No. 49, ¶5(a). Paragraph 5(a) provides examples of circumstances that meet this requirement. As discussed further therein, this condition is present if (a) a resale price guarantee exists, (b) the seller has an option to purchase the product, the economic effect of which compels the seller to purchase the product, or (c) the buyer has an option whereby it can require the seller to purchase the product.

14. SFAS No. 49, ¶5(b).

15. See SOP 97-2, ¶25.

16. See In the Matter of Stewart Parness, Accounting and Auditing Enforcement (AAER) Release No. 108 (August 5, 1986); SEC v. Bollinger Industries, Inc., et al, Lit. Rel. No. 15093 (September 30, 1996); In the Matter of Laser Photonics, Inc., AAER No. 971 (September 30, 1997); In the Matter of Cypress Bioscience Inc., AAER No. 817 (September 19, 1996). Also see SFAC No. 5, ¶84(a). and SOP 97-2, ¶22.

17. Such requests typically should be set forth in writing by the buyer.

18. See Note 16, supra.

19. Such individuals should consider whether APB Opinion No. 21, Interest on Receivables and Payables, pertaining to the need for discounting the related receivable, is applicable. APB Opinion No. 21, ¶3(a), indicates that the requirements of that Opinion to record receivables at a discounted value are not intended to apply to "receivables and payables arising from transactions with customers or suppliers in the normal course of business which are due in customary trade terms not exceeding approximately one year" (emphasis added).

20. SOP 97-2, ¶22.

21. SOP 97-2, ¶20. Also, SFAC No. 5, ¶83(b) states "revenues are considered to have been earned when the entity has substantially accomplished what it must do to be entitled to the benefits represented by the revenues." If an arrangement expressly requires customer acceptance, the staff generally believes that customer acceptance should occur before the entity has substantially accomplished what it must do to be entitled to the benefits represented by the revenues, especially when the seller is obligated to perform additional steps.

22. SFAC No. 5, ¶83(b) states that "revenues are considered to have been earned when the entity has substantially accomplished what it must do to be entitled the benefits represented by the revenues."

23. SOP 97-2, ¶13, and 68-70.

24. SFAS No. 53, Financial Reporting by Producers and Distributors of Motion Picture Films, ¶6. The FASB has issued an Exposure Draft to rescind SFAS No. 53. The AICPA's Accounting Standards Executive Committee intends to issue a new SOP that would replace SFAS No. 53 and provide authoritative guidance on accounting for motion pictures. The Exposure Draft of the proposed new SOP contains a similar criterion for revenue recognition of a licensed film (i.e., the license period of the arrangement has begun and the customer can begin its exploitation, exhibition, or sale).

25. See SFAC No. 5, footnote 51, for a description of the "earning process."

26. In a similar situation, lenders may collect nonrefundable loan origination fees in connection with lending activities. The FASB concluded in SFAS No. 91, Accounting for Nonrefundable Fees and Costs Associated with Originating or Acquiring Loans and Initial Direct Costs of Leases, that loan origination is not a separate revenue-producing activity of a lender, and therefore, those nonrefundable fees collected at the outset of the loan arrangement are not recognized as revenue upon receipt but are deferred and recognized over the life of the loan (paragraphs 5 and 37).

27. The revenue recognition period should extend beyond the initial contractual period if the relationship with the customer is expected to extend beyond the initial term and the customer continues to benefit from the payment of the up-front fee (e.g., if subsequent renewals are priced at a bargain to the initial up-front fee).

28. A systematic method would be on a straight-line basis, unless evidence suggests that revenue is earned or obligations are fulfilled in a different pattern, in which case that pattern should be followed.

29. Footnote 1 of SOP 98-5, Reporting on the Costs of Start-Up Activities, states that "this SOP does not address the financial reporting of costs incurred related to ongoing customer acquisition, such as policy acquisition costs in Financial Accounting Standards Board (FASB) Statement No. 60, Accounting and Reporting by Insurance Enterprises, and loan origination costs in FASB Statement No. 91, Accounting for Nonrefundable Fees and Costs Associated with Originating or Acquiring Loans and Initial Direct Costs of Leases . The SOP addresses the more substantive one-time efforts to establish business with an entirely new class of customers (for example, a manufacturer who does all of its business with retailers attempts to sell merchandise directly to the public)." As such, the set-up costs incurred in this example are not within the scope of SOP 98-5. The staff believes that the incremental direct costs (SFAS No. 91 provides an analogous definition) incurred related to the acquisition or origination of a customer contract, unless specifically provided for in the authoritative literature, should be accounted for in accordance with paragraph 4 of FASB Technical Bulletin (FTB) 90-1, Accounting for Separately Priced Extended Warranty and Product Maintenance Contracts or paragraph 5 of SFAS No. 91.

30. See Note 27, supra.

31. SOP 97-2, ¶31.

32. Ibid.

33. Ibid.

34. SFAS No. 125, ¶16.

35. SFAS No. 48, ¶4.

36. The staff will question further analogies to the guidance in SFAS No. 48 for transactions expressly excluded from its scope.

37. Reliability is defined in SFAC No. 2 as "the quality of information that assures that information is reasonably free from error and bias and faithfully represents what it purports to represent." Paragraph 63 of SFAC No. 5 reiterates the definition of reliability, requiring that "the information is representationally faithful, verifiable, and neutral."

38. For example, if an estimate of the expected cancellation rate varies from the actual cancellation rate by 100% but the dollar amount of the error is immaterial to the consolidated financial statements, some would argue that the estimate could still be viewed as reliable. The staff disagrees with that argument.

39. The term "remote" is used here with the same definition as used in SFAS No. 5, Accounting for Contingencies .

40. Paragraph 8 of SFAS No. 48 notes various factors that may impair the ability to make a reasonable estimate of returns, including the lack of sufficient historical experience. The staff typically expects that the historical experience be based on the particular registrant's historical experience for a service and/or class of customer. In general, the staff typically expects a start-up company, a company introducing new services, or a company introducing services to a new class of customer to have at least two years of experience to be able to make reasonable and reliable estimates.

41. SFAS No. 91, paragraph 5 and FTB 90-1, paragraph 4 both provide for the deferral of incremental direct costs associated with acquiring a revenue-producing contract. Even though the revenue discussed in this example is refundable, if a registrant meets the aforementioned criteria for revenue recognition over the membership period, the staff would analogize to this guidance. However, if neither a nonrefundable contract nor a reliable basis for estimating net cash inflows under refundable contracts exists to provide a basis for recovery of incremental direct costs, the staff believes that such costs should be expensed as incurred. See Note 29, supra.

42. Lessees should follow the guidance established in EITF Issue No. 98-9, Accounting for Contingent Rent .

43. These factors include "a) the susceptibility of the product to significant external factors, such as technological obsolescence or changes in demand, b) relatively long periods in which a particular product may be returned, c) absence of historical experience with similar types of sales of similar products, or inability to apply such experience because of changing circumstances, for example, changes in the selling enterprise's marketing policies and relationships with its customers, and d) absence of a large volume of relatively homogeneous transactions."

44. SFAS No. 48, ¶6.

45. See, for example, ARB 43, Chapter 11A, ¶20; SOP 81-1, ¶58-60; and SFAS No. 45, ¶16.

46. See Regulation S-X, Article 5-03 (b) (1) and (2).

47. See Regulation S-K, Article 303 and Financial Reporting Release No. 36.

48. FRR 36, also see In the Matter of Caterpillar Inc., AAER No. 363 (March 31, 1992).

49. SFAS No. 107, Disclosures about Fair Values of Financial Instruments .

50. Gains or losses from the sale of assets should be reported as "other general expenses" pursuant to Regulation S-X, Article 5-03 (b) (6). Any material item should be stated separately.

51. APB Opinion No. 20, ¶13 and ¶36-37 describe and provide the accounting and disclosure requirements applicable to the correction of an error in previously issued financial statements. Because the term "error" as used in APB Opinion No. 20 includes "oversight or misuse of facts that existed at the time that the financial statements were prepared," that term includes both unintentional errors as well as intentional fraudulent financial reporting and misappropriation of assets as described in Statement on Auditing Standards No. 82, Consideration of Fraud in a Financial Statement Audit .

52. SFAS No. 13, ¶1 defines a lease as "the right to use property, plant, or equipment (land or depreciable assets or both) usually for a stated period of time."

Installing the Templates

If you are using Windows 95 or above, select the Control Panel from the Start menu. Then choose Add/Remove Programs and select Install. You will be asked a series of questions. Read each question carefully and answer as indicated. To install the files on the disc using Windows 3.1, choose File, Run from the Windows Program Manager and type D:/INSTALL (or whichever drive is your CD-ROM drive) in the command line or at the DOS prompt.

First, the installation program will ask you to specify which drive you want to install to. You will then be instructed to specify the complete path where you would like the files installed. The installation program will suggest a directory for you, but you can name the directory anything you like. If the directory does not exist, the program will create it for you. The installation program will automatically install both Word and WordPerfect files.

Opening the Word Processing Files

Open your word processing program. If you are using Microsoft Word or WordPerfect 7.0 or above, choose Open from the File menu. Select the subdirectory that contains the loaded files to list the names of the files. Highlight the name of the file you want to open and click OK or press ENTER. You can also open a document from the File Manager (in Windows 3.1) or in Explorer (in Windows 95 or above) by highlighting the name of the file you want to use and double-clicking your left mouse button.

The list of the Disc Contents is also available on your disc in a file called "Contents." You can open this file and view it on your screen or print a hard copy to use for reference.

PDF Files

Some of the files on the disc are in Adobe® Acrobat® PDF (portable document format). Clicking on a PDF file will automatically launch the Adobe Acrobat Reader to enable you to view the PDF file. The Adobe Acrobat Reader can be downloaded free of charge from http://www.adobe.com/proindex/acrobat/headstep.html.

PowerPoint Files

Open PowerPoint 7.0 or higher or a compatible program. Choose "Open an existing presentation" from the file menu. Click OK or press ENTER. Select the subdirectory that contains the loaded files to list the names of the files. Highlight the name of the file you want to open and click OK or press ENTER. You can also open a PowerPoint file from the File Manager (in Windows 3.1) or in the Explorer (in Windows 95) by highlighting the name of the file you want to use and double-clicking your left mouse button.

Word Processing Tips

Wherever possible, the text of the word processing documents has been formatted so that you can modify the text without altering the format of the documents.

If you are working within a table, you may find the following tips useful. To maneuver within a table, press TAB to move to the next cell, and SHIFT + TAB to move backward one cell. If you want to move to a tab stop within a cell, press CTRL + TAB. For additional tips on working within tables, consult your word processor's manual. It might be helpful to turn on the invisible table lines in Microsoft Word while modifying the document by selecting Gridlines from the Table menu. In WordPerfect, select Reveal Codes and Show Paragraphs from the View menu to reveal all formatting codes and formatting tools such as QuickStops; this will help you to determine the shape of the table.

Microsoft Word and WordPerfect are equipped with search capabilities to help you locate specific words or phrases within a document. The Find option listed under the Edit menu performs a search in both Microsoft Word and WordPerfect 7.0.

Important: When you are finished using a file you will be asked to save it. If you have modified the file, you may want to save the modified file under a different name rather than the name of the original file. (Your word processing program will prompt you for a file name.) This will enable you to reuse the original file without your modifications. If you want to replace the original file with your modified file, save but do not change the name of the file.

If you experience any difficulties installing or using any of the documents and cannot resolve the problem using the information presented here, call our toll-free software support group hotline at (888) 551-7127. Hours of operation are 8 a.m. to 4:30 p.m., PST, Monday through Friday.

Print Troubleshooting

If you are having difficulty printing your document, the following suggestions may correct the problem:

Microsoft Word

- Select Print from the Microsoft Word File menu. Then choose the Printer function.
- Ensure that the correct printer is selected.
- From this window, choose Options.
- In the media box, make sure that the paper size is correct and that the proper paper tray is selected.
- Check your network connections if applicable.
- If you still have trouble printing successfully, it may be because your printer does not recognize the font Times New Roman. At this point, you should change the font of the document to your default font by selecting the document (CTRL + A) and then choosing Font from the Format menu and highlighting the name of the font you normally use. Changing the font of the document may require additional adjustments to the document format, such as margins, tab stops, and table cell height and width. Select Page Layout from the View menu to view the appearance of the pages before you try to print again.

WordPerfect

- Select Print from the WordPerfect File menu. Then choose Select.
- Make sure the correct printer is selected.
- From this menu, press Setup.
- Ensure the correct paper size and paper source are selected.

- You may be having difficulty because your printer does not recognize the selected font. You can correct this problem by changing the base font of the document to your default font. From the Edit menu, choose Select All (or press CTRL+A). The entire text of the document should be highlighted. Then choose Font from the Layout menu and highlight the font you normally use. Changing the font of the document may require additional adjustments to the document format, such as margins, tab stops, and table cell height and width. Select Two Page from the View menu to view the appearance of the pages before you try to print again.

All of the CD-ROM files are in a word processing format, with the exception of files 01–12, 01–13, and 11–23. File 01–13 is a PowerPoint file and files 01–12 and 11–23 are PDF files.

Chapter One: The Origin of Financial Fraud

01-01 Exhibit 1–1: A Word about Nomenclature.

01-02 Exhibit 1–2: Statement on Auditing Standards No. 53's Definition of *Errors* and *Irregularities*.

01-03 Exhibit 1–3: The Treadmill Effect

01-04 Chairman Arthur Levitt, Securities and Exchange Commission, "The 'Numbers Game,'" Remarks at the New York University Center for Law and Business, New York (Sept. 28, 1998).

01-05 Chairman Arthur Levitt, Securities and Exchange Commission, Remarks to the Committee for Economic Development, New York (May 19, 1999).

01-06 Commissioner Norman S. Johnson, Securities and Exchange Commission, Remarks at the Harvard Club, New York (Apr. 29, 1999).

01-07 Commissioner Norman S. Johnson, Securities and Exchange Commission, "Managed Earnings" and "The Year of the Accountant," Remarks at the Utah State Bar Mid-Year Convention, St. George, Utah (Mar. 6, 1999).

01-08 Chairman Arthur Levitt, Securities and Exchange Commission, "A Partnership for the Public Trust," Remarks Before the American Institute of Certified Public Accountants (Dec. 8, 1998).

01-09 Chairman Arthur Levitt, Securities and Exchange Commission, "A Financial Partnership," Remarks at the Financial Executives Institute, New York (Nov. 16, 1998).

01-10 *Fraudulent Financial Reporting: 1987–1997, An Analysis of U.S. Public Companies,* Research Commissioned by the Committee of Sponsoring Organizations of the Treadway Commission (1999).

01-11 *Financial Reporting and the Accounting Profession: The Whirlwind Continues,* American Bar Association, Section of Business Law Annual Meeting, Atlanta, Georgia (Aug. 9, 1999).

*01-12 *1998 Securities Litigation Study,* PricewaterhouseCoopers LLP.

**01-13 Lucy P. Allen, "Accounting Fraud: Is Everyone Doing It?" presented at NERA's Finance, Law and Economics Securities Litigation Seminar, Keystone, Colorado (July 2, 1999).

01-14 *Securities and Exchange Commission v. W.R. Grace & Co.,* No. 98-8942, Complaint for Injunctive and Other Relief (S.D. Fla. 1998).

Chapter Two: So Who Gets the Blame?

02-01 Exhibit 2–1: The Evolution of Financial Reporting.

02-02 Exhibit 2–2: Key Recommendations of the Treadway Commission for Public Companies.

02-03 Exhibit 2–3: Evolving Perceptions of Auditor Responsibility.

02-04 Exhibit 2–4: Arthur Levitt's September 28, 1998, Speech.

02-05 Report of the National Commission on Fraudulent Financial Reporting (October 1987).

02-06 *Rosenblum, Inc. v. Adler,* 461 A.2d 138, 93 N.J. 324 (1983).

02-07 *Bily v. Arthur Young & Co.,* 834 P.2d 745, 3 Cal. 4th 370 (1992).

Chapter Three: The Immediate Aftermath

03-01 Exhibit 3–1: Restoring Credibility.

03-02 Exhibit 3–2: Implementation Checklist.

03-03 *Accounting Irregularities: The Peril, Discovery & Cure,* Willkie Farr & Gallagher (1999).

03-04 Sample press release.

Chapter Four: Getting New Audited Financial Statements

04-01 Exhibit 4–1: Selecting an Auditor.

04-02 Exhibit 4–2: Restatement Guidance.

---

* PDF file. The Adobe Acrobat Reader can be downloaded free of charge from http://www.adobe.com/proindex/acrobat/headstep.html.

** Powerpoint file.

04-03   Exhibit 4–3: What to Expect from Auditors Auditing Fraud-Related Restatements.

04-04   AICPA Professional Standards AU §§ 561, 9561, Subsequent Discovery of Facts Existing at the Date of the Auditor's Report.

04-05   AICPA Professional Standards AU § 316, Consideration of Fraud in a Financial Statement Audit.

04-06   AICPA Professional Standards AU § 315, Communications Between Predecessor and Successor Auditors.

Chapter Five: Digging Out the Fraud: The Lawyers

05-01   Exhibit 5–1: Investigative Tasks.

05-02   Exhibit 5–2: Pros and Cons of a Written Report.

05-03   *Granite Partners, L.P. v. Bear, Stearns & Co.*, 184 F.R.D. 49 (S.D.N.Y. 1999).

05-04   *In re Subpoena Duces Tecum Served on Willkie Farr & Gallagher*, 1997 WL 118369 (S.D.N.Y. 1997).

05-05   *In re Kidder Peabody Securities Litigation*, 168 F.R.D. 459 (S.D.N.Y. 1996).

05-06   *In re the Leslie Fay Co., Inc. Securities Litigation*, 161 F.R.D. 274 (S.D.N.Y. 1995).

05-07   *In re the Leslie Fay Co., Inc. Securities Litigation*, 152 F.R.D. 42 (S.D.N.Y. 1993).

05-08   *Westinghouse Electric Corp. v. Republic of the Philippines*, 951 F.2d 1414 (3d Cir. 1991).

05-09   *John Doe Corp. v. United States (In re John Doe Corp.)*, 675 F.2d 482 (2d Cir. 1982).

05-10   *Permian Corp. v. United States*, 665 F.2d 1214 (D.C. Cir. 1981).

05-11   *Diversified Industries, Inc. v. Meredith*, 572 F.2d 596 (8th Cir. 1977).

05-12   Joseph T. Baio, *Developing Best Practices in Litigation Management: Questioning Employees,* 6 Metropolitan Corporate Counsel 7 (July 1998).

05-13   *Report to the Audit Committee of the Board of Directors of Cendant Corporation,* Willkie Farr & Gallagher and Arthur Andersen LLP (Aug. 24, 1998).

Chapter Six: Digging Out the Fraud: The Forensic Accountants

06-01 Exhibit 6–1: Key Benefits of Using Outside Forensic Accountants.

06-02 Exhibit 6–2: Typical Approach of Forensic Accountants.

06-03 Exhibit 6–3: Common Accounting Fraud Areas.

06-04 *Audit Issues in Revenue Recognition,* American Institute of Certified Public Accountants (1999).

Chapter Seven: Class Action Lawsuits

07-01 Exhibit 7–1: Typical Stages of a Securities Class Section.

07-02 Securities Exchange Act of 1934, § 10(b).

07-03 Securities Exchange Act of 1934, § 20.

07-04 Securities Act of 1933, § 12(a)(2).

07-05 Securities Act of 1933, § 11.

07-06 Securities Act of 1933, § 15.

07-07 Private Securities Litigation Reform Act of 1995.

07-08 Securities Litigation Uniform Standards Act of 1998.

07-09 Jon Koslow, Note, *Estimating Aggregate Damages in Class-Action Litigation Under Rule 10B-5 for Purposes of Settlement,* 59 Fordham L. Rev. 811 (1991).

07-10 Keith R. Ugone, Ph.D., John D. Finnerty, Ph.D., *Measuring Damages in Securities Fraud Class Action Lawsuits,* PricewaterhouseCoopers LLP (Sept. 30, 1998).

07-11 *In re Health Management, Inc. Securities Litigation,* 96CV889 (E.D.N.Y. Oct. 26, 1999) — Jury Instructions.

Chapter Eight: Dealing with the D&O Insurer

08-01 Exhibit 8–1: D&O Insurance Issues.

08-02 Michael R. Young, "Accounting Irregularities and the D&O Insurer," Willkie Farr & Gallagher (1999).

08-03 AIG Specimen Policy: "Directors, Officers and Corporate Liability Insurance Policy, D&O Gold."

Chapter Nine: Dealing with the Regulators

09-01 Exhibit 9–1: New York Stock Exchange Delisting Procedures.

09-02 Exhibit 9–2: Nasdaq Delisting Procedures.

09-03 New York Stock Exchange Listing Requirements 101.00–102.03 as Amended by SR-NYSE-99-13 (and Amendments thereto) and SR-NYSE-99-17 (and Amendments thereto).

09-04 New York Stock Exchange Delisting Procedures—Section 8 as Amended by SR-NYSE-99-29 (and Amendment No. 1 thereto).

09-05 Nasdaq Listing Requirements.

09-06 Nasdaq Delisting Procedures.

09-07 Securities and Exchange Commission Regulations on SEC Oversight of Self-Regulatory Organizations, 17 CFR Chapter 11, §§ 240.19b-4 - 240.36a1-2.

Chapter Ten: Criminal Investigations

10-01 Exhibit 10–1: Securities Act of 1933.

10-02 Exhibit 10–2: Securities Exchange Act of 1934.

10-03 Exhibit 10–3: Phases of a Criminal Investigation.

10-04 Exhibit 10–4: Federal Sentencing Guidelines: An Effective Program to Prevent and Detect Violations of Law.

10-05 Securities Act of 1933, § 24.

10-06 Securities Exchange Act of 1934, § 32(a).

10-07 Investment Company Act of 1940, § 49.

10-08 Investment Advisers Act of 1940, § 217.

10-09 Securities Exchange Act of 1934, § 3(a)(9).

10-10 Securities Act of 1933, § 2(2).

10-11 *Federal Sentencing Guidelines,* Chapter 2, Part F.

10-12 *Federal Sentencing Guidelines,* Chapter 3, Part E.

10-13 *Federal Sentencing Guidelines,* Chapter 5, Part A.

10-14 *Federal Sentencing Guidelines,* Chapter 5, Part K.

10-15 *Federal Sentencing Guidelines,* Chapter 6, Part B.

10-16 *Federal Sentencing Guidelines,* Chapter 8.

10-17 Fifth Amendment to the United States Constitution.

Chapter Eleven: What's an Audit Committee to Do?

11-01 Exhibit 11–1: New NYSE Rules: Audit Committee Composition.

11-02 Exhibit 11–2: New NASD Rules: Audit Committee Composition.

11-03 Exhibit 11–3: New NYSE Rules: Audit Committee Independence.

11-04 Exhibit 11–4: New NASD Rules: Audit Committee Independence.

11-05 Exhibit 11–5: New NYSE Rules: Audit Committee Charter.

11-06 Exhibit 11–6: New NASD Rules: Audit Committee Charter.

11-07 Exhibit 11–7: New SEC Rules to Implement the Recommendations of the Blue Ribbon Committee.

11-08 Exhibit 11–8: Delaware Law.

11-09 Exhibit 11–9: Foreign Corrupt Practices Act.

11-10 Exhibit 11–10: SEC Rule: Book and Records.

11-11 Exhibit 11–11: New Amendments to Statement on Auditing Standards No. 61 (Communication with Audit Committees).

11-12 Exhibit 11–12: New Amendments to Statement on Auditing Standards No. 71 (Interim Financial Information).

11-13 Exhibit 11–13: SEC Staff Accounting Bulletin No. 99 (Materiality).

11-14 Exhibit 11–14: Independence Standards Board Standard No. 1 (Independence Discussions with Audit Committees).

11-15 Exhibit 11–15: Auditor Independence.

11-16 Securities Exchange Act of 1934, § 10A.

11-17 AICPA Professional Standards AU § 722, Interim Financial Information.

11-18 Report and Recommendations of the Blue Ribbon Committee on Improving the Effectiveness of Corporate Audit Committees.

11-19 Statement of Financial Executives Institute at Hearing of Blue Ribbon Committee on Improving the Effectiveness of Corporate Audit Committees, delivered by P. Norman Roy, President, Financial Executives Institute (1998).

11-20 Testimony of William G. Bishop, III, The Institute of Internal Auditors Before the Blue Ribbon Committee on Improving the Effectiveness of Corporate Audit Committees of the NYSE and the NASD (1998).

11-21 Testimony of Michael R. Young, Willkie Farr & Gallagher, Before the Blue Ribbon Committee on Improving the Effectiveness of Corporate Audit Committees of the NYSE and the NASD (1998).

11-22 Securities and Exchange Commission Final Rule to Implement the Blue Ribbon Committee Report and Recommendations on Improving the Effectiveness of Corporate Audit Committees.

*11-23 Executive Summary, *Report of the NACD Blue Ribbon Commission on Audit Committees,* Produced by the National Association of Corporate Directors and the Center for Board Leadership Sponsored by Heidrick & Struggles, Inc., Washington, DC (1999).

11-24 Independence Standards Board No. 1, Independence Discussions with Audit Committees.

11-25 NYSE Corporate Governance Rules §§ 301 – 306, and NYSE Order Approving Proposed Rule Change Amending the Audit Committee Requirements and Notice of Filing and Order Granting Accelerated Approval of Amendments No. 1 and No. 2 Thereto.

11-26 Nasdaq Order Approving Proposed Rule Change Amending the Audit Committee Requirements and Notice of Filing and Order Granting Accelerated Approval of Amendments No. 1 and No 2 Thereto.

11-27 AICPA Professional Standards AU § 380, Communication with Audit Committees.

11-28 AICPA Independence Rules.

11-29 Securities and Exchange Commission Staff Accounting Bulletin No. 99.

11-30 Securities and Exchange Commission Staff Accounting Bulletin No. 100.

11-31 Securities and Exchange Commission Staff Accounting Bulletin No. 101.

11-32 AICPA Professional Standards AU § 317, Illegal Acts by Clients.

11-33 Securities and Exchange Commission Independence Rules.

11-34 *In re Caremark Int'l Inc. Derivative Litigation,* 1996 WL 549894 (Del. Ch. 1996).

11-35 Michael R. Young, Willkie Farr & Gallagher, "Today's CFO—Financial Reporting Responsibilities and Liability," Speech Before AICPA Fall National Industry Conference (1998).

11-36 Michael R. Young, "The Liability of Corporate Officials to Their Outside Auditor for Financial Statement Fraud," 64 Fordham L. Rev. 2155 (1996).

11-37 John O. Whitney, *The Economics of Trust,* Chapter 1 (McGraw-Hill 1996).

Chapter Twelve: Accounting Irregularities and the Future of Financial Reporting

12-01 Richard I. Miller & Michael R. Young, "Financial Reporting and Risk Management in the 21st Century," 65 Fordham L. Rev. 1987 (1997).

12-02 Michael R. Young, "The Future of Financial Reporting."

12-03 John O. Whitney, Executive Director of Columbia Business School's Deming Center, "There's a Rhinoceros in the Room," Speech Delivered at the XV World Congress of Accountants (Oct. 1997).

A

Accountant, forensic. *See also* Auditor; Investigation, forensiccoordination with incumbent auditor, 106–8
accounting conventions expertise, 90
billing rates, 91
defined, 89
facilitation of financial statement restatement, 62–63
forensic investigation vs. audit, 94–96
interaction with incumbent auditor, 68–69
objectives in investigation, 96–98
reasons for hiring, 89–93
retention by the law firm, 75–76
retention of, 51–52, 61–62
use of outside teams, 92–93

Accounting irregularity. *See also* Fraud
common fraud areas, 98–103
comparison to errors, 4–5
consequences, 259–61
and D&O insurance, 148–54
defined, 1, 3–6, 64
examples of, 64
future of financial reporting, 255–56
nomenclature, 4

Accounting policies, change in, as reason for restated financial statements, 65–66

Accuracy, in criminal investigations, 189

Action plan by board of directors, 49

Adjudication
in D&O insurance coverage, 151–52
in delisting proceedings, 177

Adjusting journal entry, 238

Aftermath of fraud discovery, 41
action plan implementation, 49
finding extent of the fraud, 44
initial board meeting, 42–47
initial press release, 49–50, 119–21
insurance. *See* Insurance, director and officer
limiting liability to securities traders, 42, 43–44
maintenance of operations, 46–47
preliminary investigation, 41–42
procedures to continue business, 51–54
termination of employees, 45, 83
time pressure for thorough investigation, 45

AICPA. *See* American Institute of Certified Public Accountants

Allen, William, 242

American Institute of Certified Public Accountants (AICPA)
auditor independence, 243, 244
standards for previously issued audit reports, 57

American Stock Exchange (AMEX), 169. *See also* Self-Regulatory Organization
new rules of financial reporting, 22

Analysts, Wall Street, 258–59, 263–64

Attorney-client privilege
and forensic accountants, 105–6, 108
in grand jury testimony, 194
limitation, 194–95
waiver of, 194

Attorney work-product doctrine, 194–95

AU Section 380 (Communications with the Audit Committee)
auditor discussions with audit committee, 38

Audit committee, 15–17
communication with. *See* SAS-61
as defendant in class-action lawsuit, 114
functions. *See* Audit committee functions
ignorance of, 16–17
inadequacies of, 16
inadequate configuration, 32
insufficiently diligent, 32–33
Levitt initiative concepts for, 35–36
recommendations by Blue Ribbon Committee, 36–38
recommendations for public companies, 26, 27
role in financial reporting, 25

Audit committee functions, 211–12
access to reliable information, 230
assure adequate reporting system (Delaware Law), 229
charter, 218, 225–27
checklists, 213–14
compensation, 229–30
configuration of committee, 218–20
detection of financial misreporting, 217
establish proper tone at the top, 214–16, 248–49
financial reporting responsibilities, 212–13
financial sophistication, 224–25
independence of, 220–24
information from senior management, 231–32

Audit committee functions, *cont.*
information from internal audit, 246–48
information from the outside auditor. *See*
Audit committee information from
the outside auditor
learn the business, 251
logistical capability of reporting system,
216–17, 233–35
meetings, 251–53
minimize paper, 250–51
tools, 248–53
use of good judgment, 253
willingness to work, 225–30
Audit committee information from the
outside auditor, 232–33
auditor independence, 241–45. *See also*
Independence of auditor
checking thoroughness of the audit, 241
environmental information, 233
level of cooperation, 235–36
logistical capabilities of financial
reporting system, 216–17, 233–35
managerial bias in GAAP application,
235, 236, 237
nonmaterial PAJEs, 238–40
review of quarterly information, 240–41
unusual reserve activity, 237–38
unusual revenue activity, 237–38
Audit process
evidence requested, 67
misconceptions among company
personnel, 66–67
new audit team personnel, 68
new procedures for fraud-related
restatements, 66–67
professional skepticism, 62, 68, 94
Audit reports
accuracy of prior-year, 61
effect on previously issued reports, 56–
58
Audit sampling, 62, 232–33
Auditor. *See also* Accountant, forensic
as defendant in class-action lawsuit, 114,
125–27
incumbent. *See* Auditor, incumbent
independence. *See* Independence of
auditor
independent outside counsel, 52, 75–76
outside. *See* Outside auditor
reluctance of new auditor to accept
client, 61
selection of, 59–61
Auditor, incumbent
coordination with forensic accountants,
106–8

benefits of retention, 59–61
interaction with forensic accountants,
68–69
Auditor's Responsibility to Detect and
Report Errors and Irregularities. *See*
SAS-53

B

Bank. *See* Lenders
Barter transactions, 101
Bill-and-hold transactions, 100
Bily v. Arthur Young & Co. lawsuit, 30, 31
Blame for financial fraud, 33–34
corporate management, 30–32
outside auditor, 21–23
Blue Ribbon Committee
recommendations, 36–38, 39–40
report on corporate audit committees
(1999), 22, 172
rules for audit committee composition,
218
SEC rules to implement recommendations for audit committees, 218,
227–28, 240, 245
study of corporate audit committees, 2
Board of directors
action plan, 49
crisis due to fraud, 19–20
as defendants in class-action lawsuit, 114
insurance (D&O). *See* Insurance, director
and officer
meeting in aftermath of fraud discovery,
42–47
role in financial reporting, 25
Boston Stock Exchange, 169. *See also* Self-
Regulatory Organization

C

Capacity requirement in D&O insurance,
139
Cease-and-desist orders, 168
Certified Public Accountant (CPA),
punishment for wrongdoing, 168
Charter for audit committees, 218, 225–27
Checklists for audit committees, 213–14
Chicago Board Options Exchange, 169. *See
also* Self-Regulatory Organization
Chicago Stock Exchange, 169. *See also* Self-
Regulatory Organization
Chief executive officer (CEO)
as defendant in class-action lawsuit, 114
knowledge of fraud, 44–45
Chief financial officer (CFO)
as defendant in class-action lawsuit, 114
knowledge of fraud, 44–45

pressure to misrepresent financial results, 1

releasing financial information, 260–61, 263–64

Cincinnati Stock Exchange, 169. *See also* Self-Regulatory Organization

Claim, defined, 137–38

Claims based on accounting irregularities, 1

Claims-made insurance policy, 136–37, 146

Class action lawsuits. *See* Lawsuits, class-action

Cleopatra syndrome, 230, 248

Collective-knowledge doctrine, 199

Committee of Sponsoring Organizations of the Treadway Commission (COSO). *See also* Treadway Commission
committee recommendations applicable to small companies, 39
report (1987), 22
study of underlying causes of fraudulent financial reporting, 2

Committee to investigate the fraud, 51

Common interest agreement, 166

Communication with audit committees. *See also* SAS-61
access to reliable information, 230
from internal audit, 246–48
from outside auditor, 232–46
from senior management, 231–32

Communications with the Audit Committee. *See* AU Section 380

Community of interest, 195

Company, as defendant in lawsuit, 113, 120–21

Complaint, consolidated, 116–19

Computerized
general ledger information, 104
general ledger, investigation of, 104–5
records, preservation of, 97

Concurrence by outside auditor, 61

Confidentiality of reports. *See* Privilege

Conflict of interest, 202

Consideration of Fraud in a Financial Statement Audit. *See* SAS-82

Consignment sales, 100–1

Continuous close of financial results, 266

Cookie-jar reserves, 14, 15

Corporate criminal liability for employee actions, 198–202

COSO. *See* Committee of Sponsoring Organizations of the Treadway Commission

Counsel, responsibilities during investigation, 207–9. *See also* Outside counsel; Investigation

Court cases
Bily v. Arthur Young & Co., 30, 31
Ernst & Ernst v. Hochfelder, 117

CPA. *See* Certified Public Accountant

Credibility
after fraud disclosure, 46–47
restoring of, 46, 162–63, 164

Criminal investigation. *See* Investigation, criminal

Cross-claims, 71. *See also* Lawsuits; Litigation

Customers
effect of lack of confidence in company, 59
interest in objective investigation by forensic accountants, 93
restoring of credibility to, 47

D

Damage
estimates, 129
expert, 128–29
insurance exceptions, 140–41

Database information in investigation, 78

Dates
prior acts, 138
retroactive, 138

Day-traders as shareholders in lawsuit, 129

Debt covenant implicated by financial fraud, 46–47

Defendants
in class-action lawsuits, 113–15
deliberate participants, 149
reckless, 149

Delaware Law, 229

Delisting of securities, 52–53, 157, 170
company approach to proceedings, 176–77
effect of no audited financial statements, 59
Nasdaq procedures, 174
NYSE procedures, 173
prevention and handling of, 174
suspension of trading, 175–76

Depositions, 127

Depression-era financial reporting system, 257–58, 264

Director
board. *See* Board of directors
defined, for insurance, 138
insurance exclusion for outside directorship, 139

Discounting used for revenue manipulation, 101

Discovery
adding outside auditor as defendant, 125–27
components of process, 123–24
defined, 122
depositions, 127
document requests, 124–25
process of, 123–27

Dishonesty, in fraudulent financial reporting, 11

Division of Enforcement of the SEC
final investigative report, 166–67
focus on financial fraud, 160–61
Formal Order of Investigation, 161–62, 165
initial contact by company, 164–65
penalties and sanctions, 162, 168–69
shipment timing, 262–63
subpoena powers, 161, 165

Document(s). *See also* Report(s)
request, 124
securing after fraud discovery, 53

Double jeopardy, 209

Dual-sovereignty doctrine, 209

E

E-mails
as investigative evidence, 78
revenue reports, 264

Economics of Trust, The, 249

Edgar system of electronic SEC filing, 258

Employee
identification in criminal investigations, 187–88
reluctant, 189
termination due to participation in fraud, 45, 83
welfare by corporations, 3

Endorsements. *See* Insurance, D&O, endorsements

Enforcement Division. *See* Division of Enforcement of the SEC

Environment
in development of financial misreporting, 3, 18
example of business, 6–10
pressure, 11

Equitable relief, 162

Ernst & Ernst v. Hochfelder lawsuit, 117

Errors
comparison to irregularities, 4–5
defined, 4–5, 63
examples of, 64

Estimates, inaccurate
examples of, 65
as reason for restated financial statements, 65

Events of default in debt covenant, 47

Evidence, preservation of, 97

Evolution of financial reporting, 22

Example of company fraud, 6–10

Exclusions in insurance policies. *See* Insurance, D&O, exclusions

Expectation gap
defined, 29
initiative, 29
revision of SAS (1989), 22

Expenses, manipulation of, 100, 103

F

FASB. *See* Financial Accounting Standards Board

Federal Sentencing Guidelines, 204–7

Fifth Amendment protection
civil and criminal proceedings, 209–10
corporate indemnification, 200
grand jury witness, 192–94
and immunity, 196–97
protection of company documents, 186
understanding by executives, 184
waiver, 193

Final adjudication in D&O insurance coverage, 151–52

Financial Accounting Standards Board (FASB), new scrutiny of technical pronouncements, 2. *See also specific SAS*

Financial market. *See* Stock market

Financial misreporting, causes of, 2–3

Financial reporting system, logistical capabilities of, 216–17, 233–35

Financial statements, new audited
auditor. *See* Outside auditor; Accountant, forensic
depression-era reporting system, 257–58, 264
effect of lawsuits, 70–71
future of, 255–56
involvement of outside auditor, 56
management representations, 69–70
mistrust by auditor and company personnel, 58–59
periodic, 257–65
previously issued audit reports, 56–58

Financial statements, restated, 72
audit process, 66–69
guidelines, 64
by forensic accountants, 62–63

management responsibility for, 62–63
  reasons for requirement, 63–66
Fines imposed by the SEC, 168–69
Foreign Corrupt Practices Act, 233–34
Forensic accountant. *See* Accountant,
  forensic
Form 8-K, filing upon occurrence of
  specified events, 159
Form 10-K Annual Report, 258
  effect of previously issued audit reports,
    56–57
  effect on stock prices, 259
  filing with the SEC, 159
  inclusion of audit committee letter, 38
  inclusion of audited financial statements,
    229
  placing on Web sites, 258
  Section 10(b) prohibitions, 117
Form 10-Q quarterly report
  auditor review before filing of, 38
  filing with the SEC, 159
  placing on Web sites, 258
  Section 10(b) prohibitions, 117
Formal Order of Investigation, 161–62, 165
Framing the issues, 98–99, 104
Fraud. *See also* Accounting irregularity
  common accounting areas, 98–103
  elements of, 11–13
  start of, 11–12
  surfacing of, 19
  use of the term in authoritative literature,
    3–4

G
GAAP. *See* Generally accepted accounting
  standards
General ledger investigation, 104–5
Generally accepted accounting standards
  (GAAP)
  appropriate reserve levels, 101
  expenses to be expensed of capitalized,
    103
  financial statement violations, 62–63
  forbidden financial statement restate-
    ment, 63
  forensic accountant expertise, 90
  managerial bias in GAAP application,
    235, 236, 237
  reporting changes in accounting
    principles, 66
  rules for changes in estimates, 65
GAAS. *See* Generally accepted auditing
  standards
Generally accepted auditing standards
  (GAAS)

assumption of truth by client, 94
  audit sampling approach, 62
  auditor independence, 70–71
  auditor-management relationship, 70
  auditor observation requirement, 102
  forensic investigation vs. GAAS audit,
    95–96
  jury understanding of, 22
  management representations, 69
  management's responsibility for financial
    statements, 29
  materiality thresholds of audits, 18
  professional skepticism approach, 62, 68,
    94, 232–33
  purpose of audit, 95
  quality of accounting principles, 37–38
Governance standards, 171–72
Government investigation. *See* Investigation,
  criminal
Grand jury phase of criminal investigation
  document presentation, 185–87
  employee contact with counsel, 187–88
  employee interviews, 188–91
  initial contact, 182–85
  subpoena *duces tecum*, 182, 186, 188,
    194
  testimonial phase, 191–98

I
Illegal acts, defined, 65
Immunity of witnesses, 196–98
  formal, 203
  informal, 197, 198
  letter, 197
  from prosecution, 202–3
  transactional, 197
  use, 197
Imputation from one insured to another,
  149–50, 152
In terrorem effect, 229
Indemnification
  of employees, 53–54, 80, 199–201
  of underwriters, 115
Independence Discussions with Audit
  Committees (ISB No. 1), 242, 243
Independence of auditor
  and the audit committee, 241–45
  defined, 242
  effect of auditor as defendant, 126
  effect of lawsuits on, 70–71
  NASD requirements, 218, 219, 223
  NYSE requirements, 218, 219, 221, 222–
    23
Independence Standards Board (1997), 22
  Standard No. 1 (Independence Discussions
    with Audit Committees), 242, 243

Independent outside counsel
   conducting business in the aftermath, 52
   investigation of fraud, 75–76
Injunctions, 169
Insider trading, 260
Insurance, D&O (director and officer), 43,
   133–34
   accounting irregularities, 148–54
   application process, 153–54
   body of the policy, 135
   claim, defined, 137
   claims for wrongful acts, 139–40
   claims-made policy, 136–37, 146
   in class-action lawsuit, 120
   Coverage A (individual side), 134
   Coverage B (company reimbursement),
     134
   coverage issues, 154–56
   date of coverage, 138
   declarations page, 134
   defining terms, 135
   for early settlement of lawsuits, 123
   endorsements. *See* Insurance, D&O,
     endorsements
   entity coverage, 134
   exclusions. *See* Insurance, D&O,
     exclusions
   factual determination, 151–52
   imputations from one insured to another,
     149–50, 152
   insured, defined, 138–39
   insuring clauses, 135, 136
   loose cannons on the deck, 152–53
   losses, 140–41
   notice-of-claim provisions, 146–47
   policy structure, 134–35
   retention and coinsurance, 147
   self-insurance, 147
   terms and conditions, 135
   tests of claims for coverage, 136
Insurance, D&O, endorsements
   addition of employees, 139
   defined, 135
   expansive, 145
   policy exclusions, 141–42
   restrictive, 145
Insurance, D&O, exclusions
   conduct, 142
   deliberate fraudulent acts, 148–49
   due to other policies, 142–43
   endorsements. *See* Insurance, D&O,
     endorsements
   fraud, 48
   insured v. insured, 143–44
   outside directorship, 139

pending and prior litigation, 142, 143
prior-notice, 147
section of policy, 135, 141–42
Intel market value, 262
Intent-to-benefit rule, 199
Interim Financial Review. *See* SAS-71
Internal audit
   communication with audit committees,
     246–48
   lack of viable function, 33
   recommendations by Treadway
     Commission, 26
   used to combat fraud, 17
Internet access to financial information, 256
Interrogatories, 124
Inventory, manipulation of, 100, 102–3
Inventory accounting, change resulting in
   need for restated financial statement,
   65
Interview of witnesses
   lack of subpoena power, 79–82
   by lawyers and accountants, 105–6
   list of people to interview, 78–79
Investigation
   accountants. *See* Accountant, forensic
   criminal. *See* Investigation, criminal
   effect of lack of subpoena power, 79–82
   forensic. *See* Investigation, forensic
   fraud investigation, as new system of
     audits, 233
   by the government, 76–77
   outside counsel retained for, 75–76
   preliminary, 41–42. *See also* Aftermath
     of fraud discovery
   pretrial, 122
   privileged work product, 86–87
   privileged written reports, 85–86
   purposes of, 73–75
   tasks, 77–79
   time frame, 76–77
   unresolved issues, 82–83
   written vs. oral report, 83–85
Investigation, criminal, 179–82
   cooperation vs. antagonistic stance, 183–
     85
   cooperative stance and witness
     identification, 187
   corporate liability, 198–202
   document presentation, 185–87
   employee contact with counsel, 187–88
   employee interview, 188–91
   Fifth Amendment. *See* Fifth Amendment
     protection
   initial grand jury contact, 182–85
   justification for extent of investigation,
     181

parallel proceedings, 209–10
phases, 182
plea discussions, 202–4
sentencing, 204–7
testimonial grand jury phase, 191–98
Investigation, forensic. *See also* Accountant,
   forensic
documentary evidence, 95
ending the investigation, 108–9
evidence gathering, 95–96
forensic investigation vs. audit, 94–96
general ledger information, 104–5
interviews, 105–6. *See also* Interview of
   witnesses
issues to explore, 96–103
as new system of audits, 233
purpose of, 95
scope and materiality, 96
urgency of audit, 96
use of outside teams, 92–93
Investors
institutional as shareholders in lawsuit,
   129
interest in objective investigation by
   forensic accountants, 93
momentum, as shareholders in lawsuit,
   129
Irregularity. *See* Accounting irregularity;
   Fraud
ISB No. 1 (Independence Discussions with
   Audit Committees), 242, 243
Issuers
defined, 158
information requests by Division of
   Enforcement, 161
security registration, 158
Issues common in accounting fraud, 98–99
expenses, 100, 103
inventory, 100, 102–3
reserves, 100, 101–2
revenue recognition, 99–101

J
Joint defense
agreement for reluctant employees, 189
in grand jury testimony, 195–96
multiple counsel, 166
waiver, 195–96
witnesses, 187
Joint representations, 166

L
Lawyers. *See* Investigation; Outside counsel
Lawsuits. *See also* Cross-claims; Investiga-
   tion; Litigation

civil party, 76–77, 188
class-action. *See* Lawsuits, class-action
effect on auditor's independence, 70–71
Lawsuits, class-action, 111
commencement of litigation, 112–13
consolidated complaint, 116–19
damages, 129
defendants, 113–15
defined, 111–12
discovery process, 123–27
early settlement, 122–23
handling by board of directors, 53
liability of initial press release, 119–21
motion to dismiss, 121–22, 123, 124
settlement, 122–23, 127–31
shareholders as plaintiffs, 121
sorting out parties and counsel, 115–16
stages of, 112
Learn the business by audit committees, 251
Legal counsel indemnification, 53–54, 80
Lenders
company credibility after fraud
   disclosure, 46–47
effect of no audited financial statements,
   59
interest in objective investigation by
   forensic accountants, 93
Letters, management representation, 69–70
Levitt, Arthur, 2
audit committee meeting frequency, 252
initiatives, 34–40
speech at New York University (1998),
   22, 34–35
speeches to stop "accounting hocus-
   pocus", 160–61
Liability
of corporation for employee actions,
   198–202
vicarious, 198–99
Listing requirements, 171–73
agreement, 171
delisting. *See* Delisting of securities
quantitative, 171
qualitative, 171
Litigation. *See also* Cross-claims; Lawsuits
crisis, 29
effect on auditor's independence, 70–71
use of written investigative report, 85
Loss, defined, for D&O insurance, 140–41

M
Man power for investigations, 90–91, 106
Managed earnings, 13–15
cookie-jar reserves, 14, 15
types of, 13

Management
    hiring of, in the aftermath, 52
    representations, 69–70
    responsibility for reliable financial
        reporting, 25
    responsibility for restated financial
        statements, 62–63
Material misstatement, 238–40
Materiality
    and scope of investigation, 96
    Staff Accounting Bulletin No. 99, 238–
        40
    thresholds of audits, 18
McKesson-Robbins inventory fraud, 102
Microsoft financial reports, 266
Misconceptions by company personnel
    during re-audit, 66–69
Misreporting financial, 2–3
Mistrust by auditors and company personnel,
    58–59
Motion to dismiss, 121–22, 123, 124
Mutual funds as shareholders in lawsuit, 129

N

NASD. *See* National Association of
    Securities Dealers
Nasdaq, 169–70. *See also* National
    Association of Securities Dealers; Self-
    Regulatory Organization
    delisting. *See* Delisting of securities
    delisting procedures, 174
    trading practices criticized, 171
National Association of Securities Dealers
    (NASD), 169. *See also* Nasdaq
    audit committee charter, 218, 225, 227
    audit committee composition, 218–20,
        221, 224–25
    audit committee independence, 218, 219,
        223
    Blue Ribbon Committee recommenda-
        tions, 172
    fraud investigation, 21
    new rules of financial reporting, 22
    restructuring in 1996, 171
    rules to combat financial fraud, 2
National Commission on Fraudulent
    Financial Reporting. *See* Treadway
    Commission
Negligent wrongdoer penalties, 168
Negotiated resolution with the SEC, 167–69
New Deal securities legislation, 170
New York Stock Exchange (NYSE), 169–70.
    See also Self-Regulatory Organization
    audit committee charter, 218, 225, 226
    audit committee composition, 218–19,
        224, 225
    audit committee independence, 218, 219,
        221, 222–23
    Blue Ribbon Committee recommenda-
        tions, 172
    delisting. *See* Delisting of securities
    delisting procedures, 173
    disclosure requirement, 172
    fraud investigation, 21
    interest in objective investigation by
        forensic accountants, 93
    new rules of financial reporting, 22
    rules to combat financial fraud, 2
Non-prosecution agreement, 203
NYSE. *See* New York Stock Exchange

O

Objectivity, by forensic accountants from
    another firm, 92–93
Obstruction-of-justice, 202
Off-the-record discussion, 203
Offense level for sentencing, 204
Officers
    as defendants in class-action lawsuit,
        113, 114
    defined, for insurance, 138
Operations of the company, maintaining
    credibility, 46–47
Outside auditor
    advantages of using, 56
    benefits of incumbent auditor, 59–61
    blame for misreporting, 21–23
    communication with audit committees,
        232–46
    as defendant in class-action lawsuit, 115,
        125–27
    demands for information from audit
        committees, 33
    involvement in finding irregularities, 56
    role in fraud detection, 17–19, 28
    watchdog function, 31
Outside counsel
    conducting business in the aftermath, 52
    responding to SEC subpoenas, 165–66
Outsource of internal audit function, 246–47

P

Pacific Stock Exchange, 169. *See also* Self-
    Regulatory Organization
PAJE (proposed adjusting journal entry),
    238–40
Parallel proceedings, 209–10
Passed adjusting journal entry (PAJE), 238
Penalties by the SEC, 168–69

Periodic financial reporting, 257–65
Philadelphia Stock Exchange, 169. *See also* Self-Regulatory Organization
Plea bargain, 202–4
Plea discussions, 202–4
Points added to offense level, 204
Press inquiries, response by counsel, 207
Press release
  call to SEC prior to, 164–65
  liability implications of, 119–21
  at the time of discovery, 49–50
Pressure
  element of fraudulent financial reporting, 11
  to misrepresent financial results, 1
  of senior executives, 32
  Treadway Commission report as cause of fraud, 24–25
Pretrial depositions, 127
Pretrial investigation, 122
PricewaterhouseCoopers, survey of claims based on accounting irregularities, 1
Private Securities Litigation Reform Act (1995), 22
Privilege
  attorney-client, 105–6, 108
  confidentiality of final investigative report, 166–67
  work product, 86–87
  written reports, 85–86
Professional skepticism by auditors, 94
  abandonment of approach, 232–33
  in financial statement restatement audit, 68
  GAAS approach, 62
Proffer discussion, 203
Proposed adjusting journal entry (PAJE), 238–40
Prospectus included in the registration statement, 158
Public Oversight Board, 2

R

Real-time world, 256–57, 261, 265, 266–67
Reckless participants, 149
Regulators. *See also* Securities and Exchange Commission; Self-Regulatory Organizations
  disclosure requirements, 158–59
  restoring of credibility to, 47, 162–63
  written report of investigation, 85–86
Remedial order, 204
Report(s). *See also* Document(s)
  audit, 56–58, 61

final investigative report to SEC, 166–67
Form 8-K, 159
Form 10-K. *See* Form 10-K Annual Report
Form 10-Q. *See* Form 10-Q Quarterly Report
  privileged, 85–87
  written vs. oral, 83–85
Representation letters by management, 69–70
Representations and warranties in debt covenant, 46–47
Reserves, 100, 101–2
  defined, 101
  reporting unusual activity to audit committee, 237–38
  restructuring charges, 102
Restated financial statements. *See* Financial statements, restated
Restitution by the company, 204
Restructuring charges, 102
Revenue recognition, 99
  accelerated shipments, 7–8, 99–100
  barter transactions, 101
  bill-and-hold transactions, 100
  communication to audit committee, 237–38
  consignment sales, 100–1
  discounting, 101
Rule 10b-5, 117
Rule 102(e) (proceedings against wrongdoing professionals), 168

S

Sampling, 62, 232–33
SAS-53 (The Auditor's Responsibility to Detect and Report Errors and Irregularities)
  errors, defined, 5
  irregularities, defined, 4, 5
SAS-61 (Communication with Audit Committees), 228
  amendments to increase auditor candor, 235, 236
  items to be discussed, 245–46
SAS-71 (Interim Financial Review)
  amendments to increase auditor candor, 235, 237, 246, 250
  auditor review before filing of Form 10-Q, 38, 240–41
SAS-82 (Consideration of Fraud in a Financial Statement Audit), auditor's responsibility for detecting fraud, 4
Scienter, 117, 122
SEC. *See* Securities and Exchange Commission

Section 10(b), 117, 121–22, 129
Section 11, 118–19
Section 12(2), 118
Section 12(a)(2), 118
Section 15, 119
Section 20, 117–18
Section 24, 180
Section 32(a), 180
Securities
    delisting. *See* Delisting of securities
    liability due to misleading financial
        statements, 42
    trading on basis of financial statements,
        42, 43–44
Securities Act of 1933
    registration statement requirement, 158–
        59
    Section 11, 118–19
    Section 12(2), 118
    Section 12(a)(2), 118
    Section 15, 119
    Section 24 (criminal violations), 180
Securities and Exchange Commission (SEC).
    See also specific Form, Rule;
        Regulators; Self-Regulatory Organiza-
        tions
    company cooperation, 163–64
    comparability of reporting system, 160
    confidentiality of investigative report,
        166–67
    Edgar system of electronic filing, 258
    effect of no audited financial statements,
        59
    Enforcement Division. *See* Division of
        Enforcement of the SEC
    filing of audited financial statements,
        219, 227–28, 240, 245. *See also*
        SAS-61
    fraud investigation, 21
    heightened scrutiny of reporting
        practices, 2
    initial contact, 164–65
    interest in objective investigation by
        forensic accountants, 93
    negotiated resolution, 167–69
    new rules of financial reporting, 22, 39–
        40
    penalty limitations, 162
    prosecution of responsible parties, 74–75
    regaining credibility of company. *See*
        Credibility
    regulation of company personnel, 160
    responsibilities, 157–58
    rule for books and records, 233–34
    rules to implement recommendations for

audit committees, 218, 227–28, 240,
    245
Staff Accounting Bulletin No. 99
    (Materiality), 238–40
transparency of reporting system, 160
witnesses. *See* Witnesses
Securities Exchange Act of 1934
    corporate disclosure requirements, 159
    original public reporting requirements,
        258
    Section 10(b), 117, 121–22, 129, 159–60
    Section 13, 159
    Section 20, 117–18
    Section 32(a)(criminal violations), 180
Securities exchanges. *See* Self-Regulatory
    Organizations
Securities Litigation Uniform Standards Act
    (1998), 22
Self-insurance, 147
Self-Regulatory Organization (SRO), 169.
    See also Stock Market
    corrective measures, 176
    creation of, 170
    delisting. *See* Delisting of securities
    described, 169–70
    investigation by the SEC, 171
    listing requirements, 171–73
    listing violations, 176
    registration with the SEC, 170
    suspension of trading, 175–76
Sentencing guidelines, 204–7
Settlement
    agreement, 130–31
    conference, 128
    early, 122–23
    judge as catalyst for, 127–29
    negotiated, 123
Shareholders
    as defendants in class-action lawsuit, 115
    interest in objective investigation by
        forensic accountants, 93
    lawsuits. *See* Lawsuits, class-action
    as plaintiffs in lawsuits, 128–30
Shipments, accelerated, 7–8, 99–100
Special committee appointed to investigate
    the fraud, 51, 125
SRO. *See* Self-Regulatory Organization
Staff Accounting Bulletin No. 99 (Material-
    ity), 238–40
Statements on Auditing Standards. *See also*
    specific SAS
    Expectation Gap revision (1989), 22
Stock
    halt of trading pending new financial
        information, 55

price after fraud disclosure, 52
trading on basis of financial statements, 42, 43–44
Stock market. *See also* Self-Regulatory Organizations
   delisting. *See* Delisting of securities
   inefficiencies, 261–64
   restoring of credibility in, 47
   volatility of, 14, 261, 262, 264, 266
Subpoena
   by Division of Enforcement, 161, 165
   duces tecum, 182, 186, 188, 194
   by grand jury, 182
   power in the interview process, 79–82
   responding to, 165–66
Suppliers
   effect of lack of confidence in company, 59
   interest in objective investigation by forensic accountants, 93
   restoring of credibility to, 47

T
Tasks by investigators, 77–79
Testimonial quality knowledge, 189
Time pressure for thorough investigation, 45
Timeliness of audit approach, 233
Tone at the top established by the audit committee, 214–16, 248–49
Treadmill effect, 9
   causes of, 10
   in managed earnings, 14
Treadway Commission. *See also* Committee of Sponsoring Organizations of the Treadway Commission
   consequences of report, 26, 28–30
   formation of, 23
   recommendations for public companies, 26, 27
   report (1987), 22, 24–25, 28
   study of financial fraud, 23–26

U
Underwriters
   as defendant in class-action lawsuit, 114–15
   due diligence investigation of prospectus, 118

V
Venture capitalists, interest in objective investigation by forensic accountants, 93
Volatility of stock market, 14, 261, 262, 264, 266

W
Waivers
   attorney-client privileges, 194
   conflict of interest, 202
   Fifth Amendment, 193
   joint defense, 195–96
Wall Street analysts, 258–59, 263–64
Warranties in debt covenant, 46
Watchdog function of auditor, 31
Web site
   available data, 267
   display of Form 10-K and 10-Q, 258
Wells Submission, 162
Whistleblower
   assistance in preparing restated financial statements, 45
   investigation of claims, 41–42
Whitney, John O., 249
Witnesses
   defined, 196
   Fifth Amendment privileges, 192–94, 196–97
   identity in criminal investigation, 187–88
   immunity of, 196–98
   interviewing of, 78–82
   privileges, 192–96
   representation of, 165–66
   rights of, 192
   subject, 196, 200, 201–2
   target, 196, 200, 201–2
Work product as privileged information, 86–87
Working papers of outside auditor used for investigation, 60
Wrongful act
   defined, 139
   interrelated, 141

HARCOURT PROFESSIONAL PUBLISHING SOFTWARE LICENSE AGREEMENT FOR ELECTRONIC FILES TO ACCOMPANY *ACCOUNTING IRREGULARITIES AND FINANCIAL FRAUD* (THE "BOOK")